# POLITICAL PARTIES AND ELECTIONS
## IN THE FRENCH FIFTH REPUBLIC

# Political Parties and Elections in the French Fifth Republic

by J. R. FREARS

C. HURST & COMPANY · LONDON

First Published in the United Kingdom by
C. Hurst & Co. (Publishers) Ltd.,
1-2 Henrietta Street, London WC2E 8PS
© 1977 by J. R. Frears
ISBNs
*Hardcover:* 0–903983–68–0
*Paperback:* 0–903983–28–1

For Andrea
and in memory of
Dr Christopher Frears
(1938–1976)

Printed in Great Britain by offset lithography by
Billing & Sons Ltd, Guildford, London and Worcester

# ACKNOWLEDGMENTS

The research for this book has been greatly assisted by a grant from the Nuffield Foundation (Social Sciences Small Grants Scheme). I am indebted to colleagues at the Centre d'Étude de la Vie Politique Française in Paris—notably for access to their computerised classification of election results. Professors Jack Hayward and Peter Campbell have been particularly helpful and generous with their advice and expert criticism. It was Tony Burkett's idea that I should write this book, and I am especially grateful to him for his help and comments. Finally I would like to thank Patricia King for her skill and patience in typing the manuscript.

J. R. F.

# CONTENTS

# TABLES

# 1
# FRENCH POLITICS AND THE ROLE OF PARTIES

Political observers looking at France in recent years have been rather like a group of meteorologists busy measuring rainfall who have failed to notice that the sun has begun to shine quite strongly. In a remarkably short space of time, the stereotype of France as an industrially underdeveloped, politically unstable, and socially fragmented nation has become as inadequate as the stereotype of Great Britain and the United States as the embodiment of social cohesion and enthusiastic legitimacy. So many aspects of life, economic structure, the standard of living, acceptance of the political order, have been transformed in a couple of decades. Political parties—the subject of this book because, as the vehicle for choice, they have to be at the centre of the democratic process—are part of that change. Their earlier weaknesses, the failure to produce leaders, the inability to sustain or control government, the incapacity to rise above parochialism or sectarianism, reflect the traditional weakness of France as a workable democracy. Their new strength is an important element of France's new strength.

Of course France has had almost 200 years of discord about what form of regime to have, and that discord follows several more centuries of struggle to unite the territory under one government. So the image of France as a divided and unstable political society has some historical substance and constitutional crisis and political instability could undoubtedly return. There have been sixteen different constitutions since the Revolution, and each one 'a treaty . . . a partisan procedural device . . . not endowed with the sacredness or permanence attributable to a constitution that symbolises fundamental agreement about political values as well as about political procedures'.[1] Change has been abrupt and violent. Since the 1789 Revolution, revolution has disposed of two more monarchies—the last of the Bourbons in 1830 and the last king of all, the bourgeois monarch Louis-Philippe in 1848. *Coups d'état* have sent three of the five Republics packing—the First by the first Napoleon on the 18th Brumaire 1799, the Second by his nephew Napoleon III in 1851, and the Fourth Republic by the Army revolt in Algiers as recently as 1958. The character of the dramatic and bloodless event which restored General de Gaulle to power, as well as the low level of support for the regime, was well expressed by an officer, who, seeing a demonstrator carrying off the bust of

1

Marianne, symbol of the Republic, remarked 'No casualties fortunately, except the Republic and that's not serious'.[2] Four other regimes were finished off by defeat in war. The First Empire was defeated at Waterloo in 1815, the Second Empire at Sedan in 1870, the Third Republic collapsed under the weight of German armour in the same North-Eastern part of France in 1940, and the Vichy regime that governed the southern half of France by permission of the Nazis collapsed with the liberation of France in 1944. In this turbulent history, no regime 'enjoyed unchallenged legitimacy. Each one is threatened by reactionaries or radicals or both. Efforts are made by dissident groups to weaken the existing regime and exploit its difficulties in order to create conditions which would make it possible to replace it with another political system'.[3] For revolutionaries 1789 was '*à refaire*' in 1848, in the Commune of 1871, in the Popular Front of 1936. Other movements, like Boulangism and the Anti-Dreyfusards in the 1880s and 1890s, *Action Française* in the 1920s and 1930s, or the Vichy state in the 1940s, wanted to wind the clock back to an authoritarian monarchy.

In this climate of turbulence and threats, regimes tended not merely to change violently but to oscillate from one extreme to another. Authoritarian regimes were followed by democratic regimes with no provision for firm government at all, in turn to be followed by another authoritarian regime with no provision for

Table 1.1
REGIMES SINCE THE FRENCH REVOLUTION

| | Regime | Ended by |
|---|---|---|
| Up to 1789 | Ancien Régime | Revolution |
| 1792–99 | First Republic | Coup d'état—18 Brumaire |
| 1799–1814 | Consulate of Napoleon and First Empire | Napoleonic Wars |
| 1814–30 | Monarchy—Bourbon Restoration | Revolution—the 'July Days' |
| 1830–48 | The July Monarchy—King Louis-Philippe | Revolution—the 'June Days' |
| 1848–52 | Second Republic | Coup d'état—2 Dec. 1851 |
| 1852–70 | Second Empire—Napoleon III | Franco-Prussian War |
| 1870–1940 | Third Republic | 2nd World War—the Fall of France |
| 1940–4 | Vichy—Marshal Pétain | Second World War—liberation |
| 1944–6 | De Gaulle provisional government | Peaceful transition |
| 1947–58 | Fourth Republic | Coup d'état—13 May 1958 |
| 1958– | Fifth Republic | |

liberty. The weak but democratic Third and Fourth Republics respectively succeeded the authoritarian and anti-libertarian Second Empire and Vichy. The authoritarian First and Second Empires succeeded the chaos of the First and Second Republics. Democracy and Government were in David Thomson's phrase 'two poles too far apart for the vital spark of democratic government to flash between them'.[4]

One of the propositions of this book is that in the Fifth Republic the elusive synthesis of government and democracy may have been found. It would be a rash individual who would predict how long that synthesis will be maintained but it is possible to point to a new legitimacy, a new acceptance of the political order.

The economic and social stereotypes are no more tenable today than the political. For 150 years France bore the conservative imprint of the Revolution's settlement of the land question. To a nation of small landowning peasants, who did not want to have too many sons because inheritance laws require subdivision of holdings into even smaller plots, the ideas of enterprise, risk and expansion were totally alien. France was a 'peasant's republic'.[5] The population which, in marked contrast to industrialising countries like Great Britain or Germany, remained virtually unchanged around 40 million from 1850 to 1950, was an ageing one. An industrial sector of very small firms operated on the defensive principle that the total market could not expand, and therefore that one trader's gain would be another's loss. The French call this unenterprising outlook 'Malthusianism'. All those years of the Third Republic, characterised by stagnation, weak government and rigid administration, produced the image of France as the 'stalemate society'.

Another aspect of the 'stalemate society' was the remarkable extent of rigid social cleavage. We have already referred to the great legitimacy problem where substantial sectors of the population were implacably opposed to the regime of the day, whatever it was. Related to it was the religious problem. The Catholic church had entered the camp of counter-revolution when in 1790 a measure known as the Civil Constitution of the Clergy had ended a number of church privileges, made ecclesiastical property the property of the nation, and required the clergy to swear allegiance to the civil power. Catholic parts of France, notably the Vendée in the West, resisted the Republic. For over a century the Church, the nobility and the Catholic faithful were seen by Republicans, Radicals and Socialists as upholding superstition against Reason, a hierarchical social order against equality, the authority of a single individual ruling by divine right against the authority of the representatives of the popular will. There is a Republican song of the Third Republic called '*la*

*Marseillaise anticléricale'* in which opposition to the Church is neatly equated to democratic rights. The chorus of the familiar Marseillaise runs *'Aux armes, citoyens'*, but the anticlerical version urges

> *Aux urnes, citoyens . . .*
> *Votons, Votons*
> *Et que nos voix*
> *Dispersent les corbeaux.*[6]

Clericalism—*'voilà l'ennemi'*, as Gambetta had said—was stamped out of public education so effectively that to this day there are no prayers, no religious instruction, not even Christmas carols of a religious nature, in French state schools. After the Dreyfus case, which dragged on from 1894 to 1906 and in which the Church, monarchists, the nobility and the army had for the most part resisted reopening the trial of a Jewish officer wrongly convicted for treason and championed by Republicans, Catholics were virtually purged from senior ranks of the army and scarcely a Catholic served in government for the duration of the Republic. There is 'no reference to God in any of the Republican constitutions, no prayer at official functions, no "In God we trust" on coins, no religious oath for office-holders'.[7] It was the proud boast of Viviani, a Third Republic minister, that 'our generation has extinguised for ever from the minds of the oppressed classes all hopes of salvation by divine providence'. A whole edifice of left-wing thought in France was founded on the humanism of Jaurès and the notion that it was incompatible with liberty to teach people that their every act was under the surveillance of an all-powerful deity. In consequence opposition between left and right in France tended to be reduced to opposition between partisans and adversaries of the Catholic Church, and still today as we shall see there is a strong correlation between religious practice and the propensity to vote for parties of the centre or right.[8] Catholics were seen as forming a kind of 'sub-system' in the Republic with their own schools and their own newspapers like *La Croix* or the weekly for farmers *Foyer Rural*. Catholics had their own trade unions, the CFTC (French Confederation of Christian Workers) and their own youth organisations—a lot of recent dynamism in French agriculture has come from the leadership of JAC (Young Christian Farmers). The post-war MRP (Popular Republican Movement) was a Christian-Democratic political party, although it never achieved the success of the CDU/CSU in West Germany or *Democrazia Cristiana* in Italy. Religious division in French society was a factor of the deepest importance.

Another cleavage arose from the issues of class and socialism.

We shall discuss the Socialist and Communist parties in a later chapter, but at this stage let us emphasise that a gradualist, reformist, social-democratic version of socialism never emerged. When Socialists or Communists have held office in coalition governments, as they have from time to time, their policies may have been opportunistic and indeed conservative, but their language has remained revolutionary. Working-class movements have been syndicalist in character. Far from forming their own political party to achieve progress by parliamentary means, like the British trade union movement, French trade-unionists signed in 1906 the Charter of Amiens declaring they would never have anything to do with any political party for fear of contaminating their revolutionary zeal in the shabby compromises of government. In fact today there are fairly close links between unions and parties—notably between the CGT (General Confederation of Labour) and the Communist party in the form of people who sit in the central committees of both organisations—but the ideology of no-compromise lives on.

The Communist Party itself, like the Catholic Church in the Third Republic, has all the appearance of a separate subculture that rejects the political community. It has a large and consistent electoral following—around 5,000,000 votes or a little over 20% of all votes cast. Research in the late ♦950s produced striking evidence that Communist voters had an outlook on issues and events that was quite different from other Frenchmen. Whether they were being asked what they thought caused price increases, what they thought it was like to live in the Soviet Union, what they felt about the suppression of the Hungarian revolt in 1956, the responses of Communist voters were dramatically opposite to those of France as a whole. There was in short a *'conscience communiste'*.[9] The party machine itself sedulously enfolds its activists in a *'contre-société'* with its own newspapers, magazines, training schools, youth clubs and holidays. The *raison d'être* of this whole edifice, with its discipline and its requirement of total involvement, its deep loyalty to the international Communist movement led by the Soviet Union, is revolution—the total transformation, not necessarily by violence, of the economic and political order of their country. Communism with its 'separatist' subculture on the one hand, and fear and distrust of Communism on the other, have come in the twentieth century to represent a polarising division as deep as the conflict between clericals and anticlericals in the nineteenth century.

These, in summary, are some of the elements of the traditional picture of France as a socially divided, politically unstable and economically unenterprising nation. The changes of the last twenty years have been remarkable. The economic transformation

Table 1.2

ECONOMIC AND SOCIAL CHANGE

|  | France | | | Great Britain | | | United States | | |
|---|---|---|---|---|---|---|---|---|---|
|  | 1938 | 1958 | 1972 | 1938 | 1958 | 1972 | 1938 | 1958 | 1972 |
| Population (millions) | 42.0 | 44.8 | 51.7 | 47.5 | 51.8 | 55.8 | 130.0 | 174.9 | 208.8 |
| GNP *per capita* ($) |  | 1,346 (1960) | 3,774 |  | 1,254 | 2,739 |  | 2,600 | 5,550 |
| Industrial Output (1958 = 100) | 53 | 100 | 223 | 67 | 100 | 150 | 33 | 100 | 201 |
| Ownership of cars (% of households) |  | 28 | 57 |  | 46 (1967) | 56 (1974) |  | 75 (1960) | 80 (1971) |
| New homes built ('000) |  | 290 | 637 |  | 279 | 278 (1974) |  | 1,042 (1957) | 2,058 (1973) |
| Civil employment or occupation— |  |  |  |  |  |  |  |  |  |
| % in agriculture | (1936) 37 | (1962) 20 | (1971) 12 | 6 | 4 | 3 | (1940) 17 | 8 | 4 |
| % in industry (including mining and construction) | 29 | 37 | 39 | 50 | 51 | 44 | 40* | 37* | 31 |
| % in services (including transport) | 34 | 43 | 49 | 44 | 45 | 53 | 43* | 56* | 65 |

*Transport workers included in industrial sector.

whereby France has become one of the leading and most dynamic industrial countries is too well known to need elaboration. Table 1.2 gives a few indicators.

As always in France, in the days of Colbert as in the days of Napoleon, the public sector has been the motor of innovation:

The legendary timidity of the mass of French family firms meant that it was public rather than private enterprise that innovated and took risks. Despite the dramatic industrial revolution through which France has been going in the last two decades, and is still undergoing, the weight of this long-standing *dirigiste* tradition still makes itself felt in the sense of dependence upon government, which French businessmen more or less explicitly acknowledge. In November 1968 the president of the CNPF asserted that far from the growth in foreign competition requiring a withdrawal of the national government's protective and supporting intervention, it was a further justification of such assistance. 'The salient feature of this new phase of our economic development is the decisive role that states will be called upon to play. International competition will involve the whole nation. Left to themselves, firms cannot face this competition alone.'[10]

The state, through a largely nationalised banking and insurance sector controls two-thirds of all long-term credit, and half of industrial investment. Public enterprise operates not only in the traditional public monopolies—telecommunications, railways, electricity, gas, coal—but also in aviation, armaments, electronics, oil, chemicals, building and in services like commercial radio and estate management. The role of the state as coordinator and banker for industrial development is carried out by such bodies as the Planning Commissariat, the *Caisse des Dépôts et Consignations,* and FDES (Economic and Social Development Fund). 'Where in Britain the private sector has traditionally enjoyed greater prestige and power than the public sector, in France the situation is reversed, with pervasive consequences for public policy. While the large private firms in Britain are the senior partners in the mixed economy, in France it is public enterprise that sets the pace . . . France has never officially adopted the ideology of free competition.'[11] Galbraith has argued in *The New Industrial State*[12] that the enormous cost and complexity of modern advanced technology and the vast size of large modern corporations have made the rhetoric of enterprise and competition in private corporations and the rhetoric of democratic accountability in public corporations completely obsolete. The modern corporation cannot be governed by shareholders or the public, and it has to depend on the state for its supply of educated manpower, overall management of demand, and finance for very advanced technology in the form of public programmes like defence contracts or space research. Private corporations in sectors like aviation or electronics can be private only in name. History and public attitudes may not have equipped France very favourably for the great era of *laissez-faire* industrial growth, but today, with no last-ditch antagonism to *dirigisme* from the private sector and no expectations of real public discussion of the investment priorities determined by technocratic criteria, France is rather well-equipped to be a 'new industrial state'. All the indices of prosperity have risen remarkably, from ownership of cars and refrigerators to the numbers of roads, homes, schools and new towns built.

Social change cannot of course be separated from economic change. The rise in living standards and the progress of industrialisation have made immense inroads into the peasant population and the peasant outlook. The proportion of French people deriving their living from the land is only a quarter of what it was before the last war. Industrial affluence has cut into class distinctions, into the kind of widespread discontent that would menace the economic and political order, and into religion as a traditional referent. It is therefore hardly surprising to find that the social cleavages based on the Communist faith and the Catholic faith have all but disappeared. Ever since Catholics fought in the Resistance, there has never been any question of systematic Catholic opposition to the Republic. In fact Catholic votes provide the electoral basis of the Republic in its present form, and they support its institutions. The Christian-Democratic MRP, once a haven for Catholic votes, has disappeared, and anyway it supported the Republic. In 1964 the CFTC dropped the word Christian from its title and became CFDT (French Democratic Confederation of Labour) and has moved close to the Socialist Party. There is now scarcely any argument about state aid to church schools: an issue which maintained a flicker of anticlerical life in the 1950s and mid-1960s. The only relic of this old cleavage is in the extraordinary and continuing geographical correlation whereby strongly Catholic parts of France always vote for political parties and candidates of the centre or the right. As for Communism, it is very difficult to explain the actions of the Communist Party, especially at times of dislocation and crisis like the general strike of May 1968, other than as the action of a party whose leadership has concluded that its supporters, notably the prosperous skilled industrial workers of the economic miracle, do not want the revolutionary overthrow of the economic system. The PCF plays its part in the normal functioning of the regime— elections, parliament, municipal government. It described itself, in those extraordinary days of May 1968, as the 'great and tranquil party of order' trying to stop industrial workers being led astray into leftist 'adventures', Jean Ferniot's conclusion on those days was that while the attachment of the Communist leadership to democratic values remains highly suspect, the Party is demonstrably no longer working for the overthrow of the system.[13] About its supporters Georges Lavau writes: 'the Communist vote . . . does not signify fundamental disagreement with all the bases of legitimacy of the political system'.[14] The PCF in one sardonic view actually upholds the system by providing a safety valve. 'The PCF's reformist action', says Edgar Morin, 'meets the material needs of large sections of the working class and the revolutionary myth affords satisfaction to the frustrations of life at work.'[15] It appears possible today to affirm that for the first time since the eighteenth century no major social group challenges the institutions of the Republic. One must add, though, that it remains to be seen whether that institutional consensus could survive the victory at the polls of a left committed to a radical economic and social policy.

The legitimacy accorded to the Fifth Republic is naturally related to the economic developments and social changes it has brought about. What people regard as the test of the effectiveness of their political system will vary[16] but will usually include such elements as economic wellbeing, order and freedom. In some regimes legitimacy is very conditional—Almond and Verba claimed in 1960[17] that in West Germany commitment to the political order was largely dependent on the regime's continued effectiveness as a provider of prosperity. In some regimes 'rain or shine' commitment appears greater—Great Britain in the 1930s for example, where severe economic depression posed no serious threat to constitutional monarchy, parliamentary sovereignty, or other basic institutions. But 'a breakdown of effectiveness, repeatedly or for a long period, will endanger even a legitimate system's stability'.[18] The institutions of the Fifth Republic appear to have that wide measure of public acceptance called legitimacy. The central institution of a strong and directly elected President is widely supported. Opinion surveys have shown that this is the type of regime people want, and the enormous interest shown in presidential elections bears this out. In 1974 the two principal candidates for the Presidency were addressing vast public meetings, and the electoral turnout reached a record 89%. In addition the public for twenty years has continuously granted parliamentary majorities to a coalition which has made support for the Fifth Republic, its institutions and its government, the central point of its appeal.

The events of May 1968, to which reference has already been made, have often been presented as evidence that the legitimacy of the regime is built on sand. That is the difficulty with countries which have a myth of revolution—it makes them rather unpredictable. 'The tradition, nay the cult, of insurrection, of Michelet's concept of the Revolution as Goddess, is still alive and numbers many worshippers.'[19] In 1968 there was a general strike and the government appeared to totter. Revolution, however, is a serious matter. In May 1968 there was all the folklore— cheerful *comités de grève*, symbolic road-blocks, romantic barricades—but nobody turned the power or the water off, and above all nobody did any shooting. Substantial quantities of blood flowed only at the Whitsun weekend when, by permission of the strike committee, petrol distribution was resumed and 120 people were killed in holiday road accidents. Who can doubt that the Communist Party was correct to conclude that 1968 was not the moment for the discontents of relatively affluent industrial workers to face the tanks?

However, while affirming our conviction that the present political institutions enjoy the highest legitimacy of any regime since the Revolution, the turbulent French political tradition must cause us to show some caution. A decline in effectiveness, either by serious economic recession or by a new period of unstable government, could quickly call this legitimacy into question. France still has to undergo the critical test of democratic stability— the peaceful alternation of power whereby after an election the opposition without violence becomes the government. In Great Britain and the USA it happens all the time. In West Germany it happened in 1969. In France it has not yet happened. Popular commitment to the institutions of the Republic has not really been tested.

Political parties, the focus of this present study, have been a part of this transformed political and social order. They were part of the old weakness; they are part of the new strength. It is right, therefore, that this introductory chapter should conclude with a brief examination of what political parties are for, what they contribute to the political process, how they failed to make that contribution in the past, and how a renewed party system is making a more effective contribution now. Political parties are central to the democratic process. Disraeli believed that 'without party parliamentary government is impossible'. Just as bureaucracies emerged at the stage of history where administration became too much for the prince's household, 'the political party materialised when the tasks of recruiting political leadership and making public policy could no longer be handled by a small coterie of men unconnected with public sentiments . . . the emergence of a political party clearly implies that the masses must be taken into account by the political élite.'[20] This notion may derive from the belief that people have a right to participate in the determination of public policy and selecting leaders or from a dictatorship's need to find some means of control. By most definitions, the object of political parties is control of the government. For instance 'political parties are associations formally organised with the explicit and declared purpose of acquiring and/or maintaining legal control, either singly or in coalition or electoral competition with other similar associations, over the personnel and the policy of the government of an actual or prospective sovereign state'.[21] Richard Rose places a slightly different emphasis upon the same theme: 'A political party [I presume he means in a liberal democracy] is an organisation concerned with the expression of popular preferences and contesting control of the chief policy-making offices of government.'[22] The idea that parties are interested in the objectives of government as well as merely occupation of government office has a long tradition. Burke wrote that a political party is 'a body of men united for promoting by their joint endeavours the national interest, upon some particular principle on which they are all agreed'. François Borella, in a recent book on France, leans to this normative view when he suggests there are three notions in party—a group of people with a common purpose, a programme of government, and an activity related to the quest for or exercise of political power.[23] Whatever their motives may be—principles, interest, the gratification of office, power goals and policy goals in infinitely varying degrees— parties aspire to govern. The other functions of political parties are subsidiary to that aim.

One of their most important functions is the recruitment of political leaders. Selection of candidates and support of their nominees fill a large part of the activity of political parties because they want their nominees to govern. Another function is the formulation of policy. As intermediaries between the populace, various interest groups and the institutions of government, parties seek to aggregate a diffuse mass of demands into reasonably coherent policy alternatives which they intend as government policy. A third function is the mobilisation of the citizenry for political participation. Popular support for party leaders and party policies is a prerequisite of party government in competitive systems and a far from negligible preoccupation in dictatorial government. All these functions support the principal aim of government. From the standpoint of democratic theory, it could scarcely be otherwise. Competition between parties for the power to govern is an indispensable part of the democratic process, and if such electoral victory does not confer the power to determine policy then electoral choice has no meaning.

One of the great weaknesses of the political order in France until recently was precisely the failure of political parties to perform these functions. Parties were too small to aggregate the demands of a large part of the electorate into coherent policy programmes, and were thus more like interest groups, so that a Radical Deputy from the Aude or the Hérault never really represented Radical policy or opposition policy but was simply transmitting the parochial demands of his constituents such as an increase in prices for wine-growers. French parties hardly ever produced mass organisations capable of mobilising the electorate. Voter identification with parties was very low. In an article published in 1962, Converse and Dupeux found that only 45% of Frenchmen identified 'psychologically' with a party, in comparison with 75% of Americans. Ninety-five per cent of Americans knew their fathers' electoral choices while only 29% of the French did.[24] The characteristic French political party was an internally created electoral committee for a few prominent local notables. 'Except for the extreme left, French party organisations have remained most of the time as skeletal as were parties in many countries at the time of their nineteenth-century beginnings.'[25] The French party system failed for the most part to recruit political leaders for the nation. Many national leaders, like Marshal Pétain or General de Gaulle, have come from outside the party system. The diplomat Maurice Couve de Murville was appointed Foreign Minister in 1958 and faced his first parliamentary election in 1967. The first the public ever heard of Georges Pompidou, banker, former teacher and member of General de Gaulle's personal staff, was when he was appointed Prime Minister in 1962. He too faced his first election in 1967.

Finally, and most important of all, parties failed to govern. In a fragmented multi-party system elections never conferred the right to govern upon a majority, no party saw as its role support for the government of the day and the defence of its record before the electorate. Government reposed not upon the popular will as transmitted by political parties but on deals and combinations in the corridors of the National Assembly. Ehrmann writes:

Only once, after the Liberation of France in 1944, has there existed a serious chance for a thorough overhauling of the party system. The representative regime of which the Third Republic had been the prototype was thoroughly discredited. Three parties, the Communist, the Socialist, and the *Mouvement Républicain Populaire,* emerged in the first elections of the new republic with a combined following of about 75% of the electorate. All were intent on forming disciplined mass parties and on governing the country by an effective coalition government. Yet after a few transitional years, and due to the cold war as well as to domestic pressures, the country reverted to the traditional forms of atavistic and atomistic representation and to the rule by shifting coalitions of the Center which now included the socialists.[26]

General de Gaulle, who despised political parties, described this anarchic situation of no responsible government and no responsible opposition as '*Le régime des partis*'. A regime of parties, though, was exactly what it was not and we have to wait till a party composed of the General's own supporters starting to win parliamentary majorities, ready to see sustaining the government as their main job in Parliament and defending it as their main job outside, that we can talk about a party regime in France.

Indeed it is the emergence of such a majority, of such dependable support for the government, that has perhaps been the most remarkable change of all. It is an indicator of a new legitimacy for the Republic. It has contributed greatly to the new governmental stability. The existence of a cohesive majority party—the UDR (Union of Democrats for the Republic)—enabled the Republic to survive the resignation of its charismatic founding father, the first defeat of Gaullism, without a tremor. It enabled the Republic to pass smoothly through the second defeat of Gaullism—the election of Valéry Giscard d'Estaing to the Presidency of the Republic after the death of Pompidou in 1974—by continuing its role as the principal element of the parliamentary support for the government. The motives may have been various—the desire to maintain the UDR's occupation of so many top posts in government, administration and public bodies, fear of possible socialist and communist electoral victories, the unlikelihood that Giscard d'Estaing would in reality challenge cherished articles of Gaullist faith like strong executive leadership at home or national self-assertion abroad. Whatever the reasons, a cohesive pro-government majority has been a supremely important part of democratic stability in the Fifth Republic—certainly since 1962. The functions in the political system that parties should perform are now being performed at any rate to a much greater extent than in previous regimes. Political leaders are party men. If Giscard d'Estaing himself has always led a small electoral-committee type of party like the parties of the Third Republic, his actions as President show, as we shall see, a lively sense of the need to lead a cohesive majority and not try to be a lonely prophet in direct communion with the people. His first Prime Minister, Jacques Chirac, who followed the classic non-party path into political life (civil service training, and membership of President Pompidou's personal staff), learned, like Pompidou, the importance for those who want to become national leaders of becoming party leaders first. The strong hold on power by a disciplined majority has had its effect on the opposition too, as we shall see. The *Union de la Gauche*—an electoral alliance of the new Socialist Party, the Communist Party and a part of the Radical Party with an agreed programme of government—has been able, despite some difficulties and internal stresses, to present itself as an effectively led and effectively organised political force.

In the last twenty years, therefore, an expanding and dynamic economy, a decline of traditional social conflicts and a new acceptance of the country's political institutions have changed almost all the traditional reference points for observers of French society. Political leaders, on the basis of electoral victory in the country and consistent support in Parliament, give political direction to government policy. That is a very large part of democratic government, and political parties are at the centre of this new democratic strength, as they should be. The next chapter will suggest that the transition to this far happier state of affairs was the extraordinary contribution of Gaullism.

## NOTES

1. Jack Hayward, *The One and Indivisible French Republic*, Weidenfeld and Nicolson, 1973, p.1.
2. Aidan Crawley, *De Gaulle*, Collins, 1969, p. 337, and P. Williams and M. Harrison, *De Gaulle's Republic*, Longmans, 2nd edn. 1961, p. 55.
3. R. Pierce, *French Politics and Political Institutions*, Harper and Row, 1968, p. 7.
4. *Democracy in Modern France*, Oxford University Press, 1958, p. 14.
5. See Gordon Wright, *Rural Revolution in France*, Stanford University Press, 1964.
6. 'To the ballot-box, citizens . . . vote, vote, and may our votes scatter the crows [priests].'
7. Henry W. Ehrmann, *Politics in France*, Little, Brown & Co., 1968, p. 48.
8. See, for example, Vincent McHale, 'Religion and electoral politics in France', *Canadian Journal of Political Science*, Sept. 1969, pp. 295–311.
9. Pierre Fougeyrollas, *La Conscience Politique dans la France Contemporaine*, Paris, Denoël, 1963, pp. 38–56.
10. Hayward, *The One and Indivisible French Republic*, p. 152.
11. Hayward, *Ibid*, p. 214.
12. Hamish Hamilton, 1967.
13. *Mort d'une Revolution*, Paris, Denoël, 1968.
14. 'Le Parti Communiste dans le système politique français' in F. Bon, *et al.*, *Le Communisme en France*, Paris, Colin, 1969.
15. Edgar Morin *et al.*, *La Breche*, Paris, Fayard, 1968, p. 28.
16. See S. M. Lipset, *Political Man*, Heinemann, 1969 edition, p. 77.
17. *The Civic Culture*, Princeton University Press, 1963.
18. Lipset, *Political Man*, p. 80.
19. S. E. Finer, *Comparative Government*, Allen Lane, 1970, p. 326.
20. J. La Palombara and M. Weiner, *Political Parties and Political Development*, Princeton University Press, 1966, p. 4.
21. J. S. Coleman and C. G. Rosberg, *Political Parties and National Integration in Tropical Africa*, University of California Press, 1964, p. 2.
22. *The Problem of Party Government*, Macmillan, 1974, p. 3.
23. *Les Partis Politiques dans la France d'aujourd'hui*, Paris, Editions du Seuil, 1973.
24. 'Politicisation of the Electorate in France and the United States', *Public Opinion Quarterly*, Spring, 1962, pp. 1–23.
25. H. Ehrmann, *Politics in France*, p. 198.
26. *Ibid*, p. 205.

# 2

## THE IMPACT OF GAULLISM

'In the sweeping changes which transformed French life in the twenty years after 1945, the political sector lagged behind.'[1] The economic transformation was on the way as the old conservative employers, discredited by collaboration with the Nazis in the war, were replaced by more dynamic managers. Growth and expansion were preached with missionary zeal by Jean Monnet, founder of the French experiment in national economic planning. A more expansionist economic outlook was accompanied by profound social changes. The birth-rate, static for a century, began to rise. The old social divisions based on religion began, as we have seen, to decline in importance. Fewer and fewer small farms meant less and less influence for the small farm mentality.

The political class, however, had failed to give expression to these changes in the form of coherent and forward-looking government. No majority could be found to keep any government in office longer than a few months. Ostrich-like and pusillanimous, the regime faced crisis, particularly colonial crisis first in Indo-China and then in Algeria, with nothing more vigorous than parliamentary intrigue. On 13 May 1958, the Republic was threatened by a military *coup d'état* in Algiers. There was no will to resist. 'The Republic was not murdered; it committed suicide.'[2]

France needed to be equipped with a new and more effective political order, and it was. The next few years saw the solution of France's colonial crises, the building of a new legitimacy for political institutions which' has made the Fifth Republic a more widely accepted regime than any of its predecessors since the Revolution, and the transformation of the party system into one which gives expression to the majority will and to the democratic requirement of accountability. The enormous contribution of one man to this process of change entitles us to explore the notion of charismatic legitimacy and its role in the emergence of a new political order.

Charismatic authority is a title to rule based on 'devotion to the specific and exceptional sanctity, heroism or exemplary character of an individual person'.[3] It characteristically appears as a transitory phenomenon in countries going through periods of great turmoil and change; most particularly it is found in countries that are in transition from traditional society to modern nation-

15

state. As societies turn away from an unresponsive traditional élite or colonial occupier, often a single leader—such as Gandhi in India, Nasser in Egypt, Nkrumah in Ghana, Mao Tse-tung, Nyerere, or Kenyatta—emerges to embody the legitimacy of the new nation. The word charisma is often used to describe the exceptional popularity or capacity to inspire loyalty and devotion that we find in leaders like Winston Churchill or President Kennedy. This is a misuse. Charismatic leadership occurs where a single leader's capacity to inspire creates legitimacy for a new political order. The examples above are from the Third World, but in post-war Western Europe in nations with special problems of transition to modernity two important leaders at least stand out as charismatic in the sense that confidence in them as individuals enabled the rebuilding of a legitimate political order: Adenauer in West Germany[4] and General de Gaulle in France.

General de Gaulle clearly regarded himself as being in the heroic mould of a charismatic chieftain. In a famous broadcast on 29 January 1960, at the time of another Algiers uprising, he actually claimed *'une legitimité nationale que j'incarne depuis 20 ans'*. It was a personal claim to represent the legitimacy of the nation, despite the intervening Republics and Constitutions and parliamentary elections, since the day of his most famous broadcast of all—the London declaration of 18 June 1940 calling for resistance to the surrender of France. The whole life and style of this remarkable man looks like a self-conscious preparation for and performance of the role of hero. The earlier writings like *Le Fil de l'epée,* a series of presumptuous but magnificent staff college lectures, set out the qualities of leadership—reserve, dignity, mystery and contempt for the rules which bind lesser men.[5] Part of his leadership style lay in his command of heroic symbolism. At moments of crisis he would withdraw into the wilderness like some holy prophet as if seeking renewed sources of strength (an example was his disappearance for a few hours at the height of the general strike on 29 May 1968); he chose Bayeux, the first French town to be liberated in 1944, for a speech containing the whole Gaullist constitutional doctrine of a strong state and a strong executive; he used to choose radio and not television for speeches to the nation at moments of great crisis like 23 April 1961 when Paris was threatened by the paratroops in another Algiers revolt, or again in the general strike on 30 May 1968, because it reminded people of 18 June; at his press conferences he would sit enthroned like Louis XIV, the *Roi Soleil*. His memoirs and his speeches might have been written by Chateaubriand. The literary style, the richness of historical sweep, the elegance of language, the Delphic subtlety, the monstrous egotism place them among the most remarkable documents of our time. Some have claimed that the cult of the hero in de Gaulle makes him a kind of fascist leader; let those who would do so compare the speeches of de Gaulle with the demented raving of Hitler or Mussolini. It is not within the scope of this essay to write the biography of General de Gaulle. The purpose of this brief evocation of his leadership style is to examine his own claim to charismatic legitimacy.

There can be little doubt that the legitimacy of the new political order, the Fifth Republic, was founded upon charismatic Gaullism. In particular, three critical elements of the new order could not have come into being in any other way: the preservation of the state and of national unity during the solution of the Algerian crisis, the emergence of new political institutions based on a directly elected Presidency of the Republic, and the emergence of a modern party system. It was the crisis in Algeria, with the army in revolt against the legal government of France, that destroyed the Fourth Republic. The French army, from its ignominious defeat in Indo-China at Dien Bien Phu in 1954 at the hands of a certain Ho Chi Minh, and the 1,000,000 settlers who had made Algeria more like an exotic region of France than a colony, were determined to hold on to this jewel of the imperial crown. More and more troops, more and more resources, more and more brutal repression, were all failing to suppress the movement to national independence. When a sell-out to the rebels was believed imminent, the army itself rebelled. Convinced that the old soldier, with a nationalistic vision of the greatness of France, would stand by '*l' Algérie Française*', the army supported the return to power of General de Gaulle. In fact de Gaulle was always careful not to commit himself to the maintenance of French rule in Algeria. He spoke to Louis Terrenoire in 1955 of 'a wave which sweeps all peoples towards emancipation. There are fools who will not understand this'.[6] He knew that '*l' Algérie de Papa*' was dead, that colonial rule over a subject people could not be maintained in the modern world, that France's economic strength and her prestige in the world— particularly with the newly emerging nations— would depend on a solution that respected a population's rightful desire for independence. The problem was to make the French accept that vision. On 16 September 1959 he proclaimed the principle of self-determination for Algeria. Algerians were to be offered three choices: complete independence, integration in France or self-government in association with France. This was clearly his own preference when he invited them, in the manner of an oracular riddle, to pronounce for '*la solution la plus française*'. On 24 January 1960, Algiers began the 'week of the barricades' in Algiers as the civilian *Ultras* of *Algérie Française* rebelled and the paratroops did nothing to help restore law and order. De Gaulle appeared on television in uniform and ordered the army to restore order. It did. New units were brought into Algiers to replace the *Paras*. The principle of self-determination was massively adopted by the French in a referendum on 8 January 1961. There was a 75–25 majority for Yes. Preparations were made for a conference at Evian to discuss arrangements for independence. Then, on 22 April 1961, came the *'putsch des généraux'* when four of the most prominent leaders in the French Army, Generals Salan, Challe, Jouhaud and Zeller, supported by some battalions of *Paras* seized Algiers. The invasion of Paris was hourly expected. Over the radio he ordered the soldiers not to obey their officers if the latter joined the rebellion. He assumed emergency powers under Article 16 of the Constitution and ordered the total blockade of Algiers. The rebellion collapsed. Most observers agree that it was his leadership that saved the day. Without it, it is not hard to recognise in the situation after the *coup* the elements of panic and reinsurance with the supposedly stronger side which had brought down the Fourth Republic. De Gaulle's personal preponderance had never been so clearly demonstrated.[7]

The storm was not over. The generals, in hiding, continued their struggle in the OAS (Organisation of the Secret Army) which carried out continuous acts of terrorism in France and Algeria for more than a year, including assassination attempts on General de Gaulle himself. But when Algeria chose complete independence, the French people backed it by a huge 91% majority in the referendum of 8 April 1962. The achievement: civil war avoided, excellent relations with former colonies established, French prestige enhanced by this 'peace with honour'—so different from the Nixon retreat from Vietnam to which that phrase was to be applied. 'For a man of my age and my background', he says in his memoirs, it was difficult to have to break the spirit of the French army and give up French territory.[8] It is unlikely that anyone else would have been able to accomplish such a task. 'The Algerian settlement was the final proof of de Gaulle's political genius'.[9]

The political institutions of the Fifth Republic are of course Gaullist ideas given form and substance. The famous speech at Bayeux in 1946 proposed a regime at whose centre was a head of state endowed with executive authority. The 1958 Constitution puts four powerful weapons into the hands of the President of the Republic. He can invoke special powers in a situation he considers to be an emergency (Article 16), he can call for referenda on certain issues (Article 11), he can dissolve Parliament (Article 12), he appoints the Prime Minister (Article 8) and can exercise certain presidential powers without the Prime Minister's counter-signature. The powers of the President, as defined by the constitution, are by no means absolute. It was the constitution, the

Algerian crisis and General de Gaulle's *persona* together that ensured presidential supremacy at the outset. The supporters of his successor President Pompidou had a large majority in Parliament, hence presidential supremacy was always accepted. President Giscard d'Estaing has to be a little more circumspect because the Gaullist party (RPR—*Rassemblement pour la République*) forms by far the largest element of his majority. Nevertheless Presidential leadership is a strong element in the constitution and was made stronger by the 1962 amendment, initiated by General de Gaulle, which lays down the election of the President by direct universal suffrage. The other theme of constitutional Gaullism is that the strong executive, on which stability and progress depend, can only be strong if it is free from the interference and harassment traditionally practised by the French Parliament. The 1958 Constitution, to a remarkable degree, lays down in minute detail just how an enfeebled Parliament can be kept in its place.

In what sense can the legitimacy that attaches to the constitutions of the Republic be considered charismatic? It is scarcely conceivable that any other political leader, even in the crisis situation of 1958, could have gained the agreement of a political class steeped in Republican fears of Bonapartism for a such a fundamental change of institutions, and won the assent of the public by a 79/21 majority in a referendum. In 1958, 'Frenchmen wanted before all else the solution of the Algerian problem and only very incidentally the reform of the State. For de Gaulle the order was the opposite'.[10] The General, at the outset and throughout his period in power, linked his indispensability in a crisis to support for the institutions he considered indespensable if the country was to surmount crisis. In 1958 the message was 'if you want peace in Algeria adopt my constitution'. In 1962 and 1969 it was 'if you do not want to risk the chaos that might follow my resignation, adopt my constitutional amendments'. One may deplore these methods, but it is hard to see how the regime could have been established in its present form without them. There was a generalised desire for institutions making possible stronger government. Opinion surveys since 1945 have even revealed a preference for a directly elected head of state. The institutions are now widely accepted, as the enormous public interest in presidential elections and the calm that attends them show, and the Republic appears to face no challenge by any major social group. The contribution of de Gaulle's leadership to this new legitimacy has to be recognised. Perhaps we can allow him his last boast. In the fragment of memoirs on which he was working at the time of his death appears this sentence:

In France has the state ever had the stability it now possesses without damaging our liberties? When did the world last see such assurance and serenity in the exercise of public authority. Have I not served France well by leading her people to so miraculous a change?[11]

The third element of the new political order in France that stems from the presence in power of General de Gaulle is the modernised party system that has emerged and which is the subject of this book. Gaullism has proved, up to 1974 at any rate, to be the federator of almost all the electors that used to vote for small parties and local notables in the centre and on the right. It is true that this concept of Gaullism as federator of the centre and right needs some refinement after the victory of Giscard d'Estaing, officially a non-Gaullist but a member of many Gaullist governments. The future majority may be more Giscardian than Gaullist but the majority habit is a Gaullist legacy. Gaullism's success as a federator of the right and centre has also had an effect on the left, pushing the parties of the left into the more effective cooperation which, despite fluctuations, has been an important feature of the evolving party system in recent years. The contribution of the 'Gaullist phenomenon' to the transformation of the French political system is the thesis of Jean Charlot's influential study.[12] The phenomenon is the growth of a large, disciplined and pragmatic party, which came into existence to give organised support to the action of General de Gaulle, and which saw its role, according to Charlot, as making a coherent parliamentary majority system possible in a country with a long tradition of loose and unstable multi-party coalitions.[13] It represented a 'veritable mutation' of French politics: 'the movement from a weak multi-party system to a dominant party system in recent years. The contribution of the 'Gaullist adds that this is one of the phenomena which 'could doubtless not have occurred without General de Gaulle'.[14]

The rise of 'Party Gaullism' to replace the gradually waning appeal of 'personal Gaullism' is the central theme of Charlot's study. It enables us to return to the theoretical question of charismatic legitimacy because the rise of 'Party Gaullism' is central to any analysis of the 'routinisation of charisma'. 'Routinisation' means the transformation of the authority of a charismatic leader into the kind of authority more readily transferred to his successors. As D.E. Apter has pointed out, 'maintenance of charismatic authority is dysfunctional to the maintenance of secular forms of authority'.[15] The stability and development of the system require that a solution be found to the problem of the heroic leader's departure. It has been the argument of this chapter that in France charismatic authority was necessary for crisis to be surmounted, for new institutions to gain acceptance, and for political development in the form of a modern party system to begin. But if France is a model of the timely rise of charismatic leadership in a period of crisis, it is also an admirable example of its timely fall when 'normalcy' returned. The smooth and peaceful transition to a 'secular form of authority' is an intriguing aspect of legitimacy in the Fifth Republic.

The year 1962 is widely regarded as the watershed of the Fifth Republic and a critical year in the routinisation of legitimacy. Up to 1962, the country was dominated by the Algerian problem. General de Gaulle ruled alone and autocratically with no guaranteed parliamentary majority to support his ministers. There were periods of crisis and for five months from April to September 1961 a period of 'constitutional dictatorship' under the emergency powers of Article 16. After 1962, Algerian independence and a safe Gaullist parliamentary majority enabled the regime to sail in calmer domestic waters and broaden out into spectacular international diplomacy. Maurice Duverger calls the years 1958 to 1962 'Authoritarian Gaullism' and the years from 1962 'Parliamentary Gaullism'.[16] Michael Steed[17] and François Borella both regard 1962 as the great caesura in the transition from the traditional weak multi-party system to a modern majority party system. '*En réalité*', says Borella, '*le nouveau régime est véritablement né en 1962*'.[18]

April 1962 represents the apogee of personal Gaullism. The Evian agreement granting independence to Algeria is overwhelmingly adopted at the referendum of 8 April, with only 9% of votes being cast against. In the same month one of the generals who played a leading part in the 1961 Algiers putsch and the OAS, Jouhaud, is condemned to death by the supreme military tribunal and another, Salan, is arrested. In the summer of 1962, the question of routinising the legitimacy of the Presidency is broached. The 1958 constitution laid down that an electoral college of some 80,000 local councillors and other officials should choose the President of the Republic. Direct election of the President of the Republic by the people had been raised before. In April 1961 at a press conference, de Gaulle had said it 'could be envisaged', though at another press conference as late as May 1962, he added 'not for the moment'. However by June he had made up his mind. In his broadcast of 8 June he said 'We are a great and united people as we have decided, massively and solemnly, by universal suffrage, to be . . . *Françaises, Français,* we must, by the same method, make certain, when the time comes, that in the future, though men come and go, the Republic can remain strong and well-ordered, and will endure'. The presidential car was machine-gunned at Le Petit Clamart on 22 August 1962. De Gaulle's miraculous escape from this incident forcefully underlined how men come and go, and on 20 September a referendum was announced: the French people would be asked to decide on 28 October whether they wished the President of the Republic to be elected in future by direct universal suffrage. 'The President must have the direct confidence of the nation. Instead of having that confidence implicitly—as was the case with me in 1958 for a historic and exceptional reason—it is necessary that henceforth the President be elected by universal suffrage.' 'From the very beginning', he added in his broadcast, 'I knew that before the end of my term of office I would have to propose to the country that this change be made'. According to Article 89, constitutional changes are supposed to be approved by the two assemblies of Parliament before being submitted to popular referendum. General de Gaulle loftily dispensed with this formality, and Parliament was furious. The President of the Senate, Gaston Monnerville, invoked the Constitutional Council and the National Assembly passed, on 4 October by 280 votes out of 480, a motion of censure on the government. This remains the only occasion during the whole Fifth Republic in which a censure motion has been successful. As the constitution provides in Article 50, the censured government resigned. General de Gaulle, accepting the resignation tendered by his Prime Minister George Pompidou (an almost unknown former personal assistant of the President called from the obscurity of Rothschilds bank in April 1962 to lead the Government), dissolved Parliament and asked the government to remain in office until the referendum and new elections had revealed the popular will. All the old parties campaigned in the referendum for a 'No' vote: from the Communists to the '*Cartel des Non*', which grouped together the old right-wing Independents, the Christian-Democratic centre represented by the MRP, the Radicals, and the Socialists. On 18 October General de Gaulle hinted that he might retire if the referendum result was '*faible, médiocre ou aléatoire*'—weak, mediocre or uncertain. The result on the 28th was not a triumph like the earlier referenda of the Fifth Republic. 62% of those voting voted Yes,—but, thanks to abstentions, that 62% only amounted to 46% of those eligible to vote. Pompidou, the Prime Minister, declared that the result was '*ni faible, ni médiocre, ni aléatoire*', so there was no question of the President retiring. Nevertheless the October referendum was a first sign that the appeal of General de Gaulle would not accomplish in normal times what it could in times of turmoil.

From the parliamentary elections of the following month, however, dates the emergence of the cohesive majority party which was to represent the real transformation of French politics. The November 1962 elections were a triumph for the Gaullists—at that time called UNR—UDT (the Union for the New Republic, which had absorbed the smaller 'left-wing Gaullists' group, the Democratic Union of Labour). They increased their first-ballot share of the vote from 17·6% to 31·9%. With their allies the Independent Republicans (RI—led by Valéry Giscard d'Estaing—the yes-voting pro-governmental element of the old National Centre of Independents and Peasants) they won 270 seats, an overall majority. 'Thus for the first time in history the French electorate voted to approve a government's record. The election of 1958 had registered no confidence in the Fourth Republic; that of 1962 recorded approval of the Fifth; the referendum was designed to prevent a return to the old system![19] The autumn of 1962 is an important stage in what is surely a classic case of the routinisation or dispersal[20] of charismatic authority. Furthermore no connoisseur of political strategy can fail to admire the consummate timing. 'General de Gaulle engaged the battle with his opponents at the most favourable moment, on the most favourable terrain, and by forcing them to combine against him in a negative coalition which brought back to the electors too many unhappy memories to have the slightest chance of victory.'[21]

In the years that followed, 'personal' Gaullism steadily weakened as an electoral force. In December 1965 General de Gaulle only obtained 43·9% of the first ballot votes in the first presidential election to be held under the new universal suffrage. In April 1969, in a referendum on regionalisation and the reform of the Senate, the Yes-vote was only 46·9%, and the General resigned as head of state. However the Prime Minister, Georges Pompidou, emerged, after the first-ballot setback for the General in 1965, as an able leader of a majority party who realised the necessity of organising the majority so that it could maintain its cohesion and its effectiveness when charismatic authority was gone.[22] Pompidou directed the second ballot campaign for de Gaulle in 1965; he directed the parliamentary election campaigns of 1967, in which the government just returned with an overall majority, and of 1968 in which it had a massive majority. Party Gaullism, in the shape of the UDR survived the resignation of General de Gaulle: its candidate Pompidou won the presidential election of 1969 and it retained leadership of government and Parliament, winning, with its allies, a further election victory in March 1973.

France in the period of the Pompidou Presidency was often called *l'état-UDR*—the UDR state. Heroic Gaullism had yielded to party Gaullism. Nominees of the UDR controlled nearly every important office—Presidency, Government, Parliament, civil service appointments, appointments to public bodies like the television network or the nationalised industries. The power of the President was based not upon his own electoral appeal but upon the universal presence of his party at all levels of national decision-making life. 'What distinguishes the Fifth Republic from the Fourth Republic', writes Ezra Suleiman, 'is not so much the altered institutional arrangements in favour of the executive, nor the relative ministerial stability, as the existence of a majority party which dominates the executive, the legislature, and probably the bureaucracy'.[23]

Party Gaullism has not only survived the resignation of General de Gaulle, it has so far survived the defeat of Gaullism. In the presidential election of May 1974 which followed the death of Pompidou, the UDR candidate Jacques Chaban-Delmas, who campaigned on the image of heroic Gaullism, could only obtain 15% of the votes cast. Heroic Gaullism has disappeared—it already had under Pompidou's Presidency—but the UDR, especially when Jacques Chirac was Prime Minister, remained a prominent, indeed predominant, element in the government and the parliamentary majority which supports President Giscard d'Estaing. The UDR began by adapting to the leadership of a non-Gaullist President of the Republic, who in turn was aware that the power, lustre and prestige of his office was dependent, for some time at any rate, upon the goodwill of the UDR. In late 1976, with Chirac out of the government, the 'Giscardisation' of the UDR was put into reverse and the RPR, a throwback to a more aggressive and combative style of Gaullism, emerged under Chirac's vigorous leadership. Nonetheless both President of the Republic and RPR understand the need to maintain the majority system in a Republic which has moved on from the period of charismatic legitimacy associated with its turbulent early years 1958 to 1962.

Gaullism has also had its effect upon the opposition. Presidential leadership of the executive and election of the President by universal suffrage—an important part of the General's legacy—have had the effect of personalising leadership and polarising political life somewhat into a joust between two champions. The left, as we shall see in a later chapter, has done much better at presidential elections when it has a single champion in the lists, as it did with François Mitterrand who, in 1965 and 1974, played a very 'presidential' part and took care not to appear a mere party nominee or delegate. Furthermore, the effect of 'party Gaullism' as an electoral force capable of grouping together nearly all the electors of the centre and the right, who in the Third and Fourth Republics used to be scattered over many parties and over none, has forced the parties of the left to work together or be crushed. The two-ballot electoral system, to boot, imparts what Jean Charlot calls a '*coup de pouce majoritaire*'[24]—an inbuilt impulsion in favour of would-be majority parties who can attract second-ballot votes from a wide spectrum of opinion. The system also, as we shall see, tends to crush small parties, isolated parties, extremist parties, parties in decline. The Socialists, after various attempts to build a centre-left alternative to Gaullism, realised from 1965 onwards that the only chance of the opposition winning power was for the democratic left to draw the Communist Party out from its ghetto and work with them and their 5,000,000 voters. There have been setbacks, notably in the period 1969-71; there are problems, notably that an alliance with the Communists can be, electorally, a poisoned chalice because the Stalinist image of the PCF frightens many moderate voters into voting for the Government. The logic of the party system created by the 'Gaullist phenomenon' is bipolar. Majority Gaullism condemned the parties of the left to live together. One of the most important tasks of this book is to explore whether the majority system and the majority habit are sufficiently strong to withstand, over a long period of time, the transition to a non-Gaullist presidential leadership, or whether both majority and opposition will shake down into their separate elements and return to opportunistic coalition-building.

A great deal depends on the 1978 elections: whether there will be many first-ballot 'primaries' between candidates from different elements of the majority; whether the *Giscardien* Independent Republicans gain many seats; whether the Socialists will be detachable from the Communists in the event of a success for the Left—there have been suggestions that M. Mitterrand would be willing to form a government under the Presidency of Giscard d'Estaing, whereas the Communist leadership would not. It is not for this chapter to analyse these important questions. Its aim has been to assess the impact of Gaullism: of charismatic Gaullism and the foundation of the legitimacy of the Republic, and of party Gaullism by which charismatic authority was routinised and dispersed into a more 'secular' system of government.

## NOTES

1. Philip M. Williams and Martin Harrison, *Politics and Society in de Gaulle's Republic,* Longman, 1971, p. 63.
2. Dorothy Pickles, *The Fifth French Republic,* Methuen, 1960, p. 17.
3. Max Weber, *Theory of Social and Economic Organisation,* Collier-Macmillan, 1964 edition, p. 328.
4. See Tony Burkett, *Parties and Elections in West Germany,* C. Hurst, 1975, p. 22 and Ch. 2.
5. He also adds: 'La perfection évangélique ne conduit pas à l'Empire. L'homme d'action ne se conçoit guère sans une forte dose d'égoisme, d'orgueil, de dureté, de ruse' (*Le Fil de l'Epée,* Paris, 1944), p. 87. So the historic leader must be a cunning egoist as well.
6. Louis Terrenoire, *De Gaulle et l'Algérie: Témoignage pour l'histoire,* Paris, Fayard, 1964, p. 41.
7. Anthony Hartley, *Gaullism: The Rise and Fall of a Political Movement,* Routledge and Kegan Paul, 1972, p. 180.
8. *Mémoires d'Espoir* Vol. 1: *Le Renouveau 1958–1962,* Paris: Plon, 1970, p. 41.
9. Raymond Aron, quoted in Williams and Harrison, *Politics and Society,* p. 42.

10. Jacques Chapsal quoted in Hartley, *Gaullism*, p. 157.
11. *Mémoires d'Espoir II: L'effort 1962*, Paris: Plon, 1970, p. 104.
12. *The Gaullist Phenomenon*, Allen and Unwin, 1971.
13. See *L'UNR, Étude du pouvoir au sein d'un parti politique*, Paris: Colin, 1967, p. 306.
14. *The Gaullist Phenomenon*, p. 17.
15. *Ghana in Transition*, Princeton University Press, 1963, p. 203.
16. *Les Institutions françaises.*
17. In S. Henig and J. Pinder, eds. *European Political Parties* (PEP—Allen and Unwin, 1969), Ch. 4.
18. *Les Partis politiques dans la France d'aujourd'hui*, Paris: (Editions du Seuil, 1973), p. 9.
19. Philip Williams, *French Politicians and Elections 1951–1969* (Cambridge 1970), pp. 145–6.
20. The term is E. Shils's: see *American Sociological Review*, 1965, pp. 199–213.
21. 'Le Référendum d'Octobre et les élections de Novembre 1962' in *Cahiers de la FNSP* (directed by F. Goguel, Paris: Colin, 1965), pp. 436–7.
22. See Frank L. Wilson, 'Gaullism without de Gaulle' *(Western Political Quarterly*, 1973, pp. 485–506).
23. *Politics, Power and Bureaucracy in France*, Princeton University Press, 1974, p. 164.
24. *Le Point*, 3 Nov. 1975, p. 52.

# 3

## THE *MAJORITÉ*

The last chapter discussed the emergence since 1962 of a bipolar
'government and opposition' party system in France. The impetus,
it has been suggested, came from Gaullism: Gaullism as a federator
of almost all the electors of the centre and right, Gaullism as a
creator of majority government and the majority habit, Gaullism
as a force compelling its opponents to unite. An interesting
paradox, however, is that government and opposition polarity
does not appear to be leading to a two-party system. Small groups
of the centre have suffered the same kind of consequences of a
polarising trend as the British Liberals did in the half-century from
1920 or as the West German FDP did in the 1960s. On both sides of
the divide between government and opposition, however, we find
distinct groups stressing their own identity, conducting
relationships with their allies in a spirit of quite considerable rivalry
and even tension, and presenting candidates against each other
(systematically in the case of the left) but cooperating effectively
when it comes to governing, opposing, voting legislation and
winning elections. Within the *Union de la Gauche,* which has a
manifesto for government,[1] Socialists and Communists stress their
separate personalities and their mutual suspicions. In parliamentary
elections, each party contests every constituency in the first ballot,
agreeing that whichever candidate does best shall be supported by
both at the second ballot. On the Government side, the subject of
this chapter, rivalry has been on the whole more discreet. Electoral
and parliamentary discipline have been well maintained.
Indeed it is a remarkable and curious fact that for most of the Fifth
Republic, in a country where the word coalition has for
generations been synonymous with instability, the pro-
government coalition of Gaullists and other groups has been
indissoluble and practically unwavering.

It is for this reason, and to express the singular nature of the Fifth
Republic's party system, that the word coalition is never used to
describe the French government and its parliamentary support.
The word always used is *Majorité.* The *Majorité* is more than a
coalition but less than a party. It is a term that embraces all parties
and groups that give disciplined electoral and parliamentary
support to the President of the Republic and to the government
appointed by him. The presidential element is of great importance.
It is the components of his support that define the *Majorité,* but the

27

term can only be used when the President has the support of a parliamentary majority in the National Assembly.

This odd conjunction of elements—presidential and parliamentary—which constitutes a *Majorité* requires explanation. First we need to examine the parliamentary component and the importance of a parliamentary majority in a country in which Parliament's powers in relation to the executive have been so vastly enfeebled. Then we must look at the presidential element, and illustrate how each President has had the support of a wider *Majorité* than his predecessor.

The powers of Parliament in general and its relation with the executive were a major issue in French politics in the 1950s. The return to power of General de Gaulle in 1958, the passage of the 1958 Constitution, the strengthening of the Presidency by the introduction of direct presidential elections, and the repeated electoral victories until 1974 of the General's supporters, all underlined one victorious theme: stability and progress depend on a strong executive free from interference and harassment from the dividers and wreckers traditionally to be found in the French Parliament. The Parliaments of the Third and Fourth Republics had never produced any majority willing to give regular support to a government in difficult times when unpopular decisions had to be faced. There had been ninety-four governments in the seventy years of the Third Republic, and in the twelve years of the Fourth, eighteen (not counting five that lasted less than one month). Decisive government was impossible. There was an infinite number of procedures whereby parliamentarians could obstruct business, harass ministers and bring down governments. The constitutional doctrine of General de Gaulle and his supporters was to strengthen the Executive and the chances of stable government by restricting the divisive role of Parliament with its multi-party obediences. The 1958 Constitution expresses this reaction against an over-mighty Parliament in elaborate detail. It is very unusual for a constitution to lay down minuscule aspects of Parliamentary procedure. In the 1958 document, however, the way motions of censure can be introduced and carried, the way the government can break a deadlock between the two houses of Parliament, how the government can guillotine amendments, the maximum time permitted for discussion of the Finance Bill, priority on the order paper for government business, every detail is included. It tells us when Parliament can meet and for how long, what it can legislate on and what it must leave to the executive sphere, how it can delegate its legislative power to the Executive. Every detail gives the executive an additional weapon against parliamentary harassment.

In contrast to all this is the growing power of the Presidency. It has been said that the President of the Republic in France has all the powers of an American President or a British Prime Minister but does not suffer the limitations and constraints of either. He is not responsible to Parliament; there is no Supreme Court to rule on the constitutionality of his acts; there is no federalist counterbalance to his executive power in the form of local or regional autonomy. The constitution of the Fifth Republic arms the President with important powers—ill-defined but absolute powers in a national emergency (Art. 16), the recourse to referendum (in theory 'on the proposition of the government'—Art. 11), dissolution of the Assembly (Art. 12), nomination of the Prime Minister (but no constitutional right to dismiss him—Art. 8). He also has the legitimacy of direct popular election—but then so has the President of Austria, who reigns but does not rule. Certainly during the rule of General de Gaulle and President Pompidou, presidential supremacy was never questioned. De Gaulle went so far as to say:

'It must of course be clearly understood that the indivisible authority of the State is conferred in its entirety upon the President by the people who elected him, that no other authority exists, ministerial, civil, military, judicial, which is not conferred by him; finally that it belongs to him alone to make changes in this area of supreme responsibility which is his alone and those areas whose management he has delegated to others.'[2]

Jacques Chaban-Delmas, who ironically had been the only Prime Minister of the Fifth Republic to try implementing his own ideas and to enlarge the scope of prime-ministerial responsibility, enunciated the doctrine of the presidential supremacy of President Pompidou. The Prime Minister was not on the same level as the President because he was not chosen by the people but appointed by the President. His task therefore was to direct the government along the lines traced by the President (*'dans le sens des orientations présidentielles'*). The President is the captain of the ship, the Prime Minister his first lieutenant.[3] 'A Prime Minister worthy of the name could not remain a moment in office against the wishes [*sentiment*] of the President of the Republic . . . to contest this principle, over any issue no matter how small, would be to fling down a direct challenge to the institutions of the Republic.'[4]

In view of all this, why does a parliamentary majority matter to the President? An American President always hopes, of course, that Congress will have a majority for the President's party. That makes it easier to get the necessary legislation and money; however, it is only mildly inconvenient if the opposing party has a congressional majority and it very often occurs. Why should it apparently create more difficulty for a French President to have the enfeebled national Assembly in opposition to his policies than for an American President to see Congress, with all its very wide and independent powers, controlled by the opposition party? There are two answers. First, American parties are not like European ones. A Democratic Congress will not oppose a Republican President on everything. Conservative Democrats will vote with Conservative Republicans against Liberal Democrats voting with Liberal Republicans. Secondly, the Executive in the United States is quite separate from the Legislature, and cannot be removed other than by impeachment. Although in France the President cannot be removed by Parliament, the government still can be; the separation of powers is not complete. The President appoints the government which is responsible to the National Assembly. The Constitution makes it as difficult as possible for the Assembly to harass the government, but the government is still obliged by the Constitution (Art. 50) to offer its resignation if the National Assembly passes a motion of censure or rejects the government's programme or a general statement of government policy. It is very difficult to pass a censure motion. It needs the signatures of one-tenth of the Assembly's membership, and the same signatories cannot introduce another in that session. Censure motions are not voted on for forty-eight hours after their introduction—time for the crisis to die down and the government to rally its support. Only votes in favour of the censure motion are counted so that the absent, the sick, and the abstainers are constitutionally held to be supporters of the government. To be carried, a censure motion must receive the votes of a majority of the total membership of the Assembly—in today's Assembly, 246 votes. It is difficult to censure the government but it can be done. It has been done only once in the Fifth Republic—on 4 October 1962 over the issue of calling a referendum on direct presidential elections.

A President of the Republic who wants to continue the Fifth Republic practice of presidential leadership in all important fields of policy must be able to appoint a Prime Minister and a government team sympathetic to his aims. Such a government could survive only if there is a parliamentary majority prepared to allow it to do so. Indeed, what happens if the *Majorité* is defeated in a parliamentary election is one of the unsolved riddles of the constitution, and a crucial issue at each election. If the Socialists and Communists had jointly won the 1973 election or if they jointly win the 1978 election, what should the President do? The people elected him against a candidate of the left, and he believes in presidential leadership, so he cannot meekly appoint a Socialist Prime Minister and become no more than an honorific head of state. On the other hand he cannot ignore the election result, because a government that supported him would be brought down by the newly composed Assembly. Hence the importance of the parliamentary aspect of the term *Majorité*. We shall return to this interdependence of President and *Majorité* arising from the semi-presidential ambiguity of the Fifth Republic's institutions.

The second aspect of the term *Majorité* is presidential. The boundaries of the *Majorité* are defined by the President. General de Gaulle, a somewhat uncompromising figure, defined his *Majorité* on a take-it-or-leave-it basis: these are my policies, the nation is behind me, reject them at your peril. His successors, however, have felt the need, during the election campaigns which brought them to office, to devise policies which would create a wider base of support, to attract leaders from the opposition to their campaign and subsequently into the governments they appointed. In consequence, each President of the Republic has had a wider *Majorité* than his predecessor—wider, that is, in the sense of encompassing more shades of opinion.

## 1. *The* Majorité *of General de Gaulle*

Up to 1962 there was no *Majorité*. This was the period of charismatic authority when the General ruled virtually alone, living on his direct relationship with the French people. The National Assembly could have overthrown the government of M. Debré, appointed by the General, but that would have provoked the General's resignation and a political crisis. De Gaulle was seen by the Right and the Centre as the nation's sole protector against chaos and Communism, and by the Socialists (for example, during the Algiers revolts of January 1960 and April 1961) as the sole defence against military dictatorship. After 1962 there was a *Majorité*. The Gaullist party UNR (Union for the New Republic) did not have a parliamentary majority on its own, but they were able to rely on the Independent Republicans (RI). This group, led by Valéry Giscard d'Estaing who had been a member of the government since 1959, was composed essentially of Independents from the 1958 Parliament who had not campaigned for a No vote in the 1962 referendum on direct presidential elections. As we shall see in chapter 5, they were not unconditional supporters of every Gaullist initiative, but they repeatedly made clear that they supported the Fifth Republic and the new institutions making stable government possible, and never threatened the government by supporting motions of censure in Parliament. Orthodox Gaullists and Independent Republicans have maintained an electoral *concordat* since 1962. It was formalised in 1967 when they contested the elections together under one common banner: Fifth Republic. In 1968 they were together under the banner 'Union for the Defence of the Republic' and in the 1973 elections 'Union of Republicans for Progress' (URP). Normally they agree which party contests which constituency on behalf of the *Majorité* under the common banner.

## 2.    The Majorité *of President Pompidou*

Under the Presidency of Georges Pompidou, the *Majorité* was widened to include further elements. The last year of the General's reign had revealed some cracks in the *Majorité*, and Giscard d'Estaing, dismissed as Finance Minister in 1966, had gone as far as to announce with considerable *éclat* that he would not support the April 1969 referendum on Regionalisation and Reform of the Senate. Many Gaullists then blamed Giscard d'Estaing for the defeat of the referendum and for the General's resignation which was the immediate consequence, and some continue to do so. Pompidou, who had been Prime Minister up to June 1968 and who was the obvious and natural Gaullist successor to the Presidency, immediately declared his candidature which received the endorsement of the UDR (Union of Democrats for the Republic—the Gaullist party's latest label). It looked, however, as if he might have some difficulty in getting elected. It appeared that the population had turned away from the solitary and arbitrary use of power, and from the heroic style of the General. The amiable and indisputably unheroic President of the Senate, Alain Poher, who had been thrust into the limelight during the campaign to defeat the referendum and, more especially, by his constitutional role as temporary President of the Republic until the new election, had a lead over Pompidou in the opinion polls. Consequently, Pompidou, despite the large parliamentary majority which the UDR had earned as a result of the 1968 elections, felt the need to attract a wider spectrum of support to his candidature. Above all, he felt he needed the endorsement of Giscard d'Estaing and the Independent Republicans, who in urgent meetings had been considering a number of possibilities including support for Poher or a Giscard d'Estaing candidature. After some uncharacteristic hesitation, Giscard d'Estaing decided that his hour had not yet come and he declared for Pompidou who therefore proclaimed his candidature as expressing '*continuité et ouverture*': continuity of the achievements of Gaullism and an opening towards more liberal policies in certain fields, notably European integration. His campaign obtained the support not only of Giscard d'Estaing and his friends but also of part of the Centre. The various groups of the old centre and right, like the Independents or the MRP (Popular Republican Movement), had long seen their electoral edifice and their leadership crumble away under the appeal of Gaullism. A number of MRP leaders like Maurice Schumann, Marie-Madeleine Dienesch or (in a more cautious and reluctant manner) Pierre Pflimlin had over the years taken themselves and their electorates off to join the Gaullists. Pompidou now attracted to his campaign and into the government he subsequently appointed a number of important Centrist figures like Jacques Duhamel, René Pléven and Joseph Fontanet, who had remained in the opposition while de Gaulle was President. Twenty-five out of thirty-six Centrist Deputies joined the new *Majorité,* formed the CDP (Centre for Democracy and Progress) and joined the URP banner at the 1973 elections.

## 3.   *The* Majorité *of President Giscard d'Estaing*

The Presidency of Valéry Giscard d'Estaing has widened the *Majorité* still further. This, as in the case of his predecessor, is explained by the need to build as wide a base of support as possible during the presidential election campaign of 1974. When Giscard d'Estaing declared his candidature, the UDR had already endorsed Jacques Chaban-Delmas, who had proclaimed, with barely decent haste, his desire to succeed the dead President Pompidou. Giscard d'Estaing said he felt it right that a member of the outgoing government, which had worked with the late President, should stand. He agreed to stand aside for the Prime Minister, M. Messmer, if Chaban-Delmas would do the same—an offer that was declined. Giscard d'Estaing therefore had to campaign against the Gaullists, although it was clear from the start that he had the support of some important members of the government and leading figures. This group, 'the 43', were led by Jacques Chirac, subsequently Prime Minister and leader of the UDR and of its 1976 metamorphosis the RPR *(Rassemblement pour la République).*

Giscard d'Estaing, however, was able to attract to his campaign, and into the government he appointed after the election, what little of the old MRP and centre that had remained in opposition to President Pompidou. The leading figure of this group was Jean Lecanuet, who had been a centrist candidate against de Gaulle in 1965 and the leader of CD (Democratic Centre). In 1971 these opposition centrists, whose MRP origins go back to a Christian Democratic tradition, had joined forces with the Radical Party, which belongs to the tradition of the old anti-clerical left, to form the 'Reform movement'. The Radical Party split over this alliance which was an alliance essentially of those who rejected both Gaullism and a Union of the left which included Communism. The leading 'Reformers' brought some valuable support to the Giscard d'Estaing candidature—Lecanuet, Michel Durafour (mayor of St-Etienne), Pierre Abelin and, after much hesitation, the leader of the Radical Party element of the Reformers, Jean-Jacques Servan-Schreiber. After the first ballot collapse of the Chaban-Delmas candidature, which had foolishly restricted its appeal to the epic of the Resistance and the appeal of heroic

Gaullism, the UDR, apart from a few 'barons' of historic Gaullism, gave its powerful support to Giscard d'Estaing. In consequence the new *Majorité* extends from the Gaullists to parts of a Radical party that for most of the 1960s had been linked to the Socialists. The trend whereby each presidential *Majorité* has been wider, though not necessarily more numerous, than the previous one is summarised in Table 3.I. The diagram in Table 3.2 schematically presents the lure of the *Majorité* and the regrouping throughout the Fifth Republic of both *Majorité* and opposition.

Table 3.I EVOLUTION OF THE *MAJORITÉ*
*(Parliamentary Seats)*

| President: | · De Gaulle 1958-1969 | | | | Pompidou 1969-1974 | | Giscard d'Estaing 1974- |
|---|---|---|---|---|---|---|---|
| Parliament: | *1958* | *1962* | *1967* | *1968* | *1968* | *1973* | *1973* |
| Total membership of Nat. Assembly | 552 | 482 | 487 | 487 | 487 | 490 | 490 |
| No. required for absolute majority | 277 | 242 | 244 | 244 | 244 | 246 | 246 |
| Components of the *Majorité:* | | | | | | | |
| UNR/UDR | 199★ | 233 | 201 | 296 | 296 | 183 | 183 |
| RI | — | 37 | 44 | 64 | 64 | 55 | 55 |
| PDM | *(OPPOSITION )* | | | | 25 | 30 | 30 |
| *Réformateurs* | *(OPPOSITION ........)* | | | | | | 34 |
| Total *Majorité* | — | 270 | 245 | 360 | 385 | 268 | 302 |

★ a true figure for the *Majorité* in the period 1958–62 would include a number c Independents who gave reliable support to the Government throughout.

Giscard d'Estaing's presidential *Majorité* is less cohesive than the *Majorités* of his predecessors, since Gaullism can never be entirely happy with national leadership in ﾉon-Gaullist hands. The government of the non-party Raymond Barre has the support of the RPR, but of a less unconditional kind than that which the UDR gave to Chirac's government, and *that* support was much

## Table 3.2: THE CHANGING PARTY SYSTEM

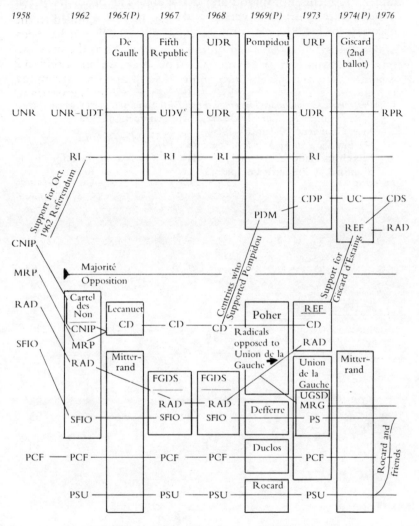

*(P)* Presidential election. For other abbreviations, see Appendix 1.

less unconditional than it gave to the governments that served under Presidents Pompidou and de Gaulle. The problem of the *Majorité* is to combine diversity and even rivalry with the unity necessary to face the electoral challenge of the left.

## NOTES

1. *Programme Commun de Gouvernement du Parti Socialiste, Parti Communiste, et Mouvement des Radicaux de Gauche*, Paris: Flammarion, 1973.
2. Press Conference, 3 January 1964.
3. See interview in *Le Monde* 4 September 1970.
4. Speech to National Assembly 24 May 1972 (a few weeks before being dismissed by President Pompidou).

# 4

## PARTIES OF THE *MAJORITÉ*:
## I. THE GAULLIST MOVEMENT

This chapter is the first of several in this book to deal in detail with the background, the ideas, the men, and the organisation of a particular political party. Most of the political parties in France have changed greatly in character as a totally new party system has emerged based on a majority prepared to give disciplined support to the President of the Republic and his government. Gaullism, the most important catalyst of the new party system, is its most diverse and constantly-changing element. As René Rémond has put it, 'there is no unique, stable, and permanent Gaullism'.[1]

Gaullism and *Majorité* were so nearly synonymous for so long that it is hard to realise that they are synonymous no longer. Gaullism transformed the French political order producing majority government with a new force and a new legitimacy. The non-Gaullist parts of the *Majorité* up to 1969 consisted of men like Giscard d'Estaing, who had supported the main Gaullist initiatives—notably the election of the President by universal suffrage. Many key men in high ministerial office under President Pompidou from 1969 to 1973 were vintage Gaullists: Jacques Chaban-Delmas (Prime Minister 1969–72), Pierre Messmer (Prime Minister 1972–4), Michel Debré (Minister of Defence until 1973), Olivier Guichard (Minister of Education up to 1972), Roger Frey (Minister responsible for Relations with Parliament up to 1973). The Gaullist party (UNR, then UDR, and subsequently RPR) was—and still is—by far the largest and best organised parliamentary group and electoral force in the *Majorité*.

However, as we saw in Chapter 3, the *Majorité* has changed. A non-Gaullist is President of the Republic after defeating the representative of 'heroic' Gaullism, Jacques Chaban-Delmas, in the first ballot of the 1974 presidential elections. Anti-Gaullists are prominent in the government—especially Jean Lecanuet, Minister of Justice and presidential candidate against the General himself in 1965. Until the phoenix-like return of M. Guichard as Minister of Justice and coordinator of the *Majorité* in the August 1976 Government changes, it looked as if the 'barons' of heroic Gaullism had all gone. The strong man of Gaullism today is Jacques Chirac, who helped to defeat heroic Gaullism by supporting Giscard d'Estaing at the Presidential election of 1974 and by serving as his Prime Minister for two years. In December

1976, in scenes of feverish hero-worship, he was able to seize personal control of the movement, to reverse the UDR's tendency to become more moderate and more democratic, to curtail its unconditional support for the President, to sow the dragon's teeth and see militant Gaullism spring fully-armed from the ground. The Gaullism of Jacques Chirac's new RPR is not the Gaullism of the UDR of 1975 or 1968. The Gaullism of the UNR in 1958 to 1962 was not the Gaullism of the post-war RPF. Yet all have been nourished by a common tradition and served by the same men.

### 1. *Gaullism in the Fourth Republic and its antecedents*

Rémond (in the book just quoted), Philip Williams[2] and others have commented on the affinity between classic Gaullism and the French political tradition known as Bonapartism. Indeed Rémond refers to a 'real kinship of inspiration',[3] though he warns against taking the parallel too far. The hallmarks of Bonapartism and its appeal are a strong state under a strong leader, a vigorous emphasis on nationalism, a non-aristocratic and indeed progressive notion of equality—the Napoleonic idea of careers in the service of the state being 'open to all the talents'—and popular sovereignty, its democratic expression preferably expressed in plebiscites and referenda rather than squabbling parliaments. The parallel between this and Gaullism should not be taken too far: the Napoleons were dictators and crushers of liberty which General de Gaulle never was.[4]

After the shortlived Gaullist Union, founded by René Capitant in 1946 and winner of 300,000 votes in the November 1946 election, the first seriously organised political expression of Gaullism was the RPF, the Rally of the French People (*Rassemblement du Peuple Français*), launched at Strasbourg on 7 April 1947. Stridently anti-Communist, hostile to the parliamentary regime of the Fourth Republic, nationalistic and a structured, organised, well-financed mass movement, the RPF at its height had 1,000,000 members. It won almost 40% of the votes at the municipal elections of 1947, 22% and 120 seats in the parliamentary elections of 1951.

The main elements of the Right were found grouped in the RPF and, as Malcolm Anderson has observed, 'virtually all conservative politicians engaged in electoral politics considered coming to terms with the RPF at some time during its history'.[5] In Parliament the RPF was uneasily divided between intransigent opposition to the system (which meant voting with the Communists) or joining the system. The group split in 1952 over whether to support M. Pinay for Prime Minister. Twenty-eight members defied the General and did so. In 1953 de Gaulle withdrew, and the RPF was at an end. The demagogic language and style, the violent behaviour of some supporters, and the authoritarian character of the movement make the RPF the most discreditable and Bonapartist phase of Gaullism.

Various parliamentary groups succeeded the demise of RPF. There was Republican and Social Action (ARS), the group of RPF deputies who had supported the Pinay government. When de Gaulle had withdrawn, Loyalists formed URAS (Union of Social Action Republicans) and subsequently RS (Social Republicans). These, in contrast to the mass movement RPF, were little groups of notables—the most prominent being Jacques Chaban-Delmas who served in various Fourth Republic governments, in particular that of Pierre Mendès-France in 1954.

## 2. *The UNR*

The RPF period was something of an aberration in the history of Gaullism but, two aspects connect the RPF to the Gaullism of the Fifth Republic: the men and the conception of Gaullism as an organised and popular mass electoral force. 'Gaullism', says Philip Williams, 'was the movement of a generation. . . . Twenty years later the core of the party was still formed by men who had answered the call [in 1940] as Resisters or Free Frenchmen. Very many original followers became devotees for life who willingly subordinated their own views (and careers) to the General's successive policies and appeals'.[6] 'Ten telephone calls', recalls Jean Charlot,[7] and the little team of faithful supporters from the 1945 to 1947 period, even those who had been disillusioned by the RPF, were reassembled in 1958: Capitant, Michelet, Debré, Foccart, Pompidou, Chaban-Delmas, Malraux, Frey, Christian Fouchet, Soustelle and the others.

The Union for the New Republic (UNR) was founded on 1 October 1958. Jacques Soustelle, Minister of Information, former Secretary-General of the RPF, who was later to be expelled from the UNR because of his refusal to accept Algerian independence, called the different strands of Gaullism together three days after the referendum triumph in which the Constitution of the Fifth Republic had been adopted. The Social Republicans (Chaban-Delmas and Frey) and Soustelle's *Union pour le Renouveau Français* (Union for the Renewal of France) were there. So was another group, formed in July 1958 from Resistance veterans and RPF militants: the Republican Convention, whose leading members were Marie-Madeleine Fourcade and Léon Delbèque, a conspiratorial Gaullist active in the Algiers Committee of Public Safety and, like Soustelle, subsequently to be removed from the UNR. These elements formed the UNR to fight the Parliamentary elections in October, which it did with great success, becoming the basis of majority government.

Jean Charlot begins his study of the UNR with this sentence that admirably sums up the early days of Gaullism in the Fifth Republic:

What a curious party the UNR is: its *raison d'être* General de Gaulle will have nothing to do with it in principle; it was born with political power in its cradle; it won an electoral triumph before it had the time to organise. The UNR is first and foremost a ministerial team, then a central committee for the selection of candidates in Parliamentary elections, thirdly the largest parliamentary group in the National Assembly, and only lastly a party.[8]

The whole ethos of General de Gaulle and his followers was that political parties were sordid and petty, so the General could not possibly be the UNR's President; he made it clear at his press conference on 23 October 1958 that his name could not be used, 'even as an adjective', to describe any group or candidate. Nevertheless the UNR managed to use the famous name in the party's statement of aims, and ten times in the model election address suggested to candidates[9]—the general message being: support de Gaulle's government, the new Constitution presented by de Gaulle, and the renewal of France inspired by de Gaulle, by voting for those who have always backed de Gaulle. That, essentially, was the party's policy. The statement of aims talks of 'maintaining the Fifth Republic in the spirit of liberty and renewal embodied by General de Gaulle'. The UNR pledged itself to 'defend in all circumstances . . . national independence'. The commitment to 'maintain Algeria in the framework of French sovereignty' did not prevent the party from continuing its faithful support of the General when he declared for Algerian self-determination.

It is a remarkable testament to political flexibility and the power of leadership that the party, formed to support a man brought back to power by those determined to keep Algeria French, held together when Algerian Independence became the aim of national policy. General de Gaulle's speech on radio and television, announcing the principle of self-determination, was on 16 September 1959—eighteen months before the referendum on this question. The first conference *(Assises Nationales)* of the party—or movement as it prefers to be called—in November 1959 centred round the issue of whether fidelity to Gaullism meant fidelity to the French Algeria commitment which had inspired the action of 13 May 1958, the *coup* that had restored de Gaulle to power, or simply fidelity to whatever the General's policy was at any time. Soustelle and the partisans of *'Francisation'* of Algeria were soundly beaten, the party line being best summarised in a letter written by its Secretary-General Albin Chalandon to the rebellious Soustelle a month before the Conference: 'We have no other role than that of demonstrating in discipline and unity our total confidence in the head of state and his Prime Minister. It is a historic role that we are playing',[10] and in the Conference motion defining part of the movement's 'mission' as 'seeing itself as a party of government, closely associated, in initiation and in responsibility, to Government action'.[11] This last phrase would serve admirably as a description of the functions of Great Britain's two major political parties.

With the *Ultras* of *Algérie Française* eliminated—by resignation along with Delbecque, or by expulsion along with Soustelle—the UNR was able to attract to it groups of 'Gaullists of the Left'[12] like Louis Vallon and Léo Hamon who had never been advocates of *Algérie Française*. This group, known as UDT (Democratic Union of Labour), merged with the UNR to form UNR–UDT. Under this lengthy label the Gaullists victoriously fought the parliamentary elections of November 1962 and faced the calmer years of majority government from 1962–7.

### 3. *The UDR State*
Georges Pompidou, appointed Prime Minister in April 1962, is the principal figure in the second act of Gaullism in power. After de Gaulle failed to win an overall majority at the first ballot of the presidential election in 1965, it was clear that simple reliance upon the General's capacity to inspire would be insufficient to maintain Gaullism in power. The Prime Minister turned Party leader and Party organiser. Pompidou and de Gaulle had 'complementary attitudes towards party affairs'.[13] The General despised even the party of his own supporters; Pompidou—from the second ballot in December 1965 onwards—organised. The 1967 and 1968 election campaigns saw Pompidou in the role of Prime Minister/Party Leader with which British electors are familiar. He directed the campaign,[14] addressed the big meetings, and made the election broadcasts.

After the narrow electoral victory of March 1967, and the Lille party conference in June, the Party was reorganised. UNR and UDT were fused into the single Union of Democrats for the Fifth Republic (UDVe), which had been the election banner for all candidates of the *Majorité*. A new Secretary-General too young to have been in the Resistance (Robert Poujade—no relation of the celebrated shopkeeper who created Poujadism, the revolt of the small man, in the 1950s), a new emphasis on recruiting a mass membership, and a new concentration on constituency organisation were the main hallmarks. There were organisations for women and for the more vociferous young Gaullists. The UJP (Union of Young people for Progress), led by the energetic Robert Grossmann, was independent from the Party, but had quite a large and fervently Gaullist membership.

The 1968 elections, held after the great disorders of May, were heralded by a vast rally of Gaullists who filled the entire mile and a half of the Champs Elysées on 30 May straight after the General's broadcast calling for civic action to counter the threat to constitutional government. The local Party organisations became the nuclei of Committees for the Defence of the Republic. The Party and its allies contested the June election in this combative spirit under the label Union for the Defence of the Republic. With these initials UDR, Gaullism had its greatest-ever election victory and they were retained as the movement's title: Union of Democrats for the Republic.[15] The dismissal of Georges Pompidou as Prime Minister in July 1968 and the resignation of the General after the unsuccessful referendum in April 1969 had surprisingly little impact on the cohesion and effectiveness of the UDR as an electoral force.[16] Although presidential candidates like to present themselves as men of union, above party, and never, as in the United States, the candidates of a single party, in fact the backing of a well-organised political party is absolutely indispensable.

During the Pompidou presidency there were some stresses inside the UDR—some unhappy left-wing Gaullists like Capitant and Hamon drifted away from the *Majorité,* and some of the most Gaullian Gaullists in the parliamentary Party, for instance the General's brother-in-law Jacques Vendroux formed a group called 'Presence and Action of Gaullism'. Power, however, is an amazing political adhesive, and in the Pompidou years the expression UDR-state came to be used. In the Elysée, the Government, Parliament, public service bodies like television or the banks, and in the higher ranks of the civil service, UDR men were in charge—perhaps the most effective example of party government, in Richard Rose's sense of the phrase,[17] in the Western world. However the 'barons', the high-priests of the orthodox Gaullist faith, were still strong. At the national conference of the movement at Nantes in November 1973, the 'pragmatists' (supporters of President Pompidou such as Jacques Chirac, at that time Minister of Agriculture) were eclipsed by the representatives of fundamentalist Gaullism. Two recently dismissed ministers Jacques Chaban-Delmas, representing 'progressive' Gaullism, the creator of a new social order, and Michel Debré embodying the side of Gaullism that stresses national grandeur, prestige and influence, carried the 4,500 delegates and, in the phrase of *Le Monde* on 20 November, 'gained control of the movement'. This triumph, more apparent than real since the machinery of government was untouched, was of rather short duration.

## 4. *The UDR in the Presidency of Giscard d'Estaing*

The presidential elections of May 1974 were uncomfortable and distressing for the UDR.[18] Chaban-Delmas, the candidate endorsed by the movement, was badly beaten into third place. Moreover it was clear that many leading figures from the UDR, notably the Pompidou men in the Government, the 'pragmatists' defeated in Nantes, favoured the success of Giscard d'Estaing. The principal Pompidou protégé—Jacques Chirac, Minister of the Interior at the time of his patron's death—became Prime Minister. Chirac, a determined, ambitious and bold tactician, saw the need for the UDR to recover its morale, to resume its place as the principal element of the presidential *Majorité,* to regroup its forces and to extend its influence. A new organisational structure for the Party was worked out and a national Council convened for 14 December 1974. It was a difficult time for the UDR. The Secretary-General Aléxandre Sanguinetti, a deeply convinced Gaullist of the old school, had deep reservations about Giscard d'Estaing as President. He expressed them during the campaign and went on expressing them long after.[19] He had, however, great confidence in Jacques Chirac's capacity to see that Gaullist options were respected in the administration.[20] He therefore consented to a remarkable *coup d'état* whereby Chirac became Secretary-General and took personal control of the movement.

*Le Monde* of 14 December 1974 carried an interview with Maurice Couve de Murville, another Gaullian Gaullist and former Prime Minister, in which the letter boldly affirmed that the UDR was no longer 'the lobby-fodder of those in power' and that the bulk of UDR activists 'did not recognise the head of state as one of their own, as they used to do, even if they had voted for him at the second ballot'. Before the ink was dry, the Central Committee, convened by telegram for 8 a.m., had accepted Sanguinetti's resignation and his replacement on a temporary basis by Chirac. The 'barons' huffed and puffed. Debré and Guichard grumbled; Chaban-Delmas called the process a *'coup de force'* and a *'pantalonnade',* but the move had wide support from the Parliamentary Group and Party activitists. Chirac, at the June 1975 National Conference in Nice, announced his intention of handing over the Secretary-Generalship to André Bord, Mayor of Strasbourg and Minister for War Veterans. In April 1976 a new election took place and Yves Guéna, Mayor of Périgueux in the Dordogne and a former Minister, supported by Chirac, became Secretary-General. Chirac himself remained honorary Secretary-General—an important fact after his resignation as Prime Minister in August 1976. Just as in November 1959, at the height of the *Algérie Française* debate, the UDR had to decide what it meant by 'fidelity'. In 1959 those who thought fidelity to Gaullism meant fidelity to *Algérie Française* and the spirit of the May 13 *coup* were defeated by those who defined it as fidelity to de Gaulle, whatever policy he as head of state saw fit to pursue. In 1974–5 those who thought fidelity meant attachment to the principles and policies for which de Gaulle had stood were beaten by those who saw the role of the Party as being to support the head of state and to provide the principal element of his *Majorité,* provided no outrage was done to fundamental Gaullist options such as 'national independence' or 'strong government' (an additional reason for backing the Presidency—key stone of de Gaulle's Constitution). Thus, in one odd way, the UDR, led in 1974–5 by new men who had replaced the devotees of heroic Gaullism, had come full circle to where it was in the late 1960s. Its unchallenged leader was the Prime Minister. Its main role was to support, electorally and parliamentarily, the government of the day appointed by the President of the Republic. Several times, when trouble has threatened, the Prime Minister was able to come to Parliament and, calming perturbed spirits, gain pro-Government votes for controversial measures: for example the capital gains tax, much watered-down, in June 1976. Gaullism was never a particularly doctrinaire faith and, although it has its principles, influence in the exercise of power remained a more appealing objective.

## 5. *The RPR (Rassemblement pour la République)*
In August 1976 Jacques Chirac resigned as Prime Minister. The reason he gave was that the President would not allow him to do his job as leader of the *Majorité.* Looking ahead to a parliamentary election which might bring a victory for the left, Chirac would have preferred a more aggressive and combative approach, while the President insisted that liberal and humane social reform would win over the uncommitted. Announcing his determination to revive and enlarge the popular audience of Gaullism, Chirac made a triumphant return to Parliament with a by-election victory in November 1976 in his constituency in Corrèze. As honorary Secretary-General of the UDR he called a special Party conference *(Assises nationales extraordinaires)* at which, in the enthusiastic presence of some 50,000 activists the UDR transformed itself into the RPR. The vacuum created in the leadership of the movement by Chirac's departure from the government, the disorientation of a party craving for a strong leader which had just lost an eighteen-year tenancy of prime ministerial office, was all ended by the acclamation of Chirac as President of the new *Rassemblement.*

   *Rassemblement*: the very word is like a knell to toll us back to the days of the RPF. The UNR and the UDR never had a President. The RPF did. In the RPR, like the RPF, the President appoints the Secretary-General and the members of the Executive Committee.

The RPR, like the RPF, began life with a vast rally made up of all social classes, all come to worship a leader and to hear the call to arms against Communism and against national decadence. The President and leader of the RPF, of course, was General de Gaulle. At the Porte de Versailles on 5 December 1976, all the badges said 'Chirac—I believe in him'. The *barons* were there in full support, with the notable exception of Chaban-Delmas. There were cheers for Michel Debré when he observed '*nous sentons les hésitations du pouvoir*' and for Chirac when he declared, 'Hope returns thanks to us, it returns with us.' The aim of the *Rassemblement* was to enlarge the audience of Gaullism: 'We turn to all French people who sense that their society is in peril, whose eyes are open but whose lips remain closed.' A vigorous battle to resist 'collectivism' would be engaged. A manifesto restating the aims of Gaullism—national independence and liberty in a strong state with strong government—was launched. Not to be outdone by *Démocratie Française*, the book published a few weeks earlier by President Giscard d'Estaing,[21] the manifesto, like the President, declares its aim as being to abolish privilege and to help people to a greater sense of responsibility by permitting participation in 'the democracy of everyday life'. But it was the combative style of the RPR that, more than anything else, links it to what Gaullists see as their grand tradition—the Resistance, the RPF, the great march down the Champs Elysées in May 1968. The call to arms has come—and that is what they really like.

## 6. *Beliefs and Attitudes of Gaullism*

The UDR, it was sometimes said, was a party 'not like the others'.[22] It had no ideology, it represented no interest or class, it was not a 'militant-directed' party with doctrinal goals to be pursued even if they were electorally unpopular, it was not simply an umbrella and electoral committee for a few notables—a 'cadre party'. 'Gaullists', says Harvey Waterman: 'a collection of words (Nation, Independence, Progress, Liberty, Fifth Republic), together with caustic references to the ideologies and machinations (i.e. politics) of the "old parties", are combined with a service agency of technocrats for getting things done—and a dominant political position that allows for doing them.'[23] This was more true, perhaps, of the UDR when it was the dominant party of the French political system and the supreme pathway to influence, than in its later role as an element—albeit the largest—in the *Majorité* of a President who 'for the first time in the young history of the Fifth Republic is not one of us'.[24] The UDR had as many distinctive principles and attitudes as any large political party in the West—and as few constraints on the wide interpretation of principles to permit the continued exercise of power. Like nearly every large political party, it was not monolithic. It had a Left and a Right—it had moderates and fundamentalists.

The collection of principles and attitudes which characterises the UDR and the new RPR is of course linked to that Name, which figures reverently, enthusiastically and frequently in all speeches at Gaullist gatherings. Admiration for what the General stood for, his style, and the progress made by the country under his leadership are the basic components of Gaullism. The first phrase that expresses this best is 'national independence': a fundamental belief that the nation-state is the basic political reality, and in consequence a policy of national self-assertion in foreign affairs, defence and technology, a resistance to absorption into alliances or blocs like NATO or submersion of national identity or national interests in supranational bodies like the European Community. These ideas are not uniquely Gaullist—they touch a chord in all Frenchmen, and indeed in people from other countries—but Gaullism has given them a more consistent, triumphant and stylish expression than other political movements.

Consitutional Gaullism, is another sacred principle. Jacques Chirac, at the Nice conference of the UDR in June 1975—a conference which, a year after defeat, set out to redefine the role of Gaullism and restate its aims, proclaimed it thus: 'The Constitution of the Fifth Republic has created, without a shadow of·doubt, the best political regime we have known for centuries. Defending it and consolidating it remain fundamental objectives of our movement. We will accept on this point no compromise, no going back, no reform which threatens its basic principles.' What are these principles? A strong executive in which the President of the Republic is pre-eminent, a legislature with very limited powers to interfere with the executive, popular sovereignty expressed through referenda as well as elections, and a strong state which resists regional autonomy: a set of ideas both distinctive and bold.

A third principle of Gaullism enjoys perhaps a less unanimous consensus than the first two: an economic philosophy which seeks a middle way between 'blind capitalism and totalitarian collectivism'.[25] The word 'participation', meaning involvement by all in economic responsibilities and decision-making, is often used to express this philosophy. It was set out by General de Gaulle, who never shared decision-making with anyone, in a television interview after the events of May on 7 June 1968. Apart from a few half-hearted attempts to promote worker shareholdings in nationalised enterprises, there has been no attempt to give substance to the idea of participation—an idea which President Pompidou was said to regard with little enthusiasm. The way between 'blind capitalism and totalitarian collectivism', which is most characteristic of Gaullists in government, has been a strong belief in state intervention in the private sector, to achieve national objectives. This sets Gaullists apart from other big political parties of the Centre and the Right in the Western World. At Gaullist gatherings one does not hear praise for the virtues of private enterprise, the profit motive and market forces, as one would at a Republican, or even Democratic, convention in the United States or at a British Conservative Party conference. In this Gaullism is more like the British Labour Party, if one removes from the latter the layers of belief in public ownership as an end in itself. The Nation, a strong executive, an interventionist economic philosophy: James Callaghan would be admirably suited to membership of the Gaullist movement, except that he would not care for the Bonapartist hero-worshipping style of the new RPR. To these three central principles which characterise the Gaullist faith one can add a collection of broadly-shared Gaullist attitudes: a contempt for political parties, a Rousseauean conviction that interest groups should not be able to determine or veto public policy, a concern about moral degeneration and the family, about discipline in school and in the army, about the inadequate punishment of offenders and the maintenance of law and order, a preference for a strong and rather authoritarian style of leadership, progressive policies on public expenditure for housing, social services and education, and finally a deep attachment to the idea of Gaullism as a popular movement with an appeal to, and concern for, all classes and sectors of the population.

This combination of principles and attitudes which gives Gaullism its unique flavour is, it must at once be added, reasonably adaptable and, in a softened and moderate form, is something with which men of different political styles, and in particular President Giscard d'Estaing, can live. Although slightly more sympathetic to the aspirations of Parliament, he has always supported constitutional Gaullism. Although slightly more favourable to a liberal economy, his technocratic background predisposes him to interventionism. Above all, though slightly more European and Atlanticist, his Presidency has never called into question the pre-eminence of the nation. Indeed a leading Gaullist,[26] explaining to the writer why there had been so little Gaullist unrest over the President's attachment to a united and integrated European Community and to a directly-elected European Parliament, pointed out how Giscard d'Estaing's approach, by promoting summit meetings at head of government level—the European Council—had done much to reinforce the nation-states and '*l'Europe des Patries*' dear to the heart of General de Gaulle.

## 7. Organisation of the RPR

Writing in the mid 1960s Jean Charlot, in his celebrated thesis on the UNR,[27] his 'study of power inside a political party', describes a very oligarchic party. It was directed by a little inner circle composed in large part of ministers in the Government (almost half of the Executive body—the *Commission Politique*—in 1963).[28] Most members were the 'eternal Gaullists'[29] from the Resistance and the RPF. In 1963 46% of the Central Committee and 62% of the *Commission Politique* had been in the Resistance. Only 28% of the Central Committee and 11% of the *Commission Politique* had been neither in the Resistance, the RPF nor any other Gaullist group of the Fourth Republic.[30] The importance of coopted and *ex-officio* members grew as one approached the summit of the organisational hierarchy, the *Commission Politique,* where they formed a large majority. Outgoing office-holders were usually re-elected at all levels of the organisation. For the key posts— Secretary-General of the movement and the Presidents of the parliamentary groups in the Assembly and the Senate—the weight of the Prime Minister and of the Elysée Palace itself was in the balance for the 'official' candidate. there was central vetting of applications for Party membership, central investiture of parliamentary candidates, central nominations to the posts of Secretary-General of the local Federations in each *département,* central control of any alliances the Party might make at local level. It was a disciplined party whose job was to support Gaullism in power and keep it in power.

Demands from members for a more democratic structure led, at the Lille conference in 1967, to some reforms. Elected representatives of local organisations were to have an increased role, but the distribution of power remained basically unchanged. The passage of time was removing Resistance heroes from the leadership of the Party. After the election defeat in May 1974 of Jacques Chaban-Delmas, of heroic Gaullist pedigree and a leader of the movement, a further reappraisal took place. The Secretary-General Sanguinetti set up an inquest on what had gone wrong, and Charles Pasqua was given the job of presenting a report on 'The Life of the Movement' for the Nice conference in June 1975. Speaking of the aftermath of May 1974, Pasqua said: 'As for the movement, . . . most political observers were agreed in predicting its disappearance, its break-up. It had been deeply upset and disappointed, and doubted whether it had a future. In fact one could wonder whether henceforth the UDR still had a role to play and if it would be capable of playing one.' The inquest had found that the movement lacked confidence in its leadership, criticised its insufficient contact with the rank and file, rejected transformation into a party, and wanted to remain, under new leadership, the UDR.

New leadership the UDR certainly had. Speaker after speaker at Nice heaped fulsome praise upon the Prime Minister Jacques Chirac, and linked support of the President of the Republic to the presence of Chirac at the head of the government. The former minister Roland Nungesser even went so far as to assert that 'what, to the surprise of some, had rallied the immense majority of activists to him was that they discerned in Jacques Chirac a Gaullian style.'

In addition to new leadership, it acquired a more democratic structure. The National Council was to contain many more representatives of rank and file membership. Indeed it has a representative elected by each constituency union. In particular, it—and no longer the central committee—was to elect the Secretary-General of the movement. It was, in the words of a leading member of the Party secretariat, to be the 'real power of the movement'.[31] The metamorphosis into RPR has changed all that. Most of the leadership roles are in the gift of the President of the *Rassemblement,* and the National Council has disappeared.

The UDR, like the other two mass parties in France, the Socialists and Communists, had an intricate network of local organisations, and the RPR has retained it. Members join a *commune* section at village, suburb or town level (or possibly a professional or work-based non-geographical section). There are cantonal committees at *département* electoral division level, and constituency Unions which, as with British political parties, form the basic representative unit. All RPR members living in a parliamentary constituency elect the secretary of the constituency Union, and delegates to the departmental Federation. An average *département,* outside Paris and the big industrial areas, will group three to six constituencies. The Federation at *département* level has a departmental secretary appointed (subject to local ratification) by the Secretary-General of the movement in Paris. The Departmental Committee is the only local body empowered to correspond with the Secretary-General. It sends him its views on national policy and proposals for election candidatures. Each Federation debates Party policy before National Conference and sends voting delegaes to National Conference in proportion to its membership and the number of local councillors it can muster. Regional councils, which can call regional conferences, coordinate Federations at regional level.

At National level there are four structures. the first is National Conference *(Assises Nationales)* which meets every two years and 'defines the general action and political direction of the movement'. All RPR members can attend. Special congresses can also be called by the President of the movement. National Conference elects the President of the movement, and indeed the inaugural rally of December 1976 elected Jacques Chirac by 11,500 votes to nil (400 abstentions and spoilt votes).

The Central Committee meets at least four times a year and directs the movement in accordance with National Conference policy. It makes the final decision on the adoption of election candidates and the tactics relating to second ballot withdrawals. It also deals with disciplinary matters on the advice of a disciplinary subcommittee, the *Commission nationale des conflits*. It elects the Treasurer of the movement and a finance committee. The Central Committee also has six policy subcommittees: Organisation and Elections, Information and Public Relations, Study Groups, Economic and Social Affairs, a subcommittee dealing with Culture, Youth, Sport and Education, and finally one for Foreign Affairs, Cooperation, and Defence. Membership of these subcommittees is proposed by the Secretary-General. The Central Committee is composed of sixty parliamentarians elected by the RPR group in the National Assembly and the Senate, and seventy non-parliamentarians elected regionally by delegates to National Conference. In addition there are 100 members elected on a 'national list' at National Conference, and the members of the Political Council.

The third element, the Political Council *(Conseil politique)* is composed of the President of the movement, the Secretary-General appointed by him, fifteen members elected by the Central Committee, former Prime Ministers who are members of the RPR, and the leaders of the parliamentary groups in the Assembly and the Senate. Additional members can be co-opted by the President in virtue of 'their competence and their national stature'.

Finally the apex of the organisational structure is the Executive Committee *(Commission executive)*. It is an oligarchy appointed by the President, who can vary its composition as he pleases. The first Executive Committee of the RPR, appointed in December 1976, included

*Secretary-General:* Jacques Monod
*Political Delegate:* Yves Guéna (former minister)
*Assistant Secretaries-General:* Anne-Marie Dupuy (former *chef de cabinet* of Georges Pompidou);
  Charles Pasqua (former Deputy);
*National Delegates:* Jean de Lipkowski (former Minister)— International Relations;
  Jean Tiberi (Deputy)—Elections;
  Alain Juppé (former member of M. Chirac's Prime Ministerial cabinet)—policy studies:

Jean-Claude Servan-Schreiber (former Deputy, cousin of the leader of the Radical Party, Jean-Jacques)—relations with the press.

It also included among its membership as an adviser, and as a symbol of French national prestige, the Concorde test pilot André Turcat. The function both of Executive Committee and *Conseil Politique* is to 'assist the President'.

For a movement which has played so powerful a role in French politics for the last twenty years, Gaullism's press is remarkably slim. There used to be a daily newspaper *La Nation* which had a small circulation but was widely quoted in other newspapers and on radio and television; it was thus a useful way of giving wide circulation to the view of orthodox Gaullism. This was replaced by a daily stencilled bulletin, *La Lettre de la Nation*. A party press release, however, lacks the authority of an authentic newspaper. Other extremely modest publications include a monthly newsletter for party activists, *La Lettre des Compagnons*. The RPR plans more ambitious publications.

The UDR did not have a lot of affiliated organisations. Strenuous efforts were made to build up the youth movement *UDR-Jeune*. To the annoyance of UDR organisers, the old Gaullist youth movement UJP (Union of Young people for Progress) broke with the UDR in October 1975 and not only continued in existence but stridently denounced the movement's leadership for supporting Giscard d'Estaing and selling out the sacred principles of Gaullism.

It is hard to arrive at any estimate of the financial resources of the RPR. In comparison with the other political parties, the old UDR headquarters in the rue de Lille, just across the road from the National Assembly, were extremely modest. M. Chirac's team, on the formation of the RPR, moved into an expensive new party headquarters in the Montparnasse skyscraper. In a sense the UDR was everywhere in Paris. All those years of Gaullist domination of power at all levels—ministerial, parliamentary, public service, nationalised corporations—has left behind innumerable former ministers with private offices, and others who contribute to the work of the movement. In addition there is that vast reservoir of ministerial time and ministerial staff which has been available over the years to organise the success of Gaullism.

## 8. *Membership and electorate of the RPR*

On the eve of its transformation into RPR, the UDR claimed 282,000 members. Of these 60% were men, the best-represented age group was 30–50, and the least-represented the under-thirties. Professional, business, management and clerical occupations provided 59% of members. Manual workers (34·8% of the population as a whole) provided 22% of UDR membership. The RPR claims hundreds of new membership applications since the December 5 rally—mainly from people who have not previously joined a political party. These figures may contain an element of honest exaggeration,[32] but it is nevertheless clear that Gaullism remains a mass movement with considerable appeal to all segments of society and a very large organised force indeed.

The electorate of Gaullism today presents some difficulties. Up to 1973, as has already been observed, *Majorité* and Gaullism were virtually synonymous. The UDR accounted for 89% of the entire *Majorité* vote in 1968. Most studies of the remarkable electoral penetration of Gaullism in the 1960s took the view, quite justifiably, that groups like the Independent Republicans and, later, the 'Pompidou' centrist PDM were part of a Gaullist presidential majority which permitted them to exist by endorsing their candidates and not contesting their constituencies. It is clear that since the victory of Giscard d'Estaing in 1974, the various elements of the new *Majorité* can no longer be considered as mere appendages of Gaullism. What is Gaullism anyway? In the first part of this chapter, we saw how Gaullism has changed constantly throughout its history. The Gaullism of the RPF was not the Gaullism of the Fifth Republic and its stable Governments. The 'Gaullist' votes of confidence in General de Gaulle in referenda or in the presidential election of 1965 were not the same as the vote for Pompidou as President, not to mention the meagre support for Chaban-Delmas in 1974. Table 4.1 lists the fortunes of electoral Gaullism in many of its diverse forms. It does not include second ballots for parliamentary elections because they give an incomplete picture of the country,[33] but is should be remembered that many electors in each election did rally to the *Majorité* at the second ballot, possibly from fears of the alternatives. Jean Charlot has pointed out the dangers of interpreting the Chaban-Delmas vote as an irreducibly Gaullist vote: 'It is inaccurate . . . not to believe that some people expressed their Gaullism by voting for Giscard'[34] (who had, unlike Chaban-Delmas, after all been a minister under both de Gaulle and Pompidou).

The problem is to distinguish the support for Gaullism at its height, which includes all the voters who supported the presidential *Majorités* of the General and Pompidou, and a specific RPR electorate today. The first is a well-known and well-researched electorate, the second an unknown quantity.

Sociologically, most observers agree, the electorate of the *Majorité* in 1967 and 1968 was as near to being a perfect microcosm of the French electorate as a whole as it is reasonable to expect a political group to attain. In 1973, by losing some working-class

## GAULLISM IN ELECTIONS SINCE 1945
### (Metropolitan France only)

| | | | | Million votes | % of vote |
|---|---|---|---|---|---|
| **4th Republic** | | | | | |
| Nov. 1946[a] | Parliamentary | Union Gaulliste | | 0·3 | 1·6 |
| June 1951[a] | Parliamentary | RPF | | 4·1 | 21·2 |
| Jan. 1956[a] | Parliamentary | Social Republicans | | 0·5 | 3·9 |
| **5th Republic** | | | | | |
| Nov. 1958[a] | Parliamentary | UNR | (1st ballot) | 4·0 | 19·5 |
| Nov. 1962[b] | Parliamentary | UNR-UDT and allies | (1st ballot) | 7·0 | 37·8 |
| | | UNR-UDT alone | | 5·9 | 31·9 |
| Dec. 1965[c] | Presidential | General de Gaulle | (1st ballot) | 10·4 | 43·7 |
| | | | (2nd ballot) | 12·6 | 54·5 |
| March 1967[c] | Parliamentary | UDVe (UNR and allies) | (1st ballot) | 8·5 | 37·7 |
| | | UNR alone | | 7·3 | 32·2 |
| June 1968[c] | Parliamentary | UDR (UDVe and allies) | (1st ballot) | 9·9 | 44·7 |
| | | UDVe alone | | 8·2 | 37·0 |
| June 1969[c] | Presidential | Georges Pompidou | (1st ballot) | 9·8 | 44·0 |
| | | | (2nd ballot) | 10·7 | 57·6 |
| March 1973[c] | Parliamentary | URP (UDR and allies) | (1st ballot) | 8·5 | 36·0 |
| | | UDR alone | | 6·1 | 25·7 |
| June 1974[d] | Presidential | Jacques Chaban-Delmas | (1st ballot) | 3·6 | 14·6 |

(Note the continual name changes of the *Majorité* as a whole and of the Gaullist movement itself: 1967 UDV[e] and UNR, 1968 UDR and UDV[e], 1973 URP and UDR respectively. Now the movement is RPR).

*Sources*

[a] J. Charlot, *The Gaullist Phenomenon*, p. 38, and J. Charbonnel report *Sociologie du Gaullisme* (UDR publication).
[b] Ministère de l'Intérieur official statistics: *Les Elections Législatives de 1962.*
[c] Statistics of FNSP—Centre d'étude de la vie politique française.
[d] *Le Monde Dossiers et Documents: l'élection présidentielle de mai 1974.*

Table 4·2
SOCIAL COMPOSITION OF *MAJORITÉ* ELECTORS (%)[35]

| | France (1968 census) | *Majorité* 1967 | 1968 | 1973 |
|---|---|---|---|---|
| *Sex* | | | | |
| Men | 48 | 42 | 46 | 43 |
| Women | 52 | 58 | 54 | 57 |
| | 100 | 100 | 100 | 100 |
| *Age* | | | | |
| 21-34 | 29 | 29 | } 55 | 24 |
| 35-49 | 29 | 26 | | 29 |
| 50-64 | 22 | 26 | } 45 | 23 |
| 65 + | 20 | 19 | | 24 |
| | 100 | 100 | 100 | 100 |
| *Occupation* | | | | |
| Top management, professions | 6 | 5 | 6 | 7 |
| Small businessmen | 9 | 11 | 14 | 9 |
| Clerical, lower management | 17 | 16 | 18 | 19 |
| Workers | 32 | 28 | 25 | 21 |
| Farmers | 12 | 16 | 18 | 17 |
| Retired and non-working | 24 | 24 | 19 | 27 |
| | 100 | 100 | 100 | 100 |
| *Habitat* | | | | |
| Rural villages | 30 | 34 | 40 | 38 |
| Towns under 20,000 | 14 | 16 | 16 | 16 |
| Towns 20,000-100,000 | 14 | 14 | 11 | 12 |
| Cities over 100,000 | 25 | 19 | 19 | 20 |
| Paris area | 17 | 17 | 14 | 14 |
| | 100 | 100 | 100 | 100 |

support to the Left,[36] it came to have a more traditionally conservative composition.

As in 1967, the *Majorité* electorate in 1973 was disproportionately feminine and disproportionately rural. In 1973 support had been gained among the elderly but lost among the young, the industrial workers, and inhabitants of large cities. *Majorité* voters are also much more religious than the opposition's, it being an ancient if waning French political tradition for Catholics to vote mainly for right and centre parties.[37]

Regionally, Gaullism and the changing *Majorités* that have grown from it have been strongest in traditional Catholic bastions of the right: Alsace and Lorraine, Brittany, the Loire country, the Southern parts of the Auvergne. It has also been strong in the dynamic industrial areas of the North, the North-east, and Paris.

Its weakest areas were the old anticlerical regions with a venerable tradition of voting for the Left—the southern strip of France from the Pyrenees to the Alps, and the Centre. Gaullism made a great breakthrough into these areas, which are economically rather backward and traditionalist, in the landslide of 1968. It held these gains in 1973, but began to loose its grip on the industrial areas. The UDR remained surprisingly weak among 'notables'—those well-entrenched and indestructible local chieftains who occupy so many town halls. A vast number of mayors were described in the 1971 official electoral statistics as 'miscellaneous moderates favourable to the *Majorité*' (31·7%), but only 8·7% of mayors (including some of important cities like Bordeaux) were specifically and avowedly Gaullist. This relative lack of notables, which distinguished the UDR sharply from its centrist and independent Republican allies, is not an unmitigated source of regret. As Malcolm Anderson points out, 'The survival of the notable is of great political importance because the basis of the disciplinary authority of the Gaullist party would be at risk if a large minority of its Deputies became notables ensconced in impregnable local positions.'[38]

As for the indestructibly UDR element of this *Majorité*, we have little to go on. Some observers have argued that the Chaban-Delmas voters, discounting his personal support in Bordeaux and Aquitaine, are the hard-core of pure Gaullism. There is some evidence to support this: opinion polls during the 1974 campaign indicated that supporters of Chaban-Delmas were more nationalist than others, and that his image as a 'real Gaullist' was a reason for voting for him.[39] But it tells us nothing of the potential electorate for RPR candidates in the Parliamentary elections of 1978. The only indicators we have are the opinion polls on voting intentions. In 1975 and 1976 they gave the Independent Republicans a big lead over UDR—but this only really indicated the prestige of a presidential office still identified with the RI, not the likely fate of UDR candidates in an actual election. In late 1976, polls showed Chirac behind Giscard d'Estaing in voting intentions at an imaginary presidential election, though not very far behind. In November 1976, a final indicator, UDR candidates seemed to fare better at by-elections against the left than their colleagues from other elements of the *Majorité*, especially the Independent Republicans who lost two seats. The picture is unclear and fluctuates widely. If the *Majorité* presents a single candidate in most constituencies and restricts first ballot competition between the RPR and their centrist or Independent Republican allies, then once again there will merely be a global *Majorité* electorate and not one specifically Gaullist—or, for that matter, Giscardian.

NOTES

1. *The Right Wing in France from 1815 to de Gaulle*, University of Pennsylvania Press, 2nd edn, 1966, p. 367.
2. *Crisis and Compromise*, Longmans, 3rd edn, 1964, p. 141 and n.
3. *The Right Wing in France*, p. 380.
4. At his press conference on 19 May 1958, General de Gaulle was faced with the remark, 'Some people fear that if you return to power you will attack public liberties.' He replied: 'Have I ever done so? On the contrary, I restored them when they had disappeared [a reference to the restoration of democracy after the Liberation]. Is it credible that I am going to begin a career as a dictator at the age of sixty-seven?'
5. *Conservative Politics in France*, Allen and Unwin, 1973, p. 311.
6. *Crisis and Compromise*, p. 133.
7. 'L'UNR: étude du pouvoir au sein d'un parti politique', *Cahiers de la FNSP*, 1967, p. 303.
8. *Ibid.*, p. 23.
9. See Jean Charlot, *Le Gaullisme*, Paris, Colin, 1970, pp. 88–92.
10. *Ibid.*, p. 102.
11. *Ibid.*, p. 108.
12. It used sometimes to be said that General de Gaulle was a '*Gaullist de Gauche*'!
13. Frank L. Wilson, 'Gaullism without de Gaulle', *Western Political Quarterly*, 1973, p. 506.
14. Note his chairmanship of the Action Committee for the Fifth Republic (the body responsible for adopting the candidates of the *Majorité*) in 1967.
15. Actually the official title was still Union of Democrats for the Fifth Republic but the 'Fifth' was silent.
16. Its support for Pompidou's election is an important theme of R. G. Schwartzenburg's book on the presidential elections of 1969, *La Guerre de succession*, Presses Universitaires de France, 1969. See also below, p. 199.
17. 'The variability of party government', *Political Studies*, Dec. 1969, pp. 413–45, and E. Suleiman, *Politics, Power and Bureaucracy in France: the Administrative Elite*, Princeton University Press, 1974, pp. 164 and 361.
18. See p. 203.
19. For instance, he declared on France-Inter on 25 August 1975, in reply to the question 'Are you now an unconditional supporter of M. Giscard d'Estaing?', 'No. In politics you have to choose the lesser evil. Between abstention, Mitterrand and Giscard, Giscard was the lesser evil. We shall have to wait until the end of his mandate to see if we were right.'
20. He was also personally indebted to Chirac. *Le Monde* of 9 October 1973 recounts how the central committee was deadlocked with an equal vote for both candidates for the position of Secretary-General of the movement. Chirac, summoned from the provinces, arrived to vote for Sanguinetti.
21. Paris: Fayard, 1976.
22. Thorez's famous phrase about the French Communist Party has often been applied to Gaullism, e.g. Bernard le Calloch, *La Révolution silencieuse: du Gaullisme au pouvoir*, Paris: Eds. Didier, 1971.
23. *Political Change in Contemporary France*, Merrill, 1969, p. 126.
24. Speech of Charles Pasqua, *Assisses Nationales* (National Conference) of the UDR, Nice, 14 June 1975.

25. Speech by Pierre Messmer, former Prime Minister, at Nice Conference, 14 June 1975.
26. Jean de Lipkowski, ex-Minister of Cooperation, in an interview Dec. 1975. M. de Lipkowski is now a member of the RPR Executive Committee.
27. 'L'UNR . . .', *Cahiers de la FNSP*, 1967.
28. *Ibid.*, pp. 244 and 228.
29. *'Gaullistes de toujours'.*
30. Charlot, 'L'UNR . . .', pp. 218–9.
31. Interview with Charles Pasqua, April 1976.
32. See Charlot's assessment of UDR membership in 1970, *The Gaullist Phenomenon*, p. 131.
33. See below, p. 184.
34. In *France at the Polls*, ed: Howard R. Penniman, American Enterprise
35. Jean Labrousse and Jean-Marc Lech in J. Charlot, ed., *Quand la Gauche peut gagner*, Paris: Moreau, 1973, p. 52.
36. Note that General de Gaulle himself had a strong working-class following. According to F. Goguel, 'Combien y-a-t-il eu d'électeurs de gauche parmi ceux qui ont voté 5 déc. 1965 pour le General de Gaulle', *Revue Française de Science Politique*, Feb. 1967, pp. 65–9. Some 3 million voters who had voted for the left in 1956 voted for de Gaulle and not François Mitterrand in the 1965 presidential election.
37. See below Ch. 16; see also Ch. 7 for Socialist gains among Catholics in 1973–74 and J. F. Bizot; *Au Parti des Socialistes*, Paris: Grasset, 1975, pp. 337–57.
38. *Conservative Politics in France*, p. 167.
39. See J. Charlot in Penniman, ed., *France at the Polls*, pp. 54–5.

# 5

## PARTIES OF THE *MAJORITÉ*:
## II. *GISCARDIENS* AND CENTRISTS

There are three structured mass-membership parties in France.
Two are on the left—the Communists and the Socialists. The other
is the RPR (ex-UDR) discussed in the last chapter. The remaining
groups in the *Majorité*—the Independent Republicans and the
various groups of centrists now joined in the Centre for Social
Democracy (CDS)—are more like the traditional cadre parties
described by Duverger in his classic study of political parties.[1]
Grouped around a few leaders of local or national renown,
replying on their personal electoral positions which allow them the
maximum room to negotiate alliances and coalitions, they would
seem to most British people more like parliamentary factions than
political parties. Despite their lack of a mass-membership,
however, these centrists groupings are very important. Firstly,
'France', according to President Giscard d'Estaing, who himself led
the Independent Republicans, 'wants to be governed from the
Centre'. He means by this that the aspirations of the French are
essentially those of moderates and are not met by any of the big
battalions. Gaullism is too nationalistic and too authoritarian, and
Socialism too Marxist and too collectivist. Secondly, Giscard
d'Estaing did win the presidential election, and opinion polls in
1975 and 1976 suggested that if his Independent Republicans had a
candidate in all constituencies they would benefit from the lustre of
the Presidency, and have a chance of running ahead of the
UDR/RPR. Thirdly, the smaller parties of the *Majorité* are
indispensable to the stability of the government coalition, and the
'moderate' image of leaders like Jean Lecanuet are important
elements in its electoral appeal.

### 1. *The Independent Republicans (RI)*
Gaullism and the Independent Republicans have both belonged,
since 1962 when the latter began its official life, to the *Majorité*. In
that mighty army, however, the UDR provided the dense ranks of
the infantry, the heavy artillery and the generals. The Independent
Republicans have provided a couple of dashing and aristocratic
divisions of hussars and lancers. Gaullism and the Independent
Republicans each draw their inspiration from one man, though
not the same one. The UDR took the form of a great political
movement based on the historical role and the thought of General

de Gaulle. The Independent Republicans, on the other hand, are a club formed to promote and be carried upwards by the career of Valéry Giscard d'Estaing. Now that their man is in the Elysée, they would like to become a great presidential movement with the capacity to harness and to organise the vast electorate that gave Giscard d'Estaing such a remarkable success even at the first ballot in June 1974.

The RI grew out of a very loose-knit association called CNI (Independents' National Centre), which was formed in 1948 with the modest aim of avoiding unnecessary electoral competition between those who were neither Marxists, Radicals, nor MRP. In 1951 the association was extended to include the various peasant party federations, and it became CNIP (National Centre of Independents and Peasants). Its organiser was Roger Duchet and its leading light a conservative Independent, who became Prime Minister in 1952 and who symbolises to this day rectitude, financial orthodoxy and cautious commonsense: Antoine Pinay. The independents associated with Pinay represented what René Rémond calls 'the restoration of the essential mentality and ideology of the Orleanist Right . . . the body of thought, half-liberal and half-conservative that has continued since the July Monarchy'.[2] The liberal element of this 'half-liberal and half-conservative tradition' is that preference for a non-authoritarian parliamentary regime with a free market 'liberal' economy, associated with a certain type of French conservatism from the bourgeois monarch Louis-Philippe onwards. It is a conservatism that is distinguished from the other strands of the French Right— Bonapartism and the old Ultra Royalist tradition. The partisans of this type of liberal conservatism have traditionally been known as the Moderates and they remained important in politics throughout the Third and Fourth Republics, with their electoral strength in rural Catholicism.

In 1958 the Moderates supported de Gaulle—some of them without great enthusiasm and conditional upon an imagined commitment to keep Algeria French. In the 1958 elections, CNIP candidates had a big success. Their vote increased from $1\frac{1}{2}$ million to $4\frac{1}{2}$ million, and they formed a parliamentary group 118 strong. 'This success was to a large ... . extent due to the enthusiastic public support which CNIP candidates gave to the new Republic and to General de Gaulle personally.'[3] 'People voted for the Moderates because they were Gaullists.'[4] The Independents in Parliament, now known as IPAS (Independents and Peasants for Social Action), on the whole supported the Government, which had Antoine Pinay as Minister of Finance and other of their members in it, including Giscard d'Estaing. They were by no means unconditional. Most of them refused to support Pinay's 1959 budget, and they split over the issue of self-determination for Algeria, taking every position from support for de Gaulle (Giscard d'Estaing) to total opposition (Duchet). The CNIP wanted their ministers to follow the example of MRP ministers and resign when de Gaulle, on 15 May 1962, made his famous derisory remarks about Europe (speaking Volapük, a made-up language even more obscure than Esperanto). They did not. Finally the CNIP ship foundered on the rocks of the October 1962 referendum on direct elections for the Presidency, and it was the few survivors clinging to the spars that, after the election in November, formed in Parliament the Independent Republican group.

De Gaulle's initiative in calling that referendum in October 1962, its masterly timing after the ending of the Algerian crisis, and the way that all opponents of the referendum were made to seem like opponents of the stability and renewal for which the new Republic stood, has been described in Chapter 2. Most of the moderates, true to their parliamentary tradition, expressed their outrage at the way the Constitution and Parliament were flouted by the direct submission to the people of a major constitutional reform and their hostility to the Bonapartist idea of a directly elected Presidency. They voted for a motion of censure which brought down the Government, and then joined the motley crew of Socialists, Radicals and MRP in the ill-fated 'Cartel des Non'. After their referendum defeat, electoral slaughter followed for the Moderates who had helped to bring down the Government and campaigned against a popular reform. Those independents who had not voted for the motion of censure, and one or two others who took the precaution of breaking with the CNIP, were rewarded by having no Gaullist opponent. A parliamentary group of thirty-five was formed in December 1962 under the chairmanship of Raymond Mondon, deputy for the Moselle, but clearly under the leadership of Giscard d'Estaing—now Minister of Finance. Indeed, just as the UDR members have always commonly been called Gaullists, the RI have always been known as *Giscardiens*.

From 1962 to the present day, the RI have been committed to the support of both the regime, the Fifth Republic, and the government of the day. They have, in other words, been a reliable though not entirely unconditional component of the *Majorité*. They have sailed close to the wind on occasions, as we shall see, but in Parliament, at least, they have never used their votes to bring down the government by supporting a motion of censure. Apart from the period 1968–73, Gaullism has never had a parliamentary majority on its own. Giscard d'Estaing and his friends were able to exploit this position with great skill, never threatening to bring down the government,[5] yet managing by their strategic importance to the stability of the governing coalition to acquire an influence out of proportion to their numerical strength.[6] The RI's role as a parliamentary ginger group inside the *Majorité* is a very interesting one—and exerted on behalf of the principle of increased influence for backbenchers. Philip Williams, quoting an RI deputy's description of the group's role as 'rather like that of France within the Atlantic alliance', reports that

'it was through the RI that the leadership [of the government] was warned when the rest of the house felt strongly that the government was abusing its authority—as over the State Security Court . . . It was also through the RI that doubts within the UNR ranks, whether on the substance of policy or on its electoral implications could be conveyed without compromising the doubters' reputations for loyalty. A few—or even many—RI abstentions would not bring the government down but they acted as a useful alarm signal. UNR members might resent the greater independence of their allies . . . but they were sometimes glad of an indirect channel of protest to the government'.[7]

They have also marked their separate personality by sitting as part of the Liberal Group in the European Parliament instead of with their domestic Gaullist allies, who sit almost alone in a group called European Democrats.

Two important changes of emphasis occurred after Giscard d'Estaing was dismissed from the Government in January 1966. The RI became more openly critical of the government and, overcoming the Independents' classic dislike of organisation, organised. Giscard d'Estaing skilfully cultivated the art of attracting maximum attention for his criticisms of General de Gaulle. In a famous phrase on 10 January 1967 he described his attitude to the Government as *'oui mais'*—support but not unconditional support. He was critical of de Gaulle over various issues: condemnation of Israel in the Middle East war, his support for Quebec nationalism, and the assumption by the Government in May of special powers to revise the social security laws. Consequently, he went so far on 17 August 1967 as to attack de Gaulle's 'solitary exercise of power'. In the election that followed the Events of May 1968, Giscard d'Estaing's election broadcasts did not follow the UDR in blaming all the troubles on Communists and agitators, but allowed criticism to creep in of a government insufficiently sensitive to popular grievances. The cruellest cut, however, was his public opposition to the Referendum proposals for Senate and regional reform in April 1969.[8] This directly contributed to the narrow defeat of the Referendum, and hence to the General's resignation.[9] This was the most direct disloyalty that Giscard and his friends ever perpetrated, and Gaullists have never forgotten it.

The second change of emphasis was the formation of a party in the country, as opposed to a mere parliamentary group. The

National Federation of Independent Republicans (FNRI) was launched in June 1966. It had regional federations, and it had a youth movement—the JRI (Young Independent Republicans), which by 1967 had sixteen groups and some 300 members. Above all it had the *Clubs Perspectives et Réalités*—(clubs for political discussion called 'Perspectives and Realities'). The first one had been set up in Paris in May 1965, but in the Spring of 1966 Giscard d'Estaing made a Gaullian progress through France, which he called his 'tour of thought and action', and during which he inaugurated further branches of the club: Nice in March, Lille in June. By 1967 there were fourteen clubs with a total membership of 700, and by 1970 fifty-five clubs with 5,000 members (1,500 in Paris). The clubs held national annual conventions each of which, unlike Party conferences, had a single theme—for instance 'Europe'. Like a non-socialist Fabian society, the clubs see themselves as contributors of new progressive ideas to political debate. Like a non-socialist version of the political clubs grouped in the Convention of Republican Institutions, they recruit largely among top civil servants, intellectuals, and professional and business men and see themselves as a nursery for political talent. The clubs played an important part in the 1974 Presidential elections when they formed the nuclei of the local and national committees that organised support for Giscard d'Estaing. At their Ninth National Convention at Lyon in May 1976, a membership of 20,000, distributed over 218 clubs,[10] was claimed, entitling them to be considered one of the most dynamic movements in the Presidential Majorité and 'one of the strongest on the ground'. Their national President is Jean-Pierre Fourcade, Minister of Equipment, ex-Minister of Finance, and former member of Giscard d'Estaing's cabinet at the Ministry of Finance. Fourcade's presence indicates the strong personal interest taken in the clubs by the President of the Republic.

(a) *Philosophy of the RI.* Is there a set of ideas that can be called 'Independent Republican', or are we merely talking about the thoughts of Valéry Giscard d'Estaing? A man of remarkable ability, style and ambition, trained not in one but in both of the élite schools for top administrators, ENA and the Polytechnique, of aristocratic descent and fortune, Giscard d'Estaing is extraordinarily well equipped for that task of national leadership for which he has so sedulously prepared himself. Indeed born to rule, suggest the authors of a Communist publication on the 1974 election: 'There is a breed of partridge where one bird bears a red mark indicating that he will be the leader. Is Valéry Giscard d'Estaing one of these? . . . a chieftain marked by destiny?'[11] The Independent Republicans have been his creature, vehicle, forum, sounding-board and troops. Their ideas his ideas, their words his words, their successes his successes, the Independent Republicans have been far more the instrument of Giscard d'Estaing than ever Gaullist parties were of de Gaulle.

Paradoxically, however, this does not mean that all Independent Republicans identify with the ideas of Giscard d'Estaing, and that the party is homogeneous. This is noticeable, first of all, at the level of the élite. There are some parliamentarians, Independents and Moderates in 1958 and before, who joined up with Independent Republicans when they were formed in 1962, but who are really more Gaullist than *Giscardien*. The classic example is Raymond Marcellin, a strong-arm authoritarian Minister of the Interior under de Gaulle and Pompidou, who in his local newspaper *Le Républicain Indépendent de l'Ouest* used to attack Giscard d'Estaing's criticisms of the General and the conditionality of his support for the government.[12] In addition, it has already been observed, four-fifths of the RI Parliamentary group preferred to follow the General in voting Yes at the 1969 referendum. Finally it should be remembered that some fairly influential RIs of the 1960s like the late Raymond Mondon, at that time Chairman of the RI Parliamentary Group, and Alain Griotteray, began life in the RPF.

There is also an absence of unanimity between the ideas of Giscard d'Estaing and the RI at rank-and-file level. Many RI electors see the job of their party, rather as Marcellin does, as being to help keep law and order and to fight Communism. The President's conceptions of a liberal society—which includes, for example, the freedom to have abortions—is not really to their taste. A glance at the 'Readers' Letters' columns in the (rather intermittent) RI magazine *France Moderne* confirms this, e.g. 'one thing really worries me today: pornography in all its forms . . .'[13] The RI are not the first French political party which has had the problem of a progressive leadership and a conservative electorate, moving farther and farther apart. The MRP in the Fourth Republic was in exactly the same position.

Nevertheless the leading members of the RI organisation, its ministers in the Government, men like Michel Poniatowski, Michel d'Ornano and Jacques Dominati, and the large number of people who participated in the presidential campaign are *Giscardiens* even if they are not all quite as liberal as the President professes to be. The Giscardian philosophy is summed up in the phrase 'advanced liberal society'[14] and in two other words, 'centrist' and 'European'. 'The European theme is the one the RI exploit the most readily—for very understandable reasons: it is without doubt the issue which permits them to distinguish themselves best from their Gaullist partners.'[15] Giscard d'Estaing and his friends were always more favourably disposed than

Gaullists to the development of European Community institutions such as the European Parliament, to the enlargement of the Community to include in particular Great Britain, and to cooperation with Community partners even in matters like defence. Giscard's period as President has so far coincided with a rather negative phase in the history of European integration, and he has certainly not been associated yet with the relaunching of the 'European Dream'. He has, however, reiterated in audiences with the Centre Democrat element in his *Majorité* that he fully intends to achieve European Union, and prefers for such a union a presidential system of leadership.[16] He endeavours to reassure the Gaullist forces in his *Majorité,* on the other hand, that he is merely continuing the work of President Pompidou, who was associated with many 'European' initiatives.[17]

The word Centre has been enjoying a tremendous vogue in recent years, not only in France. It has come to mean not only moderate, rejecting extremes of Right and Left, sensible and realistic, but progressive as well—one has only to look at the 'Centrists' in the British Labour Party. As men of the Centre, the *Giscardiens* reject Marxism and the class struggle. They also reject the authoritarianism, the mysticism and the exaltation of the Nation associated with Gaullism. The difficulty with this is that the Moderates and the Centre are viewed in France very much as part of a Right-wing tradition. Colliard quotes an opinion survey of 1967, admittedly a little out of date now, showing Giscard d'Estaing perceived as a man of the Right by a large majority of voters from all points of the political compass, including electors of the Right.[18] Winning over Jean Lecanuet, leader of the Centre Democrats, and his Centrist electoral following was an important factor in Giscard's electoral victory. That success, however, was based on a more conservative and less working-class electorate than had voted for his predecessors—particularly de Gaulle. Consequently when Giscard and his associates, giving the phrase its progressive turn, say they want to 'govern in the Centre', that can only mean, according to André Fontaine, 'when one has been elected by a Right-wing majority, govern more on the Right than on the Left'.[19]

The importance of being liberal is as fundamental, and as imprecise, as being in the Centre. We are all liberals now and we are all centrists. The two terms are synonymous and equally elastic. Giscard d'Estaing expresses a fundamental liberalism in his conviction that French political life should be less tense and sectarian. 'Peaceful', 'reasonable' and 'tolerant' are the key words in the Thoughts of Chairman Giscard as presented in his book *La Démocratie Française*[20]. He would like to have reasonable contacts with the opposition such as a British Prime Minister enjoys. Other aspects of the political liberalism associated with Giscard d'Estaing and the Independent Republicans are in this vein. There is an attachment to Parliamentary institutions, a desire to give Parliament a more significant role than Gaullism would ever allow it. There is the Giscardian emphasis on civil liberties. During the presidential election campaign 1974 the two important civil liberties issues, long the subject of criticism by Independent Republicans, were telephone tapping and government interference with the freedom of information on television and radio. Since the election, it has been announced that telephone tapping, except where public safety and national security are involved, has been stopped, and the ORTF, the State Television and Radio organisation, has been abolished, being replaced by a number of separate and competing, though publicly financed, channels. A further aspect of Giscardian political liberalism is decentralisation, and greater autonomy for regions and for local authorities. Possibly because he cannot afford to raise Jacobin hackles upon the spines of his Gaullist supporters, Giscard d'Estaing has not so far been a reforming President in this matter. Paris has at last been granted a Mayor, but demands for greater Corsican autonomy, expressed with violence it is true, have met with repression. In concluding the section on the *Giscardiens* and civil and political liberties, it must be observed that M. Poniatowski, the leading Independent Republican in the Government, veteran critic of Gaullist abuses of executive power and right hand man of President Giscard d'Estaing, has not proved a particularly liberal Minister of the Interior. He has deployed his police and purged his Prefects in the strong-arm manner traditional to his office.

Liberalism, as expressed by Giscard d'Estaing and his followers, has a progressive-social-justice as well as a political aspect. The President sees himself as a social reformer. He wants to promote the equality of the sexes (indeed he appointed a 'Secretary of State for the Feminine Condition'). He wants to liberalise social legislation—on abortion, for instance—and in so doing has angered many supporters. He wants to hit the profits of land speculation, and in so doing has angered many supporters. He wants to do something about shanty towns and the conditions of immigrant workers, and to this end he has appointed another Secretary of State and engaged the involvement of Mme Giscard d'Estaing herself.

Social justice, civil liberties, representative institutions, decentralisation—these are the basic elements of the 'advanced liberal society' which is the Giscardian grand design. When the French use the word 'liberal' however, they usually do so in the economic sense of a private enterprise economy relatively unregulated by the State. Colliard confirms that while there may be some nostalgia in the ranks for a liberal economy, the RI philosophy places much more emphasis on political than economic liberalism.[21] As pointed out in the chapter on the UDR and its ideas, Giscard d'Estaing, with his background as a trained civil servant, is as convinced as the Gaullists of the legitimacy of considerable state intervention if a modern economy is to function in the interests of the community. The wide consensus on this matter in France is probably one of the reasons for the French economic miracle.[22]

*(b) Organisation of the RI.* The last section, under the guise of a discussion of the Independent Republican philosophy, mainly presented the policies and attitudes of M. Giscard d'Estaing. It even discussed the initiatives of Giscard as President, although custom insits that the President of the Republic is above party and ceases to belong to one. This is because there really is no Independent Republican philosophy which is not Giscardian, and there is no *raison d'être* for the Independent Republicans outside their support for the President. The man who masterminded the Presidential campaign in 1974 and who is the great fund-raiser for the RI, Victor Chapot, is in the President's cabinet and has an office at the Elysée Palace. Party headquarters, formerly near Parliament in the Boulevard St-Germain, have followed the President across the river. In a larger building in rue de la Bienfaisance they are handy for the Elysée and M. Poniatowski's Ministry of the Interior. The Independent Republicans are still the President's men.

After the election campaign, which produced a wave of pro-Giscard enthusiasm and young campaign workers, it was hoped that the RI would be relaunched as a Presidential movement, a mass party. The Party's ambition is to become the 'Majority of the *Majorité*'—that is to say a larger Parliamentary Group than the RPR. An important objective is therefore to create more local federations and to find influential local people who will make suitable RI candidates. There is a small team from party headquarters which scours the country for the likely and the presentable, and there is a club '*Agir pour l'Avenir*' (Action for the Future) which trains candidates when they have been discovered. The Independent Republicans parliamentary strength has gradually grown over the years as a proportion of the *Majorité*—mainly by the device of skilfully negotiating with the other groups in the *Majorité* for candidatures in winnable districts.

The RI, perhaps because they are based more on local notables than the Gaullists, perhaps because their reforming image and conditional support for the Government has distinguished them from Gaullists, have till recently been better able to withstand ebbing government popularity. Firmly believing that they have

Table 5.1

RI AS PROPORTION OF THE *MAJORITÉ*
(Parliamentary Seats)

|  | 1962 | 1967 | 1968 | 1973 |
|---|---|---|---|---|
| UNR/UDR | 233 | 201 | 296 | 183 |
| RI | 37 | 44 | 64 | 55 |
| CDP | — | — | — | 30 |
| *Majorité* | 270 | 245 | 360 | 268 |
| RI as % of *Majorité* | 13·7% | 18·0% | 17·8% | 20·5% |
| Ratio of RI to Gaullists | 1 : 6·3 | 1 : 4·6 | 1 : 4·6 | 1 : 3·3 |

more popular appeal than the Gaullists, the RI have also argued the case for Primaries—more than one candidate of the *Majorité* in constituencies at the first ballot—to see which element of the *Majorité* the electors really want to support at the second ballot.[23] In 1973, not a particularly good election for the *Majorité* defending their landslide gains of 1968, ten RIs were elected at Primaries. Three were of no significance—minor opposition from Centrists not Gaullists in safe seats.[24] Three were straightforward RI/Gaullist 'primaries'. In one, the Independent Republican won the primary against a Gaullist and took the seat from the Socialists.[25] The three others, with personal support in the campaign from Giscard d'Estaing, actually defeated sitting Gaullist Deputies.[26] If the RI want to achieve their aim of becoming the majority of the *Majorité,* they will need to continue the strategy of primaries in 1978 in the hope that the President's prestige and popularity will help their candidates. Set against this, though, is the resurgent Gaullism of Chirac's RPR, and the need of the *Majorité* to appear united against the threat from the Left.

Parliamentary and electoral tactics are therefore the main concern of the RI. Nevertheless, the aim to turn the Party from a group of notables into a mass movement is being actively pursued. A local delegate has been appointed in each parliamentary constituency to organise local committees. In each *département* there is a Federation with an elected Bureau, and there are regional coordinating bodies. At national level, Congress, held every two years, elects, among others, the president and the secretary–general of the Party. The direction of the Party is undertaken by a dovetailed hierarchy of committees. The constituency delegates sit on the National Council, as do all members of the next level: the *Comité Directeur*. The *Comité Directeur* includes all RI parliamentarians and ministers, representatives of *département* Federations, the youth movement GSL (*Génération Sociale et Liberale*) and the *Perspectives et Realités* clubs, and all members of the highest party echelon: the *Bureau Politique*. There are at present eighty members of the *Bureau Politique* including thirty-one representatives of the parliamentary group. Leading members in 1976 included:

*President:* Michel Poniatowski—Minister of the Interior
*Secretary-General:* Jacques Dominati (Deputy and Paris City Council)
*Vice-Presidents:* Philippe de Bourgoing
   Jean-Pierre Soisson—Minister for Sport
   Roger Chinaud—President of Parliamentary Group
   Michel d'Ornano—Minister for Industry
The four of the twelve national secretaries most concerned with Party organisation.
Victor Chapot—Member of M. Giscard d'Estaing's personal cabinet, a former TPG[27], *chef de cabinet* of the President when he was Minister of Finance, director of Sud-Radio and Sofirad, the state holding company which partly owns the commercial radio stations Europe 1 and Radio Monte Carlo.
Bertrand de Maigret—Organiser of the 'Committees to support the President of the Republic'
Raymond Long—Former Prefect and once *chef de cabinet* of M. Pompidou
*Perspectives et Realités* are represented by Jean-Pierre Fourcade, Minister of Equipment (Minister of Finance until the August 1976 reshuffle), an official from his *cabinet,* and by the clubs' Secretary-General Philippe Poncet, another ministerial *cabinet* official who used to be in M. Giscard d'Estaing's *cabinet.*

In the Spring of 1977, Jean-Pierre Soisson took over as Secretary-General and the RI changed its name to *Parti Républicain* (Republican Party).

Any pretension to build a mass popular movement can only be based on the appeal and prestige of Giscard d'Estaing. 'Giscard for President' committees sprang up all over the country during the election campaign of 1974. In an attempt to harness the support generated then, a *Comité National de Soutien pour le Président de la République* (National Committee to support the President) was launched in December 1976, and claimed 47,000 supporters by November 1976. These supporters are of three types: presidential campaign volunteers, members of parties in the *Majorité,* and new subscribers to the *Comité* journal, *Réformer.* The *Comité de Soutien* does not have a local organisation running parallel to the RI, though there are branches based on professions—medicine and journalism, for example. Meetings are held in various parts of the country, especially in key marginal cities where the need for cohesion in the *Majorité* is greatest. These meetings, much more

*Majorité* than RI, have successfully attracted large audiences much less upper-class in character than the RI. Speakers are usually ministers from any one or all of the parties in the *Majorité,* and local dignitaries not associated with the RI but who support the *Majorité* on the platform. The *Comité* publishes leaflets for distribution in factories and Unions. It plans a digest of the President's book *Démocratie française* of which quarter of a million will be distributed. It claims to be 'independent of all political parties'.[28] *Réformer,* addressing itself to all 'liberals', publishes contributions by ministers from all parts of the *Majorité,* and places it emphasis on support for Giscard and his reforms. Readers can cut out and send off forms requesting information on Presidential policies. Nevertheless, the *Comité* is closely associated with the RI—it is run from RI headquarters by Bertrand de Maigret, who is a member of the RI *Bureau Politique* The *Comité* has the appearance of being well-financed.

A total of 70,000 members, an exaggerated figure, is claimed by the RI, 47,000 by the *Comité de Soutien,* 30,000 by GSL (the artfully chosen G in the title makes it easy to call them the 'Young *Giscardiens'*), and 20,000 by *'Perspectives et Réalités'* with all four categories overlapping to a great extent. Over 20,000 supporters turned up to the RI National Convention at the Champ de Mars in Paris in June 1976 to celebrate two years of Giscardian rule. Members pay an annual subscription of 40F. to the local Federation and 10F. to national headquarters. Even if the figure of 70,000 members was correct, the sum thus contributed would fall far short of that required to pay the staff at the rue de la Bienfaisance. They number about forty. Part of the difference, as with all other parties except the Communists, is made up by gifts from industry, commerce and private individuals. In addition, like other parties of the Government *Majorité,* some members of the staff are in fact civil servants who are seconded by their ministries or at least allowed to spend part of their time on organisation for their minister's party. This is particularly marked in the case of the Independent Republicans. Each of the leading ministerial figures in the RI—Poniatowski, d'Ornano, and Fourcade—has, in addition to his own presence, a member of his *cabinet* on the *Bureau Politique.* The national organisers of *Perspectives et Réalités* are all ministerial *cabinet* officials. The Presidential *cabinet* is represented by Victor Chapot.

(c) *Press. France-Moderne,* which has appeared on and off throughout the history of the RI, reappeared for a time in 1975 as a fairly ambitious and serious journal with articles and comment, and was sold on a subscription basis. It failed to reach financial viability and has been withdrawn. In May 1976 a simpler, more direct campaigning broadsheet called *L'Avant-Centre* (Centre-Forward) was launched and appears approximately every fortnight. Its first edition declared it to be 'the journal of militant *Giscardiens*, of fighting *Giscardiens*', and 'we are fighting for Giscard'. Its principal stock in trade is unalloyed anti-Communism. The more interesting publication, not directly associated with the RI, as we have seen, is *Réformer*, the organ of the *Comité*. Launched in March 1976, it appears monthly with a print of 60,000 copies. Though not of course published by the Independent Republican Party, there are a number of leading economic and political weeklies like *Le Point* which are strongly *Giscardien* in orientation.

## 2. The Centre

The Independent Republicans, it will be recalled, claim to be a party of the Centre, rejecting extremes of Right and Left. The electoral successes of Gaullism too are not successes of the Right but of the Centre—progressive social policies and a strong working-class following balance Right-wing characteristics like nationalism. Socialists and Radicals, placed by tradition on the Left, have also traditionally been regarded ·as possible elements of Centre coalition governments. Indeed the Communist party suspects that even today their Socialist allies could be lured by Giscard d'Estaing into a Centrist betrayal. If almost everyone is in the Centre—and France has been governed by Centrist governments of one kind or another throughout nearly all its Republican history—a party actually calling itself the Centre should be either dominant or superfluous. In the Fifth Republic today it is nearer to being superfluous.

Inheritors of the Christian Democratic MRP (Popular Republican Movement) for the most part, the Centre Democrats held out for a long time as part of the opposition but refusing to be part of any alliance with the Communists. Some of their members joined the *Majorité* when Pompidou became President. The rest held out, and joined elements of the Radical Party to form the Reform movement in the 1973 elections, still part of the opposition. In 1974 they too joined the *Majorité* of Giscard d'Estaing.

(*a*) *Christian Democracy.* It took a very long time for Catholics in France to accept a democratic Republic at all. The quarrel between Catholics and Republicans lasted from the French Revolution well into the twentieth century.

Until the Second World War, Catholics were held by their political opponents to be reactionaries, whose real desire was a hierarchical authoritarian state modelled on their church. Democrats (in particular Socialists), on the other hand, were often seen by Catholics (and conservatives in general) as anticlerical atheists, whose main objective was to destroy the whole basis of society for the sake of an egalitarian, materialistic utopia.[29]

Even after the war there have been sporadic relapses of the old Catholic/anticlerical vendettas—notably over the issue of public funds for church schools, which divided the coalition government in 1951 and which was still an issue between the MRP and the Socialists in the negotiations for a possible Defferre presidential candidature in 1965.[30] There were throughout the Third Republic, however, various Catholic movements, like Albert de Mun's *Ralliement* in the 1880s, which tried to bring Catholicism to terms with democracy. In the early years of this century, in the aftermath of the Dreyfus affair when Catholic officers were still being purged from the army, Marc Sangnier's influential group '*Le Sillon*' preached the doctrine that one could be both 'fearlessly Christian and unreservedly democratic and Republican'. In 1924 a Christian Democratic party called PDP (Popular Democratic Party) was formed with Robert Schuman, France's most celebrated Christian Democratic statesman, as one of its leaders. It was the Resistance in the Second World War, however, which gave Catholics the opportunity to demonstrate their commitment to the Republic, to cooperate with Republicans, and to produce leaders of national stature. 'The MRP arrived spectacularly on the French Political scene'[31] after the liberation. The PDP had gained only 3% of the votes at the 1936 election. In the three elections of 1945 and 1946 the MRP's score averaged 25% of the votes cast. For a brief moment it was the largest party in France. The MRP participated in almost every government of the Fourth Republic and provided three Prime Ministers: Schuman (who with his fellow-Christian Democrats Adenauer and de Gasperi was one of the founding fathers of the European Community), Bidault and Pflimlin. When General de Gaulle left the government in 1946 and set up the RPF, vast numbers of conservative voters deserted the MRP for Gaullism. Gradually the MRP dwindled almost into a regional party, with residual strength in the strongly Catholic areas of the East and West. The MRP backed General de Gaulle when he returned to power in 1958. and various MRP leaders served in early fifth Republic governments—Pflimlin, Maurice Schumann and others. The MRP supported de Gaulle over Algeria. MRP ministers resigned however over the issue of European integration on the occasion of de Gaulle's disparaging remarks on the subject in May 1962. As the MRP slid further into opposition, Maurice Schumann and some other leading figures rejoined Gaullism, received the investiture of the UDR at elections, and eventually re-entered the Government.

Table 5.2

MRP ELECTORAL PERFORMANCE

| Fourth Republic | % of votes | seats |
|---|---|---|
| Oct. 1945 | 23·9 | 150 |
| June 1946 | 28·2 | 166 |
| Nov. 1946 | 25·9 | 173 |
| June 1951 | 12·6 | 95 |
| Jan. 1956 | 11·1 | 83 |
| | | |
| Fifth Republic | | |
| Nov. 1958 | 11·1 | 57 |
| Nov. 1962 | 9·1 | 52 |

The attempt in 1964–5 to bring the MRP and the Socialists into an anti-Communist Federation in support of the candidature for President of Gaston Defferre, the Socialist Mayor of Marseille, revealed the divisions in the MRP. Neither the MRP's Gaullists led by Schumann nor its conservatives led by Pflimlin supported the venture. What was left of the MRP decided to back the presidential candidature of Jean Lecanuet, unknown nationally but President of the MRP. He also received the endorsement of the CNIP—the old conservatives and moderates who had not rallied to de Gaulle along with Giscard d'Estaing and his friends in 1962. Lecanuet's youthful image, his articulate campaign, his opposition to de Gaulle's European policy and the exercise of 'personal power' had a successful impact especially on television. He gained 16% of the votes cast and denied General de Gaulle a first ballot re-election. Nonetheless his vote consisted of 'the hard core of the old MRP and CNI, together with disenchanted Gaullists and discontented peasants'.[32] It was from this 1965 presidential campaign, however, that Lecanuet decided to pursue his aim of forming a Centre party opposed to both Gaullism and the Left. The Democratic Centre was launched in February 1966.

(b) The Centre Democrats. Claiming 40,000 enthusiastic new members,[33] an exaggerated claim in the grand tradition, the movement nonetheless had a disappointing start. Leading figures from the Radical Party like Maurice Faure and like Mme Thome-Patenôtre joined the Executive Committee of the CD, but like Lady Jane Grey, ruled only for nine days: venerable Radical Party rules forbade membership of other parties. The CNI and the MRP declined to merge with the new party. In the time-honoured style of the smaller French political parties—built round local notables—the CD approached the 1967 elections seeking out

suitable candidates for adoption ('*investiture*') or support ('*soutien*').
Its aim 'to exist', its dream 'to hold the political balance', its
programme 'to keep the ship [the Fifth Republic] but to change
direction':[34] of such stuff was the Democratic Centre made. The
390 candidates it eventually presented were from a variety of
political backgrounds: 34% came from the MRP, 25% were
moderates (essentially CNI), 7% were from the Radicals, and 34%
were new members.[35] For a variety of reasons, the CD did not
present candidates in all constituencies; in retrospect the most
significant of these was the decision in a number of seats to 'leave
the field to the Gaullists' in order to defeat 'the more pressing
danger of Communism'.[36] Thus we find in the preparations for the
1967 election campaign the three main characteristics of the CD.
First, it is a 'parliamentary tactics' party. Secondly, it did genuinely
group together individuals from a variety of political origins (and
none) who shared a common opposition to Gaullism, at least as
practised by the General himself in the mid-1960s. Thirdly, like the
opening chords of a final movement, its fundamental opposition to
the Left signified its eventual absorption into the *Majorité*.

The CD received only 13·4% of the votes at the 1967 election. A
parliamentary group of forty-one was eventually formed, some of
whom had not strictly speaking been CD candidates in the
election. Thirteen had been MRP, ten Independents, eleven
Radicals, three UDSR (a diverse, middle-of-the-road, anti-
Communist parliamentary group of the Fourth Republic which
had originated as a federation of five non-Communist Resistance
movements[37]) and four had no previous affiliation. Jean Lecanuet
was not a candidate for the National Assembly and the leading
parliamentary figures in the group were Pierre Abelin (ex-MRP),
Bertrand Motte (ex-CNI) René Pléven (ex-UDSR and former
Prime Minister) and Jacques Duhamel (ex-Radical), who became
its leader and much more prominent than Lecanuet. The
parliamentary group was called Progress and Modern Democracy
(PDM) and, as the Centre for Progress and Modern Democracy
(CPDM), it fought the 1968 election, condemning the anarchy of
the Events of May, but still remaining in the opposition. The
Centrist vote shrank to 10·3% and its parliamentary strength to
thirty-three.

(c) *Dispersal and reunion*. The slide towards absorption into the
*Majorité* began with the resignation of General de Gaulle in April
1969. Georges Pompidou, feeling the need to attract a wider basis
of support, won over Jacques Duhamel to his camp—subsequently
rewarding him and some of his friends with ministerial office.
Two-thirds of the PDM thus went into the *Majorité*. In the 1973
election the new Centrist members of the *majorité* received

endorsement as official candidates without Gaullist opponents (except for a few 'primaries').

Jean Lecanuet and his friends remained in opposition. They backed Alain Poher (ex-MRP) in the 1969 presidential election. In preparation for the 1973 elections, they renewed the attempt begun in 1965-6 to join forces with Radicals who, like the Centre Democrats, opposed both Gaullism and any alliance with Communism. Some elements in the Radical Party found this difficult. There was the doctrinal difficulty of an ancient anti-Catholic tradition. Much more to the point, though, was the electoral dependence of most Radical deputies on second-ballot support by the left. However, those Radicals that followed the modernising vision of Jean-Jacques Servan-Schreiber joined their leader and Lecanuet in founding the Reform Movement, which also included a few Socialists who rejected the alliance with the Communists (the Democratic Socialist Movement) and a veteran Radical splinter-group, the Republican Centre. The Reformers contested the 1973 election as part of the opposition. Servan-Schreiber may have brought his magazine *L'Express* and some *éclat* to the Reformers' campaign, but he brought few troops. Out of 437 Reform Movement candidates, 359 were classified as Centre Democrat and only sixty-eight as Radicals. The Reformers achieved 13·1% of the vote at the first ballot and ended with a group of thirty-four deputies in the New Assembly: twenty-nine Centre Democrats, four Radicals, and one who had fought the election as part of the *Majorité*.[38] They would have had considerably less than thirty-four but for intensive negotiations between the first and second ballot. The maintenance of Reform candidates would have split the anti-Communist vote in many constituencies and might have permitted the left to win the election. Consequently, Lecanuet and the Prime Minister Pierre Messmer came to an arrangement whereby the Reformers gave the *Majorité* a clear run in more than 100 constituencies and the *Majorité* itself withdrew in about twenty. This helped the Reformers to win a few more seats. Meanwhile the Duhamel centrists who had joined the *Majorité* in 1969 fought the election under the *Majorité* banner but with their own label, CDP (Centre for Democracy and Progress), and set up their own Parliamentary Group with thirty members, the Centrist Union (UC).

After the death of President Pompidou in the spring of 1974, the Reformers joined their Centrist Union colleagues as part of the new *Majorité*. The CDP actually backed Jacques Chaban-Delmas at the first ballot, but Lecanuet and his friends rallied to the candidature of Giscard d'Estaing straight away. Servan-Schreiber hesitated until just before the second ballot. Both were given portfolios in the Government—Lecanuet as Minister of Justice and

Servan-Schreiber as Minister of Reforms (sic).[39] On 11 July 1974 a
new parliamentary group was formed which included the
Reformers and a large part of the Centrist Union—in total fifty-
three members. Its chairman is the ex-socialist Max Lejeune,
Leader of the Democratic Socialist Movement.[40] In May 1976 the
Centrists took a further step towards reunion. A congress was held
at Rennes in order to launch the CDS (Centre of Social
Democrats), and to re-unite the Centrists that elections of the
previous seven years had caused to disperse and wander in different
directions. The supporters and opponents of the Pompidou
presidential *Majorité* were there: Members of Parliament elected in
1973 with the endorsement of the *Majorité* and members elected in
opposition to it. The whole episode reminded some observers of a
reunion of old comrades of the MRP,[41] as many of the old guard
were there: Pierre Pflimlin, André Colin and Pierre-Henri
Teitgen, who was a founder member of the MRP in 1945. Jean
Lecanuet, elected President of the new party, assured his audience
that it was not a Christian Democratic party: 'In our ranks there are
certainly many Christians, but also Jews, rationalists, and
agnostics.'[42] The aim of the new party was to 'shift the centre of
gravity' of the *Majorité* towards its reformist elements. The idea
should be propagated that the reforming zeal of the CDS and of
the President of the Republic are closely linked. There must be
close cooperation between all those in the *Majorité* who wanted
social reform: 'I will be proposing to our friends in the Reform
Movement (the Radicals—not present at Rennes) and the
Independent Republicans that they should organise for greater
cooperation with us.'

Does this presage the birth of a big 'presidential' federation of
the Centre joining the *Giscardiens,* the Centrists and those Radicals
who have followed Servan-Schreiber into the *Majorité?* All these
groups subscribe to the same liberal and centrist values, so there is
no real difficulty of principle. There are, however, various
practical problems. The first always afflicts cadre parties built
round a small élite with strong personal electoral bases: a reluctance
to be grouped into a big battalion. Members of such an élite
subscribe readily to the view that the French voter resists
polarisation, that he likes to have his personal *tendance* to vote for,
and that support would be lost by an attempt to simplify choices.
The second problem is that the rank and file activists of the Centrist
descendants of the MRP regard themselves as separate from the
rather smart and wealthy world of the *Giscardiens.* Another
difficulty is that a merger of *Giscardiens* and Centrists, avidly
desired by Michel Poniatowski in his vigorous pursuit of the
dream of the Independent Republicans becoming the Majority of
the *Majorité,* would be an open declaration of war with the

Gaullists. The President of the Republic might well feel there were better ways of preserving harmony within the diverse camps of his *Majorité*.

(d) *CDS—Philosophy and organisation.* As the last paragraph suggested, in describing the ideas of the Centre of Social Democrats (as the Centrists have now chosen to be called), there is little to add to what has already been said of the *Giscardiens*. Both regard themselves as the Centre, with all the progressive modern connotations of that word, as liberal and pro-European. However, the CDS, it must be remembered, is a direct descendant of the MRP, the party of Robert Schuman, whose name is enough to unleash applause at any Centrist gathering. Perhaps it is true to say, therefore, that the CDS is distinctively the most 'European' of French political parties. As candidate for President in 1965, Lecanuet concentrated his attack on de Gaulle's negative policy towards Europe. It was largely because he promised to be more favourable than his predecessors to European integration that Lecanuet and his friends decided to support Giscard d'Estaing in the presidential election of 1974. The social policy of the CDS is progressive—more zealously reforming than most Independent Republicans other than the President of the Republic. Its policy declaration at Rennes includes such objectives as 'the progressive but rapid reduction of social inequalities, the primacy of the collective interest over the interests of individuals . . . greater participation of citizens and workers in decisions which affect them at national and European level [a hint here of commitment to a directly elected European Parliament] as well as in family life and life at work'.[43] In a phrase, the CDS is more Giscardian than the *Giscardiens*. It is a curious paradox that the Independent Republicans are the creature and the instrument of Giscard d'Estaing and yet the CDS is closer to those Giscardian ideas to which his RI colleagues have often expressed reservations.

Organisation, too, can be dealt with briefly, as befits small parties composed largely of a Parliamentary élite. Discipline and structure are relatively unimportant and there is little risk of challenge to the leadership from the party.

The CDS replaces the *Centre Démocrate* and the CDP though the Reform movement continues to exist as a potential electoral umbrella under which the Radicals and Centrists can potentially gather. The task of forming branches of the CDS in every *département* is still continuing. The membership is mostly Centre Democrat, since the CDP was purely and simply a group of parliamentary notables. In most cases, integration is being well-achieved though there are isolated instances of conflict between

CD activists and a local CDP Deputy who defeated their reform Movement candidate in 1973.[44] At national level a Congress will be held every two years at least. All members may attend but voting is on the basis of one *département* delegate for each fifty members. National Congress elects the President and the Secretary-General. As with other parties, the CDS is directed by a hierarchy of committees: the Political Council, a large body with the function of seeing that Congress decisions are implemented; the *Comité Directeur National,* slightly smaller, which has the important task of adopting election candidates and deciding whether or not they should be withdrawn at the second ballot; and finally the *Bureau Politique,* which directs the party and handles liason with the parliamentary group. It has thirty-nine members (thirty one of them Members of Parliament, ministers or former ministers), who included in 1976:

*President:* Jean Lecanuet—Minister of Planning and Development (CD);

*Secretary-General:* Jacques Barrot—Minister of Housing (CDP);

*Vice-Presidents:* Pierre Abelin—Former Minister (CD);
    Jean Cluzel—Senator,
    André Diligent—Senator, 1st Secretary—Reform Movement;
    Bernard Stasi—Former Minister (CDP);

*Assistant Secretaries-general:* Pierre Bernard-Reymond—Deputy (CDP);
    Loic Bouvard—Deputy (CD);

Pierre Méhaignerie—Minister of Agriculture;

André Fosset—Former Minister;

Eugène Claudius-Petit—Deputy;

Jean-Marie Daillet—Deputy, Co-Director of *Démocratie Moderne* and three Chairman of Senate committees: Edouard Bonnefous, André Colin, and Dominique Pado.

The critical organisational emphasis is on parliamentary and local election candidatures. Two members of the permanent staff are responsible for a 'local councillor' section. They have the difficult task of preparing an actual list of councillors who belong to or sympathise with the CDS, of looking for communes where Centrists might be successful, and of finding good prospective candidates. There are also policy study groups, women's groups, rural groups and a youth movement, JDS (Young Social Democrats). The optimistic figure of 30,000 members is claimed by the CDS as a whole. It is strongest in Catholic areas of the North, Brittany and Alsace, and in certain places like Marseille where there happen to be dynamic local organisers. The CDS is weakest in the old anticlerical centre of France.

There is a weekly journal *Démocratie Moderne,* serious and

Table 5.3
## OPPOSITION CENTRISM BY REGIONS 1965-73*
(% of vote—*suffrages exprimés* —1st ballot)

| | | $1965^P$ | 1967 | 1968 | 1973 |
|---|---|---|---|---|---|
| | | *Lecanuet* | | | |
| *Regions of strength* | | | | | |
| N. | Alsace | 22·8 | 28·4 | 17·1 | 23·0 |
| | Lorraine | 15·2 | 14·1 | 10·2 | 16·3 |
| | Upper Normandy | 19·6 | 11·6 | 10·8 | 17·4 |
| | Lower Normandy | 22·9 | 18·3 | 17·6 | 17·3 |
| | | | | | |
| *Average regions* | | | | | |
| N. | Champagne | 16·0 | 14·2 | 15·1 | 10·5 |
| | Picardy | 13·6 | 12·0 | 6·2 | 15·1 |
| | Brittany | 18·6 | 24·4 | 20·1 | 12·9† |
| | Loire Country | 23·2 | 19·5 | 10·6 | 13·0 |
| | Centre | 16·3 | 10·6 | 11·1 | 14·2 |
| | Paris Region | 14·4 | 12·0 | 11·7 | 14·6 |
| | Franche-Comté | 16·1 | 13·3 | 12·8 | 10·2 |
| | | | | | |
| S. | Poitou-Charentes | 16·8 | 20·6 | 16·1 | 14·7 |
| | Aquitaine | 15·4 | 16·9 | 13·5 | 12·6 |
| | Rhone–Alps | 11·8 | 18·3 | 16·5 | 14·4 |
| | Provence-Côte | | | | |
| | d'Azur | 11·7 | 13·5 | 11·7 | 13·1 |
| | | | | | |
| *Regions of weakness* | | | | | |
| N. | North | 10·6 | 7·3 | 3·5 | 9·4 |
| | Burgundy | 18·6 | 7·5 | 4·4 | 8·9 |
| | | | | | |
| S. | Limousin | 8·5 | 0·8 | — | 6·1 |
| | Midi-Pyrenees | 15·1 | 13·2 | 9·8 | 9·3 |
| | Auvergne | 16·5 | 12·3 | 8·6 | 9·6 |
| | Languedoc | 12·6 | 14·9 | 3·8 | 8·8 |
| | Corsica | 7·7 | 5·0 | 1·1 | 11·3 |
| | | | | | |
| France-Metropolitan | | 15·8 | 13·4 | 10·3 | 13·1 |

*The 1969 presidential election votes for Alain Poher (1st ballot 23·4%) have been excluded. There were too many exceptional factors (see below, p. 199).
P Presidential election
† In Brittany four opposition Centrist Deputies contested the 1973 elections as part of the *Majorité*, to which they had rallied at the time of President Pompidou's election in 1969.

moderate in tone, formerly published by the *Centre Démocrate* and now by the CDS. In addition there are various internal bulletins—*Action Démocrate, CDS Actualités* and the journal of the JDS, *Jeunesse et Démocratie*. Some local Federations publish their own broadsheets. *L'Eclair du Pas de Calais,* for instance, is a fairly ambitious publication in tabloid format.

Income from membership subscription is clearly inadequate for the smart suites of offices in two buildings on the expensive Boulevard St-Germain and for the staff consisting of some twenty persons. As with other parties, a hidden government subsidy comes in the form of a Deputy's parliamentary assistant or staff from ministries being seconded for party work.

## 3. The Radicals

There is very little to say about the Radical Party. If you go to the Place de Valois, near the Palais-Royal in Paris, an ornate seventeenth century house still bears the nameplate *Parti Républicain Radical et Radical-Socialiste*.[45] A solitary enthusiast still sits at the desk of Edouard Herriot. The Grand Old Party of the Third Republic, inheritor of the revolutionary heritage of 1789, scourge of the clerics, whose vision was the organisation of society 'according to the laws of reason', the heir of Gambetta and Clémenceau, has been a byword for conservatism and sterility for fifty years. Officially part of the Left because they were for the Republic and against the Catholic Church, the Radicals defended the conservative values of the peasant and the small town. They served in governments of all political complexions throughout the Third and Fourth Republics. They did not believe in strong central government nor, since they are the classic example of a party composed almost exclusively of well-entrenched local notables, did they believe in strong discipline in their own ranks. Today the Radicals are totally split. The official Place de Valois party is part of the *Majorité*. It has half a dozen Deputies in the National Assembly, four ministers in the Government and a few Senators. The rest of the radicals, the *Mouvement des Radicaux de Gauche* (Movement of Radicals of the Left), are closely allied to the Socialists in the *Union de la Gauche* and will be considered when we deal with the parties of the opposition. Radicals live on united in the Third Republic world of the Senate, where both wings sit in a group called 'Democratic Left' which operates on the traditionally undemanding basis of the 'free vote'.

Today's split is not of course the first in the history of the Radical Party. Founded in 1901, its capacity to survive as an institution has made the Radicals the oldest party in France. In the Fourth Republic they were utterly divided most of the time, and their leaders followed very different itineraries. Some Radicals were ardent Gaullists and went off to join the RPF. Jaques Chaban-Delmas and Michel Debré were the best known of this group but in fact there were many joint RPF-Radical lists in the municipal elections of 1947. Some Radicals became Gaullist later. The classic instance is the resilient political figure Edgar Faure, Prime Minister in 1955-6 and in 1976 an ex-member of the UDR's Executive Bureau and President of the National Assembly. Francis de Tarr relates how in 1945 Faure wanted to enter politics and could not decide whether the MRP or the Radical Party offered the most promising opportunity[46]—consideration which could quite literally have been described as heresy a generation earlier but which incidentally serves as an admirable indicator of the declining importance of religion in post-war French politics. De Tarr classifies Faure as a *'Radical de Gestion'*—a Radical who likes to manage—'political power will always be a potent attraction to those who enter political life and, for some, the exercise of power will always serve as an end in itself.'[47] There were also some very Left-wing Radicals. Pierre Cot was so confirmed a fellow-traveller that he received Communist endorsement in his elections and was still sitting with the Communist Group in Parliament up to his defeat in 1968. There were also some very Right-wing Radicals who endorsed the views of big business on economic questions and were vigorously anti-Communist. Their 'desire and ability to win Right-wing friends had found a particularly graphic expression in the RGR[48]—an organisation that despite its name was primarily devoted to gaining allies on the right.'[49]

Also on the right were the Radicals associated with André Morice, Mayor of Nantes, who split away on the issue of colonial policy to form the Republican Centre. These dissident Radicals eventually joined the Reform movement formed by Lecanuet and Servan-Schreiber in 1971 and were described in the section on the Centre Democrats. Another itinerary was followed by one of the few political lions produced by the Fourth Republic, Pierre Mendès-France. A vigorous and reforming Prime Minister, he set out in 1954 'to conquer, to renovate, and to use' the Radical Party.[50] However, having dragooned the Radical Party into supporting his progressive ideas at its special Congress in 1955, Mendès-France lost control again in 1957. In 1959 he and his supporters joined the PSA (Autonomous Socialist Party)—formed by a group of Socialists who were opposed to their party's decision to back de Gaulle's constitution, and worried about the nationalist and racialist policies Socialist leaders were supporting over the Algerian question. In 1960 the PSA became the PSU (Unified Socialist Party)—a small group increasingly to the Left of the Socialist party—and it brightest star was Mendès-France. He was triumphantly elected Deputy for Grenoble, a city with a very progressive image, in 1967; he was present at the famous Left-wing student rally denouncing Communist immobilism at the Charléty stadium in May 1968,[51] and appeared as Gaston Defferre's 'running mate', Prime Minister-designate, in the feeble Socialist campaign for the 1969 presidential elections.

For the Radicals that remained Radicals, the main drift of the Fifth Republic has been towards the *Union de la Gauche*, which will be described in the next chapter. The electoral success of Gaullism has caused the opposition parties to huddle closer together for survival. The Radicals, under the leadership of Rene Billères, joined François Mitterrand's Federation of the Democratic and Socialist Left (FGDS) in 1965 until it broke up in 1969. Some Radicals constantly felt the lure of a Centre-Right rather than a Centre-Left alliance, and the attraction of that elusive goal—a 'third-force' between Gaullism and the Left. They leant more towards Lecanuet and the Centrists despite their Catholic origins. Maurice Faure, President of the Party in 1965, actually backed the Lecanuet presidential candidature and briefly joined the executive body of the newly formed democratic Centre in 1966. In 1969 Maurice Faure was responsible for inviting Jean-Jacques Servan-Schreiber to become Secretary-General of the Party. Maurice Faure has since decided that his heart is really on the left in the Republican tradition of the Radicals—that is to say he needs Communist and Socialist support at the second ballot to hold his Parliamentary seat. He is now, therefore, a leading member of the rival establishment to the official Radical Party—the Movement of Radicals of the Left (MRG).

Servan-Schreiber, publisher of the successful weekly *L'Express*, author of '*Le Défi Americain*', a highly successful book of the mid-1960s, which argued that France and Europe must modernise themselves swiftly or become a satellite of the United States, winner of a highly publicised by-election in Nancy in 1969, determined to renovate the Radical party and win it over to progressive ideas. In 1954 he had been one of the admirers and backers of Mendès-France; Indeed the Mendès-France aim 'to conquer, to renovate, and to use' the Radical Party was actually pronounced at the first anniversary dinner of *L'Express,* and the phrase serves exactly to describe the aim of its publisher fifteen years later. The progressive and dynamic zeal of Mendès-France split the Radical Party and propelled most of the fragments to the Right, whereas that of Servan-Schreiber has split the Radical Party and propelled most of the fragments to the Left. In 1971 Servan-Schreiber became President of the Radical Party and in November the Reform Movement—the alliance of opposition centrists—was born. He hesitated longer than did Lecanuet about supporting Giscard d'Estaing in 1974, but eventually he did so.[52]

For the first time in the Fifth Republic, the Radical Party was part of the *Majorité*. Its most important figure is Michel Durafour, in 1976 Mayor of St.-Etienne and the Minister responsible for Finance under Raymond Barre. Durafour is clearly regarded by the President of the Republic as an important spokesman for the Centre-Left, but he has only recently rejoined the Radical Party. Other Radicals who have held ministerial office since 1974 include Gabriel Peronnet, Françoise Giroud, a journalist from *L'Express,* André Rossi, and Pierre Brousse— who was lured away from the Left. Apart from these ministerial portfolios, which really represent the President's hope of enlarging still further the ranks of the *Majorité* rather than the importance of the Radical Party, the grand old firm of the Place Valois has precious little left. It has no electoral base and virtually no Parliamentarians, since most of what few there were have sided with the Socialists in the *Union de la Gauche*. Now that the fragments of the Centre have been reunited in the CDS, it is hard to see that the Reform Movement, in which the Radical Party played a modest part, will have a future. In an enlarged *Giscardien* Liberal-Centre, the Radicals would be even more marginal. Jean Charlot's analysis of the 1973 elections shows, in a very brief section entitled 'the end of Radicalism', how the two wings of the party that dominated the Third Republic now account together for only 3·7% of the national vote (1·9%— Place Valois, 1·8%—MRG)—about the same as the revolutionary fringe.[53] How times can change:

> Imperious Caesar dead and turned to clay
> Might stop a hole to keep the wind away.

The Radicals have little in the way of distinctive ideas. They are more in favour of regional autonomy than their fellow Centrists and *Giscardiens*. They regard themselves as the Left-Wing of the *Majorité*. Their one modest card is their strength—if that is the right word—on local councils, where there are still a number of vintage and immovable Radicals who have not joined the Left because they want nothing to do with municipal alliances involving Communists. Do they really exist, the Radicals, or are they merely a legend? The *Canard Enchaîné* of 8 December 1948 was already doubtful: a cartoon showed two boys pointing at Father Christmas and exclaiming 'Look! a Radical!'[54]

## 4. *The MDSF*

One last tiny Centrist fragment of the *Majorité* remains briefly to be included. The Democratic Socialist Movement of France, formed in December 1973, is composed of a few former Socialists who have left the Socialist Party because they objected to the

*Union de la Gauche* strategy of alliance with the Communists. Their leader is Max Lejeune, a former Socialist minister, who is now President of the Centrist Parliamentary Group. Another prominent figure is Emile Muller, Deputy and Mayor of Mulhouse (Alsace), who stood in the presidential election of 1974 and obtained 0·7% of the vote. Associated with the group is Eric Hintermann, dismissed in 1975 as Secretary to the Socialist Parliamentary Group. There are five MDSF Deputies in all. They stood as Reform Movement candidates in the 1973 parliamentary elections, and are well-entrenched local notables.

Centrism as a third force between Right and Left, or between Gaullism and the Left, has gradually been eclipsed. One after another, the various elements have joined the *Majorité,* with the exception of a section of the Radical Party— which has joined the other big camp, the *Union de la Gauche.* Of course electoral earthquakes could reopen fissures and shake up the compact bipolar geography of 1976. It would seem, however, as if the only real unanswered question on the *Majorité* side of the electoral divide is whether the *Giscardiens* and some or all of the Centrist fragments will coalesce into a French Liberal Party.

## NOTES

1. *Les Partis Politiques,* (Paris 1951).
2. *The Right Wing in France,* p. 332.
3. Anderson, *Conservative Politics in France,* p. 250.
4. M. Chapsal, *La Vie politique en France depuis 1940,* Paris: PUF, 1966.
5. For instance, they gave their most regular support to Government legislation in 1967-8 when the majority was smallest but permitted themselves quite an amount of minor indiscipline in 1968-9 when the Government's majority was very large.
6. E.g. Jean-Claude Colliard reports their disproportionate membership of important National Assembly Committees.
7. *The French Parliament 1958-1967,* Allen and Unwin, 1968, pp. 107-8.
8. This opposition was a Giscardien initiative. 'Four-fifths of the (RI) deputies refused to follow their talented leader' (Charlot, *The Gaullist Phenomenon,* p. 119).
9. See below p. 245
10. *Perspectives et Réalités (Bulletin Intérieur)* Jan. 1976 lists 156.
11. Michel Cardoze and Jean le Lagadec, *49% naissance d'une majorité* (Editions Sociales, Paris, 1974), pp. 16–17.
12. See J. C. Colliard, *Les Republicains Indépendents: Valéry Giscard d'Estaing* Paris PUF, 1972, p. 121.
13. Letter from a widow in Montpellier, *France Moderne,* Dec. 1975.
14. The achievement of such a society is declared to be the objective of the Independent Republicans in their party statutes (Art 2). For what

it consists of see V. Giscard d'Estaing, *La Démocratie Française*, Paris: Fayard 1976.

15. Colliard, *Les Républicains Indépendents*, p. 317.
16. The author's interview with a Centre Democrat Deputy, December 1975.
17. See his interview in *Le Monde*, 3 May 1974.
18. *Les Républicains Indépendents*, p. 330.
19. *Le Monde*, 31 Dec. 1975.
20. Paris, Fayard, 1976.
21. *Les Républicains Indépendents*, p. 316.
22. See Chapter 1.
23. See below pp. 184-6.
24. Lozère 1, Ain 3, Rhône 8.
25. Haute-Loire 2.
26. Lozère 2, Yvelines 1, Meurthe-et-Moselle 2.
27. *Trésorier payeur-général*—the senior Finance Ministry official in each *département*.
28. *Réformer*, June 1976, p. 3.
29. R.E.M. Irving, *Christian Democracy in France*, Allen and Unwin, 1973, p. 12.
30. See below, p. 90.
31. Irving, *Christian Democracy in France*, p. 74.
32. *Ibid*, p. 253.
33. C. Ysmal, 'Les préparatifs du Centre Démocrate' in *Fondation Nationale des Sciences Politiques: les elections législatives de mars 1967*, Paris: Colin, 1971 p. 46.
34. *Ibid.*, pp. 46-8 and pp. 193-8 (Chapter, La campagne du Centre Démocrate').
35. *Ibid.*, p. 59.
36. *Ibid.*, p. 65.
37. See Williams, *Crisis and Compromise*, p. 174. The UDSR once contained François Mitterrand in its ranks.
38. M. de Montesquiou (Gers 2).
39. He lasted ten days in this post. Giscard d'Estaing sacked him for criticising French nuclear tests in the Pacific.
40. See p. 83.
41. See *Le Monde*, 23 May 1976.
42. The actual delegates at Rennes were nearly all Catholic (97%) and regular churchgoers (69%) (*Action Démocrate*, June 1976).
43. *Le Monde*, 25 May 1976.
44. For example, M. Desanlis (Loir-et-Cher 3).
45. Still called this 'in pious memory of its impetuous youth' (H. Lüthy, *The State of France*, Secker and Warburg, 1955), p. 166.
46. *The French Radical Party from Herriot to Mendès-France*, Oxford University Press 1961, p. 155.
47. *Ibid.*, p. 185.

48. *Rassemblement des Gauches Républicaines* (Rally of the Republican Lefts).
49. De Tarr, *The French Radical Party*, p. 129.
50. See Claude Nicolet, *Le Radicalisme*, Paris: PUF, 1961, p. 109.
51. See below, p. 94.
52. The intense expectation aroused by this hesitation, was encapsulated in a ribald comment in *Le Canard Enchaîné:* 'Plus on se retient, mieux c'est!'
53. *Quand la Gauche peut gagner*, p. 90.
54. De Tarr, *The French Radical Party*, p. 14.

# 6

## THE *UNION DE LA GAUCHE*

We saw in Chapter 2 how the sustained success of Gaullism— as an electoral force, as a disciplined parliamentary majority, as the source of legitimacy for a set of political institutions built round the strong executive leadership of a directly elected Presidency—has, among its many profound effects on French political life, brought about the birth of an opposition. Presidential elections, culminating in a gladiatorial duel at the second ballot, give great advantage to the candidate who stands at the head of a large, united and well-organised force. 'The powerful Presidency established by the constitution of the Fifth Republic was a political prize worth seeking; and the direct popular election of the President created electoral demands that the traditional parties could not meet.'[1]

The aim for a party that wants to control the government is to generate mass support for a single candidate and no longer to attempt to hold a balance of power in the centre. The parliamentary electoral system also greatly favours would-be majority parties or coalitions which can attract to a single candidate at the second ballot votes divided among several at the first. The lesson of the repeated electoral successes of Gaullism and its allies, of the whole nature of the new political order, has not been lost upon the parties of the Left. Like the band of thieves, they would have to hang together for assuredly they would otherwise all hang separately. A reasonably cohesive opposition of the Left, based upon an agreement between the Socialist Party (PS), the Left wing of the Radical Party *(Mouvement des Radicaux de Gauche*— MRG) and the French Communist Party (PCF), has emerged. It is known as the *Union de la Gauche* and it has a joint manifesto, a programme of government.[2] The story of its gradual emergence is one of tentative approaches, setbacks, conflict, contradictions, tension, rupture and renewal. It unfolds, however, with a certain Shakespearean inevitability as if there was some irresistible force 'that shapes our ends, rough-hew them how we will'. That irresistible force, we have suggested, was the transformation by Gaullism of the entire political order.

For most of the period since the war, the Left in France has been divided—often bitterly so—and it is not easy to establish criteria by which to identify its components. The terms 'Left' and 'Right' obstinately endure as part of the language of politics. They remain, and not only in France, impossible to define. David Caute has summed up the difficulty, 'To many people the left vaguely suggests an attitude towards the *condition humaine*—an attitude embracing optimism, a faith in science and rationality, love of liberty, egalitarianism, sympathy for the oppressed, anti-racism, pacifism, anti-clericalism, hostility to authority, and so forth.'[3] Does all this provide a satisfactory definition of the Left? Caute argues that such qualities are not invariably or exclusively associated with the Left, and that they are too ephemeral anyway. One traditional distinguishing mark in France was support for the Republic, another even more enduring was religion—Catholics and defenders of the Church were on the anti-Republican Right, with anti-clericals on the Republican Left. However important referents of this kind were in the Third Republic, they are—as we saw in Chapter 1—totally inappropriate today. As we shall see later, there is a Christian Left today that is active in the Socialist Party; the Socialist Party has made electoral gains in regions characterised by strong religious tradition and practice; and Catholics support the Republic.[4] In Great Britain and the United States, the word Left is associated with the word Socialism, and the word Socialism conjures up images of state intervention in the economy and redistributive welfare programmes. Differences over these matters may serve in a crude way to distinguish the ideologies of the British Labour and Conservative Parties, though hardly to distinguish their actions as governments. They will certainly not do at all to identify a Left and a Right in France. Again, the introductory chapter referred to one of the blessings heaped by generous Nature upon that fortunate country—to have no dispute about the legitimacy of economic direction by the state. 'Nationalisation, state intervention in the economy, centralised economic planning, and social welfare legislation are nowadays advocated and implemented by Parties that are traditionally on the Right, as well as by parties thought to be on the Left.'[5] The defence of private property is vigorously undertaken by, *inter alia,* the Communist Party, which has much support among small land-owning farmers in the South who, it may confidently be supposed, have no wish to share the fate of the Russian kulaks. By contrast the Independent Republicans—'the party of the President of the Republic', as they describe themselves—have as a slogan, launched in December 1975, *'Socialisme Libéral'*. Supporters of parliamentary democracy and of a more authoritarian style of government, of reform and of order, of centralised government and of devolution, are found on what is supposed to be the Left and what is supposed to be the Right.

One cannot even take nationalism and internationalism as the dividing criteria. In France the nationalism of Gaullists is outdone only by the Communist Party which waves the *Tricolore,* defends national independence against NATO and the EEC, and even supports the construction of the supersonic prestige aircraft Concorde. Frank Wilson is certainly right to conclude that the only practical way to proceed is to assert that 'the French Left is defined to include those parties that by tradition, if not doctrine, have been placed on the Left.'[6] We will therefore take it that the Left in France is composed of the Communist Party, however nationalist; the Socialist Party, however opportunist; the Radical Party, however conservative; the Unified Socialist Party (PSU), however Christian; and an anarchist fringe however anti-parliamentary.

Until the recovery heralded by the parliamentary elections of March 1973, the picture of the Left in France throughout the Fourth and Fifth Republics has been one of decline and failure to adapt to social change and political innovation. The French economy was expanding, especially in the industrial and dynamic north and east. The traditional bastions of the Left were in the rural and backward south. The institutions of the Fifth Republic brought the voters what they wanted—stability and strong government. In particular, opinion polls since the war had revealed a majority of electors, including those of the Left, in favour of a strong directly elected Presidency.[7] The parties of the Left fought to resist this constitutional innovation. The 'nationalisation' of politics, resulting from the development of national media of communication—notably television, which by the mid-1960s was in the vast majority of homes—and the appeal of national leaders like General de Gaulle, meant a decline in the importance of the local notables, those well-entrenched local mayors and opinion leaders whose influence on electoral outcomes is traditionally decisive. The Radical and Socialist parties remained far too long parties of local notables. The growing number of young voters, the decline of religion as a determinant of political attitudes, the industrialisation of the country—factors that might have been expected to favour the Left—failed to do so, at least until the 1970s. In contrast, it was 'the Gaullists [who] have been able to portray themselves as the innovators in French politics'.[8] The result was, until the 1970s, a sharp decline. In 1946 12 million people voted for the Left, which had to wait until 1973–4 to see that lost audience recovered and support of that level to be regained.

The first attempt to revitalise the non-Communist Left came from outside the party system. A number of political clubs, in the best tradition of the Jacobins of revolutionary France, began to be formed for the purpose of generating political ideas and changing the political order. There were Socialist clubs like CERES (Centre

Table 6·1
TOTAL VOTES FOR PARTIES OR PRESIDENTIAL
CANDIDATES OF THE LEFT 1946–74
*(Metropolitan France only)*

| Date | Type of election | Million votes | % of votes cast |
|------|------------------|---------------|-----------------|
| *Fourth Republic:* | | | |
| Nov. 1946 | Parliamentary | 12·0 | 58·9 |
| June 1951 | Parliamentary | 9·7 | 50·7 |
| Jan. 1956 | Parliamentary | 11·3 | 55·7 |
| *Fifth Republic:* | | | |
| Nov. 1958 | Parliamentary (1st ballot) | 8·8 | 43·2 |
| Nov. 1962 | Parliamentary (1st ballot) | 8·1 | 44·5 |
| Dec. 1965 | Presidential (1st ballot)★ | 7·7 | 32·2 |
| Mar. 1967 | Parliamentary (1st ballot) | 9·7 | 43·6 |
| June 1968 | Parliamentary (1st ballot) | 9·0 | 40·5 |
| June 1969 | Presidential (1st ballot)† | 6·9 | 31·4 |
| Mar. 1973 | Parliamentary (1st ballot) | 10·9 | 45·8 |
| June 1974 | Presidential (1st ballot)‡ | 11·6′ | 46·1 |
| | Presidential (2nd ballot) | 12·7 | 49·3 |

★ François Mitterrand's second ballot score of 10·5 million (45·5%) included too many anti-Gaullists votes from the Centre and extreme Right to be counted as a genuine total for the Left.
† The first ballot had four candidates of the Left and the second ballot had none. The score of 6·9 million probably undervalues the Left because many Socialists voted for the Centrist candidate Alain Poher who was thought to have the best chance of defeating Georges Pompidou at the second ballot.
‡ First ballot votes for François Mitterrand and the two Trotskyists, Arlette Laguiller and Alain Krivine. Environmentalists and European Federal candidates, who also urged their first ballot voters to support Mitterrand in the second, have not been included under the Left.

for Study, Research, and Socialist Education) or *Socialisme et Démocratie*. There were progressive Catholic clubs like the *Club Jean Moulin* (named after the wartime Resistance hero), or like *Citoyens 60*. There were trade-union clubs like GROP (Worker and Peasant Research Group). As the 1965 presidential elections, the first by universal suffrage, began to appear over the horizon, the clubs played an active part in the Left's preparations for that event. No longer interested only in research and discussion but ready for full partisan participation, many of the important clubs, whose members included important political figures on the Left like François Mitterrand and Charles Hernu, got together to form in 1964 the CIR (Convention of Republican Institutions), which had an organisational structure and became an important component of the FGDS (Federation of the Democratic and Socialist Left) formed in September 1965. 'The club movement went into politics with the explicit goal of creating a new, simplified party system by uniting the forces of the Left and Centre-Left in a single powerful party.'[9] The FGDS, in the creation of which the CIR played an important part, was a merger of the Socialist and Radical parties and the clubs. Wilson considers that the great achievement of the clubs was 'the integration of Catholics into the political life of the French Left—truly an innovation in French politics'.[10] They were also the source of new ideas and new leaders. However, too many clubs tended to be the personal followings of prominent politicians like Gilles Martinet *(Pouvoir Socialiste*—Left-wing) or Alain Savary *(Socialisme et Démocratie),* so in the end they added more to the fragmentation of the Left than to its unity.

For the Left the Presidential election of 1965, like impending execution, concentrated the mind powerfully. In addition to focusing the intellectual and political activity of the Clubs just described, it brought about another attempt to create a party of the democratic Left which could have a realistic chance of defeating Gaullism. This attempt was the promotion of Gaston Defferre, Mayor of Marseilles, former minister, and leading Socialist parliamentarian, as presidential candidate. The Defferre candidature was not at all a 'grass-roots' or a party phenomenon. The idea was thought up by a small group of journalists and politicians. The aim was to build a federation of all those groups who opposed both Gaullism and Communism, i.e. the Socialists, the Radicals and the Christian-Democratic MRP as well as any available clubs, independents or unions of the Centre and moderate Left. The promotion of Defferre's candidature received an immense build-up in the press, especially in *L'Express,* a weekly owned by a Defferre supporter Jean-Jacques Servan-Schreiber, which published frequent articles in 1963 about a mysterious *Monsieur X* who would be the ideal candidate to oppose General de Gaulle. As the effort to build this Centre-Left coalition around Defferre continued, it became clear that important Socialist and MRP elements had severe misgivings. Some Socialists were unwilling to make concessions on the old republican issue of state aid for church schools—regarded as indispensable by the MRP. Furthermore, some MRP leaders and many MRP voters preferred the General. A further difficulty was that the building of such a federation required a rather anti-Communist posture, and yet the support of the PCF's 4 or 5 million voters would be required for victory at the second ballot. The strategy adopted by Defferre is known as the strategy of the 'Third Force' and was familiar throughout the Fourth Republic, where most Governments were coalitions of all moderates against the extremes of both Left (PCF) and Right (Gaullism). It was inevitable that it should be attempted in the Fifth, and equally inevitable that no one would notice that Gaullism was no longer a force of Right-wing extremism. The Defferre candidature never developed the momentum to overcome the resistance of traditionalists in the parties, and in June 1965 Defferre withdrew. The idea of creating a new large moderate Centre-Left party was for the time being at an end.

The third attempt to reinvigorate the non-Communist left and give it a more dynamic impression to the electors was, like the clubs' activities and the Defferre proposals, related to the presidential elections of 1965—a supremely important contest which could not be approached by the traditional parties in the traditional way with loose lunch-based coalitions of local notables. This third attempt was the FGDS, and is inseparable from the first presidential campaign of François Mitterrand. The FGDS federation was an elaborate and structured merger between the Socialist Party (at that time still called SFIO), the Radical Party and the collective expression of the political clubs, the CIR. The aim when the federation was founded in September 1965 was the eventual formation of a single party, but in fact this never happened. Like the Trades Union Congress in Great Britain, individuals could not join the federation but had to be members of one of the affiliated organisations. Mitterrand became President of the Federation on 9 December 1965—between the two ballots of the presidential election.

The principal aim of the federation was to constitute an effective electoral force against Gaullism. The federation itself was neither long lived nor successful. The electoral decline of the Left was not halted in 1965, 1967 or 1968, and the federation collapsed after the resignation of Mitterrand as President at the end of 1968. Nevertheless the strategy upon which it was based is one to which the democratic Left has, under the same leadership, returned in the 1970s with much greater success. This strategy is simply a recognition that, in a situation where Gaullism and its allies had created an effective and cohesive majority, with a powerful electoral appeal to moderate and Centrist as well as conservative voters, the only hope for the democratic Left to win political power lay in alliance with the Communist Party and its numerous and stable body of 4 or 5 million supporters. This is quite an old idea. Léon Blum. the Socialist leader of the *Popular Front,* a Socialist-Communist-Radical coalition in 1936–8, said: 'One cannot carry out a Socialist policy in France without the support of those popular forces which look to the Communist Party.'

One difficulty with such a strategy is that Communist electoral support can be a poisoned chalice. The French Communist Party has a somewhat Stalinist aspect that moderate voters find intimidating. Sometimes the PCF exerts itself to combat this negative image—it did so in the mid-1960s and in the mid-1970s. Sometimes it does not, and seems positively to exult in being a hard-line Communist Party giving enthusiastic support to the Communist Party of the Soviet Union, dealing ruthlessly with waverers in its own ranks, rebarbative and hostile to all non-Communist elements in French society. Whatever the PCF does, however, its opponents seek to foster the Stalinist image and the fears of totalitarian dictatorship that it appears to inspire. Another difficulty of a strategy based on alliance with the PCF is that the PCF is naturally reluctant to be exploited by the electorally threadbare Socialist and Radical parties as a docile source of 5 million extra votes. It expects to be a full partner in any such alliance, with a full stake in policy formulation and, eventually, power. If the nobility wants to marry you for your money, you want higher social status to be fully and graciously accorded before you hand over the cash. From the point of view of the Socialists, the way to solve this difficulty of the new vulgar relations was to try and make them more presentable and also less in a position to dictate terms.

The Mitterrand strategy has followed this twofold pattern. He has repeatedly asserted that the millions of Communist voters are not to be regarded as untouchables but '*Français à part entière*'—full members of French political society, honest working people with a stake in the community. He has affirmed that if he doubted the attachment of the Communist Party leadership to the declarations respecting democratic freedoms of a pluralist society, he would not be its ally. By showing willingness to cooperate with the PCF, Mitterrand and his associates also hoped that the PCF itself would thereby be encouraged to evolve in a more liberal direction. In the mid-1960s this met with some response, since the PCF clearly wanted respectability and the opportunity to emerge from the political 'ghetto'. The difficulty, however, is that Communist Party attitudes in French politics seem to correlate with the international posture of the Soviet Union.[11] When the Soviet Union is pursuing a hard and uncompromising policy, as in the cold war period of the late 1940s and 1950s or in the period of the invasion and 'normalisation' of Czechoslovakia, and the renewed attacks on liberal intellectuals at home in the late 1960s and early 1970s, the PCF is hard and uncompromising too. When, however, Soviet policy emphasizes cooperation with the West or thaw or détente, as it did in the Second World War in 1941–45, in the mid-1960s and in the mid-1970s, the PCF has a more smiling aspect. It shows willingness to emerge from isolation and cooperate with others in normal democratic life. It also happened that in the mid-1960s and mid-1970s there were a number of important elections in which isolated parties with extremist postures were likely to be crushed. At the same time the Mitterrand strategy was to make the non-Communist left a stronger, more united and more electorally attractive force so that it could demonstrably be the senior partner in the alliance with the PCF, and above all be in a position to dominate any coalition government in which the Communist and non-Communist left were partners. In addition, he has kept a clear distance between himself and the Communists—taking particular care not to be identified with a pro-Soviet line in international affairs.

The FGDS, pursuing this strategy, began by publishing in September 1965 its own charter. It talked in non-doctrinaire terms of a 'new society' and of 'evolution towards justice and the flowering of true liberties which would necessitate a profound transformation leading to a new type of society'. The FGDS and the Communists supported Mitterrand's presidential campaign in December 1965. It was by no means an unqualified success in terms of recovery by the Left of the far larger percentage of the electorate that used to support it in the Fourth Republic, but Mitterrand's prestige and the hopes for a united Left were greatly enhanced. In May 1966 Mitterrand and the FGDS formed a *contre-gouvernement* or 'shadow cabinet' on the British model, the aim of which was to demonstrate to public opinion that the FGDS was a source of responsible and dynamic national leadership capable of forming an effective government. With the 1967 elections looming up, electoral pacts were established with the PCF in December 1966 and with the Left-wing PSU in January 1967. These pacts allowed for '*désistement réciproque*'. This meant that at the first ballot of the election each party of the Left would be free to run its own candidate in every constituency. However, all candidates of the Left would withdraw in favour of the one among them 'best placed' to win the constituency at the second ballot. This was usually interpreted to mean withdrawal in favour of the candidate with the most first-ballot votes, which meant that where a Communist had done better in the first round than the FGDS and PSU candidates, both the latter would urge their voters to vote Communist in the second. In some cases, however, it was agreed that if, in a close-run contest, a non-Communist candidate had a better chance of picking up those extra second ballot votes which might be withheld from a Communist but which would make all the difference between a win for the Left and a win for the

Gaullists, the Communist candidate would be the one to withdraw even though he had outscored his allies in the first ballot. The agreement worked well in 1967 for, although the total Left actually got a slightly lower share of the vote than in 1962, its parliamentary representation increased from 146 to 189 and the *Majorité* almost lost its overall control of the Assembly, holding 245 out of 487 seats. In addition, there was precious little evidence of a reluctance by Socialist and Radical voters to transfer their vote to a Communist at the second ballot. The final achievement of the FGDS was the publication on 24 February 1968 of a joint declaration by the FGDS and the PCF listing their points of agreement on a programme of government, and their points of divergence, particularly over foreign policy.

This, says Borella, was 'a text of prime importance, the first of its kind in France, which seemed at last to open the way to the winning of power by the united left'.[12] It was a false dawn. Almost at once, the pressure of singular events reopened the old fissures between the Communist and non-Communist left, and by the end of the year the FGDS was dead. First there was disagreement over the events of May—the student revolt that turned into a general strike. May 1968 was a difficult time for the Communists. They knew that the well-paid and skilled engineering workers who vote Communist were not nearly discontented enough to wish to enact the revolutionary myth to a violent conclusion. At the same time the PCF was afflicted by the deep dread that other groups might seem more revolutionary than itself, the official architect of revolution. The PCF settled for order. It employed its organisational skills to resist 'adventures' and to prevent demonstrations and strikes getting out of hand. Some Socialists, on the other hand, allowed themselves to be more affected by the mood of revolutionary romanticism. In particular, Pierre Mendès-France was prominently present at a huge rally in the Stade Charléty on 27 May organised by the PSU; this party, formed by dissidents from all the Left-wing parties in 1960, had become progressively more revolutionary in outlook. Nothing could have been more significant than the presence of the greatly admired former Prime Minister, the only dynamic leader to hold office in the Fourth Republic, the sort of man whose prestige would have been indispensable to any government the Left might have been able to form, at a rally of 35,000 students and young people in joyful revolutionary mood where speaker after speaker denounced the stuffy conservatism, the treachery and the rigidity of the PCF, who were dragging their heels on revolution and indeed trying to prevent it. The PCF was furious. For years afterwards, the single word 'Charléty' stood in the Communist lexicon for treacherous encouragement of the Leftist anti-Communism they most resent.

To add insult to injury, François Mitterrand, believing on 29 May that his hour had come and that the moment to replace a wobbly government had arrived announced at a press conference without consulting the PCF that he was ready to be a candidate for the Presidency and suggested the immediate formation of a caretaker government of the Left, to be headed by Pierre Mendès-France. That press conference cast a shadow over the Left for a long time. The overtones of illegal seizure of power seriously damaged Mitterrand's prestige and were used against the Left in the June election. The electoral pact with the Communists was grudgingly maintained, but there was no spirit behind it. The election was a disaster, and good relations between Socialists, Radicals and Communists were not re-established until four years later—when the 1973 elections were drawing near.

The climate of mutual suspicion and resentment left by the events of May, and by the very serious electoral defeat for the Left that followed it, was made worse by the Warsaw Pact invasion of Czechoslovakia in August 1968. Quite apart from the stresses and strains which this event created inside the PCF between those who favoured 'polycentrism' in the world Communist movement, implying the independent right to criticise the actions of the Soviet Union, and those who felt that the Soviet Union should be supported through thick and thin, the invasion of Czechoslovakia aroused all the old fears of totalitarian Communism, imposed by Soviet tanks. The initial reaction of the PCF leaders to the invasion was to express 'surprise and reprobation'[13] on the rather nationalistic grounds that the Czech national territory was sovereign. However, it became clear as time went on that the PCF leadership did not approve of the type of liberalising reforms known as 'Socialism with a human face' that the Dubcek regime had been trying to introduce in Czechoslovakia. It also gave its endorsement to 'normalisation'—i.e. to the re-Stalinisation of Czechoslovakia under Husak, the leader installed to replace Dubcek. This was exactly the kind of international crisis that makes people uneasy about Communist attachment to democratic values. It did great harm to the appeal of the Communist Party in France, and undermined those who felt that alliance with the Communists was the only way for the Left to defeat Gaullism. Roger Garaudy, a leading Communist intellectual and member of the Central Committee and *Bureau Politique* of the PCF, asked a most pertinent question (and was expelled from the Party for pursuing the point):

'Does it weaken the French Communist Party or, on the contrary, does it not remove an obstacle to its wider appeal, if I ask that the Party should say clearly: "The Socialism we want to bring in in France is not the Socialism imposed by Brezhnev on Czechoslovakia"?'[14]

It was no use: the PCF had sunk back into a mood of resentful truculence with its only friends East of the Iron Curtain. No important elections were expected for a long time—de Gaulle's presidential mandate should not have expired until 1972; Parliament was elected until 1973. However, at the referendum on regionalisation and reform of the Senate which de Gaulle presented to the French people on 27 April 1969, and which was opposed not only by the parties of the Left but much of the Centre and Right as well, a No vote of 52·4% provoked the General's immediate resignation. No less than four candidates of the Left entered the presidential elections that followed, including a Communist, Jacques Duclos, and Gaston Defferre, the Socialist Mayor of Marseille. The latter campaigned with Pierre Mendès-France at his side (a ticket calculated to arouse little enthusiasm from the Communists). In fact Duclos was the only candidate of the left to achieve a respectable score, and the whole Left did worse than the single candidature of François Mitterrand in 1965.[15]

Table 6·2

CANDIDATES OF THE LEFT—PRESIDENTIAL ELECTION
1 JUNE 1969 (1st ballot)
*(Metropolitan France)*

|  | *million votes* | *% of votes cast* | *% of registered voters* |
|---|---|---|---|
| J. Duclos—PCF | 4·8 | 21·5 | 16·6 |
| G. Defferre—Soc. | 1·1 | 5·1 | 3·9 |
| M. Rocard—PSU | 0·8 | 3·7 | 2·8 |
| A. Krivine—Trot. | 0·2 | 1·1 | 0·8 |
|  | 6·9 | 31·4 | 24·1 |
| (1965—1st Ballot): |  |  |  |
| (F. Mitterrand | 7·7 | 31·7 | 26·6) |

Once again it was an electoral rendezvous that gave the first sign that the climate might be thawing. In the important municipal elections of March 1971, *Union de la Gauche* lists which included Communists and Socialists were presented in several important cities and were successful in quite a number—Le Havre and Calais, to quote two towns well known to English readers. The watchword, however, was opportunism. Where the Socialists thought they could get on better without the Communists, they did so: Lille, Guy Mollet's Arras, Defferre's Marseille, or Nantes, where Socialists governed as part of a coalition led by an ancient figure from the extreme right of the Radical party—the former minister André Morice.[16] In June 1971, the new Socialist Party was launched at the famous Epinay-sur-Seine Congress of Unification, with Mitterrand as First Secretary. The strategy was the old FGDS strategy—unity of the Left, and agreement on a common programme with the PCF. The aim, in short, was to take up with the PCF the threads of February 1968—a conversion so rudely interrupted by the events of May and August of that year.

Exactly as before, Mitterrand's plan was to build up the strength and prestige of the Socialists so that they could be seen to be talking to the PCF as equal to equal. Jibes about the Socialist rabbit and the Communist cobra must be made to seem ridiculous.[17] The Socialist Party drafted its own policy programme and, exactly as in the days of the FGDS, began talks on an alliance with the Radicals before beginning negotiations with the PCF. There was serious disagreement between Socialists and Communists over the line to take in the referendum of 23 April 1972, when the French were asked to signify their approval of the admission of Great Britain, Ireland, Denmark and Norway[18] to the Common Market. The Socialists wanted Britain and the other states in, the Communists did not. Since the Referendum was largely a domestic political device designed by President Pompidou to procure a personal vote of confidence and sow discord among the Left, the sensible policy for the Left would have been to recommend abstention. This the Socialists did, but the Communists insisted on campaigning for a No vote. Forty-seven per cent of the electorate abstained—partly no doubt through boredom or indifference—but it looked as if the Socialists had more effectively judged the popular mood than the PCF, and they emerged strengthened from the referendum.

In the event, with the 1973 elections drawing nearer, the will to reach agreement on both sides was stronger than the discord engendered by the referendum, although incidents like that do reveal how fragile the unity between Socialists and Communists are on so many issues—especially foreign policy issues. Finally on 27 June 1972 'after three months of talks marked by the customary bartering, diplomatic procrastination, and simulated acrimony', as Wright and Machin put it,[19] 'the Socialists and Communists agreed upon a joint legislative programme—*le Programme Commun de la Gauche*—and a nationally binding second ballot electoral pact'. 'The present alliance', they continue, 'goes much further in linking *les deux partis frères* than either the 1934 Popular Front agreement, the liberation alliance, or the electoral pacts of 1967–8'. In July a group of so-called 'left-wing Radicals', that is to say Parliamentary members of the Radical Party who thought they would lose their seats if they followed the rest of the Radical Party into an alliance with the *Centre Démocrate* because they would be short of Socialist and Communist votes at the second ballot, defied their party and signed the *Programme Commun*. These dissident Radicals—or perhaps one should say these few Radicals who remained true to the Republican and Left-wing tradition of their party—formed a first ballot coalition with the Socialists. Reminiscent of the old FGDS but without its structure, this coalition was called UGSD (Union of the Socialist and Democratic Left).

From the days of the Popular Front in the 1930s onwards, the Left has only ever had any electoral success when it has gone into battle stressing what unites it and not what divides it. This in turn depends largely on whether world events authorise the Communist Party to co-exist amicably with non-Communist parties. These conditions were fulfilled in 1973 and the elections of that year marked a real turning-point for the Left in France. The decline of the Left, which—checked only by the previous outbreak of unity in 1967—had apparently reached disintegration with the collapse of the FGDS in 1968, the end of the old SFIO in 1969, and the humiliating failure of the 1969 presidential election, was at last reversed. The Left did not win the election, nor did it perform as well as early opinion polls had predicted. Perhaps the fears, actively canvassed by the *Majorité,* of renewed institutional instability and of Communism had an effect. Nevertheless, the Left did better than for many years.

Table 6·3

VOTES FOR THE LEFT, PARLIAMENTARY ELECTIONS
1967–73

| | *1967* | | *1968* | | *1973* | |
|---|---|---|---|---|---|---|
| | *million votes* | *% of vote* | *million votes* | *% of vote* | *million votes* | *% of vote* |
| PCF | 5·0 | 22·5 | 4·4 | 20·0 | 5·1 | 21·4 |
| FGDS | 4·2 | 19·0 | 3·7 | 16·5 UGSD | 4·9 | 20·8 |
| PSU + ext. Left | 0·5 | 2·1 | 0·9 | 4·0 | 0·8 | 3·3 |
| Other.Left | | | 0·2 | 0·7 | 0·1 | 0·3 |
| | 9·7 | 43·6 | 9·2 | 41·2 | 10·9 | 45·8 |

The new Socialist Party—which, as Wright and Machin have shown,[20] was much more dynamic, much better organised, much better led by François Mitterrand and had much greater appeal to the electorate—had achieved a new position of strength. It was from this position of strength that the dealings with the Communists were conducted. The Mitterrand strategy—the 'rebalancing' of the Left to build an alliance which the PCF could not dominate—seemed to be succeeding. The Socialist Party has grown to include leading members of the PSU like Michel Rocard, the alliance with the Left-wing Radicals (MRG) has flourished, and the presidential election of 1974— 'the occasion for a massive display of Left-wing unity'[21]—was, with almost 13 million second-ballot votes and with the support of more than 49% of those voting and of more than 42% of the entire electorate, all but a famous victory.

The *Union de la Gauche,* an association between parties of the Left into which they have repeatedly and ineluctably been driven as the only possible strategy for survival against the mighty electoral force of Gaullism, has so far survived the electoral defeat of Gaullism. In some respects this is surprising. In the first place, approaching elections are an important constituent of the bond between Socialists and Communists. After May 1974, there was no reason to suppose that there would be a parliamentary election before 1978 or a presidential one before 1981. The first contest of any importance would be the municipal elections of 1977. In consequence, the view of most observers in 1974 and 1975 was, 'If ye have aught to say, say it now'. There was plenty of Communist testiness throughout this period, for example at the PCF's special conference at Vitry-sur-Seine in October 1974. The PCF did not like losing voters to the Socialists, which it appeared to be doing, for example, at the Mont de Marsan by-election in 1974 and the Chatellerault by-election in 1975. It did not like being regarded as a docile source of 4 or 5 million votes to help its grand relations the Socialists to win power. It did not like being the junior partner at all. Furthermore, international events promised just the kind of issues to reveal the gaps between Communists and French public opinion, between Communists and Socialists. When the revolutionary events in Portugal, for example, appeared to be leading to a Communist-backed military dictatorship, the effect was strongly felt in France. The Socialists denounced all threats to liberty and in particular the suppression of the non-Communist and libertarian newspaper *Republica.* The Communists countered with innumerable declarations defending the right of workers to take over newspapers if they wanted, especially in the case of miserable fascist rags such as *Republica.* Like Czechoslovakia in 1968, Portugal in 1974–5 appeared to provide exactly the kind of issue which makes Frenchmen doubt the attachment of the PCF to democratic norms. The posture of the Soviet Union, too, suggested that a tough and uncompromising visage might be presented by the Communist world. Persecutions of dissident intellectuals, truculence and resentment at the revelations of Solzhenitsyn, active attempts at Soviet penetration in Angola to fill the chaotic vacuum after the departure of the Portuguese in Autumn 1975, seemed to point the icy way. However, at some time during 1975 the French Communist Party appeared to understand in a new way the link between its electoral chances in France and perceptions by the French public of its attachment to the Soviet Union and its anti-libertarian acts and attitudes.

The section on the structure and ideas of the Communist party in Chapter 8 will go into more detail on the question of the PCF and liberty. Declarations on the subject became more and more frequent as preparations for the 22nd Congress of 1976 were made. The dictatorship of the proletariat was considered to be an outdated concept,[22] and the existence of Soviet labour camps and savagely repressive measures taken against people for their opinions were for the first time acknowledged and denounced (to the annoyance of the Soviet Embassy in Paris). Georges Mamy summarised the change thus:

For fifty years the PCF lived in its minority-party shell, scarcely believing it could ever succeed. Since 1974 its militants have known that the attainment of power— not alone certainly, and only with a limited programme—is no longer impossible. Gradually outlooks and attitudes have been modified by this new factor, which imposes new behaviour and a different approach to problems that they might actually have to deal with tomorrow or the day after.[23]

A most important role in encouraging the apparent change in PCF attitudes has been played by the Italian Communist Party and its Secretary-General, Enrico Berlinguer. The PCI is by far the largest Communist Party outside the Communist states. Further more its prospects of winning power democratically in Italy began to seem very tangible. It has gained ground steadily in local, regional and national elections, and the chorus of voices calling for responsible Communist participation in governments with the Christian Democratic party has gradually grown in strength. The growing appeal of the PCI in a profoundly Catholic country is due essentially to three things. First, it is identified as the defender of the underpriviledged. Secondly, it has been universally acknowledged to provide, in cities like Bologna, a far more effective and less corrupt municipal government than the other parties. Thirdly, it has for many years emphasized its distance from Moscow, repeatedly making it clear that it takes no orders from the Soviet Union and that where it differs from the Soviet Union on some issue it will say so. The PCI denounced the Soviet invasion of Czechoslovakia in 1968, it denounced the apparent desire of the pro-Soviet Portuguese Communist Party to collaborate in a Left-wing military dictatorship in Portugal. It has collaborated in the European Community. It favours direct elections to the European Parliament. It is opposed to the persecution of dissident intellectuals and Jews in the Soviet Union. In other words, it has gone to great lengths to demonstrate to the Italian electorate and to the world that it does not intend to set up a Soviet-type dictatorship in Italy, and that an Italy governed by the PCI would not immediately affiliate to the Eastern bloc. Berlinguer, in meetings with his French comrades in September and November 1975, appears to have made Georges Marchais understand what an albatross it is for Western Communist parties to appear too closely identified with Soviet attitudes, and the credibility of all Western Communist parties is damaged in the eyes of Western electorates if any of the important ones convey the impression of a Stalinist outlook on Western democratic liberties. The PCF has been making steps down the Italian road—albeit in a hesitant and wobbly manner—ever since an article by the poet Louis Aragon, a member of the PCF's central committee, appeared in 1966 criticising the trial in the Soviet Union of the writers Sinyavsky and Daniel.[24] The PCF remains many leagues behind but the meeting in Rome on 15 November 1975 may have marked a decisive stage in the PCF's determination to liberalise and to catch up the PCI. If this impetus is genuine and is maintained, a large obstacle to the future success of the *Union de la Gauche* in France will have been reduced.

To summarise, the success of Gaullism from 1958 to 1974 imposed a strategy of Union on the Left as the only means of avoiding electoral destruction. No Centre-Left alternative to Gaullism has appeared remotely credible. Each anticipated election since the mid-1960s has found the parties of the left engaged in an effort to create an effective alliance—the presidential election of 1965 and the National Assembly elections of 1967 and 1973. One problem has been the need for renewal on the non-Communist Left, which has been in fragmentation and decline since the late 1940s, with its strength in declining areas and its leadership consisting of old Fourth Republic fixers and notables and not national leaders. The other problem has been the need to remove the electorate's doubts about the French Communist party and its attachment to democratic liberties. François Mitterrand, paradoxically an old Fourth Republic politician himself, has played a large part in the attempt to overcome both problems. His prestige as a presidential candidate has attracted a large, active and dynamic membership to the new Socialist Party. His strategy of rebuilding the non-Communist Left so that it was able to speak to the PCF as equal to equal, and of building an alliance with the PCF on the basis of a joint-programme in which liberties were guaranteed, has helped to overcome fears of the PCF's capacity or inclination to establish a Soviet-style dictatorship of the proletariat. The Assembly elections of 1973 were a turning-point in support for the Left, and at the second ballot of the 1974 presidential campaign Mitterrand collected the highest vote for the Left ever recorded in France. In addition, he has seen to it that an effective *Groupe de Liaison de la Gauche* (liaison group of the Left) thrashes out a joint approach to as many problems as possible, from policy to electoral candidatures.

This account of the *Union de la Gauche* completes the picture of a bipolar party system. It is far from being a two-party system. The alliances clustering round both poles—government and opposition—contain every shade of potential discord from personal rivalry to differences of principle. Gaullism, the force that legitimised the new institutions and created a vast electorate for stable majority government, imposed unity on the opposition and the will to resolve its deep internal differences in the face of so mighty an adversary. Strangely enough, by 1976 the *Union de la Gauche* was appearing in opinion surveys, local elections and by-elections to be so formidable that it was a factor in containing to some extent the renascent rivalries in the pro-government camp and imposing discipline on the *Majorité*. In short it was a bipolar system, vastly different from the disorganised coalitions of cliques which formed the fragmented party system of the Fourth Republic, but with a certain potential fragility nonetheless. So many international issues, from European integration to a multitude of Soviet foreign policy initiatives, could reopen the fissure between Socialists and Communists. If the *Union de la Gauche* collapsed, the whole edifice of the new party system might follow it, and France might be back to opportunistic Centrist coalition politics again. If the *Union de la Gauche* does not collapse but wins a majority in the Assembly at the next election (due in 1978), all kinds of problems lie ahead. It would be a test of the capacity of the Fifth Republic institutions to handle a divergence between the presidential and parliamentary majorities. It would be a test of the government élite's willingness to hand over power to the opposition—a fundamental test of a democratic political order. It would be a test of the PCF and the genuineness of its abandonment of the goal of dictatorship of the proletariat. In short, it would be a test of the legitimacy of the Republic.

## NOTES

1. F. L. Wilson, *The Democratic Left 1963-1969*, Stanford University Press, 1971, p. 141.
2. *Programme Commun de Gouvernement.*
3. David Caute, *The Left in Europe*, Weidenfeld and Nicolson, 1966, p. 12.
4. See Ch. 7.
5. Wilson, *The Democratic Left*, p. 23.
6. *Ibid.*, p. 24.
7. See Charlot, *The Gaullist Phenomenon*, pp. 56-7.

8.  Wilson, *The Democratic Left*, p. 61.
9.  *Ibid.*, p. 106.
10  *Ibid.*, p. 104.
11. See Chapter 8.
12. Borella, *Les Partis politiques*, p. 155.
13. *L'Humanité*, 22 August 1968.
14. Letter to the *Bureau Politique* of the PCF, 14 Sept. 1969. See 'A propos du blâme publique' in *Toute la Vérité*, Paris: Grasset, 1970, p. 111; see also pp. 106, 123, 151.
15. The fact that Socialist electors decided to vote for the Centrist Alain Poher, judged to have the best chance of defeating Pompidou in the second ballot, is noted on p. 199.
16. As part of the post-1973 climate of unity on the Left, the leading Socialist councillors (including a member of Parliament) in Nantes have all been expelled from the Socialist Party.
17. When, in opinion polls of late 1975, the Socialists were shown as being the first choice of 33% of the electors, ahead of all other parties, especially the PCF with 17%, the jibe was turned against the Communists: the Communist cobra had been eaten by the Socialist rabbit.
18. The Norwegians subsequently declined the invitation at their own referendum on 26 September 1972.
19. V. Wright and H. Machin, 'The French Socialist Party in 1973: performance and prospects', *Government and Opposition*, Spring 1974, pp. 142-3.
20. *Ibid.*, and 'The French Socialist Party: success and the problems of success', *Political Quarterly*, Jan.–March 1975, pp. 36–52.
21  Wright and Machin *Political Quarterly*, Jan.–March 1975, p. 37.
22. Correspondence in *L'Humanité*, 5-7 Jan. 1976; declaration by Georges Marchais on television, 7 Jan. 1976; etc.
23. *Nouvel Observateur*, 12-18 Jan. 1976, p. 27.
24. *L'Humanité*, 16 Feb. 1966: 'A propos d'un procès: une déclaration d'Aragon'.

# 7

## SOCIALISTS AND LEFT-WING RADICALS

### 1. *Socialism*

'Pre-Marxist Socialism, place of birth—France'—thus Claude Willard entitles the first chapter of this book on Socialism and Communism in France.[1] 'On French soil its luxuriant and infinitely varied vegetation germinated and grew. Only one great variety of pre-Marxist Socialism, Owenism, ripened under other skies.'[2] Gracchus Babeuf, in *Manifesto of the Equals* (1796), declared 'We are all equal, are we not? Let there be no difference between human beings but in age and sex! Since all have the same needs and faculties, let there be for all one education and one standard of life!' Saint-Simon, through his review *L'Industrie* (founded 1816), promoted a technocratic utopia in which the wasteful anarchy of a market economy would be eliminated. Fourier proposed in 1808 a social order based on harmonious communes or cooperatives. There was a Socialism of Christian and messianic inspiration associated with Lammenais. There was revolutionary Socialism (Auguste Blanqui). There was anarchist Socialism represented by Proudhon, the man who uttered the famous phrase 'Property is theft'. There was the libertarian and humanist Socialism of Jean Jaurès, the great pacifist orator murdered on 31 July 1914. Resolute Marxists and those who identify with the class struggle have had outlets in the form of the French Communist Party since 1920 or the Unions, especially the CGT (General Confederation of Labour—formed in 1895).

One would have thought, therefore, that this rich tradition of pre-Marxist and non-Marxist Socialism would have led, as in Great Britain, to a Socialist Party in which the influence of Marxism was slight. Yet while the action of the Socialist Party in France at national or local level has been reformist and moderate, its doctrine has remained anchored on Marxist and revolutionary ideology which it has never abandoned. Revolution is in France a very powerful myth, in the sociological sense of myth, i.e. in the sense of an inspiring legend that moulds behaviour. Even at its most opportunistic and anti-Communist moments, as under the leadership of Guy Mollet in the 1950s, Socialist rhetoric has always returned to the theme of revolution. Noting in 1930 this 'verbal gap which in France makes the epithets more and more terrifying at the very moment when the parties are becoming less terrible', André Siegfried recounts a visit in a traditionally Left-wing region to a comfortable farmer who owned a fine property overlooking the Mediterranean. 'How can owners of property down here such as yourself vote in such large numbers for a party whose doctrine condemns property?' With a vague and elegant gesture my companion eluded this direct aim: "It won't happen tomorrow", he replied simply and I in my naivety at last understood that one voted for the doctrine on the clear understanding that it would not be applied.'[3]

## 2. The SFIO

There were a number of competing socialist movements in France in the last years of the nineteenth century. Some were revolutionary—the Guesdistes (the Marxist Parti Ouvrier led by Jules Guèsde) and Blanquistes. Some were reformist—especially the 'Possibilists', as Paul Brousse's Federation of Socialist Workers was known. The Second International at its Amsterdam Congress in 1904 urged them all to unite. In 1905, in response to this appeal, the SFIO was founded. The 1905 programme defined it as a 'class party whose goal is to transform capitalist society into a collectivist or communist society'. That subtle word 'transform', as George Lichtheim notes, 'struck the requisite balance between the reformist and the anarcho-syndicalist trends.'[4] Its initials SFIO represented the resounding revolutionary title of French Section of the Workers' International. Most of its leadership was reformist, and this perpetual gap between doctrine and practice was the SFIO's great problem throughout the sixty-four years of its existence. Unity was less than total. Divided over how revolutionary to be, over whether Socialists should enter 'bourgeois' governments,[5] over relations with the Union movement committed by the Charter of Amiens in 1906 to a revolutionary syndicalism independent of all political parties, over whether to oppose war or to fight in it, the SFIO finally split in 1920 over the issue of membership of Lenin's Communist International.

The Bolshevik revolution in 1917 had caused great excitement and hope among Socialist movements in all countries. The SFIO sent two delegates, Marcel Cachin and L.-O. Frossard, to make contact with Russian Bolshevik leaders and discuss membership of the Third International created by Lenin in 1919. They brought back the famous '21 Conditions' for membership of the International, conditions which went a good deal further in violence, clandestinity and intolerance of divergent viewpoints than many French Socialists were prepared to go. The 21 Conditions called for a purge of reformists, clandestine organisation, rejection of 'bourgeois legality', agitation in the army, in the unions and among peasants, and rejection of patriotism, pacifism and colonialism. They insisted on support for any Soviet Republic, the form of organisation know as Democratic Centralism,[6] the name Communist Party and the obligation to accept all decisions of the International. They were debated at the Congress of Tours in December 1920. There were 3,208 votes for the Cachin-Frossard motion recommending affiliation to the International, 1,022 for a motion rejecting the 21 Conditions.[7] By a majority of 3 to 1, therefore, the Party, and in consequence all its assets, offices and newspapers—joined the Communist International. However, Léon Blum in a famous phrase proclaimed that 'Someone must stay and look after the old firm' (*la vieille maison*), and led the minority away to re-form and perpetuate the SFIO. It gradually gained membership and had a considerable success at the 1924 election in which, as part of the *Cartel des Gauches* with the Radicals, it won 101 seats.

More than a decade of intense hostility between the SFIO and the Communist Party began to thaw in the mid-1930s as the rise of Fascism in Europe became more threatening. After the famous demonstrations of the extreme Right in Paris on 6 February 1934, Socialists and Communists joined forces in a memorable anti-Fascist rally on 12 February. In 1935 the 7th Congress of the Communist Party of the Soviet Union authorised a change of line. Socialists were no longer 'social-Fascists' but allies in the common struggle against Fascism. In 1936 the Popular Front, composed of Socialists, Communists and Radicals, won its famous electoral victory. With Blum as Prime Minister, this was the lyrical period of the 40-hour week, holidays with pay and other famous social reforms. It was also the period in which France, despite its Left-wing government, joined with the other democracies in refusing arms to Republican Spain in the Civil War, and to accede to the appeasement of Hitler at the Munich Conference.

Although a large part of the SFIO, in Parliament and outside, accepted Pétain and Vichy, its leaders emerged with honour from the Resistance. Supporters and members of the provisional government of General de Gaulle, the Socialists received over 23% of the votes at the October 1945 election—a performance they have never yet equalled—and claimed a membership of 350,000, unparalleled before or since. Four Socialists served as Prime Minister in the Fourth Republic: Blum, Gouin, Ramadier (who expelled the Communist Party from the Government in 1947) and Mollet. Blum tried to seize the opportunity after the War to persuade the SFIO to drop much of its ideological baggage. He 'hoped to rejuvenate their movement as a French Labour Party emancipated from a Marxist creed which they had long ceased to take seriously, and to open it to new blood from the Resistance organisations'.[8] However Guy Mollet, whose name was to

become the synonym of opportunism, successfully carried the
1946 conference for the resolution which condemned 'all attempts
at revisionism, especially those which are inspired by a false
humanism, the real intention of which is to mask that fundamental
reality—the class struggle'. The party's doctrinal effort was 'to
enrich Marxism, . . . not to dilute it by a return, more or less
camouflaged, to utopian Socialism'. No phrase could more
graphically illustrate the stupendous and persistent self-deception
of the SFIO.

The twenty-three years with Guy Mollet as Secretary-General of
the SFIO from 1946 to 1969 were depressing years of decline,
ossification and eventually death. The SFIO in the Fourth
Republic dwindled into what the Radicals had been in the
Third—deeply conservative defenders of the old republican and
anti-clerical faith. The gap between words and actions became
wider and wider. Comfortably installed on local councils (over
half the members of the party in 1965 were councillors) or
Parliament, functioning in big towns as 'a mutual aid society of
municipal employees',[9] the party, in the name of a fearless refusal
to compromise its doctrine, rejected all progressive policies and
initiatives. In government, Socialist doctrine became 'nothing
more than a rationale for the grossest kind of opportunism'[10]
which abandoned both the humanism of Jaurès and the Socialist
dedication of Guesde, the two conflicting ideals which have always
caused such difficulties for French Socialism. This opportunism,
tricked out in revolutionary rhetoric, came to be known as *Mollet-
isme*. Guy Mollet as Prime Minister in 1956 became converted,
after an angry reception by French settlers in Algeria, to the cause
of keeping Algeria French. Just as Blum had cooperated with
Anthony Eden in denying arms to Republican Spain, so Mollet
cooperated with Eden in the cloak-and-dagger fiasco of the Anglo-
French invasion of Egypt in 1956. He opposed all attempts to build
effective alliances either with the Communist Left or the Catholic
Centre. By insisting on impossible conditions concerning the total
refusal of state aid to Catholic schools, he helped to torpedo the
Socialist-Radical-MRP alliance which Gaston Defferre was
attempting to construct on the basis of progressive policies and his
own presidential candidature. Rejuvenation of French Socialism,
the building of an effective alliance on the Left, and electoral
recovery came, as we saw in the last chapter, from outside the
SFIO—from the Left-wing clubs, from the initiatives of François
Mitterrand (never a member of the SFIO), from the phoenix of the
new Socialist Party which eventually arose in 1971 from the ashes
of the discredited SFIO.

## 3.   *The PS*

The SFIO became extinct in 1969. The FGDS, the Federation of
the Democratic Socialist Left, that for a time, under the impulsion
of François Mitterrand had successfully fused Socialists and
Radicals and acquired the authority to negotiate an alliance with
the Communists, had died in 1968—a victim of electoral débacle, a
new outbreak of Stalinist intransigence in the Communist camp,
and the development of Centrist longing in the hearts of Radicals.
The metamorphosis of Socialism is marked in the best tradition of
the French Left by the names of four congresses in the Paris
suburbs: Alfortville, Bagneux, Issy-les-Moulineaux and Epinay.
At Alfortville in May 1969 the SFIO made the disastrous decision
to 'go it alone' in the presidential election with its own candidate
Gaston Defferre, and the more promising decision to form a new
Socialist Party. At Bagneux in June, a smaller conference
attempted to work out a 'basis of agreement for all Socialists'.[11]
Rejection of Centrist alliances, the regrouping of all currents of
democratic Socialism, the will to build an alliance with the
Communists, a guarantee of representation for minorities in the
direction of the new party—these were the essential principles. In
July at Issy-les-Moulineaux a Congress established the new party
with Alain Savary as Secretary-General. By no means all 'currents
of democratic socialism' were present: Mitterrand and the
Convention of Republican Institutions (the Federations of Clubs
that played an important part in the short-lived success of the
FGDS) were not there. Issy however was an important turning
point. In particular the indispensible rejuvenation and renewal
could begin. With Savary as party leader, Vincent Wright and
Howard Machin have shown, 'between 1969 and 1971, 70% of the
secretaries of departmental federations had been replaced and the
average age of the holders of these key posts fell by 20 years'.[12]

   François Mitterrand and the Convention decided in December
1970 that they would join the new party. In June 1971 at Epinay-
sur-Seine, therefore, the Congress of Unification was held and the
new party decided upon a strategy of Left-wing unity (a joint
programme of government with the PCF) and by a narrow
majority[13] elected Mitterrand to the post of First Secretary. Since
1971 the new Socialist Party has been remarkably successful. In
1972 the 'common programme' with the Communists—a
manifesto containing a number of guarantees of democratic
liberties— was signed. Most of the Radicals were retrieved from
their Centrist adventures and encompassed, for the 1973 elections,
in the UGSD (Union of the Socialist and Democratic left)—their
humbler position in relation to the reinvigorated Socialists being
neatly reflected in the inversion of initials S and D from the old
FGDS. Finally the electoral performances of the UGSD, the

functioning of the *Union de la Gauche,* and the Mitterrand presidential campaign of 1974, all indicate the remarkable renewal of French Socialism.

There remain all kinds of difficulties. The new party, as we shall see, is a very heterogeneous mixture and there are constant outbreaks of tension with the Communists. The PS, however, unlike the old SFIO, has a dynamic and successful air about it. The smart new offices[14] opposite the Palais Bourbon, with their tasteful lettering, the beige and hessian shades, their elegant and nubile personnel, are reminiscent of a busy and fast-growing advertising agency. The opinion polls throughout 1976 were giving the PS over 30% of voting intentions. The party made tremendous gains in local elections and by-elections. The parties of the *Majorité* have done the PS the honour of considering it, and not the Communists, as their principal adversary.[15]

In October 1974 the PS was given added strength by the arrival of new forces: Michel Rocard, the leader of the PSU, which had grown from a splinter group that had split off from the SFIO in 1958 into an increasingly Left-wing and revolutionary sect, and 2,500–3,000 PSU members; Edmond Maire and some 1,500 activists from the CFDT, France's second largest and increasingly militant trade union; and even some refugees from the *Majorité* like Jacques Delors, assistant to Jacques Chaban-Delmas when he was Prime Minister. The absorption of these new elements, and the debate on *'autogestion'*, or workers' control, which they have provoked, were the main themes of the Party Congress at Pau in January 1975. At its previous conference (Grenoble 1973) François Mitterrand declared, 'We must make the Socialist Party the first party of France.' In 1975 and 1976 the 'First Party of France' is what the PS continually proclaimed itself to be.

*(a) PS—Ideas and policies.* The PS gained unity at Epinay in 1971, and renovation, because it was willing to be diverse. Indeed one extremely original feature of the PS organisation, as we shall see, is that representation for different minority currents of thought on the governing bodies of the Party is guaranteed in the Party's constitution. Diversity is institutionalised. It is enriching because of the continuous ferment of ideas, and it is dangerous because 'parties within the Party' can form. It is difficult, therefore, to present a single set of ideas which encapsulate French Socialism. The Party's official 'Declaration of Principles' starts unpromisingly with sonorous abstractions about 'liberating the human person from every alienation which oppresses him', but forms presumably a core of ideas common to all components of the party. A number of themes are embraced. There is considerable emphasis on freedom of expression, freedom of conscience, openness to new knowledge,

and democratic liberties. There is stress on the goal of replacing capitalism not transforming it, the 'progressive socialisation of the means of investment, production and exchange'. Thus far the constitution of the PS is much the same as that of the British Labour Party. There is, however, a Marxist coloration which is absent from the Labour Party's declarations. 'Socialists believe that such democracy cannot exist in capitalist society. It is in this sense that the Socialist Party is a revolutionary party'. 'The emancipation of the workers will be accomplished by the workers themselves.' They must 'take conscience that they are the majority and that they can therefore, democratically, put an end to exploitation.' Finally, there is a commitment, in the good old French Republican tradition, to *'la laïcité de l'école et de l'Etat'*—secular education and complete separation of church and state.

Besides this common fund of beliefs, there is considerable debate about such concepts as 'class collaboration' and the class struggle. To what extent is the PS an instrument of the class struggle? Completely, says the Left wing in the shape of CERES (Centre for Socialist Study, Research and Education) which has promoted the idea of *'Sections d'entreprise'*—units of membership based on the workplace. The Communists have always done this, and are not at all pleased to see the PS invading their territory. The Party's 'Guide for new members' emphasises the role of the PS as a 'class front for a class struggle in the Marxist sense of the term'.[16] Another debate concerns *autogestion* (workers' control) in which the PS is increasingly coming to represent the aspirations of those who believe that individuals should have a greater say in decisions that affect them at work and in the community—in a phrase, a more participatory democracy. This is seen as being possible only when the Left is in power and has transformed the state and its apparatus as well as the centres of private industrial and financial power. This debate figured largely in the months that followed the 1974 presidential elections and centred round the *Assises du Socialisme* in October 1974 and the arrival in the party of *autogestionnaires* from the PSU and the CFDT. Policies, as opposed to beliefs, are also, as in all democratic parties, the subject of intense debate. Unlike the parties of the *Majorité,* the Socialists do have a specific programme. The central policy document at the moment is the *Programme Commun* the joint manifesto, the 'contract of government' which forms the basis of the *Union de la Gauche',* the alliance with the PCF. The *Programme Commun* contains a number of pledges on improvement of working conditions, pensions, security of employment, and social security. It includes a specific commitment to nine nationalisations in aviation, electronics, chemicals, steel, etc. It promises decentralisation of government including, interestingly, the ending of supervision and control of local

government by the *Préfets*. It commits itself to improving civil
liberties: Habeas Corpus will be introduced, *garde à vue* (detention
by the police) will disappear, and there will be a Supreme Court to
see that the constitution is applied. In foreign and defence policy
the French nuclear deterrent will cease, conscription will be
reduced to six months, and the European Community will be
rescued from capitalism and transformed into 'Europe of the
Workers'. A government of the Left would establish with its
parliamentary majority a 'legislative contract' committing itself to
the achievement of its programme.

*(b) PS—organisation.* In a mass-membership political party,
organisational structure is important. In the smaller parties
grouped round a parliamentary and ministerial élite, the structural
arrangements whereby the party in the country is represented on
the executive bodies are relatively unimportant; the party is run by
and for its leaders. In mass-membership parties this is also
largely so—did not Michels speak of the 'iron law of oligarchy'
whereby any large-scale organisation, even of a political party
dedicated to democracy, leads to the concentration of power in the
hands of the leadership? Nonetheless, in mass-membership parties
organisation and structure remain important. A well-organised
mass-membership party is a powerful electoral force and an
important instrument in the handship of its leader. We have
already seen seen how vital an element in President Pompidou's
success was the organised force of the Gaullists Party. It is the mass-
membership aspect that makes the Gaullist Party continue to be so
important even after the defeat of Gaullism, and it is the several
thousand trained and disciplined activists that give the Communist
Party its muscle in French politics. Organisation and structure are
important too, because they are a key to how the party is
controlled by its leadership. The organisation is a problem for the
leadership of a large party, as well as an instrument in its hands.
Party management, the way support is built and maintained, the
internal power structure of a party are, in a large party, important
constraints and opportunities for the exercise of political power. In
two of the large parties in France—the RPR and the PCF—the
organisation and membership are powerful effective, and
essentially pliant instruments in the hands of the leadership. In the
case of the Socialist Party however, like its sister the British Labour
Party, the leadership has a continuous struggle, compromising,
balancing, manoeuvring to maintain its rule over an unruly and
factious rank-and-file. 'My strategy', Mitterrand is reported to
have remarked, 'is to remain master of my tactics.'[17]

The organisation of the PS can be schematically summarised:
*Section.* Basic unit of membership. Sections (minimum five

members) are formed in localities (towns, villages, *quartiers*). There can also be workplace sections *(sections d'entreprise)* or university sections. Represented in Departmental Federation in proportion to its membership. Its delegation must reflect the different shades of opinion in the section.

*Federation—Département* level: The sovereign unit as far as the local application of party policy is concerned. Minimum membership for representation at national level: fifty members (paid up to date) and five sections. The Federation sends delegates to National Convention, National Congress, and to Regional Coordinating Committee.

*National Congress.* The supreme decision-making body of the Party. It meets every two years (further exceptional congresses may be convened by the *Comité Directeur*). Delegates are elected by Federal Congresses. Federations with 50–100 members send one delegate, those with 100–250 send two. Each additional 250 members (or part thereof if greater than 125) entitles a Federation to one more delegate. Thus a Federation with 900 members would send five delegates. Delegations have a voting strength on the following basis: one vote per Federation plus one vote for every twenty-five paid-up members. A Federation with 900 members would therefore have thirty-seven votes. Three very large Federations with memberships of several thousand have traditionally dominated Socialist congresses: the Nord, Pas de Calais, and Bouches-du-Rhône (Marseille). The last-named has 12,000 members (487 votes).

Preparation for a National Congress is interesting. As in the British Labour Party, resolutions are submitted by Federations and circulated to all. But unlike the British Labour Party, in which 'composite resolutions' are cooked up the day before Annual Conference opens, the PS *Comité Directeur* prepares *textes de synthèse* and sends them to Federations a month before Congress. The Federations have an 'information day' to discuss the various resolutions and *textes de synthèse*. Then, having got themselves fully informed, the Sections vote. Finally, on the basis of the Section votes, a Federal Congress decides how the Federation will vote at National Congress.

*National Convention.* Composed of one delegate per Federation, it meets at least twice a year to ensure contact between the *Comité Directeur* and the rank and file, and to see that the Congress decisions are being respected. *Comité Directeur* and Parliamentary Group members attend.

*Comité Directeur.* Elected by National Congress, it directs the party between the National Congresses, carries out Congress and Convention decisions, controls propaganda and the Party's press, and directs the parliamentarians, councillors and party activists. It has 131 members, of which the *Mitterrandiste* majority has 87 and the CERES minority 35,[18] and 26 substitute members (19 and 7). Associated bodies such as Youth, Student or Study and Research organisations are represented in a consultative capacity. It elects the Executive Bureau *(Bureau Executif)* to which it delegates day-to-day control of the Party.

*Executive Bureau.* Administers and directs the party on the basis of powers delegated by the *Comité Directeur.* It has twenty-seven members, and in 1976 included the leader (First Secretary) and the other 14 National Secretaries as follows:

François Mitterrand—*First Secretary*
Pierre Mauroy—*Coordination*
Louis Mermaz—*Federations and Workplace Sections*
Pierre Bérégovoy—*External Relations*
Edith Cresson—*Young Socialists (JS) and Socialist Students (ES)*
Claude Estier—*Press and Information*
Marie-Thérèse Eyquem—*Associated Organisations*
Roger Fajardie—*Elections and Disputes*
Lionel Jospin—*Third World*
Charles-Emile Loo—*Finance*
Gilles Martinet—*Study Groups*
Robert Pontillon—*International Relations*
Jean Poperen—*Propaganda*
Michel Rocard (former leader of PSU)—*Public Sector*
Dominique Taddeï—*Cultural action*

The remaining members of the Executive Bureau are: Gaston Defferre, Gérard Jaquet, Pierre Joxe, Georges Fillioud, André Acquier, Jean-Pierre Chévènement,★ Didier Motchane,★ Paule Dufour,★ Georges Sarre,★ Michel Coffineau,★ Michel Charzat,★ Pierre Guidoni★ (★ = CERES).

The list includes a few relatively unknown trade unionists and militants, some long-serving party organisers, some *ministrables*—the likely holders of ministerial office in any Socialist government—the leaders of the main tendencies in the party (Chévènement on the left, Mauroy and Defferre in the Centre, and so on). Nine of its members in 1976 were Socialist Deputies in the National Assembly.[19]

A full organigram of the PS would include the General Delegates who assist the different National Secretaries, and the National Secretaries, and the National Delegates who have been appointed as Socialist spokesmen for areas of national policy. For instance Jean-Pierre Cot, a member of Parliament, speaks on European Affairs, Jacques Delors on International economic affairs, Louis Mexandeau (member of Parliament) and Roger Quilliot (professor, mayor of Clermont-Ferrand) on Education. In addition there is the numerous, young, ENA-trained, Mitterrand 'brainstrust': Jacques Attali, Christian Goux, Jean-Claude Colliard,[20] Jean-Marcel Bichat and others.

The constitution of the Party, in addition to defining the organisational structure already described, contains some interesting features. The first is the insistence throughout on the proportional representation of different shades of opinion *(tendances)*. Although Article 4 says that no organised *tendance* will be allowed, the tolerant structure of the Party makes it all too easy for 'parties within the Party' to be organised. Candidates for National bodies like the *Comité Directeur* are attached to resolutions submitted to Congress. The number elected depends on the number of votes those resolutions obtain. At local level the same thing happens: the fate of candidates for office is determined by the success of the resolutions for submission to National Congress. A minority must attain 5% to secure representation. At least 10% of all successful candidates for office at any level must be women.

The interplay of *tendances* in the PS is positively Florentine in its subtlety. The dominant tendency is a Mitterrand—Mauroy—Defferre coalition. Pierre Mauroy (Mayor of Lille) controls the block vote of the Nord delegation, Gaston Defferre (Mayor of Marseille) that of the Bouches-du-Rhône. Defferre's lieutenant in Marseille, Charles-Emile Loo is treasurer of the party. Allied to this group is the *autogestionnaire* (workers' control) tendency led by Michel Rocard. The *Mitterrandistes* achieved 68% representation after the voting on resolutions at the Pau Congress in January 1975. The opposition to the Mitterrandistes is led by the extreme Left of the party in the shape of CERES,[21] revolutionary, Marxist, *autogestionnaire,* critical of the personal power regime of the First Secretary. CERES dominates the big Paris Federation. This group, whose main leaders are Chévènement (a young and elegant *énarque*, deputy for Belfort), Motchane and Sarre, were cut down at the Pau Congress to 26%. These main groups favour the Party's central strategy—alliance with the Communists in the *Union de la Gauche*. CERES is closer to the Communists on various issues of policy such as reticence over European integration. Another small Left-wing current favourable to the alliance with the PCF is the *Poperéniste* tendency (Jean Poperen, Deputy from the Lyon area, and his friends). There is another anti-Mitterrand tendency of rapidly declining importance. Called *Bataille Socialiste* after its news sheet, it groups the old associates of Guy Mollet (who died in 1975) and the *Vieille Maison*. A lot of these have been losing their seats on the *Comité Directeur,* and have even been expelled from the Party—for instance the Socialist councillors in Nantes who refused to end their membership of a Centrist municipal coalition.[22] The leading *Molletiste* is Claude Fuzier.

Another interesting aspect of the Party constitution involves selection of candidates. The PS is far more democratic in this respect than the other French political parties, where central designation of candidates tends to be the rule. Parliamentary candidates of the PS are chosen by all Party members living in the Constituency. Candidates thus chosen are subject to ratification by the Federation and the National Convention. A similar procedure applies to local elections. A further rule (Article 50) states that if Party membership is less than 1/500th of the electorate in a locality, the local section can only choose a short list for Federal or National bodies to take the final decision. This avoids the travesty of democracy which prevails for example in many solid Labour areas of British cities, where a tiny handful of ward Party members determines local council candidatures. A special National Congress decides on any Socialist candidature for the Presidency of the Republic—but (Article 49) local Sections are consulted.

When a candidate, thus chosen, is elected to Parliament or a local council he undertakes in writing to resign his seat if he leaves the Party—a promise more honoured in the breach than the observance. Socialist members must vote in accordance with Group decisions or face disciplinary sanctions (Article 72). The votes of the Socialist Group in the National Assembly (Chairman Gaston Defferre) are determined by the Group, the *Comité Directeur,* and the National Convention. Members of Parliament are all assigned, in Parliament, to various standing committees: Foreign Affairs, Defence, Finance, etc. Socialist members must join Party study groups corresponding the parliamentary committees they are on.

The Party study groups, organised by Gilles Martinet, a writer and journalist who was once in the PSU, are related to parliamentary work in the sense that they prepare legislative proposals, but they go much further. 'In looking to an early accession to power by the Left', writes Martinet, 'we must examine all possible scenarios and provide the party with answers to the problems which will inevitably arise.'[23] There are no fewer than 130 socialist study groups covering broad areas like taxation or the public sector as well as narrow areas like architecture or the police. Some groups work with the PCF and the MRG in the framework of the *Groupe de Liaison de la Gauche.*

The financial resources of the Party are hard to estimate—as always with political parties. A budget at national level of 7 million francs for 1975/6 was proclaimed[24] based on membership subscriptions and the obligatory percentage of parliamentary salaries which are automatically paid to the Party by its members of Parliament. Individual membership subscriptions, much higher than for British political parties, are proportional to income, but 45 francs of each subscription goes to National Headquarters.

*(c)  Associated organisations.* The PS has links with various organisations. First, of course, it has its own associated groups: *Jeunesse Socialiste*, open to all Party members aged between fifteen and twenty-five and *Etudiants Socialistes* for party members who are students. Students and staff Party members can form a GSU (University Socialist Group) at their university. These go in for theoretical research and study sessions on topics like 'Analysis of the Crisis of Capitalism' or 'Is Marx out of date?' There are also industrial workplace groups—*Groupes d'Entreprise*. There is some dispute in the Party about how autonomous the workplace sections should be. The left, led on this issue by Georges Sarre, sees them as vital in making the PS a real party of the working class like the PCF. They have mainly been formed in white-collar sectors like banking, but they are also present in the Post Office, and in major industries like Michelin or steel. The older traditions, represented by leaders like Pierre Mauroy, think that workers should not be stuck in party sections which confine them to their factories; they must have a say in the conduct of municipal affairs as well. These people prefer to set up *groupes* not *sections d'Entreprise*. Other directly associated bodies include the various study groups like CERES, already referred to, or CORAN (Convention of Officers of the Reserve for a New Army).

The PS is indirectly associated with a number of other organisations—especially unions. The old tradition of separation between trade unions and political parties is breaking down. The interlocking directorates of the CGT and the Communist Party have been a feature of post-war French politics. A more recent characteristic has been the 'full entry of the CFDT into the great Socialist family'. The CFDT (French Democratic Confederation of Labour) grew out of the CFTC (French Confederation of Christian Workers) in 1964 and has moved steadily to the Left. It is Marxist, libertarian, *autogestionnaire* and non-Communist. It has some 750,000 members. It has a strong revolutionary current close to the PSU which has led a number of work-ins, for instance at the Lip watch factory at Besançon, and which agitated for union rights for soldiers in 1975. Its leader, however, is a Socialist, Edmond Maire, and the leader of its 130,000 strong engineering section Jacques Chérèque is a Socialist. The CFDT came to the Pau Congress in 1975 and is a force to be reckoned with in the Party, though it is not directly affiliated like a British trade union to the Labour Party. The experienced militants of the CFDT will make a great contribution to the socialist Party. By the same token, party members will increasingly, when they join a union as the Party rules oblige them to do, choose CFDT rather than CGT.[25] Socialists have been powerful in teacher unions for many years— especially FEN (Federation of National Education) and SNI

(National Union of Teachers)—and in the smaller industrial union *Force Ouvrière* whose General Secretary André Bergeron, an extreme moderate, is a Party member.

Other organisations linked to the PS and worthy of note include the *Foyers Léo Lagrange*—a network of youth clubs and holiday centres named after the Popular Front's Minister for Leisure (the first in French history). They have 50,000 members, their useful guidebooks recommend good Socialist restaurants. *Urba Conseil,* run by Guy Marty, is an architecture and planning consultancy agency which is available to advise the 4,000 Socialist-run towns and villages in France. It employs a staff of forty and has about 100 town modernisation or housing development contracts in being.

*(d) Press.* There has been no official party daily since *le Populaire* quietly faded away in 1969. *Le Provençal* in Marseille, a daily owned by Gaston Defferre, and *Nord-Matin,* one of the Lille dailies, support the PS. So, less officially, does the *Quotidien de Paris.* The Party launched a national weekly in 1971—*L'Unité.*[26] There is in addition a monthly, *Combat Socialiste,* and *Le Poing et la Rose,* named after the Party emblem of a fist holding a rose, which is for Party members. *La Nouvelle Revue Socialiste,* heir to a famous old journal, concentrates on theory and doctrine and appears ten times a year. JS (Young Socialists) and ES (Socialist Students) publish a journal characteristically entitled *L'Insurgé* (The Insurgent). There are also a number of specialist publications for different groups in the Party. *Communes de France,* for instance, is for local councillors, and *Armée Nouvelle,* published by the Party study groups on military affairs, campaigns for a more democratic army with more civil liberties for soldiers, and publishes articles like 'NCOs: a proletariat'. A further example is *L'Unité Agricole*[27] which backs the Party's campaign, led by a young Deputy Pierre Joxe, to get more support from farmers and more say for farmers in the formation of Party policy.

*(e) PS—membership.* The Ps claims a membership today of 150,000 which is considerably lower than the peak of 355,000 at the liberation in 1944 and than the membership at the time of the Popular Front (1937:281,000).[28] It is a great improvement on the largely fictitious SFIO membership of 81,000 in 1968.[29] There has been a brisk growth in party membership and a great rejuvenation of activists and leaders. J. F. Bizot's *Au Parti des Socialistes* is a valuable book which, while composed in a rather nauseating style of revolutionary bogus-working-class lyricism,[30] conveys very well the diversity of the PS and its members. There are ex-Communists who wanted a revolution in May 1968 and who were subsequently spurned by their Communist colleagues. There are chromium-and-glass-coffee-table Leftists fresh from the rigours of

San Francisco. There are serious-minded young people from working-class and middle-class backgrounds. There are very ancient figures (even one who had met Jaurès). There are Unionists, women and peasants. There are the *archéos* or Brontosauri—old SFIO local notables who do not hold with enforced municipal alliances with the PC. There are modish entrepreneurs like Gilbert Trigano—owner of the *Clubs Mediterranées,* journalists and intellectuals like Pierre Uri, who advise Françoise Mitterrand.

Bizot reports on the life of the Party. He describes, for example, crowded section meetings where conference resolutions are to be discussed. He also looks at the big Federations in the Nord and Marseille, where Socialists have been in command of municipal affairs for years. The Nord is to French Socialism rather what Durham or South Wales is to British. Jules Guesde himself captured the Roubaix municipality for Socialism in the 1890s. The Federation of the Nord has an annual fête—the *Phalempin*[31]—presence at which is as obligatory for Socialist leaders as that of a British Labour Prime Minister at the Durham Miners' Gala or of the Democratic candidate for the U.S. Presidency at the Detroit rally on Labour day.[32]

The Socialists' most effective organisation is that which dominates Marseille, France's largest provincial city. The PS runs everything. Bizot describes the remarkable network of 152 CIQ's *(Comités d'Intérêt des Quartiers),* which enable citizens to participate in municipal affairs but which are dominated by Party members who can get things done for their locality because, as far as relations with the Town Hall are concerned, they are on the inside track.[33] Socialists control the issue of taxi licences and the port. The President of the Cooperative that runs the port of Marseille is Charles-Emile Loo, National Treasurer of the PS, city councillor and Deputy.

The godfather of it all is Gaston Defferre who has a formidable record as Mayor: he has cleaned up Marseille, from both the criminal and the sanitary points of view, and modernised it to a remarkable extent. If anyone says French local authorities have no powers because the French system is so centralised, let him visit Marseille. Defferre owns a yacht and a newspaper—*Le Provençal,* the leading local daily.[34] He runs a very tight ship. Only 3% of Marseille Party members are CERES: 'On cultivated ground weeds do not grow.'[35]

*(f) Socialism and Christianity.* A particularly interesting aspect of the newer memberships of the PS is worth considering in some detail. French political tradition, it is well known, has it that Catholics all vote for the Centre and the Right, anti-clericals for the Left. It is a

very long time, however, since all good Republicans regarded the Church as the enemy of the Republic just waiting for its moment to bring back an authoritarian monarchy that would destroy the godless works of the French Revolution. Nevertheless, there is still a sociological correlation between going to church and the propensity to vote for the *Majorité* and not for the Left.[36] Anti-clericalism is not dead among Socialists. The right-wing Socialists leadership in Nantes, for example, blames its expulsion on a kind of Christian plot—'strange collusion between the Socialist Party, heir to the secularist thought and anti-clerical combats of its precursors, and this Christian militantism attracted to a form of Communism which comes from those Catholics moulded by *JAC, JEC,* and *JOC.*'[37] It is now claimed that half the new members of the Party are Catholics. According to Bizot 34% of all Catholic priests vote for the Left (25% PS, 7% PCF) and 64% of priests under forty (42% PS, 15% PSU, 7% PCF).[38]

On the whole, the expelled notables from Nantes are correct, the Catholics have flowed into the Left wing of the Party. The PSU, which originated with disillusioned Socialists in 1958, which was joined by various other currents especially *Jocistes* (Catholics from the Young Christian Workers movement), moved steadily further to the left. The Left-wing Catholics, grouped in the grand tradition of French radical catholicism round journals— *Témoignage Chrétien* and *Vie Nouvelle*—mainly chose the PSU for political action. Some like Charles Piaget, the Catholic CFDT leader who was the revolutionary hero of the Lip factory work-in, prefer to keep their revolutionary ideals uncompromised by remaining in the PSU. Since 1972, however, a large part of the leadership and members have felt the PS was a more realistic instrument for the kind of social change they had in mind. Christians now constitute 43% of the membership of CERES where, as the CERES leader Jean-Pierre Chévènement has it, 'We have achieved a synthesis between secular progressivism and revolutionary Christianity.'[39]

*Témoignage Chrétien* is a singular publication. Indignant Right-wingers were scandalised to find *Témoignage Chrétien* folders distributed to all delegates at the Grenoble Party Conference in 1973—'as if that paper had taken over the whole congress'.[40] Bizot gives some examples of its style. Its version of 'Give us this day our daily bread' runs 'Let our bread each day be not earned by the sweat of our brothers, but let it serve to give us force to combat all injustice.'[41] A tract which its readers produced and distributed in some villages in the 1974 presidential election, entitled *'Chrétien comment votes-tu?'* (Christian, how do you vote?), read: 'Does being a Christian mean always being the mainstay of a reactionary conservative Right allied to the powers of money? Did not Christ in the Gospel denounce all-powerful money?'[42] The class struggle, Marxist Christians: how things have changed since Vatican II!

*(g) The Socialist electorate.* The attraction of the PS to Catholics has profoundly affected not only the internal life of the Party but its electoral fortunes too. The Socialist Party was the only Party of the Left to gain a higher share of the vote in 1973 than in 1967. The greatest gains made by the PS in 1973 and by the Mitterrand campaign in 1974 were in Catholic regions which traditionally vote for the Centre or the Right: Brittany, Normandy, Alsace, Lorraine. In Côtes du Nord (Brittany), the Socialist vote went from 8,000 in 1967 to 36,000 in 1973 and a seat was actually won.[43] In Lorraine the Socialist vote doubled from 1967 to 1973 and in one Lorraine *departement* (the Moselle) increased from 17,000 to 66,000. these gains in regions of traditional weakness are the most hopeful electoral signal for the PS. The second most hopeful signal is that they are regressing in areas of traditional strength—the Party appears to be losing some of its appeal in its backward, rural, economically declining bastions. This is no bad thing. Gaullism in its dynamic years, 1962 to 1967, made all its gains in the economically dynamic regions. It was the problem of law and order in 1968 that, bringing out the innate conservatism of the peasant, made him stop voting Socialist and start voting Gaullist.

The traditional bastions of Socialism are mainly where Catholicism never caught on: the South from the Pyrenees across to Provence, Burgundy, Limousin and parts of the Auvergne. In industrial areas the Communists have usually done better than the Socialists, especially in the relatively non-Catholic Paris region. The mining and textile area of Nord-Pas de Calais, a fairly strongly Catholic region, has always been a bastion of French Socialism, but Gaullism throughout the Fifth Republic has made heavy inroads. In these areas of traditional Socialist strength the PS has not always recovered the losses incurred in 1968: M. Giscard d'Estaing carried Lille in 1974. Some examples of old rural backwoods of French Socialism that have figured on maps of left-wing strength since manhood suffrage began in 1849 further reveal this tendency: Limousin down to 25% in 1973 (31% in 1967), Burgundy down to 26% (30% in 1967), the Aude Departement round Carcassonne down to 36% (42% in 1967). Nonetheless Socialism remains stronger in the southern half of the country than in the North: France South of the Loire chose François Mitterrand for President in 1965 and 1974.

The social composition of the PS electorate is very varied: it includes peasants, industrial workers and, increasingly, white-collar workers. The PS is less strong among industrial workers than the Communist Party. It is younger and less feminine than the

Gaullist electorate, though less markedly masculine than PCF voters. François Mitterrand would have been President of France in 1965 and 1974 if women did not have the right to vote.

Table 7·1
SOCIALIST ELECTORAL PERFORMANCE,
PARLIAMENTARY ELECTIONS 1945–73

|  |  |  | *million votes* | *% of vote* |
|---|---|---|---|---|
| *Fourth Republic* | | | | |
| SFIO | Oct. | 1945 | 4·5 | 23·4 |
|  | June | 1946 | 4·2 | 21·1 |
|  | Nov. | 1946 | 3·4 | 17·8 |
|  | June | 1951 | 2·7 | 14·6 |
|  | Jan. | 1956 | 3·2 | 15·2 |
| *Fifth Republic (first ballot totals)* | | | | |
| SFIO | Nov. | 1958 | 3·2 | 15·7 |
|  | Nov. | 1962 | 2·3 | 12·6 |
| FGDS (SFIO + RAD) | Mar. | 1967★ | 4·2 | 19·0 |
|  | June | 1968★ | 3·7 | 16·5 |
| UGSD (PS + MRG) | Mar. | 1973★ | 4·9 | 20·7 |

★ Socialist candidates on their own totalled 3·5 m. in 1967 (15·5%), 3·0 m. in 1968 (13·4%), and 4·5 m. in 1973 (19·0%). Note, however, that in accordance with their alliance with the Radicals, they were not present in all constituencies. Socialists did not oppose Radical candidates, Radicals did not oppose Socialist candidates.

Socialists are traditionally strong in local administration— Socialist notables being, as one would imagine, a rather conservative element in the Party. According to Harvey Simmons, there were 40,000 Socialist councillors in 1965 (over half the Party membership) and in 1967 fifty-five out of seventy-seven Socialist Deputies were also mayors.[44] After the 1971 municipal elections, Socialist mayors presided in forty of the 193 French cities with a population over 30,000. Most were Socialist-led coalitions either with Centrists (Marseille, Lille, or Aix for instance) or Communists (Arras, Carcassonne). Some were straight Socialist (Clermont-Ferrand, Limoges, Pau). In some cities Socialist councillors were junior members of Centrist coalitions (Nantes or Epinal, for example) or Communist-led *Union de la Gauche* coalitions (Le Havre, Calais). The PS laid down for the 1977 municipal elections that the strategy of *Union de la Gauche* would be applied. Centrist councillors were swiftly dismissed in 1976 from their posts as *adjoints* (similar to Committee Chairmen in Great

Britain) in Lille and Marseille. The Nantes Socialist councillors who adamantly refused their municipal offices were, as we have seen, expelled from the Party. Some, of the rejuvenation of the PS in recent years has been at the expense of entrenched notables.

Table 7·2

SOCIALIST ELECTORAL PERFORMANCE BY REGION

*FGDS (Socialists + Radicals), 1967 and 1968*
*UGSD (Socialists + Left-wing Radicals), 1973*

| | % of vote (suffrages exprimés)— 1st ballot | | |
|---|---|---|---|
| *Regions of traditional strength* | *1967* | *1968* | *1973* |
| N. Nord | 28·0 | 24·6 | 26·6 |
| Franche-Comté | 26·8 | 23·0 | 27·4 |
| Burgundy | 30·0 | 25·6 | 26·0[a] |
| | | | |
| S. Languedoc | 24·8 | 24·4 | 27·0 |
| Midi-Pyrénées | 30·2 | 29·7 | 31·3 |
| Aquitaine | 27·2 | 26·5 | 25·3 |
| Limousin | 31·4 | 26·5 | 25·3[a] |
| Auvergne | 28·6 | 24·8 | 24·4[a] |
| Corsica (mainly Radicals) | 29·3 | 30·5 | 27·5 |
| | | | |
| *Average regions* | | | |
| N. Picardy | 19·4 | 13·5 | 18·6 |
| Upper Normandy | 15·2 | 12·1 | 16·8 |
| Champagne | 18·7 | 17·2 | 20·7 |
| Centre | 21·5 | 17·0 | 18·7 |
| | | | |
| S. Rhone-Alps | 16·6 | 13·8 | 20·8 |
| Poitou-Charente | 18·5 | 19·1 | 21·1 |
| Provence—Cote d'Azur | 22·1 | 17·2 | 22·3 |
| | | | |
| *Regions of traditional weakness* | | | |
| N. Alsace | 8·7 | 9·0 | 12·4[b] |
| Lorraine | 10·2 | 12·1 | 18·5[b] |
| Paris Region | 12·4 | 8·4 | 14·9 |
| Brittany | 9·3 | 7·3 | 17·1[b] |
| Loire Country | 13·6 | 12·1 | 18·5[b] |
| Lower Normandy | 12·1 | 9·6 | 17·7[b] |
| | | | |
| France Metropolitan | 19·0 | 16·5 | 20·8 |

(a) Regions of the rural centre where the substantial losses, incurred in 1968, have not been recovered.

(b) Regions of the Catholic East and West where substantial gains have been achieved. See also *Union de la Gauche* figures, p. 257.

'*Eventrer du notable*' (the disembowelling of notables) is part of the fearsome reputation of the young lions of the PS. Jean-Pierre Chévènement, in order to win his seat in Belfort, had to get rid of M. Dreyfus-Schmidt, a former Socialist Deputy, who in fact stood against his young rival as a Reform Movement candidate.

*(h) Leadership and Perspectives.* The PS is a very diverse party. Revolutionaries, administrative experts, dynamic city bosses, old-fashioned notables, workers, intellectuals, farmers, moderates, Christians, anti-clerical Freemasons, all coexist in an unstable equilibrium. What it loses in cohesion, however, it gains in richness. The fusty image of the 1950s and 1960s has been immeasurably brightened up.

That a lot of this is due to François Mitterrand is undeniable. Despite an undistinguished political past as a minister in the Fourth Republic, he has emerged as the Left's most persuasive and popular figure in the 1970s. His oratory, encompassing irony and passion, is most effective and fills vast halls anywhere in the country. His skill in retaining the support of the diverse currents in his party is remarkable. It is not an easy task to present progressive and libertarian policies and to make the necessary genuflection to the rhetoric of revolution and the class struggle without sinking back into the dispiriting quagmire of opportunism or *Mollettisme* or simply losing all electoral appeal. His own followers, 'the great tribe which follows the prophet',[45] represents perhaps a third of the Party, and he is supported by the left-wing *autogestionnaire* newcomers from the PSU, Michel Rocard and his friends, and the old SFIO led by Mauroy and Defferre. So vertiginous a coalition is obviously subject to disagreements, particularly over thorny matters like the alliance with the PCF. Bizot, however, quotes Gaston Defferre as stating firmly, 'When today I find myself in disagreement with him, I give an honest warning to his other opponents that, in the end, it is with François Mitterrand that I shall side.'

His management of the Communist alliance is skilful. It was noted in the last chapter that since 1965 Mitterrand has been firmly in favour of a *Union de la Gauche* strategy, because he clearly saw that no victory for the Left was possible without it. He has pursued that goal steadily, but has always been aware of the dangers. His aim has been to build the Socialist Party into an organisation that was on equal terms with the PCF, to persuade the PCF to become more respectable by accepting the rules and institutions of pluralist democracy, and to show the public clearly where he disagreed with the Communists—notably over their attachment to the Soviet Union—and to persuade them to change. François Mitterrand is not a figure of the intellectual and moral stature of

Jaurès or Léon Blum, but his leadership has been remarkably reinvigorating to the Party. Indeed it is hard to see anyone who might replace him. Among the younger leading Socialists only Michel Rocard has comparable style and appeal.

## 4. Left-wing Radicals—Mouvement des Radicaux de Gauche (MRG)

The long history, modest achievements, and nebulous ideas of the Radical Party were related in Chapter 5, which dealt with the Centrist elements of the *Majorité*. That is where the official radical party with its headquarters in the Place Valois now belongs. Many a Radical, however, would find this arbitrary treatment of their party a little unfair for two reasons. First, does not Radicalism, defender of the Republic and the achievements of 1789, scourge of the Church and of would-be authoritarian governments, belong to the Left? Secondly, the bastions of Radicalism in the rural south-west and most Radical parliamentarians have split from the Place Valois, are part of the *Union de la Gauche,* and sit in a joint parliamentary group with their Socialist colleagues. Indeed these Radicals, who have not followed the Place de Valois into the *Majorité,* take the view, expressed by their leader Robert Fabre: 'There is only one Radical Party: us.'[46]

The Radical parliamentarians, who found themselves in the minority at the 1971 Radical Party Conference when it backed Jean-Jacques Servan-Schreiber and his aim to ally the Party with progressive-minded Centrists rather than the left, formed in October 1972 a 'Movement of the Radical Socialist Left'. They fought the 1973 elections under a joint electoral banner with the Socialists—UGSD (Union of the Socialist and Democratic Left)—participated in the alliance with the Communists, subscribed to the left's collective manifesto the *Programme Commun,* and opposed their brother-Radicals. On 1 December 1973 in Paris, a Congress established the MRG as a new party with a structure, rules and organisation. Unwavering in its conviction that it represents true Radicalism, the MRG, for its constitution, has adopted almost word for word, phrase for phrase, article for article, the constitution of the official *Valoisien* Radical Party. The lists of those entitled to attend Party Congress is virtually identical (the MRG includes members from its youth section—the Movement of Young Left-wing Radicals). Both parties have a *Comité Directeur* with almost the same composition. It includes all parliamentarians and all local councillors for the MRG, only some for the *Valoisiens.* The National Bureau of the MRG is slightly larger than the Bureau of the *Valoisien* Party. The responsibilities of each body, and the rules on candidatures and membership are the same for both parties.

Both parties, too, see themselves in an identical role within their respective formations. In the presidential *Majorité* the official Radical Party sees itself as the guardian of progressive, republican and libertarian values—the very values in fact which the MRG professes to defend within the opposition. The MRG, anxious to demonstrate that it is not merely an electoral appendage of the Socialist Party, published in February 1975 a voluminous report of some sixty pages. Entitled 'The Left in the Service of Man', it sets forth MRG—indeed Radical—attitudes on the great questions of the day—freedom, the economy, international affairs. Justifying the decision of the MRG ('Party of the heart and of reason'[47]) to 'commit itself, with its eyes open, to the road to Socialism, to Socialism on a human scale',[48] the report stresses the need to reconcile Socialism and Liberty. In case any sceptics were wondering 'why Radicals have accepted a programme of government which includes the nationalisation of some very large firms—a limited number at that—when everyone knows that they are not fanatical supporters of such measures',[49] they may rest assured. Radicals will insist on fair compensation for shareholders and a form of nationalisation that is not just state control. It has been somewhat cynically remarked already that the real bond that ties the MRG to the Left is the loss of their parliamentary seats which would occur if they were unable to rely on the absence of a Socialist candidate at the first ballot and on the withdrawal in their favour of Communist candidates at the second. Besides, people vote Radical in the South where most of them come from, because Radicalism has always been on the left. It is hard to see, for example, how MRG Deputies like Zuccarelli and Alfonsi (Corsica), Maurice Faure (Lot), Mme. Thome-Patenôtre (Yvelines), Antonin Ver (Tarn et Garonne) or Georges Bonnet (Dordogne) could have won without these arrangements. By contrast, the *Valoisien* Radicals were able to reject as a matter of high principle any alliance with Communists because they visibly had no need of them. Gabriel Péronnet (Allier) and Jean-Jacques Servan-Schreiber ran well ahead of all the left combined, as well as the UDR at the first ballot.

The MRG is completely separate from the Radical Party. The *Majorité* has succeeded in enticing away one or two of their parliamentarians—Senators Caillavet and Brousse for instance. Any possibility of reunification, however, is excluded by the leaders of MRG in terms as rigorous as Radicals can formulate.

There is not in present conditions any perspective of some sort of reunification between two political formations one of which is practically an unconditional supporter of the *Majorité,* and the other in the opposition with totally different social and economic choices. It is not therefore in the name of certain friendships, it is not in the name of memories of the Place de Valois, it is not in the name of a radical philosophy to which we, for our part, remain faithful, that we could tinker with the political and strategic choice we have made. M. Peronnet is free to indulge in fantasy . . . the true Radical tradition is still on the Left. That is to say with us.'[50]

The MRG boasts 12 Deputies in the National Assembly compared to 6 *Valoisiens,* 16 Senators (who are still members of the same group as the 19 *Valoisiens),* 96 *Conseillers Généraux (Département* Councillors) of which 9 are Chairmen of the council, and a larger but unspecified number of Municipal Councillors.[51] It occupies a small suite of gleaming new offices at the Rue de Grenelle, in the smart Boulevard St-Germain quarter. It publishes a monthly journal *Mouvement.* It claims 25,000 members (an improbable figure). Its strength is in the deep South—Midi-Pyrenees and Corsica. The most prominent leaders of the movement today are Robert Fabre, a Deputy from the South (Aveyron), and Michel Crepeau a dynamic figure who is not from the South. He is in fact Mayor of and Deputy for La Rochelle in the West. The MRG vigorously attempts to differentiate itself from its ally the PS. It believes there is the need for the reassuring presence of a third political force on the left to balance the Communists. It claims that it is prepared to leave the *Union de la Gauche* if negotiations for the reform of the *Programme Commun* are refused.[52] In fact it is hard to see how they could survive if they did. Jean Charlot describes their electoral performance in the 1973 as the 'end of Radicalism' (1·8% of the national vote, *Valoisiens* 1·9%). Within the FGDS (Federation of the Democratic and Socialist Left) in 1967 and 1968, the Socialists and the Radicals decided not to compete against one another at the first ballot. The Socialists stood in three-quarters of all constituencies, the Radicals in one quarter. Charlot notes that 'in 1973, within the UGSD (Union of the Socialist and Democratic Left)—the passage of the adjective "Socialist" before the ephithet "democratic" is significant—the new PS carves out nine-tenths for itself with the Radicals . . . reduced to forty-three candidates . . . through the lack of any real negotiating strength'.[53]

A dwindling band of notables, they either huddle for shelter under the Socialist tree, or dash helplessly for cover to the Giscardian Centre where warm ministerial portfolios are waiting for some. But if they do that, what would happen to them at the elections? This the dread that 'Makes us rather bear the ills we know, Than fly to others that we know not of'.

## NOTES

1  *Socialisme et Communisme Français*, Paris, Colin, 1967.
2  *Ibid.*, p. 5.
3. A. Siegfried, *Tableau des partis en France*, Paris; Grasset, 1930, pp. 162-5.
4. *Marxism in Modern France*, Columbia University Press, 1966, p. 35.
5. They almost invariably did when asked—e.g. Millerand, Viviani and Aristide Briand.
6. See next chapter.
7. See Jacques Fauvet, *Histoire du Parti Communiste Français*, Paris; Fayard, 1964, Vol. 1, p. 37.
8. Williams, *Crisis and Compromise*, p. 89.
9. An ex-deputy quoted by Williams, *Ibid.*, p. 99.
10. Harvey Simmons, *French Socialists in Search of a Role 1956-1967* (Cornell University Press, 1970), p. 92.
11. See Jean Poperen, *L'Unité de la Gauche 1965-1973*, Paris: Fayard, 1975, p. 267.
12. 'The French Socialist Party in 1973: performance and prospects', *Government and Opposition*, *Spring 1974*, pp. 127-8. See also Christiane Hurtig, *De la SFIO au nouveau parti Socialiste*, Paris: Colin, 1970, pp. 114-15.
13. 43,926 mandates to 41,757, with 3,925 abstentions, Poperen, ibid., p. 333.
14. It is said that Jacques Chaban-Delmas had had his eye on them for the UDR if he won the presidential election.
15. Yves Guéna, in his first letter to Gaullist activists after his election as Secretary-General of the UDR, wrote: 'It is quite clear that the Communist party is static, despite its doctrinal contortions. With some 20% of the vote in the country, it has no chance of acceding to power without the help of the Socialist Party which appears as our principal adversary. In order to cut down that Party, we must not pander to it but attack it, not adopt its doctrine or vocabulary but proclaim our own ideas' ('La Lettre des Compagnons', *UDR Monthly*, April 1976).
16. *Guide du Nouvel Adhérent (Bureau National d'Adhésions*, PS, Sept. 1975), pp. 33-4. The Guide quickly adds, 'This is the place to recall that Marxism, method of analysis and guide for action, is not a rigid doctrine, and that its operational character is compatible with philosophical or religious options' (p. 34).
17. Wright and Machin in *Government and Opposition*, *Spring 1974*, p. 133 (quoting *Le Nouvel Observateur* 25 June 1973).
18. Proportional to the results of voting on rival resolutions at the January 1975 National Congress at Pau.
19. Mitterrand, Mauroy, Mermaz, Loo, Poperen, Defferre, Joxe, Fillioud, Chévènement.
20. Whom we have encountered as the author of *Les Républicains Indépendents*.
21. *Centre d'Etudes de Recherches et d'Education Socialistes* (formed 1967).
22. See André Routier-Preuvost; *Lettre inquiète à François Mitterrand* Nantes: Europlan, 1976.
23. *Le Poing et la Rose*, April 1976.
24. See *Le Poing et la Rose*, January 1976.
25. Bizot (*Au Parti des Socialistes.*, p. 285) quotes a February 1974 poll in *Le Point* which suggested that a third of Socialists belonged to the Communist-dominated CGT and only just over a quarter to the CFDT. In Paris, however, it is suggested that half of all party members are in the CFDT.

26. Circulation 4,500-5,000 in 1973, according to Wright and Machin, in *Government and Opposition* 1974, p. 136n.
27. It claims 2,000 subscribers *(Le Poing et la Rose*—Nov. 1975).
28. Figures from *Guide du Nouvel Adhérent* (PS 1976).
29. Borella (*Les Partis Politiques dans la France d'Aujourd'hui*, p. 159) claims that in 1970 there were 15,000 members accredited to National Headquarters!
30. Just to give a couple of examples—
    Letter from a new militant to his mother after the Pau Congress:
    'I have seen my comrades and I know now that they really are my comrades . . . Yes, *maman*, it really is a Great Party, you ought to join . . .'(pp. 258).
    'She is a small girl—very *soignée*. Never the same dress twice at the big party meetings . . . a trace of rouge on her cheekbones to highlight an amber tint. Well-turned waist and ankles, grecian profile, fresh body. She is 19, has will and intelligence. She works in order to be independent, studies law, party activist for a year now. Her father, a top civil servant, is a little shocked . . .'(p. 21).
    The interviews with revolutionary workers, larded with class struggle slang, are untranslatable. Nothing but '*tu*' and '*quoi*' and '*mecs*'.
31. See Bizot, *Au Parti des Socialistes*, p. 114.
32. A tradition not followed by Mr. Jimmy Carter in 1976.
33. Bizot, *op. cit.*, pp. 180-1.
34. The Party Constitution has a special provision relating to people who own newspapers. Art. 86 states that they can 'be summoned before the Bureau of the Party to give explanation, if the need arises, for the behaviour of their paper.'
35. Bizot, *An Parti des Socialistes*,p. 184.
36. See below, p. 252 and V. McHale, 'Religion and electoral politics in France', *Canadian Journal of Political Science*, 1969, pp. 295 *et seq.*
37. A. Routier-Preuvost, *Lettre Inquiète à François Mitterrand*, p. 41. *JAC:* Young Christian Farmers. *JEC:* Young Christian Students. *JOC:* Young Christian Workers.
38. Bizot, *Au Parti des Socialistes*, p. 342, quoting opinion polls from *Le Point*, 1973.
39. 'Nous avons réussi la synthese du progressisme laïc et du christianisme révolutionnaire'— *Ibid.*, p. 31 and p. 338.
40. A. Routier-Preuvost, op. cit., p. 39.
41. *Au Parti des Socialistes*, p. 341.
42. *Ibid.*, p. 338.
43. Charles Josselin (a Catholic) beat the former Centrist Prime Minister René Pléven.
44. *French Socialists in Search of a Role*, pp. 281 and 284.
45. Bizot, *Au Parti des Socialistes*, p. 15.
46. *L'Année Politique*, 1973, p. 68.
47. '*La Gauche au service de l'homme*' (Report adopted by the Bordeaux Congress of the MRG, Feb. 1975, p. 58.
48. *Ibid.*, p. 16.
49. *Ibid.*, p. 44.
50. Robert Fabre interviewed in *Le Quotidien de Paris*, 12 Dec. 1975.
51. *Mouvement* April 1976.

52. Interview with François Loncle (National Bureau member responsible for Union with the Left). May 1976.
53. *Quand la gauche peut gagner,* Paris: Alain Moreau, 1973, p. 90.

# 8

## COMMUNISM

It is almost impossible to write about Communism or to evaluate what others have written. In a Jesuitical manner, Communists write only what serves the cause. Anti-Communists frequently discuss Communist aims in terms that can only be described as hysterical. To make matters worse, non-Communists are in a real sense anti-Communist even if they are not hysterically or systematically so. It is all very well for Waldeck Rochet, the honorary President and former General Secretary of the PCF, to write : 'Communists are not the members of a mysterious sect or a secret society.'[1] To all Western non-Communists that is exactly what they seem to be. To the inheritors of an intellectual tradition which stresses tolerance and the freedom to criticise and to oppose, the total unanimity of a Communist congress, the blind certainty, the five hour speeches couched in alien jargon, the constant self-congratulation that the Party is always right, are quite literally incomprehensible. Or at least they are incomprehensible in a country where there is no systematic persecution, denial of rights, or exceptional deprivation inflicted on the working class which leaves disciplined and organised revolution as the only hope for change. It is especially incomprehensible when, faithful to the aspirations of its supporters, the Party in question no longer has revolution as an objective. The *Parti Communiste Français,* however is a most important element of French political life. The attempt at comprehension must therefore be made, though no claim to objectivity can honestly be sustained.

The relationship between the PCF and the Soviet Union, a relationship which can literally be described as umbilical since the PCF was born a child of Lenin's Comintern, is at the centre of this chapter. It is the focal point of our brief account of the history of the PCF, because that history has consisted of a series of phases very different in character one from the other, which have coincided with the different phases of Soviet policy and attitudes. It is the focal point of our analysis of the ideas and doctrine of the PCF because emancipation from the values represented by the Soviet regime are a critical indication to people in France and elsewhere of the role the PCF would be willing to play in the government of a pluralist democracy. Its electoral fortunes, the nature of debate inside it, the relationship with other parties in France, and a whole host of other aspects of Communist activity are connected to the state of its fidelity to the Soviet mother-church.

## 1. History of the PCF

*(a). Origins and Bolshevisation 1920-34.* The Party was formed, as the last chapter related, when the Socialist Party (SFIO) decided at the Congress of Tours in December 1920 to join Lenin's Communist International by subscribing to the 21 Conditions.[2] For Annie Kriegel, therefore, 'French Communism is the specific and original product of a grafting process: the grafting of Russian Bolshevism on the body of French Socialism'.[3] Those of the Socialist Party who voted to join the Communist International included the big working-class Socialist federations in Paris and its suburbs, and these still remain the stronghold of French Communism today. A miner called Maurice Thorez, along with his local Pas de Calais Socialist Federation, also voted to join.[4] The new Party inherited too the support of much of rural Socialism— that is to say, a large element of peasant anti-establishment, anti-clerical hostility. 'In the South', wrote Siegfried many years ago, 'the Communist is often no more than the reddest of Republicans.'[5] 'Bolshevisation', therefore, had to be imposed. Lenin told two PCF leaders in Moscow in 1923: 'There is at present no Communist Party in France. Do you want to build one?'[6] The next few years were 'a period of organisational and ideological assimilation of the Leninist model, as progressively modified by Stalin after Lenin's death'.[7] The appropriate leadership for this type of organisation was eventually achieved in the person of Thorez, elected General Secretary in 1930 and, from 1931 on, schooled and supported by a team of advisers sent by the Comintern Executive Committee.[8]

French Communism in this period was of extreme intransigence and dogmatism. It purged, it expelled, it denounced. Considered to be a public enemy by Government,[9] it was also persecuted. Thorez and most of the other leading Communists were rounded up and imprisoned.[10] Membership declined steadily from 109,000 in 1921 to 28,000 in 1933,[11] as the rather sectarian tactic of 'class against class' was followed. Everyone was an enemy—in particular, the Socialists were 'Social Fascists'. 'The bourgeois state', proclaimed the Party in 1934, ' . . . will be smashed in all its parts because each part serves only the task of crushing the workers.'[12]

*(b) The Popular Front 1934-39.* The riots of the extreme Right in Paris on 6 February 1934, the rise of Fascism all over Europe, and

the change of attitude this provoked in the Communist International at its 7th Congress in 1935, all made possible a complete change of PCF attitudes and its reintegration into French political life. This was the period of the 'outstretched hand'. Socialists, Catholics, Radicals, all men of goodwill, were invited to join in a united front against Fascism. The Popular Front electoral alliance of Socialists, Radicals and Communists won a famous victory at the polls in 1936. The Communist vote at $1\frac{1}{2}$ million (15%) was double that of 1932. Parliamentary representation increased from 12 to 72 seats. Membership recovered. As in other countries, many leading intellectuals rallied to Communism or at least to joint action with the Communists during this period, because Communism seemed the one effective and disciplined anti-Fascist force in Europe. While Hitler and Mussolini supplied arms to Franco in the Spanish Civil War and the democracies (including France under the Popular Front) did nothing, Stalin alone supplied the Republican Government. In consequence, the Nazi-Soviet non-aggression pact in 1939 unleashed a wave of shock and dismay. The PCF, loyal to this new Moscow line, called on people not to fight in an 'imperialist war'. Paul Nizan, the French novelist, accepting call-up into the army to defend France against Hitler, wrote to Jacques Duclos on the Central Committee; 'I address to you my resignation from the Party. My position as a mobilised soldier dispenses me from adding any more.'[13]

*(c) Disgrace 1939-1941.* Stalin had dealt the French Communist Party an almost lethal blow by imposing upon it a policy which it has never subsequently been able to explain away.[14] PCF denuniciation of the war led to a new ban on the Party, and clandestine Communist publications advocated neutrality and even conciliation with the Germans after the Occupation in 1940. There was even a request to the German authorities requesting permission to recommence publication of *L'Humanité*: its task 'to denounce the agents of British imperialism'.[15] The communists themselves contest his version of history—and the charge that they only commited themselves to the Resistance when Hitler's invasion of Russia in June 1941 put an end to the Nazi-Soviet pact.[16]

*(d) Resistance and Government 1941-7.* When the Communists did join the Resistance they played a heroic and characteristically well-organised part. Many activists were deported, imprisoned, executed or killed in action. They played an important part in the insurrection that preceded the liberation of Paris in 1944.[17] The Party's role in the Resistance and the part played by the Soviet Union in the Allied war effort contributed greatly to the prestige

of the PCF. Thorez remained throughout the war in Moscow—against his own will[18]—and when he returned to France at the Liberation entered de Gaulle's provisional government. Communist resistance fighters disarmed and Communist ministers continued as loyal Government ministers, urging workers to increase output and not to strike for higher wages. This was the peak period of Communist membership (800,000 in 1946)[19] and electoral strength (5.5 million voters—28·6% of the national total—in November 1946).

There was no question at this period of revolution. However, international tension between the Western allies and the Soviet Union, as well as industrial unrest at home, brought difficulties between the PCF and its government partners. The Socialist Prime Minister Ramadier dismissed the Communist ministers on 4 May 1947. The PCF has never participated in Government since.

*(e) The Cold War 1947-62.* The Cold War between the Soviet Union and the West was matched by the cold war between the PCF and the rest of the French political system. The PCF disappeared into truculence, intransigence, parliamentary obstructionism and total isolation. It was in this period (30 September 1948) that the *Bureau Politique* made its famous declaration, 'The people of France will not, will never, make war on the Soviet Union.' The Party supported the Soviet repression of the Hungarian uprising in November 1956. As the PCF's support for the Nazi-Soviet pact had done, this posture lost the Party many members and supporters.[20] Herbert Lüthy in the 1950s was able to write that 'since 1948 the Communist Party has counted only as a dead weight . . . and has sterilised the votes, wishes and demands of 5 million Frenchmen'.[21] The PCF opposed the Fourth Republic, it opposed the return of power of General de Gaulle, it opposed the Fifth Republic, it opposed the Consitutional Amendment of October 1962 introducing direct election of the Presidency by universal suffrage. At this point it was joined in its opposition to Gaullism by the Socialists, and the election of November 1962 represents another turning-point in the history of the PCF. There was no formal electoral alliance but, in the interests of defeating Gaullism, reciprocal withdrawal of candidates at the second ballot occurred.[22]

*(f) The road to Union de la Gauche 1962*-Thorez died in 1964. A reader, a teacher of revolution, a devoted Leninist, an organiser, a disciplinarian—the Party was his whole life. This instrument, which he had controlled so effectively, he had dedicated from the very start to the defence of the Soviet Union. The PCF, however, was one of the last Communist parties to respond to the wind of

change in the world Communist movement that followed the death of Stalin in 1953. The era of 'de-Stalinisation' was inaugurated at the XX Congress of the Soviet Communist Party by Nikita Kruschev in 1956, and 'peaceful coexistence' with the West began to thaw the Cold War. Furthermore, world Communism was ceasing to be monolithic. China and Cuba developed versions of Communism different from the Soviet Union. Indeed relations between China and the USSR eventually reached a point little short of war. Various other Communist parties claimed the right to choose their own road to Socialism— Italy, Romania and, with tragic consequences, Czechoslovakia in 1968. The notion that the Soviet model was the only possible model for Communist parties was increasingly rejected. These gradual changes produced a gradual response in the PCF. The PCF also had to take into account the problem of the affluent worker. Living standards in France rose very fast in the 1960s as they did elsewhere and revolutions, as Bismarck used to say, are made by people who are discontented in the stomach not in the head.

Thorez's successor, Waldeck Rochet, despite his solid training at the Lenin school in Moscow, was incontestably a 'moderate'. He wanted to open up and rejuvenate the Party, to shed its secret-society image, to bring it out of the political ghetto. Between the lines of lengthy speeches attempting to redefine the nature of revolutionary goals, phrased in stupefying bureaucratic jargon and crammed with quotations from the prophets Marx and Lenin, a change of mood can be sensed. The events that followed this change of mood, the Communist support for Mitterrand's presidential canditure in 1965, the electoral pacts in parliamentary elections from 1967 on, the signature of the *Programme Commun* joint manifesto with the Socialists and left-wing Radicals in 1972, the support for Mitterrand's second presidential campaign in 1974, all belong to the story of the evolution in the Fifth Republic of the *Union de la Gauche,* told in Chapter 6. That chapter also indicates the setbacks and vicissitudes that have beset that enterprise, particularly in the period 1968-9. The events of May 1968, which appeared to be revolutionary but which were neither started nor controlled by the PCF, brought out the Stanlinist reflexes of the Party as it reacted to criticism of its role as 'vanguard of the proletariat'. Support for 'normalisation' (the suppression of liberal tendencies) in Czechoslovakia after the Soviet invasion of August 1968 revived old fears about where Communist hearts really lay. Finally the total disarray of the presidential campaign of 1969 revealed the collapse, for a time at any rate, of the spirit of cooperation that had existed between the PCF and the non-Communist Left from 1965 to 1968.

Since 1968 Waldeck Rochet—physically and spiritually

broken, it is said, by the Soviet-led invasion of Czechoslovakia and its effect on the PCF policy of reintegration into normal French political life—has been too ill to direct the Party. Georges Marchais deputised as leader and was elected General Secretary in 1972. His aggressive and sarcastic tone give him a far more Stalinist aspect than Rochet with his mild air and unbelievable Burgundian accent. Nevertheless Marchais has presided over a period in which the PCF has gone still further than under Waldeck–Rochet towards dispelling its totalitarian image. As we shall see in the next section, it has critised presecution in the Soviet Union, it has made repeated declarations on respect for civil liberties, it has officially abandoned the Leninist notion of the dictatorship of the proletariat, and it has committed itself to working within the *Union de la Gauche*. As always in the periods when loyalty to the Soviet Union is not compelling it to defend the indefensible, its membership and electoral support have recovered, although at 21·3% in 1973 it still has a lower share of the vote than the 22·5% it gained in 1967. In 1976 it claimed 500,000 members with a year-end target of 600,000. The relationship between PCF attitudes. Soviet attitudes and support for the PCF are schematically summarised in Table 8.1.

## 2. Doctrine

'Changeless and changing': the phrase has been applied to French society and to the French Communist Party. The brief survey of the PCF's history concentrated on change, the alternation from phases of relative integration to phrases of total isolation. Changes in the Communist world, in international relations, in French political life and society were reflected by changes in the PCF. However, throughout this change certain unchanging themes have characterised the doctrine and marked the style of the Party. The constant themes of Communist doctrine are: the party as vanguard of the working class, the crisis of capitalism and loyalty to the Soviet Union, the last-named blended in a curious way with nationalism. Change has come from a further theme, which has profoundly modified and overlaid but not obliterated the others: the Communist attitude to participation in liberal democracy. Like the tide, this theme has rolled in from time to time in Communist history and ebbed away leaving the beach more or less as it was before.

*(a) Vanguard of the proletariat.* The revolutionary role of the working class and of the Party, vanguard of the proletariat, are of course fundamental tenets of the Marxist-Leninist faith. History is seen as a continuous series of phases in which one class exploits another and thereby precipitates its overthrow by the exploited

Table 8.1
PCF SUPPORT AND THE SOVIET UNION

| Election Dates | PCF vote—parliamentary elections | | PCF Membership* ('000) | Soviet Union (H = 'Hard', C = 'Conciliatory') | PCF |
|---|---|---|---|---|---|
| | m | % of vote | | | |
| May 1924 | 0·8 | 9·5 | 60 | | |
| April 1928 | 1·1 | 11·3 | 50 | Rise of Stalin, 'Socialism in one country' (H) | 'Bolshevisation' (H) |
| May 1932 | 0·8 | 8·4 | 30 | | |
| April 1936 | 1·5 | 15·3 | 329 (1937) | 7th Congress. (C) United Front against Fascism. | Popular Front (C) |
| 1939–41 | — | — | 300 (1939) | Nazi-Soviet pact (H) | Denunciation of Imperialist War (H) |
| Oct. 1945 | 5·0 | 26·0 | 545 | Wartime ally (C) | Resistance and Government (C) |
| June 1946 | 5·1 | 25·9 | 804 | | |
| Nov. 1946 | 5·4 | 28·2 | | | |
| June 1951 | 4·9 | 25·6 | 250 | Cold War, Hungary (H) | Isolation, Obstructionism (H) |
| Jan. 1956 | 5·5 | 25·7 | | | |
| Nov. 1958 | 3·9 | 19·0 | | | |
| Nov. 1962 | 4·0 | 21·8 | 275 | Peaceful coexistence (C) | Towards Union de la Gauche (C) (1968–9) (H) |
| Mar. 1967 | 5·0 | 22·5 | | | |
| June 1968 | 4·4 | 20·0 | 450 | (Czechoslovakia—1968) (H) | |
| Mar. 1973 | 5·1 | 21·4 | | Détente (C) | (C) |

*Approximate figures based on estimates by Kriegel, *The French Communists*, pp. 32, 33 and 370 and Tiersky p. 18?

class, which becomes dominant in its turn. The bourgeoisie, owners of capital, having thrown over the aristocratic social order which bound it, becomes the class that exploits a new class of manual industrial workers—the proletariat. Just as Laius King of Thebes fathered the son Oedipus by whom he was destined to be killed, so Capitalism fatally and inevitably produces the very instrument of its own destruction. An ever more severely exploited, ever more numerous, ever more class-conscious proletariat would with absolute inevitability one day rise up and cast off the shackles of its oppressors. The emancipation of the proletariat could only be the work of the proletariat itself, but its class-consciousness and revolutionary destiny required the leadership of a disciplined party consisting of professional revolutionaries. Tiersky rightly insists on the PCF's Leninist view of itself and its role.[23] Even at the 22nd Congress of the PCF in February 1976, when Leninist notions like 'dictatorship of the proletariat' were removed by resolution from the Party's statutes, it was repeatedly made clear that such changes in no way involved 'any attenuation of the directing influence of the working class and its Communist Party'.[24] 'Today the working class is in the vanguard of the struggle for the transformation of society.'[25] The Leninist notion of the Party as vanguard explains in part the style of Communist discussion. Most non-Communists regard diversity as a hallmark of genuine debate and massive unanimity as something that results only from intimidation. However, the constant invocation of virtual unanimity in every Federation, on every issue, for every vote, is regarded as demonstrating 'profound unity'.[26] Why not have amendments and critical debates at Congress? 'We should be taking precious little interest in leading to success the struggle of the working class if we acted like that. If others want to do that, that is their business . . . The workers, who need a party which gives force and effectiveness to their struggle, are grateful to the Communists for having a quite different conception of their responsibilities.'[27]

*(b) The Crisis of Capitalism.* Frédéric Bon reminds us that this concept 'covers the entire history of Communism. The idea of a general crisis of capitalism was present in the analyses made by the Comintern right from the first meetings of its directorate. International Communism's debates on strategy usually take as their central focus an up-to-date assessment of the phase or stage reached by the general crisis of capitalism.'[28] Capitalism, by its very nature, exploits more and more people in the accumulation of profit, renders them more and more impoverished, leads to war as capitalists from different countries battle for markets and resources, and, as huge monopolies eliminate competition, an

authoritarian regime will emerge aggressive for empire and conquest, and known as state monopoly capitalism.

The interesting analysis by F. Bon, already cited, shows how the crisis of capitalism theory was progressively refined and modified by the impact of economic expansion and rising living standards (usually denied or regarded as sectoral or temporary), the development of the EEC, and the establishment of the Fifth Republic under which France has made spectacular political and economic gains. The general crisis theory is still alive and in good health in French Communism. It appeared at the 21st Congress in 1974, when delegates were reminded of 'the fact that state monopoly capitalism . . . has thrown society into a global crisis signifying that . . . a profound change of social structures is objectively necessary'.[29] In 1976, 'everything confirms that Lenin's general description can be applied as we showed in 1971, to the period of crisis into which French society has entered.'[30] 'The present crisis, as opposed to what the big capitalists and their political representatives claim, is not a simple economic crisis. It is a deep global, and durable crisis which affects every aspect— economic and monetary, social, cultural, political, and moral—of national life . . . The same crisis affects the whole capitalist world.'[31] 'Sixteen million people in France live in a state of wretched poverty.'[32] It all goes to prove that the PCF is correct in holding true to the 'living theory of scientific socialism founded by Marx, Engels and Lenin',[33] which predicts the end of the capitalism followed by the edification of socialism as day follows night.

*(c) The Soviet Union and the Nation.* The strange mixture of nationalism and loyalty to the Soviet Union is the third permanent theme of PCF doctrine. Our historical survey showed how closely the PCF has followed and supported Soviet attitudes and initiatives. Loyalty to the Soviet Union has coexisted with a doctrine of national independence ever since the famous remark of Thorez in 1934 that 'we have recovered the Marseillaise and the Tricolore flag of our ancestors, the soldiers of the Year II'.[34] Apart from the period of the Nazi-Soviet pact from 1939 to 1941, this has been maintained in the form of a rather chauvinistic patriotism. National independence in the face of European integration, national independence from NATO and the Western alliance, national independence from economic domination by American multi-national companies—these are perpetual demands. In the name of national independence the PCF. like the Gaullists, vigorously supports the construction of Concorde, attacks *Franglais* and is suspicious of direct elections to the European Parliament. It was in the name of Czech national independence

that the PCF criticised the Soviet invasion of Czechoslovakia in 1968. When confined to France, however, the doctrine of national independence has been wholly compatible with Soviet foreign policy since the war. 'Socialism in the colours of France' is the PCF's slogan today. It neatly combines a straightforward national appeal with a hint of something much more complex—the validity of non-Soviet model of Socialism.

It is around this—the validy of a non-Soviet model—that the whole drama of the PCF's loyalty to the Soviet Union and its desire to participate in democratic government revolves. Absolute unconditional loyalty has given way in the last decade to a mysterious and elaborate ritual involving periodic criticism of the Soviet Union intermixed with unbelievably uncritical expressions of admiration and warnings against anti-Sovietism. For instance, the invasion of Czechoslovakia in 1968 was greeted with 'surprise and reprobation'.[35] 'It was a brutal interference in the internal affairs of the Czechoslovak Communist Party . . . We do not have to approve of everything [done by the Soviet Union]. That would be a form of subordination which would not correspond to true friendship.'[36] However the Party backed 'normalisation' (suppression of liberalising tendencies) that followed, and in 1970 expelled one of its leading intellectuals, Roger Garaudy, for, among other crimes, writing that the PCF should 'say clearly that the Socialism we want to establish in France is not that imposed by Brezhnev in Czechoslovakia'.[37]

There are a few other instances of criticism of the Soviet Union. The trial of the writers Sinyavsky and Daniel in 1966 was attacked by the Communist poet Aragon in L'Humanité, which resulted in that day's edition being banned in Moscow. The Party criticised the 'Leningrad trials' in 1970 of some Jews who planned to seize an aircraft and leave the country. In 1973 the non-appearance in the USSR of Solzhenitsyn's books was reproved. In October 1975 the PCF came out strongly against the detention and treatment of the Soviet mathematician Leonid Plyushch. Most notably of all, the PCF reacted vigorously to a film on French television which reported on conditions in a Soviet labour camp.

The film gave an intolerable picture of conditions of detention in this camp. In addition the commentator declared that some of the detainees were political prisoners. This is all the more serious because in the USSR there are in fact trials of citizens for their political opinions. In these circumstances the Bureau Politique of the PCF declares that, if reality corresponds to the broadcast pictures and if no public rebuttal is forthcoming from the Soviet authorities, it will express its profound surprise and its most formal disapproval. Such unjustifiable facts can only prejudice Socialism and the renown which the Soviet Union has justly acquired in the eyes of the workers and peoples of the world, thanks to the immense successes achieved by its own people in so many different fields.[38]

*Pravda* and the Soviet Embassy in Paris took the PCF to task, but declaration after declaration reaffirmed that 'while we are conscious of the immense contribution of the Socialist countries to the progress of history and of the need for solidarity of workers in the world, that does not lead us to give our support blindly to everything which happens in the Socialist countries.'[39]

As the statements show, these clear and important condemnations, Italian-style, of repression in the USSR are always shaded with protestations of admiration for the achievements of the Soviet regime in general, and of its leading role in the struggle for Socialism. In addition, the statements never fail to denounce 'anti-Sovietism'. The 22nd Congress both registered the tremors of disagreement with the Soviet Union, and orchestrated the fundamental harmony of these relations. Speaking of the Socialist countries, George Marchais quoted the 'gigantic achievement' they had already accomplished,

what a demonstration of the superiority of Socialism they have already given! It is Socialism which, in the Soviet Union, has achieved that immense historic advance represented by the disappearance of the exploitation of man, the building of a powerful economy that develops without crisis, without unemployment, without galloping price increases, a considerable advance in living standards, the access of workers to responsibilities, democracy at work, equality of opportunity, . . .'

(quite unlike capitalism in crisis in fact). The PCF had thus been led to criticise 'certain facts which have come up in the Soviet Union'. This disagreement did not, however, 'enfeeble our will to cooperate with [the Soviet Union] in the common struggle against imperialism and for our great common objectives'.[40] The fraternal delegate from the Soviet Communist Party was nonetheless a little acid when he spoke of the great fuss made by Western countries about the 'defence of the rights of man' in the Soviet Union where they were in fact 'entirely assured'.[41]

*(d) Participation in Liberal Democracy.* All these persistent themes—vanguard of the proletariat; crisis of capitalism; loyalty to the Soviet Union; nation—have undergone modification and revision, as we have seen, but have remained fundamentally intact. Such changes as there have been result from the one big change in Communist doctrine—the Party's attitude towards participation in liberal democracy. Indeed, spurred by this issue, the Party has been undergoing a period of intensive doctrinal revision, and even in Thierry Pfister's phrase a 'crisis of identity'.[42] The development of the *Union de la Gauche* into an effective alternative to Gaullism and the present *Majorité*, it was noted in Chapter 6, is dependent to a significant extent on the PCF's ability to convince the public of its emancipation from those anti-libertarian attitudes represented

most notably by its Leninist and Soviet attachments. Yet to renounce the Leninist conception of the Party's role, to allow free rein to anti-Sovietism, to ape the manners and style of social democracy, would be to abandon all the distinctiveness and certitude involved in being a Communist. Furthermore, the first steps along this road of abandoning Leninist myths in the interests of cooperation with the non-Communist Left led to electoral gains not for the Communist Party but for the Socialists at Communist expense. This was demonstrated at by-elections in 1974 and 1975 and local elections in 1976. The Left as a whole made big gains but the PCF made none.

Nevertheless the will to participate in democratically elected government has led the PCF down the path of doctrinal change which relates closely to the permanent themes of Communist doctrine already examined. The first set of changes involves the entire Leninist myth of the revolutionary seizure of power and the transition to Socialism by means of the dictatorship of the proletariat. The first time the question of a 'French road to Socialism' was seriously put forward was in Thorez' interview with *The Times* on 17 November 1946: 'The progress of democracy across the world . . . enables one to consider other roads to socialism than that followed by the Russian Communists.' On the occasions since the war when one might have supposed the Communists to be in a position to bring about revolution—after the liberation in 1944 to 1946 or in the general strike of May–June 1968—they have significantly refrained from doing so. In December 1968 the 'Champigny Manifesto' appeared. It affirmed the PCF's desire to participate in government, explained what it would do in government, stressed the need for the *Union de la Gauche* and for Socialism to come—not all at once in a violent overthrow of capitalism but step by step. It 'constituted the first attempt by the Party to define a method for taking power and for the transition to Socialism which was free from Leninist mythology and corresponded to the realities of French Society'.[43]

The official abandonment of the notion 'dictatorship of the proletariat' at the 22nd Congress in February 1976 has already been referred to. It was preceded by a remarkably open debate in the columns of the Communist press which published numerous letters from readers. The phrase 'dictatorship of the proletariat' describes the transitional regime that is supposed to follow the overthrow of capitalism by the working class led by its revolutionary Party. It is a period in which the lingering traces of the values and structures of capitalist exploitation would be eliminated. It therefore follows that if one no longer envisages the insurrectional overthrow of capitalism, then the notion 'dictatorship of the proletariat' is 'out of date . . . [and] no longer has its place'.[44] It is open to two further objections. The word 'dictatorship' has a pejorative sense which contradicts the PCF's undertaking in the *Programme Commun,* signed with the Socialists, to respect democratic liberties. Secondly, the word 'proletariat' 'evokes the central core, the heart of the working class. While its role is essential it does not represent the whole of the working class'[45] nor the other exploited groups who share the desire to participate in the transformation of society envisaged by the *Union de la Gauche.* The world has changed and, PCF leaders affirm, what was necessary in Russia in 1917 is not so in France in the 1970s.

The second set of doctrinal changes brought about by the PCF's desire to participate in the government of a liberal democracy involves its attitude to the Soviet Union. Loyalty to the Soviet Union, its leaders. its policies, its achievements, its regime, remain, as we have seen, a constant theme of French Communist thought. The occasional criticisms of Soviet practices, such as the persecution of intellectuals or the invasion of Czechoslovakia, occur against a background of constantly repeated solidarity and admiration. The PCF has never gone as far in criticising the Soviet regime as the Italian Communist Party, whose leader Togliatti even in the 1950s was denouncing the bureaucratic degeneration, the violation of legality, the stagnation of Soviet life under Stalin.[46] However the PCF's statement condemning labour camps in the Soviet Union is regarded, for instance by the Socialist party in a special report on the Communists' 22nd Congress, as 'the most important step since the 1968 condemnation of the entry of Warsaw Pact troops into Czechoslovakia'.[47] At the 22nd Congress the PCF certainly went further than ever before in reaffirming that 'there does not exist and cannot exist a 'model' of Socialism that it would be possible to transpose from one country to another or to copy'; that 'no party or group of parties can lay down the law for others'; and that 'one must be on one's guard against the temptation to substitute for the democratic effort to convince . . . the convenience of authority and repression.'[48]

The final aspect of doctrinal change flows on from these modest declarations of independence from the Soviet version of Socialism, and can be summed up in the word 'liberties'. The PCF's will to participate in the government of a liberal democracy has been orchestrated with repeated affirmations of the Party's attachment to the civil and political liberties practiced in Western democracies. In May 1975, the PCF presented its proposals for a 'Declaration of Liberties'. 'The struggle for freedom', it affirmed, 'is, logically and naturally an integral part of all the activity of the PCF . . . For us Communists our aim is to liberate the worker from the exploitation of which he is a victim.'[49] The document presented is like a constitution or Bill of Rights with eighty-nine articles containing every conceivable protection for the citizen, the guarantee of the rule of law, and various political and social rights like worker participation in management. 'All these freedoms . . . the Communists undertake to respect and to see that they are respected.'[50] That is to say the document would not be treated like that other landmark of libertarian prose, the 1936 Soviet Constitution.

There have been other signs of a tentative liberalisation. It is easier to approach and to join the PCF. Public meetings are less stage-managed and have trailing microphones for the audience to put questions. Some features in the Communist press take the form of debate not affirmation. The divergent views of readers about 'dictatorship of the proletariat' have been referred to. On 19 May 1976, *L'Humanité dimanche,* a popular weekly with a sale of 500,000, contained a debate between a member of the PCF *Bureau politique* and the editor of the non-Communist economic journal *l'Expansion.* The latter was able to put forward cogent arguments as to why Communist analyses of the current economic crisis and what to do about it were completely wrong-headed! There are other examples in the same vein.

One should perhaps add that participation in the functioning of democracy is nothing new for the PCF. It has always contested parliamentary elections – with candidates bearing the Party label, too, and not camouflaged by *ad hoc* alliances. It is experienced in municipal government with some 20,000 councillors and seventy-two mayors of large towns from Le Havre to Nîmes. It pays close attention to parliamentary activity, which it takes seriously. The PCF has in this and many other ways, as Lavau has argued, contributed to the smooth functioning and legitimisation of the democratic process in France.[51] Nevertheless it is a 'partial legitimisation'[52] only. The PCF is still a very pro-Soviet Leninist party. It has modified its doctrine 'because it is constrained to do so by events and not because it has so thought and decided'.[53]

## 3.   Organisation and Style

The original 21 Conditions imposed by the Communist International on all would-be Communist Parties included the requirement that the Party be organised on the principle of Democratic Centralism. In very simple terms, this means that the lower echelons of the Party elect the higher ones,[54] but decisions flow in the opposite direction. Decisions taken at the higher levels of the pyramid are binding upon all lower ones.

Members join at the lowest level of organisation—the cell (*cellule*). There are three types of cell—workplace cells (*cellulles d'entreprise*), local cells (street, estate, or *quartier*) and rural cells (villages). The development of workplace cells is considered to be of primary importance and fits in closely with the Party's notion of itself as the spearhead of the class struggle, in the front line against exploitation of the worker. The PCF has been exceedingly displeased by recent efforts of the Socialist Party to develop workplace sections.[22] André Vieuguet reported to the 22nd Congress in 1976 the existence of

|  | 8,072 | Workplace cells |
|---|---|---|
|  | 9,649 | Local cells |
|  | 5,457 | Rural cells |
| Total | 23,178 | cells (19,520 in 1972)[56] |

Each cell has a Bureau which includes a secretary and a treasurer.

The cells are grouped in sections, either territorially or, in the case of very large factories, at workplace level. There are some 2,500 sections which hold conferences to elect their committee which in turn elects the Section Bureau and the Secretariat. Communist activity in each of the ninety-five French *départements* is coordinated by the Departmental Federation.[57] As with the Section, its conference elects a committee which in turn elects a Bureau and Secretariat. In big Federations which have a proper administration, the Secretary and the Bureau will all be permanent Party officials. The Federal Secretary is a key figure and his nomination has to be ratified by the Central Committee. At national level the same pattern is repeated. The supreme body of the party, the Congress, is composed of delegates elected by all the Federal conferences. In theory all power emanates from Congress but in fact congresses that occur every three years or so tend to be 'a ritual reunion where delegates re-immerse themselves in a communal atmosphere both studious and joyful and in the truths of the faith. The real discussions and decisions occur before'.[58] Congress is a medium for diffusing the up-to-date Party line to the active membership. Because its proceedings are open to the press and are subsequently published, Congress is a medium for communication between the PCF and the outside world. Like all party conferences it has the fascination of being both a private high mass and a public shop-window.

The Congress delegates elect, on the basis of a list submitted to them by the ·Candidatures Committee, the Central Committee, the 'cardinals of the Communist church'.[59] Party statutes lay down that the 'Central Committee directs the political, ideological, and organisational activity of the Party'. It has at the moment 121 members (including twenty-four apprentice members or *suppléants*). Fifty-eight are manual workers by background. The Central Committee elects its Secretariat and the *Bureau Politique*. These bodies constitute the leadership of the Party.

The composition of the 21-member *Bureau Politque* in 1976 was as follows:

| | |
|---|---|
| Georges Marchais (S) | General Secretary (D) |
| Gustave Ansart | Chairman of Central Political Control Committee. (D) |
| Guy Besse | Director of Centre of Marxist Studies and Research (CERM) |
| Etienne Fajon | Education Section (D) |
| Paul Laurent (S) | Party Organisation (D) |
| Roland Leroy (S) | Director of *L'Humanité* and *L'Humanité Dimanche* (D) |
| René Piquet (S) | Propaganda Section |
| Gaston Plissonnier (S) | Coordination |
| Claude Poperen | Liaison with Federations |
| Georges Séguy | Secretary-General of CGT |
| André Vieuguet | Director, *Cahiers du Communisme* |
| Madeleine Vincent | Woman's Section |
| Mireille Bertrand | Health and Social Security Section |
| Jacques Chambaz | Intellectuals and Culture (D) |
| Jean Colpin (S) | Industry and Immigrant workers |
| Guy Hermier | Youth Section |
| Jean Kanapa | Foreign Policy Section |
| Charles Fiterman (S) | Economic Section |
| Maxime Gremetz | Preparation of elections, relations with Christian organisations |
| André Lajoinie | Agriculture Section |

(S)  =  Member of Secretariat
(D)  =  Member of Parliament—Deputy
CGT =  General Confederation of Labour

A number of leading Communists are not on the *Bureau Politique* but are members of the Central Committee. Examples are Georges Gosnat (D), the Party treasurer; Pierre Juquin (D) a young parliamentarian in charge of the 'Quality of Life' section; and Robert Ballanger (D), President of the Communist Group in the National Assembly. Some 'historic figures' have recently been removed by death or retirement from the directorate of the Party—Jacques Duclos, Benoît Frachon, and Jeannette Thorez-Vermeersch, the lifelong companion of Thorez. The departure of those unconditionally pro-Soviet figures has incidentally made it less difficult for the PCF to criticise Soviet practices. Georges Marchais himself was born in 1920 of working-class family in Calvados. He joined the Party after the Communists left the

Government and retreated into isolation in 1947. A protégé of Jeannette Thorez-Vermeersch, he joined the Central Committee in 1956 and in 1961, under Thorez, moved to the key post of Secretary for Party Organisation. Unlike Waldeck Rochet, he was always regarded as a hard-line Stalinist. He is, however, leading the Party in the abandonment of Leninist concepts he himself has vigorously defended.[60] His relative moderation is challenged by Roland Leroy, who expresses the fears of those who see the PCF losing its distinctive identity.[61] 'Liberals' on their way up in the Party include Paul Laurent, in his forties and a highly successful former secretary of the Paris Federation.[62]

The PCF now claims a membership of 500,000, or approximately one in ten of Communist voters. Members come and go, as in all parties, but the great strength of the PCF lies in the existence of a core of several thousand dedicated activists, trained and disciplined, capable of working in a most efficient and organised manner. In May 1968, when the whole country was in the grip of a general strike, Communist militants were, within a few hours of *Bureau Politique* decisions, able to put up posters indicating the new Party line even in the most distant provinces.

Many writers have commented on the total character of Communist party membership. Annie Kriegel has analysed the PCF as a *'contre-sociéte'*, a 'counter-community', a private world with its own schools, leisure activities, youth groups, books and newspapers, a separated 'minority community' thus enabled 'to preserve its immunity and, by maintaining the homogeneity and fullness of its own internal world, to defend it daily against assimilation'.[63] Edward Upward in his novels about life in the British Communist Party in the 1930s paints a similar picture of Communist activity filling his entire life, including marriage and personal relationships.[64] Gabriel Almond in his study *The Appeals of Communism*[65] links this total immersion to abnormal personality traits like exceptional feelings of hostility or isolation or self-rejection. A famous collection of essays by prominent intellectuals who eventually abandoned Communism repeatedly recalls the 'emotional fervour and intellectual bliss' which comes from being admitted to a world of total certainty and all-demanding dedication.[66] Absorption into the hermetically sealed Communist world, described by Annie Kriegel and others, obviously varies at different levels of the Party. The level of assimilation and involvement one would find in leaders and Party officials is very different from that in the lives of the 220 Communists in the four cells at the Chausson bus factory in Gennevilliers. These later, and a wide variety of different sorts of people, figure in an interesting book by André Harris and Alain de Sedouy.[67] This impressionistic collection of interviews and visits paints a picture of a diverse and often quite iconoclastic membership, and not of a closed secret sect at all.

A number of writers have commented on the error of regarding the whole edifice of the PCF as a monolithic army of disciplined robots. Denis Lacorne, for instance, has described in an interesting essay[68] the lengths to which officials go in order to explain the Party line to members and to convince them of its correctness. For instance, the need for electoral alliances at local level with anti-Communist Socialists and Radicals causes long and stormy meetings.

Some of the most important institutions in this private and all-embracing world, if that is what it is, are the schools for the education of activists. There are innumerable Federal and sectional schools—usually evening classes—and at national level the central schools. They used to be at the 'University of Bobigny', Thorez's house near Paris. They now occupy a modern building not far away at Choisy-le-Roi. There are one-month and four-month courses. A 'four-month school' militant is destined for higher things. The students are usually Federation leaders or even central committee members. Work is intensive, with lectures on Marxism, the history of the PCF and the Soviet Communist Party, and the policy of the Party. There are also lectures on art, literature and science by the Party's leading intellectuals.[69] Out of 1,522 delegates at the 1976 Congress, 228 (15%) had attended the four-month course, 450 (30%) the one-month, 848 (56%) a Federal school, and 959 (63%) an 'elementary' Party school. 283 (30%) had attended none.[70] Tiersky quotes the figures of Léon Feix for the period 1967-9: 408 Federal courses teaching 5,036 students, thirty central courses teaching 997.[71]

All this vast organisation is run from the headquarters of the Party, a remarkable curving glass and concrete building, located at the Place du Colonel Fabien[72] in Paris XXe, the East End. It is very hard for outsiders to penetrate beyond the concrete entrance hall lined with Party publications. Legends, denied by Party spokesmen, have grown up about the building: facilities are said to exist which enable it to withstand military, even nuclear, attack!

## 4.   Finance

At the 1976 Congress an income for the preceding year of over 100 million francs was proclaimed. According to the Treasurer, George Gosnat,[73] it was made up as follows:

|  | *Million francs* |
|---|---|
| *Membership dues (approx. 1% of salary)* | 45 |
| *'Ristournes des élus'* | 20 |

(This is a strange and characteristic system whereby Communist members of Parliament or Councillors hand over their salary to the Party and are paid by the Party the average wage for a skilled industrial worker. A Deputy's salary in 1975 was 12,000 F. per month, a skilled worker's considered to be 3,120 F.

| Special subscriptions (lotteries, fêtes, sales etc.) | 40 |
|---|---|

In addition, the Central Committee receives the proceeds of the sales of certain Party publications. The Central Financial Control Committee report in 1976 referred to some 3 million francs from this source.[74] There are various companies owned by the PCF, such as that which publishes *L'Humanité*. There are also a number of property development and trading consortia controlled by the PCF which deal primarily with Communist municipalities, and import-export companies dealing with the Soviet Union and Eastern Europe. A firm called Interagra run by Jean Doumeng (the 'Communist billionaire') arranged the famous deal to export the EEC butter mountain to the Soviet Union. The PCF claims to spend half its income on propaganda, a quarter on administrative expenses, and a quarter on staff salaries and benefits. It claims to have 600 permanent staff which include all elected Communists who have handed over their salary to the Party.[75]

It is by far the largest and best-financed of French political parties – in this, as in so many other respects, 'a party not like the others'.

## 5. Associated Organisations

The CGT, the largest labour union in France with some 2 million members is often regarded as being under the control of the PCF. Certainly the PCF has in the past fought very hard to control it and in 1947 split it in order to do so. The CGT Secretary-General, Georges Séguy, is a member of the Party's *Bureau Politique,* along with Henri Krasucki who is also on the CGT Confederal Bureau. However French unionism has a tradition of relative independence from political parties. There are probably 250,000 Communist activists in the CGT,[76] and they play a preponderant role inside the organisation. But the CGT, with its image as the toughest and most powerful union, has a wide non-Communist membership, and its candidates usually attract 45-50% of the vote for social security boards or works councils—elections that are not confined to Union members.

In agriculture a rather *Poujadiste* organisation, called MODEF, the role of which is the vigorous defence of the small peasant farm,[77] was founded in 1959 and includes many Communists among its 200,000 members. It is strongest in the West and South-west of France. Its campaigns and its decisions feature in the Communist press, but in fact the PCF probably no longer has a majority on the MODEF Executive.

Other organisations which are controlled or dominated by the PCF include.

*Jeunesse Communiste*—the Young Communist movement which publishes a 'sectarian and unreadable'[78] magazine *Avant-Garde,* and has a separate section for girls.

UEC—Union of Communist Students

UFF—Union of the Women of France

*Mouvement de la Paix*—Peace Movement, supported by prominent non-Communists like Jean-Paul Sartre.

ARAC—Republican Association of War Veterans

*Secours Populaire Français* which, reminiscent of *Secours Rouge* in the Spanish Civil War, campaigns on behalf of victims of repression in Vietnam, Chile, or elsewhere.

*Union des Vieux Travailleurs de France* for retired workers.

## 6. *The Communist Press*

The best-known PCF publications are the daily newspaper *L'Humanité* (200,000 circulation) and its sister weekly *L'Humanité Dimanche* (500,000). These relatively high circulation figures are achieved to a large extent by *la vente militante*—sales by activists. *L'Humanité* has a flavour all its own. It tends to be crammed with communiqués, Soviet CP declarations, resolutions and motions, especially after meetings of the Central Committee—all of which indicates its primary function as a medium of internal Party communication. It has its own private language: in the Vietnam war one would see headlines like 'Puppets crushed', which all readers would know referred to a further defeat for the South Vietnamese forces. André Barjonet, the lapsed Communist already quoted, characterises the style of *L'Humanité* as 'falsehood through omission'.[79] For instance, the account of the Italian Communist Party conference in 1968 made no reference to the freedom of expression allowed to Left-wing critics of the Party but only to the applause for Soviet and Vietnamese delegates. *L'Humanité Dimanche* is lighter and more popular in presentation. There are various provincial Communist dailies—*La Liberté du Nord* (Lille), *La Marseillaise* (Marseille) and *L'Echo du Centre* (Limoges). In addition there are twenty-six local weekly newsheets like the *Côte d'Azur Patriote* or the *Languedoc Ouvrier*. Nineteen of them are published by Federations in the Paris area, for instance *Echo des Métallos* (Renault) or *Saint-Denis Républicain*.

Other periodicals include:

*La Terre* (100,000)—an excellent agricultural weekly, with useful technical information for the peasant. There are few political articles but when there are, they are clear and easy to understand. Waldeck Rochet was editor for a long time.

*France Nouvelle*—the weekly for higher echelon party activists.

*Cahiers du Communisme*—the theoretical monthly of the Central Committee.

*L'Ecole et la Nation*—monthly for teachers.

*La Nouvelle Critique*—(NC) a very orthodox Marxist philosophical monthly.

*Economie et Politique*—(E & P) a relatively independent and authoritative monthly economic review.

Finally the publishing house *Editions Sociales* publishes the writings of Marx, Lenin, and other prophets, books by Party leaders and intellectuals, books on Party policy, CGT handbooks, in short it satisfies almost every need for political, practical, literary, economic, philosophic or even musical material that an activist might feel.

## 7. Membership and electorate

The social composition of PCF members, according to the report by Georges Marchais to the 1966 Congress, was by occupation:

|  | % |  |
|---|---|---|
| Industrial workers | 57 | (13·5% in the public sector) |
| Clerical | 19 | (10·5% in the public services) |
| 'Intellectuals' | 9 |  |
| —teachers, technicians, students, etc. |  |  |
| Shopkeepers, artisans | 6 |  |
| Farmers | 7 |  |
| Farm-workers | 3 |  |

According to André Vieuguet's report to the 1976 Congress, only 45% of new members in 1975 were industrial workers. In 1967, 75% of members were men. The Vieuguet report in 1976 indicated that women were now 30% of the Party. In 1967 58% of members were over forty. M. Vieuguet claims that of new members three out of four are under thirty-five. 48% of delegates at the 1976 Congress were under thirty.[80] The PCF thus gives the impression of a party growing younger and gradually widening its membership outside the traditional male working-class. Membership is not static. Some 10% of members leave every year and in 1975 there were 94,000 new members.[81] About 30% of Communist members are Catholics who go to church from time to time.

The PCF is particularly strong, in members and electors, in the Paris region.[82] It had 27% of the vote in the Paris region in 1973 (30% in 1967) and thirty of its seventy-three members of Parliament represent constituencies there. It is particularly strong in the 'Red Belt' of suburbs round the city boundary—the Départements of Seine St-Denis, Hauts de Seine, and Val de Marne That is where most of the Communist municipalities are—Aubervilliers, Nanterre, Ivry or La Courneuve, where the huge annual festival, the *Fête de l'Humanité*, is held. The PCF also has strength on the South coast around Marseille and Nîmes, in the mining areas of the North, and pockets of strength in rural areas in the Limousin, parts of the Pyrenees and, for some reason, the Côtes du Nord in Catholic Brittany. It is weakest in the Catholic West and Catholic Alsace. Unlike the Socialists, it does not seem to be making gains among Christian voters. Table 8.2 (next page) shows regional strengths and weaknesses of the Communist vote and its amazing stability. Some regions vary internally: for instance, Lorraine (Catholic) is an area of PCF weakness except for the highly industrial areas of Meurthe-et-Moselle. The tremendous Communist strength in the Red Belt is offset to some extent in the Paris region by the large middle-class suburban and residential areas in and around the capital.

According to an opinion survey taken in December 1972, 58% of Communist voters are men, 52% are industrial workers or their families, 54% live in large cities (over 100,000 population) or the Paris area, 71% do not go to church, and 34% are under thirty-five. Peasants, who represent 12% of the population as a whole, only constitute 2% of the PCF vote.[83]

Municipal Communism is well-established in France. Before the 1977 municipal elections, there were some 1,100 Communist mayors of towns and villages—four in cities of over 100,000 population: Le Havre, Amiens, Nîmes and St-Denis, Thirty-four of the fifty Communist mayors in towns over 30,000 governed communes in the Paris region. The 1977 municipal strategy of *Union de la Gauche* alliances has brought more Socialist councillors into these Communist municipal bastions.

## 8. *Image and perspectives*

The PCF, as Lavau, Tiersky and others have pointed out, plays many parts in French political life. It sees itself and is seen by others in a variety of roles. In certain periods of its history it has emphasised its 'vanguard of the proletariat' and its sectarian 'counter community' aspects. These periods are associated with truculent isolation from the French political system, and with hard-line Soviet policies towards the West. The cold war period from 1947 to the late 1950s was an example. Tiersky[84] has

Table 8.2
COMMUNIST ELECTORAL PERFORMANCE BY REGIONS
1967–73
*% of vote (suffrages exprimés)—first ballot*

| | 1967 | 1968 | 1969[p] Duclos | 1973 |
|---|---|---|---|---|
| *Regions of Strength* | | | | |
| N. Picardy | 27·5 | 25·8 | 27·1 | 28·0 |
|    Upper Normandy | 27·3 | 24·6 | 24·6 | 25·7 |
|    North | 26·6 | 24·8 | 27·9 | 26·9 |
|    Paris Region | 29·9 | 26·5 | 25·8 | 27·1 |
| | | | | |
| S. Limousin | 31·3 | 29·5 | 32·6 | 29·9 |
|    Languedoc | 28·8 | 25·2 | 26·6 | 28·2 |
|    Provence—Côte d'Azur | 27·6 | 26·3 | 26·8 | 28·2 |
| | | | | |
| *Average Regions* | | | | |
| N. Champagne | 23·3 | 20·3 | 22·0 | 22·4 |
|    Burgundy | 21·3 | 18·2 | 21·0 | 19·3 |
|    Centre | 21·5 | 17·0 | 21·2 | 18·7 |
|    Lorraine | 19·0 | 15·4 | 16·6 | 16·9 |
| | | | | |
| S. Auvergne | 20·4 | 19·0 | 22·7 | 20·2 |
|    Rhone–Alps | 21·0 | 18·8 | 20·3 | 19·6 |
|    Poitou–Charentes | 19·6 | 16·4 | 18·3 | 18·0 |
|    Aquitaine | 17·6 | 15·5 | 19·6 | 17·5 |
| | | | | |
| *Regions of Weakness* | | | | |
| N. Alsace | 9·1 | 7·2 | 6·4 | 7·9 |
|    Lower Normandy | 12·2 | 10·1 | 11·9 | 11·7 |
|    Brittany | 17·1 | 16·6 | 16·8 | 16·0 |
|    Loire Country | 14·0 | 10·8 | 12·8 | 11·7 |
|    Franche-Comté | 15·1 | 12·1 | 16·5 | 14·0 |
| | | | | |
| S. Midi-Pyrenees | 16·4 | 14·3 | 18·3 | 16·3 |
|    Corsica | 12·1 | 12·8 | 16·4 | 14·5 |
| *France (Metropolitan)* | 22·5 | 20·0 | 21·5 | 21·3 |

[p]Presidential election

convincingly argued that these aspects, while not disappearing as we have seen from our references to the 22nd Congress in 1976, are turned aside Janus-like to reveal a more conciliatory face. In conciliatory mood, the PCF stresses two particular roles. One is its role as a party of government, which it plays responsibly and effectively at municipal level. Laying claim to a share in national government, it extends the hand of cooperation to non-Communist parties of the Left, accepts the modification of its Leninist myths, and undertakes to respect the rules of the liberal-democratic game. To underline this it augments its criticism of illiberal undemocratic practices in the Soviet Union and Eastern Europe. Its final role, as a relatively integrated part of the French political system, is as 'tribune'.[85] The tribune function, it is proposed by Lavau, is 'principally that of organising and defending plebeian social categories . . . and giving them a feeling of strength and confidence'.[86] It is as tribune on behalf of the workers and the lower-paid that the PCF criticises government policy on unemployment, prices, wages, housing or social security. It is as tribune that the PCF takes up the cause of the subsistence peasant farm. It is as tribune that the PCF is associated with the toughest and strongest union, the CGT. This role is the alternative, within the norms and rules of the political system, to the revolutionary role 'vanguard of the proletariat' with its full panoply of Leninist myths. It is as tribune and would-be government party that the PCF has repeatedly made clear over the past few years that the peaceful transformation of society and not the violent overthrow of capitalism is its objective—though of course it remains haunted by 'a lingering nostalgia for its distinctive if no longer revolutionary mission'.[87]

The new image of the PCF is more pleasing to public opinion than 'the fist on the table and the esoteric tirade'.[88] A SOFRES opinion poll survey conducted in January 1976,[89] compared where possible in Table 8.3 with one of February 1968,[90] reveals an improved image as far as its relationship with the Soviet Union and its will to reduce social injustice are concerned. However it was regarded in 1976 as even more 'different', more likely to take power by revolution, and more likely to eliminate other parties than in 1968.* Furthermore respondents considering Communist participation in government desirable, though more numerous than in 1964 (31%) or in 1966 (40%), are down compared with 1968. Those with no view on the matter in 1968 seem to have become hostile to the idea by 1976.

The image of the Communist Party is, as we saw in Chapter 6, fundamental to the prospects of the whole *Union de la Gauche*. Doubts about the PCF's attachment to liberal democratic values, symbolised particularly by its loyalty to the Soviet Union, are major constraints in the battle to bring about the alternation of power in France. The debate tends to centre on whether the PCF has 'really changed', and has gone beyond Stalinism. Tiersky's

Table 8.3
ATTITUDES TO THE PCF, 1968 and 1976

| | Agree % | (1968) | Disagree % | (1968) | No opinion % | (1968) |
|---|---|---|---|---|---|---|
| It is very different from other parties | 48 | (41) | 33 | (32) | 19 | (27) |
| In power, it would reduce social injustice | 39 | (34) | 37 | (30) | 24 | (36) |
| It takes too much account of Soviet interests | 38 | (44) | 29 | (20) | 33 | (36) |
| It would, if it thought the situation favourable, take power by revolution | 35 | (27) | 41 | (36) | 24 | (37) |
| If it came to power in a coalition of the left it would seek to eliminate the other parties | 46 | (30*) | 31 | (36) | 23 | (34) |
| It has moved further away from Soviet Union | 42 | | 32 | | 26 | |
| Communist ministers in Government in the next five years a good thing | 46 | (48) | 35 | (20) | 19 | (36) |

*The question in 1968 was 'Would it ban all other parties?'——a different emphasis.

reasonable view is that 'the PCF continues to move away from the Stalinist mentality of the past' and that the important question for the future is 'whether the party's leaders, whatever their personal preferences, act—or are made to act—in practice on the premise that the abandonment of old ideas is both necessary and desirable'.[91]

He further suggests—and this is supported by a survey of new members by Anne Andreu and Jean-Louis Mignalon[92] that the recent influx of newly-joined Communists are not particularly attached to Soviet achievements or Leninist myths. The commitment to the *Union de la Gauche* has required the PCF to challenge Soviet practices and to abandon certain Leninist concepts. Like Samson, 'eyeless in Gaza at the mill with slaves', or Sisyphus eternally rolling his stone in Hades, it may now find itself condemned to a task from which there is no release.

## NOTES

1. *L'Avenir du Parti Communiste français,* Paris: Editions Sociales, 1969.
2. See above, p. 105.
3. 'The French Communist theory of power', *Government and Opposition,* 1967 pp. 255-6.
4. J. Fauvet, *Histoire du Parti Communiste français,* Paris: Fayard, 1964, Vol. 1, p. 108.
5. *Tableau des Parties en France,* Paris: Grasset, p. 170.
6. R. Tiersky, *French Communism 1920-1972,* Columbia University Press, 1974, p. 23.
7. *Ibid.,* p. 33.
8. *Ibid.,* p. 32.
9. In 1927 the Minister of the Interior, Sarraut, proclaimed Communism to be the enemy 'because of the Party's anti-colonialist and anti-militarist declarations'.
10. They were still able to pursue political activities. In Autumn 1927 Pierre Semard called a conference in his prison cell with imprisoned members of the *Bureau Politique* and delegates of the Comintern! (A. Kriegel: *The French Communists,* Univ. of Chicago Press 1972, p. 125).
11. *Ibid.,* p. 32.
12. Cited by G. Lavau, 'Le Parti Communists dans le système politique français', in F. Bon *et al., Le Communisme en France,* Paris: Cahiers de la Fondation Nationale des Sciences Politiques, 1969, p.12.
13. W. Redfern, *Paul Nizan,* Princeton University Press, 1972.
14. D. Caute, *Communism and the French Intellectuals,* André Deutsch, 1964, p. 138.
15. This is documented by Auguste Lecoeur, *Le Parti Communiste et la*

*Résistance: août 1939—juin 1941,* Paris: Plon, 1968, p. 76. It must be remembered that Lecour, expelled from the Party, had an axe to grind. Nevertheless, his documentary evidence is very persuasive. See also J. Fauvet, *Histoire au Part Communiste français,* Vol. 2, p. 56 and A. Kriegel, *The French Communists,* p. 120n.

16. .See for instance *Le Parti Communiste dans la Résistance* Paris: Institut Maurice Thorez, Editions Sociales, 1967, or Jacques Duclos, *Memoires,* Paris, Fayard, Vol. 3.

17. For whether the insurrection was useful as a morale-restorer or was a useless waste of lives as the liberation forces were on their way, see Dominique Lapierre and Larry Collins, *Paris Brûle-t-il?,* Paris: Editions Robert Laffont, 1964, esp. part 2, chs. 9 and 16.

18. See Fauvet, *Histoire du Parti Communiste,* Vol. 2, p. 139.

19. Membership cards actually taken up: Kriegel, *The French Communists,* p. 33, and Fauvet, *Histoire,* Vol. 2, p. 364.

20. For figures showing the drop in PCF support at the time of the Hungarian events and a countervailing argument that the electoral setback of 1958 had little to do with Hungary but was mainly to be explained by the appeal of General de Gaulle to working-class voters, see Jean Ranger, 'Le vote Communiste depuis 1945', in Bon *et al., Le Communisme en France,* pp. 216 and 232–4.

21. *The State of France,* Secker and Warburg, 1955, p. 161.

22. See below, p. 210.

23. *French Communism,* Ch. 8.

24. Delegate from Pas de Calais at 22nd Congress of the PCF, in *Cahiers du Communisme,* Feb.-Mar. 1976, p. 98.

25. 'Ce que veulent les Communistes pour la France', document adopted by 22nd Congress, in *ibid,* p. 381.

26. Gaston Plissonnier (Bureau politique), reporting the results of the Congress vote on the Central Committee's list of candidates for the 127 Central Committee and Finance Committee places: 113 candidates received 1,501 votes out of 1,501, 13 received 1,500, one received 1,498 (*ibid.,* p. 397).

27. Jean Kanapa (Bureau politique), 22nd Congress, *ibid.,* p. 356.

28. 'Structure de l'idéologie communiste' in Bon *et al., Le Communisme en France* p. 109n.

29. Georges Marchais, report to 21st Congress: *Le Parti Communiste propose* (PCF, 1974), p. 37.

30. Georges Marchais address to 22nd Congress, in *Cahiers de Communisme,* Feb-Mar. 1976 p. 20.

31. 'Ce que veulent les Communistes', *Cahiers de Communisme,* 1976, p. 363.

32. *Ibid.,* p. 362.

33. Marchais's address, in *ibid.,* p. 69.

34. 1793/4 in the French Revolution Calendar.

35. *Bureau Politique* communiqué, Aug 21 1968.

36. Gaston Plissonnier, report to Central Committee, *L'Humanité*, 23 Oct. 1968.
37. Letter to *Bureau Politique*, 14 Sept. 1969, 'A propos du blâme publique', in R. Garaudy, *Toute La Vérité*, Paris, Grasset, 1970, p. 111.
38. René Andrieu, editorial in *L'Humanité*, 22 Dec. 1975.
39. 22nd Congress, *Cahiers de Communisme.*, p. 64.
40. *Ibid.*, p. 63.
41. Andrei Kirilenko, 22nd Congress, *ibid.*, p. 477.
42. *Le Monde*, 13 Nov. 1975.
43. Thierry Pfister, *Le Monde, ibid.*
44. Gustave Ansart, Deputy for the Nord and *Bureau Politique* member, 22nd Congress, *Cahiers de Communisme*, p. 110.
45. G. Marchais, address to 22nd Congress *ibid.*, p. 44.
46. See for instance '9 Domande sullo Stalinismo' *(Nouvi Argomenti*, 16 June 1956).
47. L. Jospin, '*Rapport sur le XXIIe Congrés du PCF, L'Evolution du Mouvement Communiste International et les Relations PS-PC*', Bureau Executif of the Socialist party, 21 Jan. 1976).
48. G. Marchais, report to 22nd Congress, *Cahiers du Communisme*, pp. 62–4.
49. 'Vivre Libres!' published by *L'Humanité*, 1975, p. 4.
50. *Ibid.*, p. 17.
51. See Lavau in Bon *et al.*, *Le Communisme en France*, pp. 50-3.
52. Lavau, p. 53.
53. Jospin *Rapport*, p. 12.
54. Candidature committees decide who they can vote for.
55. See above p. 112.
56. 'Un grand parti communiste pour une grande politique', 22nd Congress, *Cahiers du Communisme*, p. 149.
57. Finistére and Meurthe-et-Moselle have two Federations each.
58. Fauvet, *Histoire du Parti Communiste français*, Vol. 2, p. 330.
59. *Ibid.*, p. 331.
60. E.g. 17th Congress, 1964: Temporary dictatorship of the proletariat is among the 'general laws valid for all countries' in the transition to Socialism.
61. See Ian Campbell, 'The French Communists and the Union of the Left 1974–76', *Parliamentary Affairs*, Summer 1976, pp. 246–63.
62. For the new generation of Communists see A. Laurens et T. Pfister, *Les Nouveaux Communistes*, Paris: Stock, 1973.
63. Kriegel, *The French Communist Theory of Power*, p. 257.
64. *In the Thirties* and *The Rotten Elements*, Heinemann, 1962 and 1969.
65. Princeton University Press, 1954.
66. A. Koestler in R. Crossman, ed., *The God that Failed*, New York, 1950, p. 19.
67. *Voyage à l'intérieur du Parti Communiste*, Paris, Editions du Seuil, 1974.

68. 'Left-wing unity at the grass roots: Picardy and Languedoc' in Donald L. M. Blackmer and Sidney Tarrow, eds., *Communism in Italy and France*, Princeton University Press, 1975.

69. Barjonet, *Le Parti Communiste français*, p. 132, describes the censored reading and the students listening in absolute silence to the lectures while the director of the school takes copious notes ; Harris and de Sédouy, *Voyage à l'intérieur.*, pp. 59–64, present a less forbidding view 'Nous avons rencontré des élèves heureux'. They quote a lady militant: 'a girl-friend wrote saying the school was a good place to find a husband . . . [but] the boys were all young enough to be my children' (p. 31). She did in fact meet her husband at the school!

70. C. Poperen, *Rapport de la Commission des Mandats: 22nd Congress, Cahiers du Communisme*, p. 318.

71. *Cahiers du Communisme*, Feb. 1970, p. 185 (Tiersky, *French Communism*, p. 318).

72. Colonel Fabien was the code name of a Communist Resistance hero.

73. 22nd Congress, *Cahiers du Communisme*, p. 353.

74. Report of Pierre Doize, 22nd Congress, *Cahiers de Communisme*, p. 347.

75. For these figures see *L'Humanité Dimanche Spécial: Les Communistes* 1975.

76. See G. Seguy, *Lutter*, Paris; Stock, 1975.

77. *Mouvement d'Organisation et Défense des Exploitants Familiaux.*

78. Barjonet, *Le Part Communiste français*, p. 103.

79. *Ibid.*, p. 121.

80. 22nd Congress, *Cahiers de Communisme*, p. 150.

81. Vieuguet report, *ibid.*, p. 149.

82. The Paris Federation itself celebrated 25,000 members in 1976.

83. IFOP, see *le Monde* 23 Feb. 1973. Industrial workers at that time formed 32% of the French electorate, non-churchgoers 41%, under 35's 29%.

84. See *French Communism 1920-1972*, Chs 8-12 (esp. 12), and 'French Communism in 1976', *Problems of Communism*, Feb 1976 in Bon, pp. 20–47.

85. See Tiersky, *French Communism* Ch. 10, and Lavau, in Bon *et al.*, *Le Communisme en France*.

86 Lavau, *ibid.*, p. 18.

87. Ian Campbell, 'The French Communists and the Union of the Left 1974–76', *Parliamentary Affairs*, Summer 1976, p. 250.

88. R. Barrillon, *Le Monde*, 3 Feb 1976.

89. *Le Nouvel Observateur*, 2-8 Feb. 1976.

90. A. Lancelot and P. Weill in Bon *et al.*, pp. 282-303.

91. 'French Communism in 1976', *Problems of Communism*, Feb. 1976.

92. *L'Adhésion*, Paris: Calmann-Levy, 1975.

# 9

# FRINGE PARTIES—LEFT AND RIGHT

Fringe movements of sporadic and extremist character have been a feature of French politics for generations—since the Jacobins in the French Revolution if not earlier. Often they have a brief day of glory, then fade away as quickly as they came. The *Boulange*—a brief and inglorious period of remarkable popularity for the mediocre General Boulanger in 1887-9—was of this character. So apparently was the Gaullist RPF in the Fourth Republic, which did not exist in 1946, had 4 million votes (21%) in 1951, and had disappeared by 1953. Poujadism had a hectic and brief success at the 1956 election. The Fifth Republic, however, has seen no successes for extremist movements, and there are today scarcely any small parties at all, extremist or otherwise, which are not integrated into the bipolar party system. The camps of the *Majorité* and the *Union de la Gauche* virtually encompass all.

## 1. The PSU

The only party of any moment which remains outside is the dwindling Unified Socialist Party (PSU). The PSU was formed in 1960 by the merger of three discontented groups. The main one was the PSA (Autonomous Socialist Party) composed of Socialists who objected to the policies of the Mollet government and in particular to its colonialist Algerian policy. Also in the PSA was Pierre Mendès-France, the brightest star in the Radical firmament in the 1950s, who lost control of the Radical Party in 1957. The other components of the PSU were *Tribune du Communisme*—a group of Communists and ex-Communists who opposed the sterile sectarianism of the PCF—and UGS (Union of the Socialist Left). This latter group contained a strong Christian element derived from the *Jociste* movement (Young Christian workers), which we have already encountered as an important element in the new and revitalised Socialist Party. Composed of moderates and revolutionaries, elder statesmen and young militants, the PSU in the late 1960s was remarkably diverse. In 1967 it joined in the electoral pact with the other parties of the Left. It presented 101 candidates and won four seats. One of them was Mendès-France, who had been adopted by Grenoble, a progressive and fast-growing city with much new high-technology industry. He played a leading role in the campaign of the Left and took part in a memorable debate in Grenoble with the Prime Minister Georges Pompidou. May 1968 was 'the divine surprise'[1] for the PSU. Enthusiastically supporting the students in revolt, it saw itself as the one party which, unlike the stick-in-the-mud reformists of the PCF, the Socialists and the unions, was willing to embrace a revolutionary alternative. It presented over 300 candidates in 1968, obtained 4% of the vote, but lost all its seats. Its leader Michel Rocard stood as a revolutionary candidate for the Presidency in 1969, with the support of 3·7% of those voting, and won a parliamentary seat at a famous by-election in October 1969 when, still arguing for revolution, he defeated the ex-Prime Minister Maurice Couve de Murville. In 1973, challenged by even more revolutionary Trotskyist groups, the PSU's 208 candidates could only manage 1·9% of the total vote and one solitary Deputy— Yves Le Foll, the Mayor of St. Brieuc in Brittany.

The PSU has no pretensions to being a reformist parliamentary party. It has become increasingly revolutionary in its aims since 1968. Its finest hour, apart from May 1968, was the work-in at the Lip watch factory in Besançon in 1973. PSU *autogestionnaires* in the CFDT union were the leading figures in the prolonged but unsuccesful attempt to keep the company going after its bankruptcy. PSU members from all over France took part in marches and demonstrations to sustain the protest. The hero of this revolutionary epic was Charles Piaget, who was almost persuaded to stand in the 1974 presidential elections.

In 1974 the PSU split. Michel Rocard, increasingly regarded as excessively moderate, persuaded the PSU to support François Mitterrand in the election, to take part in discussions about re-uniting the different strands of socialism, and to attend the *Assises du Socialisme* in October 1974 to argue the case for *Autogestion*. After the *Assises*, Rocard found himself in a minority in the PSU, and, feeling anyway that 'the Socialist revolution is not felt in France by the workers to be their great hope',[2] led some 2,500 to 3,000 PSU members off to join the ranks of the Socialist Party. The sect of pure and committed revolutionaries (including Piaget) which remains behind continues as a revolutionary *autogestionnaire* movement. At its Congress in December 1974 it indicated a will to embrace other revolutionary groups—like the *Alliance Marxiste Revolutionnaire* which applied to join. The PSU maintains its little office full of tracts and pamphlets in the rue Borromée, physically and spiritually miles from the Boulevard St. Germain where most of the parties inside the system cluster. In 1975 the PSU played a leading part in the campaign to create union branches in the armed forces, publishing anti-militarist tracts,[3] and in December receiving the honour of having its headquarters raided by the police instructed by the government to crack down on subversive plots to weaken army morale.

What strength the PSU has left is centred on Paris, the CFDT and the universities. It publishes a weekly *Tribune Socialiste,* which has articles on workers' control, discussions on the Church and the class struggle (reminiscent of its Christian origins), reports on the PCF, banks and other enemies, Portugal, strikes, struggles and, throughout 1975, repression in the army.

## 2. *Anarchists, Trotskyists, and Maoists*[4]

A bewildering profusion of revolutionary outcrops are to be found on the Left of the PSU. The best known are:

LCR—*Ligue Communiste Révolutionnaire* (Trotskyist)
Banned in various forms at various times (JCR in 1968, LC in 1973), the LCR's most prominent activist is Alain Krivine, twice a candidate in presidential elections. It publishes a daily newspaper, *Rouge,* and is evidently not short of funds—its rotary press cost 750,000 francs.[5] The *Ligue* presents candidates at parliamentary and local elections but considers that 'the real battles take place not in the polling station but in the factories'.[6]

LO—*Lutte Ouvrière* (Workers' Struggle—Trotskyist)
Grouped round the revolutionary journal of that name, *Lutte Ouvrière* is best known through Arlette Laguiller, who, like Alain Krivine, contested the 1974 presidential elections. Her revolutionary ardour and feminist rhetoric won her a very respectable 600,000 votes (2·4%). They also present rival candidates to LCR at local and parliamentary elections. Why do they not unite? 'The cult of organisation and of doctrinal purity leads them by a sort of fatality . . . to tear at each other for ever.'[7]

PCMLF—Marxist-Leninist Communist Party of France (Maoist)
Also manages to publish *L'Humanité Rouge,* a daily devoted to the 'application in France of Marxism-Leninism and of the thought of Mao Tse-tung'. Their preference for spontaneity in political action has earned them from Trotskyist rivals the derisive nickname of Mao-Spontex.

PCR—Revolutionary Communist Party (Marxist-Leninist)
It publishes yet another daily: *Le Quotidien du Peuple.*

As if three revolutionary dailies were not enough, there is a fourth *Libération,* a rather anarchistic, or at least iconoclastic, weekly *Charlie Hébdo,* and before it was siezed (and Jean-Paul Sartre with it) there was once *La Cause du Peuple.*

## 3. *Autonomist movements*[8]

In the parts of France that have a separate language there have from time to time been regional political parties and separatist movements. In Alsace there has been no trace of separatism since the Second World War: 'Hitler did more for the cause of the French state in Alsace than all the "patriots" put together.'[9] Basque autonomists in the region near the Spanish border, who have an organisation *Enbata,* occasionally but not very often erupt in protest. Anyone who motors in Southern France will have seen references to *Occitanie Libre*—a movement to 'free' the whole South—but a few paint pots do not constitute a political movement. The most vigorous autonomists in France are the Bretons. Brittany, like Wales, has an ancient Celtic culture and language which is still widely spoken. There is a strong regionalist movement which takes all forms from serious economic and social study groups like CELIB (Study and Liaison Committee for Breton Interests) to terrorist organisations like FLB (Breton Liberation Front). The latter have carried out various bombings and attacks and there have been the usual sequence of arrests followed by hunger strikes. The regional nationalism of the Basques has tended to be associated with figures from the extreme Right, and Breton nationalism, in recent years any way, with the extreme Left. For instance, in 1972 two young Breton separatists were refused permission to enter Great Britain to attend an international conference of far-Left organisations. In 1975 and 1976 the most violent demonstrations for regional autonomy came from Corsica.

## 4. *The Extreme Right*

Nothing, of course, could be more unfair than to include the extreme Right in a chapter that discusses the revolutionary Left. They have nothing whatsoever in common except—and this is the reason why they appear in the same chapter—the fact that they all reject the norms of the party system and stay outside it.

The Fifth Republic has virtually no native extreme Right at all. Political stability and rising prosperity are not conducive to the growth of Fascism or of movements that imitate or resemble it. Up to the Second World War there were many such movements— anti-Jewish, anti-democratic, anti-Communist, nationalistic and violent—collectively known as the *Ligues* (Leagues).[10] The most important was the *Ligue de l'Action Française,* successor to the *Ligue de la patrie Française. Action Française* was led by a remarkable polemical writer, Charles Maurras, who fulminated against all ideas that smacked of the democratic or the libertarian from the Dreyfus affair in the 1890s right through to the Vichy regime of Marshal Pétain in the 1940s. The violent activists of the League were known as the *Camelots du Roi* (a reference not to their leader but to their royalist aspirations). The inter-war years saw in France, as elsewhere, a great increase of political violence. The *Jeunesses*

*Patriotes* and the *Croix de Feu* both engaged in street fighting against the Communists and in the riots of 6 February 1934 which helped in their way to promote Left-wing unity.[11] The *Croix de Feu*, led by Colonel de la Rocque, was dedicated to the task of 'smashing the internal enemies of our fatherland',[12] and at one time had 60,000 members.[13] When the *Croix de Feu* was dissolved by the Popular Front Government in 1936, de la Rocque founded the *Parti Social Français* which, as a force of the anti-parliamentary Right, built up a considerable mass membership. Another party of the extreme Right in the 1930s was the *Parti Populaire Français* founded by Jacques Doriot, a populist and an ex-Communist. Doriot's movement was much more like classic Fascism or National Socialism in character than the more aristocratic *Action Française*. Finally there were the sinister and violent *Cagoulards* (hooded-men) who carried on with political killings after the dissolution of the Leagues. The most famous *Cagoulard* act of terrorism was the murder of the Rosselli brothers, two leading Italian anti-Fascists, at Bagnoles de l'Orne on 9 June 1937. 200,000 people marched to their funeral at Père Lachaise cemetery.[14]

After the war 'the extreme Right was more isolated within the political community than ever before'.[15] Collaboration with Vichy and the Nazis marked many for life, while the purges carried out after the liberation and the trials which condemned Pétain, Laval, Maurras and others thinned their ranks. Since 1945 there have only been three extremist movements of any note which could be classified as Right-wing by their continuation of anti-parliamentarism and nationalism. We have already examined one of them, the RPF, in our account of Gaullism.[16] The second was the UDCA (Union for the Defence of Shopkeepers and Artisans)[17] otherwise known, after its founder and leader, as Poujadism.[18] Pierre Poujade, a shopkeeper from St. Céré in the Lot, led a local tax strike which rapidly developed into a mass movement of discontented small traders. At the 1956 elections $2\frac{1}{2}$ million people voted Poujadist, attracted to a campaign in which every conceivable discontent was grouped under the slogan '*Sortez les Sortants!*' ('Throw the Rascals Out!'). Roger Quilliot describes the arrival in Parliament of the successful Poujadist candidates: 'These fifty-one newcomers, intruders with heavy boots and strong language . . . a noisy, excessive group, ready for all forms of demagogy.'[19] Poujadism has given a new word to the vocabulary, and it serves to express the periodic outbursts of protest by groups who feel threatened by the progress and change of the modern world. It is reactionary in the genuine sense of the word: it seeks to put the clock back to a world where the small grocer was not threatened by the supermarket, the small craftsman by mass production, the small farmer by bureaucracy and taxes, the small employer by unions and social legislation. There have been a few incidents in the Fifth Republic reminiscent of Poujadism. Peasants rioting against low prices for wine or vegetables for instance, sometimes sack a tax office, block roads or dump thousands of tons of artichokes on a main railway line. There is a latterday Poujade called Gérard Nicoud who sees himself and is seen by his followers as a legendary folk hero. In September 1969 he and his friends, after taking three civil servants hostage, took to the Maquis. In March 1970, Nicoud, now the leading figure of CID (Committee of Information and Defence—a small traders, defence movement), led 30,000 shopkeepers and artisans in a vast demonstration in Paris. His various terms of imprisonment have been met with riots and demands for his release. Nicoud and CID, however, have never had the mass following, still less the brief day of electoral glory, of Pierre Poujade.

The third important movement of the extreme Right in the post-war period has been the OAS (Organisation of the Secret Army). The OAS lies well outside the scope of a book on political parties because it was a terrorist group of Ultras bent on keeping Algeria French. It was led by General Salan who, after the unsuccessful military rising against de Gaulle's Algerian policy in April 1961, had gone underground. OAS bombings and murders in Algeria and France culminated in the attempted assassination of de Gaulle at Le Petit Clamart in August 1962. Just as the violence of the *Croix de Feu* against the Left helped the Left to unite and win power in the 1930s, so the OAS attempt to assassinate de Gaulle, by underlining the need to establish presidential legitimacy on a permanent basis, contributed to the longevity of Gaullist institutions.[20] French-Algeria extremism lived on in the 1965 presidential candidature of Jean-Louis Tixier-Vignancour, a right-wing lawyer who defended General Salan at his trial. Tixier got 5% of the vote, mainly from resettled French-Algerians, and so great was his loathing for de Gaulle that he urged his supporters to vote Mitterrand at the second ballot. In 1969 Tixier backed Georges Pompidou for the Presidency, indicating that for the extreme Right the Algerian issue was in the past.

In the last decade there has been virtually no activity by the extreme Right. May 1968 produced some clashes between Right and Left-wing students and led to the birth of *Ordre Nouveau* (New Order) which was eventually banned in 1973. Many of its activists joined the *Front National*, founded in 1972, and then left it again to form *Faire Front* Committees. A further recent regrouping has produced the *Parti des Forces Nouvelles*. The founder and leader of the *Front National* is a figure who appears throughout the post-war history of the extreme Right, Jean-Marie Le Pen. A Poujadist Deputy in the 1950s, a fanatic of *Algérie-Française*, supporter of the insurrections in Algeria in 1960 and 1961 and of the OAS, and a partisan of Tixier-Vignancour in 1965, he himself stood in the presidential elections of 1974 where he managed to obtain only 0·75% of the first ballot vote.[21]

'The history of the extreme right in the quarter of a century after 1945 is a confused record of feuds, violence, and inefficiency.'[22] There are also deeper reasons for the silence and failure of the extreme Right. The first is the much higher level of consensus and legitimacy that, up to now at any rate, the Fifth Republic, with its stable and accepted institutions and its background of great economic development, has known. It is economic crisis and political instability that are the recruiting sergeants of extremist movements—Left and Right. The second is that Right-wing discontents about Algeria, taxation, French military weakness, lax treatment of offenders, supermarkets, or anything else now take second place to the fear of a Left-wing victory at the polls which would bring the Communists into government.

## NOTES

1. Borella, *Les Partis politiques dans la France d'aujourd'hui*, p. 207. Professor Borella used to be a leading member of the PSU, which figures prominently in his book. He has now, along with a large part of the PSU, joined the PS and is a member of its *Comité Directeur*.
2. See Bizot, *Au Parti des Socialistes*, p. 157.
3. One, entitled *PSU Documentation: Militer contre le Militarisme*, urged soldiers to join IDS (Information for the Rights of Soldiers) and 'break the wall of silence which surrounds the barracks' and to fight against repression of soldiers.
4. *Le Monde*, 3 April 1970, gives details of about thirty groups. See also Ehud Sprinzak, 'France—The radicalisation of the New Left' in Martin Kolinsky and William E. Paterson, eds, *Social and Political Movements in Western Europe*, London: Croom Helm, 1976, pp. 275–303.
5. *Le Monde*, 22 Oct. 1975.
6. *Le Monde*, L'election presidentielle de mai 1974 *(Dossiers et Documents* 1974), p. 72.
7. Borella, *Les Partis politiques*, p. 221.
8. See the excellent section in Anderson, *Conservative Politics in France*, pp. 97–124.
9. *Ibid.*, p. 113, quoting Frederic Hoffet, *Psychanalyse d'Alsace*, Paris 1951.
10. See Anderson, *Conservative Politics in France*, esp Chs 3 and 4; Ernst Nolte, *Three Faces of Fascism: Action Française, Italian Fascism, National Socialism*, (Weidenfeld and Nicolson, 1965), and J. McLelland, ed., *The French Right*, Cape, 1970.

11. See above, p. 131.
12. Preface by Col. de la Rocque to a *Croix de Feu* publication *Le Complot Communo-Socialiste,* Paris: Eds. Grasset, 1935, p. 9.
13. Anderson, *Conservative Politics in France,* p. 203.
14. See Charles F. Delzell, *Mussolini's Enemies—the Italian Anti-Fascist Resistance,* Princeton University Press, 1961.
15. Anderson, *Conservative Politics in France,* p. 267.
16. See above, p. 38.
17. It also came to be known as UFF *(Unité et Fraternité Française).*
18. S. Hoffman, *Le Mouvement Poujade,* Paris: Colin, 1956.
19. *La SFIO et l'exercice du pouvoir 1944–1958,* Paris, Fayard, 1972, p. 561.
20. See above p. 21.
21. Reward came at last to M. Le Pen in the form of an enormous legacy from a wealthy supporter in 1976.
22. Anderson, *Conservative Politics in France,* p. 297.

# 10

## SOME COMPARATIVE ASPECTS

There are certain aspects of the life of French political parties which have appeared from time to time in this book that are better drawn together in a single chapter. Finance of political parties (and especially state subsidies to political parties), selection of candidates and the activity of parliamentary groups are conveniently dealt with in this manner, and interesting differences between parties as well as international comparisons can be revealed.

### 1. *Finance of political parties*
Political parties are rarely forthcoming about their sources of funds. In Great Britain the Labour Party is open about its financial support from trade unions but the Conservative Party considerably less so about the size and extent of contributions from companies. Indeed the 1964–70 Labour Government felt obliged to bring in legislation requiring disclosure by companies of all political donations. In the United States illicit and secret campaign contributions lie behind a number of political scandals, from Watergate to the humblest Congressional contest. French parties are secretive too. The detailed research that would be required to arrive anywhere near the whole truth about party funds is well beyond the scope of this book.

The party that appears most open is the one that in everything else is the most hermetic; the Communist Party. They proclaim a budget of 100 million F, which appears roughly to correspond to the scale of organisation they are clearly able to maintain. The source of funds is clearly indicated: membership dues, collections and sales, salaries of Deputies turned over to the Party. Even so, Communist finance is surrounded by hints of profits from property companies and firms supplying Communist municipalities. The parties of the *Majorité* and, it is alleged, the Socialists receive gifts from the business world, but the amount is unknown. Certainly every party except the Gaullists and the Communists appears to occupy office accommodation which could not possibly have been provided by the subscriptions and fund-raising activities of members.

In most discussions of the financing of political parties, large private gifts are regarded as objectionable for the obvious reason that the price in terms of private political assurances is undemocratically high. What about state subsidies to political

167

parties? The West German method of a fixed annual subsidy calculated on the quantity of votes obtained by a party in the previous general election has been recommended to the British Parliament.[1] It is justified on the argument that democratic choice cannot occur effectively if political parties do not have the means to present that choice effectively. Therefore democracy needs adequately financed political parties, and it is preferable that this finance should not come from vested interests which might dictate policy. In France there is no such open subsidy at all, but the state does contribute to the financing of political parties in a number of ways—to some of which reference has already been made. In the chapters on elections, the sensible arrangements for printing and delivering election literature at public expense and the free broadcasting time on radio and TV will be discussed. There is, however, an important hidden subsidy in the presence of ministerial personnel, paid as public servants, working in party headquarters. This is quite openly the case in the parties of the *Majorité*. In France a minister, a President, a mayor of a large city, even a senior public official like a Prefect, has his *cabinet,* paid from public funds. The *cabinet* is his own team of personal collaborators. Most *cabinet* members these days are picked for their technical prowess, their administrative training and competence, but naturally the minister will be looking for people who share his political ideas and who will want his political success. This of course greatly increases the minister's capacity to impose his political will on his civil servants, and, as such, was a reform advocated by the British Labour Party in its evidence to the Royal Commission on the Civil Service in 1968,[2] and explains why outside advisers have increasingly crept into Whitehall over recent years.

The tradition of the ministerial *cabinet,* plus that of political parties being little more then electoral committees for a ministerial and parliamentary élite, has added up to a very indistinct separation between party activity and government activity. In Britain, America and France, the staff of a member of government is 'political' in the sense that it deals with the presentation of policy and the generation of support for it. Speech-writing, speaking engagements, travel—these sorts of things fall within the purview of the public service. So too would correspondence from constituents and interest groups. In France and America, however, direct electoral affairs take up much more of the time of officials paid from public funds than in Britain, where public funds cannot be deployed for any purpose which is explicitly of a party or electoral nature. In France a minister, though he is obliged by the Constitution (Art. 25) to give up his parliamentary seat, continues to contest it at each election, to take a close interest in it, and in all probability to be mayor of a town in it. Relations with constituents, town hall, local interests, the Prefecture, and party workers will be handled by a member of his *cabinet*. So too will relations with party colleagues in Parliament and the country. So too will administrative and transport arrangements for ministers in election campaigns. Ministers, as we have seen, second staff to party headquarters to organise the party and to sit on its executive committees. In addition members of the National Assembly are allowed one assistant, paid from public funds. These are often seconded to help with party organisation—indeed they are indispensable to the smaller parties like the Left-Radicals (MRG). Finally people who have been ministers or have held similar high public office appear, after they have left office, to be able to keep on their secretaries and assistants, still nominally attached to and on the payroll of their old ministries. These too are available for party and electoral work.

In addition to government financial support in the shape of seconded personnel there are direct (though not public) subsidies to political parties. Neither the extent nor the recipients of these funds are disclosed. My information, from a senior organiser of one of the *Majorité* parties, is that they are not confined to the *Majorité* but go to the Socialists and MRG as well.

All these factors help to explain how French political parties, in contrast to their British and West German counterparts, are able to live so far beyond their means.

## 2. *Parliamentary Groups*
Parliamentary Groups in France have in many cases an existence almost separate from their parties. As one might expect this is more marked in the case of the Senate than of the National Assembly, and in the case of the Centrist groupings than of the mass-parties—Gaullism, Socialism, Communism. The minimum number of Deputies required to constitute a parliamentary group is thirty and desperate efforts, alliances, and deals are made in elections to ensure that a party that wishes to preserve an independent existence gets at least thirty seats. This was the big problem for the Reform Movement in 1973 and for the PDM opposition Centrists in 1968. After elections quite a number of Deputies move around. For instance the Independent Republican Group only had fifty-five members after the 1973 election. By 1976 it had been joined by a number of members from the *Union Centriste* group and various unattached independents and had grown to seventy. The Socialists and MRG sit together in a group called *Parti Socialiste et Radicaux de Gauche*. The Reform Movement (Radicals, Centre Democrats, and ex-Socialists) and the *Union Centriste* have joined forces in a parliamentary group

fifty-one strong of whom twenty-four belong to the new Centrist party CDS. Only the Communists and the Gaullists sit in homogeneous Groups. Some deputies do not become full members of a Group, they merely become 'attached' to one *(apparentés)*. At the moment only the Communists have no *apparentés,* but they too have had them in the past.

Each group has a president and a bureau or executive committee which sometimes includes non-parliamentarians. For instance Yves Guéna, when Secretary-General of the UDR, was a member of the UDR Group Bureau. As 'political delegate' of the RPR he remains a member. For each of the six permanent committees of the Assembly—Foreign Affairs, Finance, Defence etc.—each Group appoints a spokesman or leader. The Groups meet regularly and Group members on a permanent committee meet before their committees meet. Group decisions as to voting are binding on the three mass parties with sanctions applicable to dissidents, while Centrists and Independent Republicans permit, indeed glory in, freedom of the vote.

The UDR had the most elaborate group constitution laying down in detail the powers of its president (very considerable), the mode of election for president, vice-presidents, and Bureau members (the latter by region). The new RPR preserves the UDR structure unchanged. Each vice-president is given a special area of responsibility—social problems, economic problems, political problems, public relations, cultural affairs—and they take in turns to be 'on duty' in the chamber to act as a kind of 'whip'. The Group's *bureau politique* nominates Group members to the Assembly committees and to the European Parliament, it authorises (or forbids) bills, amendments, and questions and even speeches in debates. The group organises six 'permanent study groups' on broad themes: the family, the environment, taxation, agriculture, social security, work and company reform. These parliamentary study groups are quite separate from the study groups or commissions organised by party headquarters. The party commissions (which include parliamentarians among their membership) formulate ideas and policy on health, education, and so on. The parliamentary study groups apply themselves only to the legislative application in bills, amendments, and committee reports of the policies formulated by the movement outside.

The other parliamentary groups tend to base their study groups on the six permanent committees of the Assembly. Thus, unlike in the RPR Group, sacred matters such as foreign policy, defence and the law are matters to which they are entitled to give parliamentary consideration as well as financial, economic and social affairs. Socialist Deputies are also required by the party statutes (Art. 53) to participate in the Party study groups outside

Parliament which correspond to the work of the Assembly committee they serve on. As we saw in chapter 7, the Party's study groups cover a wider area than the parliamentary arena but legislative proposals are generated: for instance the party's agriculture group led by Pierre Joxe produced in 1976 a bill relating to land.

The parliamentary groups employ a number of staff, paid not from public funds but by the Deputies, who contribute a percentage of their parliamentary salary. The PSRG Group, for instance, has a secretary and three assistant-secretaries as well as clerical employees to service the 106 Socialist and MRG members. This does not, of course, include the private secretaries or assistants of individual Deputies. The Communist Group secretariat consists of eleven people, paid by the Party on the same scale as the Deputies who, having turned over their parliamentary salary to the party, receive the average wage of a skilled manual worker.

A fruitful field for study would be the parliamentary life of political parties. In France the spectrum ranges from the Communist Group, which is to all intents and purposes an extension of the Communist Party, to the Centrists and Independent Republicans whose parties are extensions of the Parliamentary Groups. In the former case, Group action is in conformity with Central Committee decisions, in the latter the behaviour of the group and its members is dedicated by a variety of factors: conscience, negotiation, pressure, political judgement, electoral calculation. Between the two come the Socialists and the Gaullists: each of these two acts as a disciplined Group. Each Group has tensions within it. Each has a structural relationship with the party organisation so that the policies of the party as a whole are brought to bear on group decisions. The Socialist Group designates a member of its bureau as responsible for relations between the Party and the Group, and Party statutes (Art. 37) provide for the *Comité Directeur* and the parliamentary group to discuss and vote together on important matters. If they cannot agree the *Comité Directeur* makes the decision. The rules of the UDR/RPR Group, though detailed and strict, do not contain provisions of that kind. It is true that the 'political delegate' of the movement, Yves Guéna, is a member of the Group's bureau. Nonetheless liaison with the party has a different meaning and is secured in a different way. The entire *raison d'être* of the UDR Group throughout the Fifth Republic was to give organised and disciplined support to its government. In consequence the Socialist conception of a liaison between party and group is replaced by a liaison between group and government. In every government there is a 'minister responsible for relations with Parliament', and while Gaullism reigned supreme it was his job and that of his cabinet to devote themselves to keeping the UDR Group happy and in full support of government policy, and to ensure that no one was tempted to rock the boat by intemperate parliamentary questions (not allowed under Group rules) or speeches. The August 1976 government changes presented the UDR Group with an identity crisis. Throughout the Fifth Republic it had been *the* ministerial party. In 1974 Gaullism lost the Presidency of the Republic but it conserved prime ministerial office, till in 1976 it lost that too. Keeping the new RPR Group contented and loyal is going to be much more difficult; in consequence it has been seen fit to ensure that the Minister for Relations with Parliament remains a Gaullist.[3]

In summary, there are two important variables that determine the character and actions of Parliamentary Groups in the National Assembly. One is the government or opposition role of the Group. The second is the nature of the party itself. A party with a Leninist view of its function as vanguard of the proletariat assigns to its parliamentary group a very different role from that of a group of Centrist notables who take a Burkean view of party as a loose collection of like-minded individuals.

## 3. *Parliamentary candidatures*

In Great Britain, where the local connections of a candidate and local issues count for little in general elections, the parliamentary candidates are locally designated with very little control from party headquarters. A list of approved hopefuls, a little advice or pressure (usually counter-productive in the case of the Labour Party), ratification of the local branch's choice: these represent the limits of central involvement. Candidate selection is a local affair. In France, where local connections are of great importance and 'parachuted' candidates usually fail, party headquarters play the preponderant role in candidate selection.

Of course local considerations are given great weight. The views of local activists are sought and the absolute importance of local connections for a good candidate is fully understood. The reasons why party headquarters play so great a role are perfectly simple. The first and most important is that the party system is bipolar but not two-party. Both *Majorité* and opposition are composed of coalitions and alliances, and electoral strategy has to be worked out jointly. The *Majorité* has the very delicate task of deciding in the case of each constituency whether just one of the *Majorité* parties—RPR, CDS, or RI for example—should present a candidate, or whether several should be allowed to take part in a 'primary'. If a single candidate is to be presented, from which party should he come? Should the outgoing member of Parliament have a prescriptive right to unchallenged re-adoption? All this requires lengthy negotiation and liaison. In 1976 liaison committees at party, general-secretary, and ministerial levels worked at this task. The major questions of electoral strategy, the approach of the *Majorité* to 'primaries', and the difficult constituency cases were to be dealt with in 1976 by the top government 'Troika'— Olivier Guichard (RPR, and designated, in succession to Jacques Chirac, as 'Coordinator of the *Majorité'*), Michel Poniatowski (RI) and Jean Lecanuet (CDS). Also associated were Michel Durafour (Rad), regarded as the main spokesman for the Centre Left. The Prime Minister Raymond Barre and, above all, the President of the Republic himself would be directing the general orientation of strategy.

On the opposition side things are somewhat different. The Communist Party presents a candidate everywhere. Local sections are closely consulted on candidatures but the Party decides on the basis of Federal recommendations to Central Committee. Within the *Union de la Gauche* the Socialists and MRG have their own alliance. They work out together which constituencies shall have a Radical and which a Socialist candidate. Fighting under a common banner (in 1973 it was UGSD—Union of the Socialist and Democratic Left), they do not compete with each other. In 1973 only 10% of constituencies were allocated to MRG Radicals, normally cases where a Radical candidate or tradition is deeply entrenched. As far as actually selecting candidates the Socialist Party is the most 'British' of French political parties. The Party membership in the constituency, subject to certain constraints and to ratification, selects its candidate. If party membership is less than 1 in 500 of the constituency electorate (that is, in an average constituency, there are less than 100 members) the National Convention consults the local members and selects the candidate. This is an excellent means of ensuring that good candidates are presented in areas where the party is weak and needs to make a breakthrough.

This Socialist practice illustrates the second reason why party headquarters play a greater role in France than in Great Britain as far as candidate selection is concerned. A major activity of many parties is, as we have seen, looking for good prospective candidates. The Independent Republicans and the CDS devote considerable efforts to this end. Parties are not the sole route to power in France as they are in Great Britain. Non-party figures can be influential in local and national government. The Prime Minister M. Barre is an excellent case in point. The UDR and the FGDS a few years ago, the RI, the CDS, and the Radicals now, the Socialists too where they are weak, spend muchtime looking for influential or dynamic local figures likely to be sympathetic to their aims and willing to be party parliamentary candidates and local leaders.

## 2. *Presidential candidatures*[4]

It is odd that in a country where presidential elections have become the most important political event and the Presidency the dominant political office political parties have so little role to play in designating candidates for that office. It is particularly strange because the kind of organised support that a party can give is a critical factor in the success of a presidential candidature. Pompidou in 1969 and Giscard d' Estaing (at the second ballot at any rate) in 1974 had the organised support of the UDR, Mitterrand in 1974 that of the PCF and the Socialist Party. Yet declarations of candidature are, for the most part, individual acts. MM. Pompidou and Chaban-Delmas in 1969 and 1974 respectively declared themselves candidates and then obtained endorsement by the UDR. Giscard d'Estaing in 1974 was not the 'Independent Republican candidate'. Mitterrand, in conformity with Socialist Party statutes, was designated a candidate by a special Party congress. The decision, however, had effectively been taken. Discussions had taken place with the Communists to secure their support, which was granted on condition that Mitterrand stood as the common candidate of the Left not just of the PS, and no other candidate was placed in nomination at the Socialist Congress. The Congress was thus merely the first election rally.

This is in stark contrast to the tremendous primary campaigns and nominating conventions of the United States, where the rank and file registered party member can play a part in candidate designation. In fact the primary campaign is a more gruelling test of a candidate's appeal, capacity, and endurance than the presidential election itself. Parties in the United States are far less cohesive and organised at national level than the big European parties, including the French. Yet it would be inconceivable for an American party merely to ratify a self-declared candidature for the supreme political office.

## NOTES

1. *Report of the Committee on Financial Aid to Political Parties* (Houghton Report), Cmnd. 6601, 1976.
2. *Report of the Committee on the Civil Service 1966–8* (Fulton Report), Cmnd. 3638, 1968.
3. He is Christian Poncelet.
4. For a historical perspective see Roy Pierce 'Presidential selection in France: the historical background', in H. R. Penniman, ed., *France at the Polls,* pp. 1–40. Washington: American Enterprise Institute of Policy Research, 1975.

# 11

## ELECTIONS IN THE FIFTH REPUBLIC— INTERPRETATION

The next section of this book deals with elections in the Fifth Republic. It will examine, firstly, the general characteristics of the system of voting in France and how French elections can be understood and interpreted. Chapters will then follow on presidential, parliamentary, and local elections and referenda. These will deal with the particularities of each, the results of the important elections in the Fifth Republic, a brief comment on the political context and significance of each electoral test. Electoral behaviour will constitute a final part of this section.

### 1. The electoral system—general characteristics

(a) Voting in France. All persons over eighteen have the right to vote if they are French by birth (or naturalised for five years), not declared officially to be mad,[1] or bankrupt. Men over twenty-one have had the vote since 1848, women were accorded the right to vote in 1944. Young people between eighteen and twenty-one received the vote as one of President Giscard d'Estaing's first reforms in 1974. Electors register in the commune where they live, on a list annually revised. Voting in France is not compulsory. As far as the secrecy of the vote is concerned, the French are better protected than the British. In France the elector in the polling booth puts his ballot paper in an envelope which he then places in the ballot box. In Great Britain the papers are simply folded and the curious practice exists of issuing to the elector a ballot paper with his electoral register number on the back. This is done so that allegations of fraud or disputed elections can be investigated. It should perhaps be added as a cultural parenthesis that the British, more than most other people, have no particular wish to conceal their electoral choice. They do not go quite as far as the Americans, who in many states publicly register as Democrats or Republicans, but, unlike the French, the British will usually (though perhaps not always truthfully) tell door-to-door canvassers from political parties how they intend to·vote and even put up posters in their windows. That type of campaigning would be unacceptable in France.

There is one potential threat to secrecy in France.[2] How a voter voted cannot be discovered, but unlike in Great Britain, whether or not he went to vote can be. The electoral register showing who voted and who did not is available for public inspection after each election, again to assist in the detection of fraud. Each polling station's list is also available during the vote, and party representatives can see who has been to vote and who has not. Thus when the Communist Party, in the second ballot of the 1969 presidential election, advised its supporters to abstain, it was in a position to some extent to monitor their response. Furthermore, when an elector goes to vote he is supposed to produce his electoral registration card (in small towns and villages it is not compulsory, and even in large towns an identity card will do), which is stamped when he has voted. Consequently in 1969 the holder of an unstamped *carte d'électeur* might be thought to be a Communist.

The French method of voting by placing in an envelope a paper printed with the name of the candidate the elector supports is far less confusing than American or British methods. In America the confusion results from the large number of offices, national, state, and local to be filled by electoral choice at the same time. The elector can be faced by a voting machine and a bewildering number of choices—which, incidentally, can usually be resolved by voting 'straight Democrat' or 'straight Republican' where a single lever directs the machine to record one vote for every candidate of the party the elector preferes. In Great Britain the electoral arrangements seem designed to make voting difficult for the ignorant or ill-informed. The elector has to rely almost exclusively on political parties for information about the election. The only official information about candidates is provided by posters, printed in bureaucratic language and in small type, on official sites. Worse still, most British electors, because they understand their system of government, prefer to vote for a party rather than a candidate; but up to 1969 this useful information was totally absent from the ballot papers. Party affiliation can now be discerned in small print by the patient reader: it is called 'description' and follows the candidate's home address. When the elector has finally worked out who is the candidate of the party he wishes to support, he consummates his choice by making a mark that in England normally signifies rejection or error: X.

There are three other admirable characteristics of the French system of voting. First, the elector is given a great deal of information about the election by the public authorities. A declaration by each candidate and sample ballot papers are sent to each registered elector for all elections, local and national. Candidates and parties normally pay nothing, except, as we shall see, the *'fantaisiste'* candidates who in national elections fail to reach 5% of the vote. Secondly, if the elector finds no candidate for whom he wishes to vote, he can go along and cast a positive abstention. The figures for *blancs et nuls* (blank or spoilt papers) are separately listed. The Trotskyist candidate for the Presidency of the Republic in 1969, advised his supporters on the second ballot, from which he had been eliminated, to vote with a blank red card. In Britain the people who write on their ballot paper 'There is no honest man to vote for' end up in the same statistical heap as those who went fishing or stayed at home watching TV. The spoilt papers are eliminated when arriving at a total figure for electoral turnout. In France, turnout includes those who have taken the trouble to go and vote but have spoiled their papers.

Finally there is the counting of votes. In England the operation is enfolded in bureaucratic importance. Only a few 'agents' are admitted after annoying formalities, and judicial declarations of secrecy; the public is definitely excluded. In France the count is carried out by the public and not by officials. The president of each polling station is an ordinary citizen, one of whose tasks during the day is to recruit twenty or so volunteers from among the voters to help him with the count. Quite a crowd will have gathered when the poll closes and the votes are counted, then and there, by these recruited volunteers with the public around them, not by officials in some central city hall.[3] The whole thing is open to the general public; indeed the more members of the public there are, the more legitimate the exercise, the more likely it is that fair play will be ensured, the more the ethos of popular participation in the democratic process is perpetuated. What about security? No doubt it would be slightly easier in France to drop, unseen, a lighted cigarette end into a pile of ballot papers, but not much. In Corsica, it is true, electoral fraud is a highly developed industry which local counting assists. Ballot boxes are occasionally stolen and hurled into the sea. But it is the vast and fraudulent postal vote that plays the most prominent part in Corsican politics, leading, for example, to the annulment by the constitutional council of the election in 1967 of Faggianelli, the Gaullist Deputy for Bastia. For the 1973 National Assembly elections, the authorities began to introduce in Corsica some fraud-proof voting machines. Unfortunately they were thwarted by the sudden presence of twenty-eight independent candidates in Ajaccio and forty-three in Bastia—more candidatures than the machines were designed to handle![4] The authorities were also astonished in the 1973 election to receive the official voting returns from the tiny village of San Damiano (Bastia constituency). Its registered electorate of 165 had suddenly grown to 6,122 and the Gaullist candidate, a local councillor, had received 5,998 votes. The assistant mayor of San Damiano was found in hiding by the police and suspended.

*(b) The two-ballot electoral system.* The two-ballot electoral system is a curious variant of a system widely used in other countries for

'private' elections: the system of repeated ballots. American party nominating conventions, British Labour Party candidate selection conferences, the College of Cardinals choosing a new Pope, all use repeated balloting until one candidate emerges with the support of an absolute majority. In a papal election the cardinals vote as many times as is necessary, sometimes for days or weeks on end, until a candidate who at least has the merit of dividing the Church least has succeeded in gathering an absolute majority of cardinals in his support. The successful candidate thus expresses the capacity to unite, to embody harmony, to be not necessarily the first choice of many but the final choice of most. The French variant has only two ballots (if no candidate has an absolute majority over all others at the first) and at the second the winner is the candidate who comes top whether he has an absolute majority or not. The French first used this mode of election in the Second Empire in 1852 and, oddly enough, it became the characteristic system of the Third Republic in use for all but ten of the Republic's seventy years.[5] Just as vegetarians eat nut cutlets moulded to resemble sizzling steaks, the anticlerical Republic turned nostalgically to the Papacy and the Empire for a model of its electoral system. In the Fourth Republic various crude versions of proportional representation were used,[6] but the Fifth Republic has returned to the two-ballot system.

This was in many ways a surprising choice. 'A regime, avid for innovation, contemptuous of previous parliamentary systems, exhumes the old voting method of the Radical Republic which no other country has practised since 1914.'[7] One can see its virtues for the old Third Republic—virtues which would scarcely have commended it to the austere founder of the Fifth. 'The raffish, entertaining, and degenerate France of the *Belle Epoque* with its scheming Deputies in an over-mighty Parliament had a political system whose only virtue was that it divided a divided people least. The two-ballot method expresses this admirably. The elector can vote in the first ballot for a candidate, however extreme, who takes his fancy, who comes nearest to expressing his precise point of view, who has done him a favour, who is sound on the religious question, who promises the lowest taxes and the highest agricultural prices. If no candidate wins in the first ballot, then in the second the elector can adopt a different perspective and use his vote to prevent the victory of the candidate he dislikes most: hence the formula 'at the first ballot you choose, at the second you eliminate'. Consequently, the second ballot slogans are nearly always negative: '*Barrons la route à . . .*' ('block the road to . . .') Communism, personal power (an opposition expression for Gaullism), reaction, the bad old days of the Fourth Republic, and so on. Block the road—that is exactly what the second ballot elector can do by transferring his vote to a candidate he thinks might carry the day against the one he really cannot abide. The system tends therefore, to work against extreme candidates and produce a winning candidate who divides his electors least—a sort of consensus.

The problem with the search for consensus in France in the past is that the sum of consensuses in each village or constituency, thus obtained by the single-member two-ballot election, was not the same as a national consensus. It was considered very surprising that General de Gaulle should have preferred this system for the new parliamentary elections—a prescription, one would have thought, for preserving the old Centrist local notables, the wheeler-dealers who could cook up a local consensus. Perhaps de Gaulle's well-known contempt for political parties extended to his own supporters, whom he forbade to use his name 'even as an adjective', even to the point of choosing an electoral system contrary to their own interests. Certainly the single-member constituency two-ballot system was not the choice of his advisers and supporters. Duverger has suggested[8] that de Gaulle, after the remarkable success of the Constitutional referendum in September 1958, did not want a *'chambre introuvable'*[9]—too massive and too embarrassingly enthusiastic a parliamentary majority. So the method of election chosen was a kind of 'breakwater' to check the tide of Gaullism and leave a few of the old notables intact. Furthermore such a system would enfeeble the one important anti-system extremism—the Communist Party—because the second ballot is fatal to candidates who cannot make alliances or attract support from a wide spectrum. This was how things turned out at the November 1958 elections, the first of the Fifth Republic. The Gaullists were seen as uniters not dividers, and they rallied voters from all quarters at the second ballot—though not so much as to annihilate all other groups. The Communists, on the other hand, saw their parliamentary representation all but destroyed. Their electoral support fell from 25% in 1956 to 19% in 1958 and their parliamentary strength dropped from 150 seats to 10.

## 2. *Interpretation and analysis*

The interpretation and analysis of elections in France present certain problems to Anglo-Saxons familiar with two-party politics in simple majority electoral systems.

*(a) Turnout.* Electoral participation in France is rightly and properly expressed as the percentage of registered electors who actually go to the polling stations (or who vote by post or proxy). As we have seen some of those who participate in the election cast blank or spoiled ballots. When these are deducted the total of valid voters (*suffrages exprimés*) is left. It is this figure that should be compared with countries like Great Britain which do not count

spoiled papers separately. The results of French elections are usually presented in this form:

| | |
|---|---|
| *Inscrits* | (Total number of registered electors) |
| *Votants* | (Turnout: electors who have participated) |
| *Abstentions* | (Abstainers: *inscrits* less *votants*) |
| *Blancs et nuls* | (Blank and spoiled ballots) |
| *Suffrages exprimés* | (Valid votes cast: *inscrits* less *votants* less *blancs et nuls*). |

When elections or regions where turnout has fluctuated a great deal are being compared, it is advisable to consider the percentage of the electorate (*inscrits*) which has supported a candidate or party rather than of *suffrages exprimés*. Such a comparison, for three elections where turnout varied considerably, is shown below.

Table 11.1
PRESIDENTIAL ELECTION WINNERS—
*EXPRIMES/INSCRITS*
(Metropolitan France—2nd ballot)

| | % of suffrages exprimés | % of inscrits |
|---|---|---|
| 1965 de Gaulle | 54·5 | 44·8 |
| 1969 Pompidou | 57·5 | 37·2 |
| 1974 Giscard d'Estaing | 50·7 | 44·0 |

Pompidou in 1969 gained a bigger victory in terms of his share of the votes cast but a smaller proportion of the French nation turned out to support him than his predecessor General de Gaulle or his successor Giscard d'Estaing. For most of the election results in this book, however, it will be most practical to express them as % of actual votes counted (*suffrages exprimés*).

*(b) Geography of results.* The first and most obvious requirement is a national result: to know who has won the election. The national result is derived from the second ballot over the whole of France which includes the various tropical islands and territories which form the Overseas *départements* and Overseas Territories (DOM and TOM). Every vote in a presidential election and every constituency, even in the Pacific Ocean, in a parliamentary election counts towards victory.

Most comparisons of results, however, which aim to show the trend of votes from one election to another in terms of party strengths, are confined to the ninety-five *départements* of metropolitan France. This makes sense for several reasons. First, they include nearly all the electors—at the first ballot of the 1974 presidential elections the figures were Metropolitan France 29·8 million electors, Overseas France 800,000. Secondly, Overseas France votes in a thoroughly untypical way. There is a tradition of electoral fraud and docility towards candidates in whom the local administration has confidence: it was not rare in the past to find votes of 98% or 99% for pro-government candidates.[10] During the campaign in 1974 François Mitterrand sent out a team to investigate reports of electoral pressure by tribal leaders on their followers in various territories. General de Gaulle in 1965 got over 80% of the votes in the DOM–TOM. In 1974 Chaban–Delmas, heavily defeated in Metropolitan France, came top in the Overseas Territories with 54%. Thirdly, Metropolitan France remains a constant entity but Overseas France is always changing as territories become independent. In 1958, the first election of the Fifth Republic, Algeria and the Sahara sent sixty-six Deputies to the National Assembly. In 1962, independent, they sent none. Since 1974 parts of the Comores Archipelago have become independent, other parts want closer association with France. In 1976 the independence of Djibouti (the Territory of the Afars and Issas) was under consideration. Though the results are national, the figures and comparisons given in this book will be metropolitan.

The grand totals for Metropolitan France can then be subdivided in various geographical ways to reveal patterns of support for different parties or candidates. France breaks down into twenty-two programme regions, and, to localise patterns still further, into ninety-five *départements* which are very similar in size but not in population. However one can distinguish rural *départements* from urban ones, *départements* with a Catholic tradition from those without, or *départements* traditionally voting left. The *département,* even more than the parliamentary constituency, remains in France the preferred geographical subdivision for broad analytical purposes. If this book relies more on the twenty-two regions, it is because they are sufficiently distinct for broad geographical characteristics of electoral behaviour to be discernible and yet not so numerous that they confuse the non-French student with excessive and unfamiliar detail.

Of course the way the votes are counted means that in France figures for individual polling stations are available to the public. The Americans have precinct returns for national elections. The British do not. In France much of the science of predicting election results is based on analysis of individual polling station results. The excitement of election night has been ruined in France by the capacity of computers to give an accurate prediction of the final result the very moment the last polling station closes. It works like this. Most polling stations close at 6 o'clock in the evening but some, for local reasons such as the need to work a full day on the wine harvest, remain open until 8 p.m. No comment on early results is allowed before 8 o'clock on the grounds that it might influence those electors who still have an opportunity to vote.[11] Most polling stations have finished their count by 6.30 or 6.45 p.m. though collation to obtain city or constituency totals naturally takes longer. The different radio networks receive direct information from 200 or 300 representative polling stations in different parts of the country. Computers process these results and compare them with results from the same polling stations in previous elections. The computer is able to take account of regional and other variations and calculate the national result. This is then declared on radio and television at exactly 8 o'clock before the Prefects in the ninety-five *départements,* or the mayors in large cities have even announced the official local results. Although the duel between Mitterrand and Giscard d'Estaing in 1974 was extremely close and could have provided a nail-biting spectacle lasting until the last few results were in, in fact at 8 o'clock the exact percentage each candidate finally obtained was accurately predicted. The availability of individual polling district results makes possible great refinement of analysis. One can measure abstention by type of occupation—by, for instance, comparing polling stations having an exclusively agricultural electorate with others. One can see how villages with a high percentage of church-goers differ from villages in the same locality without. One can see how the Left is performing in industrial neighbourhoods. After the British general election of 1970, at which the surprise Conservative victory gave rise to much speculation, Richard Crossman expressed the view that the result was explained by differential turnout, i.e. that many traditional Labour voters in industrial neighbourhoods had stayed at home. In France such assertions can easily be checked, but in Great Britain they cannot. Finally, results by polling station give infinite flexibility: one can combine a number of polling stations to get results for a neighbourhood, a suburb, a town, a city.

*(c)　Candidates and parties.* Changing parties and changing alliances present difficult problems for the interpretation of elections in France. In the Fifth Republic a number of new parties have appeared which often have affinities with predecessor groups but which are not really comparable, because they have either found new support or lost some of the old. The Gaullism of the UNR (subsequently UDR now RPR) is not the same as the Gaullism of the RPF. The Independent Republicans are quite different from the heterogeneous moderates and conservatives which made up the loose-knit National Centre for Independents and Peasants. The Centre Democrats are remnants of the old MRP but have long ago

lost most of the MRP leaders and most of the MRP voters to Gaullism. The new Socialist Party is more than the old SFIO writ large. The PSU is a Fifth Republic party but most of its leaders have joined the Socialists and the PSU has dwindled into a revolutionary sect. The Radicals have taken more shapes than Proteus, now in alliance with the Socialists, now not, now half-and-half.

Alliances change even more than parties. Consider, for instance, the difficulty of interpreting the change in the votes cast for opposition Centrists from 1967 to 1973:

Table 11.2

VOTES CAST FOR OPPOSITION CENTRISTS

*(Metropolitan France, 1st ballot, % of valid votes—suffrages exprimés)*

| 1967 | Centre Democrats | 13·4% |
|------|------------------|-------|
| 1968 | Centre for Progress and Modern Democracy | 10·3% |
| 1973 | Reform Movement | 13·1% |

The 1967 and 1968 results are reasonably comparable, the most important change being the group's name. By 1973 a large number of Centrist Members of Parliament, hence representing areas where Centre electoral support was strongest, had joined the *Majorité* and contested the 1973 elections under that flag. At the same time the Centrists who still wanted to remain in the opposition had joined those Radicals led by Jacques Servan-Schreiber (who did not want to associate with the *Union de la Gauche*) to form the Reform Movement, and this brought some extra support into the Centre camp. In addition one has to consider that 419 candidates were presented in 1973 against only 397 in 1967. In the 251 constituencies where the opposition Centre was present in all three elections, the results show that its setback in 1973 was greater than in 1968:

Table 11.3

DECLINE IN OPPOSITION CENTRISTS

*(Metropolitan France, first ballot, % of registered electorate—inscrits)*[12]

|  | 251 constituencies | | |
|--|------|------|------|
|  | *1967* | *1968* | *1973* |
| Centre/Reform | 14·9 | 14·2 | 12·5 |

By the same token, the alliance of the non-Communist Left—FGDS in 1967 and 1968, UGSD in 1973—has changed. The

UGSD has a far weaker Radical and far stronger Socialist composition than the FGDS. The alliance known as the *Majorité* has grown to embrace more and more of the Centre and at the next parliamentary elections will presumably include the Reform Movement, whose leaders are either members or supporters of the government.

If this does not make difficulties enough, there is in addition the propensity of individual candidates to change sides but still retain their electoral following. For instance Mlle Dienesch in Loudéac (Côtes du Nord) or Maurice Schumann (Armentières-Nord) were originally MRP but fought later elections as Gaullists. To some extent, therefore, the decline of votes for the MRP and the gain of votes for the Gaullists were composed of some electors who just went on voting for the same candidate. By doing so, however, such electors did in a way represent growing support for the government.

The constantly changing shapes of alliances, allegiances of candidates, composition of parties, all help to explain why the favourite British analytical instrument for electoral analysis— 'swing'—is so singularly inappropriate in France. The notion of national swing can be used in elections only where the two major parties have very stable electorates and around 90% of the votes, where there are no excessively wild regional fluctuations, and, above all, where the parties do not keep changing, forming different alliances, losing groups to other parties, and performing other mischievous and un-British metamorphoses.

*(d) Importance of the first ballot.* Such swing as can be measured— that is to say the percentage of gains or losses by parties or coalitions from one election to another—can be measured only at the first ballot. The first ballot is a snapshot of public opinion which can be compared with the first ballot at previous elections. The problems referred to in the paragraph above have of course to be taken into account—the *Majorité* that scored 44·7% of valid votes in 1968 is not quite the same *Majorité* that scored 36·0% in 1973. However there is some vague comparability. With second ballot results there is not—in parliamentary elections at any rate.[13] Not all constituencies vote in a second ballot, as some are decided at the first; those that do are not always the same ones, and the types of contest vary as alliances cause first ballot candidates to withdraw in favour of others. For comparisons of party strengths from election to election always use the first ballot.

*(e) 'Primaries'.* Although the French do not have primaries like the Americans, in which voters can designate the man they would like to be their party's candidate, the word has some aptness for a two-

ballot electoral system. The first ballot of the French presidential election of 1974 was, in a way, a primary to see which candidate of the *Majorité* should face Mitterrand (whose first round leadership was never in doubt) in the duel which the constitution requires the second ballot to be.[14] That primary was won by Giscard d'Estaing and lost by his former ministerial colleagues Chaban-Delmas and Royer.

The word 'primary' has however crept into the French electoral language in parliamentary elections to designate first ballot contests between candidates from the different formations of the *Majorité*. Normally the *Majorité* has preferred to designate in each constituency a single candidate, be he UDR, Independent Republican, or, in 1973, Centre for Democracy and Progress. However, competition has been permitted or has occurred in a large number of cases. There were fifty first-ballot contests between supporters of the *Majorité* in 1968 and sixty-one of these primaries in 1973. The *Union de la Gauche* has a primary in all of the 490 constituencies in the sense that there is in every case a Communist candidate and one candidate representing the Socialist-Radical UGSD. In many cases there is a PSU candidate as well. They compete for the privilege of being the sole candidate of the left in the second ballot. All withdraw in favour of the 'best-placed'.[15] Within the UGSD there are no primaries—no competitions between Socialists and Left-wing Radicals for a place in the second ballot. The UGSD designates a single candidate in each constituency.

Since the Left always has a primary, should not the *Majorité* do so too? It would, some argue, have the advantage of allowing the elector a free choice of which group in the *Majorité* he preferred, so that the group which emerged as the most important element of the government coalition would have done so as a result of genuine unimpeded popular choice. For instance, is the RPR to be allowed to retain its dominant position in the *Majorité* merely because electoral alliances protect its candidates from challenge by those who identify more closely with President Giscard d'Estaing like the Independent Republicans? Or, put another way, should *Giscardien* incumbents be protected from challenge by Chirac's energetic RPR? In addition the wider the range of first ballot choice for electors basically sympathetic to the *Majorité* the greater would be the total first ballot national score for the *Majorité*.

The first point is a normative one and is being actively debated by the parties of the *Majorité*. The last point is more open to factual analysis. Jean Charlot has worked out that at the first ballot the relative performance of the *Majorité* was 3·6 percentage points better than average in 1968 and 4·6 better than average in 1973 in the constituencies where primaries occurred. At the second ballot in these same constituences the *Majorité* failed on average to attract as many extra voters as in France as a whole—3·5 percentage points less in 1968, 4·8 less in 1973. 'The advantage gained by competition in the first ballot was more than wiped out by the second.'[16]

When comparing first-ballot election results, the number of candidates presented by a party, whether in primaries or not, needs to be considered. For instance within the setback experienced by the *Majorité* as a whole in 1973 (down by over 9 percentage points compared with 1968), it might be said that the Independent Republicans held up better than their partners. In France as a whole they declined from 8·3% of the vote in 1968 to 7·1% in 1973. However, in 1968 they had 76 candidates, in 1973 they had 116. Similarly the PSU and other groups of the extreme left had 461 candidates in 1973 against 320 in 1968 but still lost a quarter of their votes.

*(f)  The second ballot.* If the first ballot of an election is the electoral snapshot of public opinion that one uses to compare one election with another, the vote that decides the result of the election is the second ballot. The first ballot has a quality of levity about it—the vote is not decisive, the elector can indulge his fancy, however extremist, knowing that at the second ballot the damage, if any, can be undone. The second ballot is serious, and its fascination lies in the transfer of votes that occurs between the two.

No new candidate can enter at the second ballot and a number of first ballot candidates are automatically eliminated (all but the top two in a presidential, all who have failed to win the support of 12·5% of registered electors in parliamentary elections). Other candidates in parliamentary elections withdraw, often in favour of one of the others. In presidential elections the whole nation votes at the second ballot, in parliamentary elections only the constituencies undecided at the first—in Metropolitan France 398 in 1967, 316 in 1968, 424 in 1973. The turnout usually drops at the second ballot and the number of spoilt papers increases because a number of electors find the simplified choice gives them nothing they can support. In the National Assembly election of 1973 and the presidentials of 1974, however, the percentage poll was higher at the second ballot. Jean Charlot suggests a link between 'the drop in second ballot abstentions and the confrontation, seen as decisive, between two different conceptions of society'.[17] In other words the real possibility of a Left wing victory mobilises the electorate, particularly those who oppose such an outcome.

The tactical and analytical problems of the second ballot can be illustrated by a close result from the Rhone-Alps Region in the 1973 parliamentary elections:

Table 11.4
EXAMPLE—SECOND BALLOT: 1973
*Drôme 1st constituency (Valence)*

|  | 1st ballot | | 2nd ballot | |
|---|---|---|---|---|
| Turnout (*votants*) | 60,095 | 79·0% | 63,384 | 82·4% |
| Spoilt papers (*blancs et nuls*) | 524 | | 2,891 | |
| Valid vote (*suffrages exprimés*) | 59,571 | 77·4% | 60,493 | 78·6% |
|  | | % of vote | | % of vote |
| PCF | 14,564 | 24·5% | 29,610 | 49·0% |
| Extreme Left | 1,437 | 2·4% | | |
| PS | 14,012 | 23·5% | | |
| Other Left | 10 | 0·02% | | |
| (Total Left) | (30,023) | (50·4%) | | |
| Reform/Centre Democrats | 9,464 | 15·9% | | |
| UDR | 20,084 | 33·7% | 30,883 | 51·0% |
| (Total Centre + *Majorité*) | (29,548) | (49·6%) | | |

No candidate had an overall majority of valid votes (29,786) so there was a second ballot. The fringe candidates of the left were automatically eliminated. The Socialist candidate, in conformity with the electoral alliance of the *Union de la Gauche,* withdrew in favour of the Communist candidate who marginally defeated him in the first ballot. The Centre Democrats, who in 1973 were still an opposition party, were in a tactical position of some significance. If their candidate remained in the contest at the second ballot he would be denying vital anti-Communist votes to the *Majorité.* If he withdrew he would be helping to ensure the survival in power of a government his party opposed. He withdrew. On paper the combined forces of the Left had enough first ballot votes—just—to win the seat. However it is an oversimplification to suppose that the second ballot total for the Communist candidate represents all the first ballot votes for the Left less 400 electors who fell by the wayside (perhaps spoiling their papers). Equally it is too simple to say that the UDR success at the second ballot is due to a solid vote from his own and the Centre Democrat's first ballot supporters with the addition of some 1,300 electors who had abstained at the first ballot. Research has shown that behaviour varies considerably between ballots: 'crude figures often hide multiple and reciprocal transfers which thus pass unnoticed'.[18] A candidate's second ballot score is made up of fractions of the votes of each first ballot candidate and a fraction of first ballot abstainers. Espositio and Gaillac, in the article just cited, have demonstrated this by a complex linear regression analysis of a large number of constituencies. This method applied to the 139 constituencies (of which Drôme-Valence is one) where the second ballot in 1973 was a duel between the *Majorité* and the Communist Party, finds that on *average* the following movements shown in Table 11.5 occurred.

Table 11.5

TRANSFER OF VOTES: 1

*(139 Majorité—PCF second ballot duels 1973)*[19]

| 1st ballot votes for: | Transferred at 2nd ballot to: | | |
|---|---|---|---|
| | PCF | Majorité | Abstention/ spoilt votes |
| PCF | 89 | 11 | 0 |
| Non-Communist Left | 56 | 31 | 13 |
| Centre | 25 | 62 | 13 |
| *Majorité* | 12 | 84 | 4 |
| Abstention/spoilt votes | 9 | 8 | 83 |

It seems that, in this type of contest in 1973, most (though not all) Communist voters, *Majorité* voters, and abstentions went on to do the same at the second ballot. Socialists and Centrists are less homogeneous. One Socialist voter in three switches to support the pro-government candidate. One Centrist in four gives his second ballot vote to the Communist Party. If one refines the analysis still further to the 100 *Majorité–PCF* duels where Socialists not Centrists had come third, one finds that more centrists abstained rather than support the government.

In close contests like Drôme-Valence it is probably true that the Left would have picked up those few extra votes if their second ballot candidate had not been a Communist. The linear regression analysis suggests that this is not because, as in popularly supposed, Centrist voters are more willing to support a Socialist than a Communist in the second ballot but because the Socialist reluctance to vote Communist is removed:

Table 11.2
TRANSFER OF VOTES: 2
*(166 Majorité—Non-Communist Left second ballot duels—1973)*[20]

| 1st ballot votes for: | Transferred at 2nd ballot to: | | |
|---|---|---|---|
| | Non-Communist Left | Majorité | Abstention/ spoilt votes |
| PCF | 83 | 11 | 6 |
| Non-Communist Left | 85 | 11 | 4 |
| Centre | 22 | 65 | 13 |
| *Majorité* | 9 | 91 | 0 |
| Abstention/spoilt votes | 15 | 9 | 76 |

Apparently the voters of the Communist Party and the *Majorité* remained equally disciplined whatever the character of the second ballot duel. First ballot abstainers seemed a little more willing to turnout for a Socialist at the second ballot.

Not all second ballot contests are duels. In 1973 there were sixty-four three-cornered contests between the Left, the *Majorité*, and the Centre. In twenty-one of these there was a Communist candidate and in the other forty-three a candidate of the non-Communist Left.

Although it is in general the first ballot that should be used for assessing gains and losses in support for the different parties from one election to another, the more politics in France becomes polarised between the *Union de la Gauche* and the *Majorité* the more one can use second ballot Left-*Majorité* duels for purposes of comparison. Although one must bear in mind that Mitterrand's second ballot score in 1965 included a lot of anti-Gaullist votes from the Centre and even the extreme-Right, comparison of second ballot scores in the 1965 and 1974 presidential duels between the *Majorité* and the Left is revealing. In the next chapter, Table 12.6 showing parts of France that went the same way at both election and the *départements* 'gained' by M. Mitterrand, clearly demonstrate the progress of the Left in industrial areas of the north and east.

One can do the same with cities or constituencies. The comparison of appropriate Left-*Majorité* duels is revealing. Consider, for example, recent results of duels in the town of Reims:

EXAMPLE—SECOND BALLOT DUELS: COMPARISON
*Reims (Marne)—2nd Ballot*
*(% of valid votes—suffrages exprimés)*

|  | Parliamentary | | | Presidential | |
|---|---|---|---|---|---|
|  | *1967* | *1968* | *1973* | *1974* | |
| *Majorité* | 56 | ★ | 57 | Giscard d'Estaing | 47 |
| Left | 44 | ★ | 43 | Mitterrand | 53 |

★No second ballot. *Majorité* won both Reims constituencies at the first ballot with 55% of all votes cast.

For second ballot comparisons, it is advisable to proceed with care, to compare like with like, and to consider duels only.

## NOTES

1. Code Civil art. 489, refers to '*interdits judiciaires*' who are in an '*état habituel de démence, d'imbécilité, ou de fureur*'.
2. Counting by polling station is a threat to secrecy in the case of tiny villages. One polling station has only four electors. To preserve confidentiality all four always turn out but always cast blank ballots.
3. This means, incidentally, that, as in America but not England, researchers have at their disposal figures for individual polling districts (see page 181).
4. In the election the 43 'independent' candidates in Bastia only managed a joint total score of 22 votes. In Ajaccio the 28 got 175.
5. For a further six years in the 1870s and 1880s a two ballot system with multi-member and not single-member constituencies was used. See Peter Campbell, *French Electoral Systems and Elections since 1789*, Faber, 1958.
6. See Appendix VI.
7. M. Duverger in *Association Française des Sciences Politiques: 'L'etablissement de la Vème République: Le Référendum de Séptembre et les elections de Novembre 1958'*, Paris: Colin, 1960, p. 221.
8. Ibid., p. 226.
9. The original *Chambre Introuvable* was the excessively royalist assembly of 1815 which out of 402 members, contained 350 ultras, rabid royalists who wanted a purge, discriminatory laws, and the re-establishment of aristocratic privileges.
10. See 'L'élection présidentielle de mai 1974', *Le Monde—Dossiers et Documents* 1974, p. 110.

11. One sometimes hears this argument used in the United States, where, because of the differences in time zones, Californians still have hours in which to vote while results from the East Coast are being declared.
12. Charlot, ed., *Quand la Gauche peut gagner*, p. 96.
13. There is some valid comparability between the second ballot presidential duels of de Gaulle–Mitterrand in 1965 and Giscard d'Estaing–Mitterand in 1974, (see p. 204).
14. See p. 193.
15. Nowadays this invariably means the one with the most first-ballot votes. There were, however, instances in 1967 where a Socialist candidate, who did less well than the Communist at the first ballot, was nonetheless deemed to be best-placed to win over crucial middle-of-the-road votes in a close run second ballot.
16. Charlot, *Quand la Gauche peut gagner*, p. 140.
17. *Ibid.*, p. 129.
18. Emile Espositio and Jean-Paul Gaillac, 'Les inconnues du second tour', in Charlot (ed.), *Quand la Gauche peut gagner*, p.167.
19. Source: Espositio and Gaillac *ibid.*, p. 169. For the mathematics of this method of analysis see pp. 211–14.
20. *Ibid.*, p. 169.

# 12

## PRESIDENTIAL ELECTIONS IN THE FIFTH REPUBLIC

Presidential elections by direct universal suffrage have become the most important in the Fifth Republic—in terms of deciding the configuration of power and in terms of public involvement and interest. However, they were not part of the original conception of the Fifth Republic and were introduced as a constitutional amendment adopted by referendum in October 1962. Many have argued that the amendment was adopted unconstitutionally[1] because Article 89 specifies that Parliament has to agree constitutional changes before they are submitted to the people. However, the change was adopted by referendum, and it has legitimised itself as there is now an utterly overwhelming majority of people who prefer the direct popular choice of the President.[2] It is a change, of course, which has greatly altered the power of the Presidency which can now claim, as the direct expression of the popular will, a role as head of the executive that the constitution confers somewhat ambiguously.

The system of direct presidential elections began in 1965, when General de Gaulle's first seven-year term expired. The General's original election as President in 1958 had taken place in the manner originally inscribed in the Fifth Republic Constitution, a manner which followed closely the constitutional doctrine of General de Gaulle as outlined in his famous speech at Bayeux in 1946. The President of the Republic should be chosen by an 'electoral college which includes Parliament but is much wider than Parliament'. Thus it was. The 1958 electoral college consisted of all members of both houses of Parliament, *Conseillers Généraux (Département Councillors)*, representatives of overseas territories, and a number of delegates from municipalities determined by size of commune and chosen by the municipal council. The one 'indirect suffrage' presidential election of 24 December 1958 produced the result: shown in Table 12.1

Table 12.1

*Presidential election (indirect suffrage), 1958*

| | | |
|---|---|---|
| Registered electors | 81,761 | |
| Votes cast | 79,470 | |
| General de Gaulle | 62,394 | (78·5%) |
| M. Marrane (Communist) | 10,534 | (13·1%) |
| M. Chatelet (Union of Democratic Forces) | 6,722 | (8·4%) |

The constitutional amendment of 1962 has ensured that the successors of General de Gaulle possess an authority which in normal circumstances a President chosen by 80,000 local notables could not expect. There are examples of directly elected Presidents fulfilling an honorific not a leadership role—in Austria or the Irish Republic for instance—but in France, the prestige of the office, its central position in the institutions of the Fifth Republic, and the further deliberately added lustre of direct elections make it inconceivable that Presidents of the Fifth Republic will, as in the two previous Republics, 'be content with opening flower-shows'.[3] The election of the President by direct universal suffrage, introduced by the constitutional amendment of October 1962, operates in the manner described below. It is a two-ballot election, with the second ballot to be a run-off between two candidates only. The election must, according to Article 7 of the constitution, take place not less than twenty and not more than thirty-five days after the expiry of the existing President's term of office or after a vacancy caused by his resignation or death. For this brief interval between a President's resignation or death and the election of a new President, the President of the Senate becomes temporary Head of State. Senator Alain Poher has had to do this twice: in 1969 after the resignation of General de Gaulle, and in 1974 after the death of President Pompidou.

Any citizen can be a candidate for the Presidency—in 1974 it seemed as though most were. All the would-be candidate needs is a deposit of 10.000 Fr. and 100 signatures gathered from mayors, Departmental councillors, or members of Parliament, located in at least ten *départements*. Nominations are presented to the Constitutional Council, which presides over the running of the election, eventually declares the result and repays the 10.000 Fr. deposit to all candidates who obtain at least 5% of the votes cast. Nominations close eighteen days before the first ballot. After the 1974 election in which there were twelve candidates, including two Trotskyists, two European Federalists and a Royalist, there was a suggestion from the new President that constitutional reforms would be proposed which would make it much more difficult to be a *'fantaisiste'* candidate (with equal rights to free radio and television time as the 'genuine' candidates) and thus restore to presidential elections their full solemnity and dignity.

A considerable amount of assistance with candidates' election expenses is provided by the state. This admirable French practice, applicable to all elections not just presidentials, contrasts with the British practice of imposing a legal limit on a candidate's right to spend his own money or gifts, and the old American private enterprise approach where if you were not a millionaire or supported by one, you did not need to trouble running for office.

In addition to the declaration by each candidate, printed and delivered to every elector at public expense, the French state also pays for and puts up official posters setting out each candidate's declaration and, in presidential elections, the posters announcing his public meetings and election broadcasts. Thereafter each candidate can spend as much as he likes or his backers will provide and the state will refund 100,000 Fr. to each candidate who obtains 5% of votes cast.

Like Great Britain, but unlike the United States, France has no television commercials paid for by candidates. Instead each candidate has an equal free allocation of broadcasting time on radio and television, which he can use personally or share with his party or other supporters. Thus in 1969, the Socialist candidate Gaston Defferre used to appear on television with the man he intended, if victorious, to appoint as Prime Minister, Pierre Mendès-France. By the same token in the 1974 elections one of the Trotskyist candidates Arlette Laguiller used to introduce revolutionary printing workers to the intrigued viewers. The principle of equal broadcasting time is rigorously respected at presidential elections—unlike at referenda, where supporters of 'oui' and 'non' have not always enjoyed equality. In both 1969 and 1974 the Trotskyist Alain Krivine was a presidential candidate. In 1969 he was doing his military service; nevertheless Infantryman Second Class Krivine A., representing a proscribed student revolutionary movement, was able to address the nation on the need for armed revolt for a stupefying one hour and forty minutes of free television and radio time which, like all the other candidates, he had been accorded—surely a unique instance in the annals of free speech.

To be elected at the first ballot a candidate needs an absolute majority of votes cast (at least 50% + 1). If this does not occur, a second ballot is held a fortnight later—voting takes place on a Sunday, as always in France. As in other elections for public office in the Fifth Republic, no new candidate may enter the contest after the first ballot. But unlike other elections, the constitution (Art. 7) lays down that there shall, in a presidential election, be only two candidates in the second ballot. This ensures that the President of the Republic will be the final choice of an absolute majority of those voting. The rule is that the only candidates allowed at the second ballot are the two who had most votes at the first ballot. If either, for some reason, prefers to withdraw, then it is the candidate with the next highest first ballot score who would contest the second ballot. At all events the second ballot is a run-off between two, and only two, candidates. In America the successful presidential candidate has to carry a majority of states, or at least the most populous ones with a majority of electoral votes, and he could conceivably win without an absolute popular majority. Nothing analogous to this happens in France: each elector's vote counts towards one national total.

The President of the Republic is elected for seven years. President Pompidou was intending a change to five years to bring the term of office into line with that of the National Assembly. The idea was not that presidential and parliamentary elections should take place together (impossible when the power to dissolve Parliament exists), but that the presidential mandate should always be fresh enough to withstand the threat to presidential legitimacy that would arise if a parliamentary election late in a President's term returned an Assembly majority which was in opposition to the President. The shorter term would thus strengthen the President's authority. There have so far been three presidential elections by direct universal suffrage: 5 and 19 December 1965, and 1 and 15 June 1969, 5 and 19 May 1974.

## 1. *The presidential election of 5 and 19 December 1965*
The 1965 presidential election aroused great public interest, and has been much analysed. It was the first 'television election' in the sense that ownership of sets was sufficiently widespread for the whole nation to participate in a national political event, and also in the sense that the public, thanks to the provision of equal time on the air, got the chance to have a good look at the opposition to de Gaulle. What the issues were, and the incidents of the campaign, are not important at this distance in time: the enduring interest centres on three things. It marked the turning-point from 'personal' Gaullism to the development of Gaullism as an organised party machine. It marked the first relative success for the *Union de la Gauche* concept of a single candidate to represent all the Left, and the making of François Mitterrand as a national figure. It revealed, thirdly, in the candidature of Jean Lecanuet, the probable limits of centrist attempts to oppose both Gaullism and the Left. Four years later, in the unusual circumstances of 1969, a Centrist candidate Alain Poher was to obtain more votes than Lecanuet's 1965 total. In 1974 Giscard d'Estaing presented his candidature, backed by Lecanuet, as Centrist, but the anti-Gaullism of the Finance Minister who had served the General and President Pompidou was one of nuance rather than fundamental principle. The Lecanuet candidature seems to represent the Fifth Republic limits of an anti-Gaullist anti-*Union de la Gauche* movement.

The main issue of the campaign was General de Gaulle himself. Despite his immense prestige he was vulnerable in terms of his age (seventy-five), the 'contemptuous impression'[4] given by the apparent haughtiness of his candidature at the outset, and his foreign policy—most notably European policy. This was the period of the 'empty chair' when France simply refused to take part in European Community decision-making for several months until the other countries had agreed to drop demands for decisions to be based on majority voting, not unanimity. Opposed to General de Gaulle were a *fantaisiste* candidate (Barbu), a Senator with no party backing (Marcilhacy), a right-wing lawyer (Maître Tixier-Vignancour) who campaigned against de Gaulle's 'treachery' in selling-out French Algeria, Jean Lecanuet, president of the MRP and mayor of Rouen, and François Mitterrand. The latter obtained the support of the Socialist Party (SFIO) and the Radicals, who grouped together to form the Federation of the Democratic and Socialist Left (FGDS—see chapter 6), and the Communist Party. He was thus the 'sole candidate of the left'. Both Mitterrand and Lecanuet presented their candidatures as representing a first step toward the creation of a new political movement. The creation of the *Centre Démocrate* and the alliance six years later in 1971 of its persistent anti-Gaullist elements with Servan-Screiber's Radicals to form the *Mouvement Réformateur* (Reform Movement) was the outcome of Lecanuet's pledge. The FGDS, and six years later the creation of the new Socialist Party under Mitterand's leadership and the building of the *Union de la Gauche* with its joint programme of government agreed with the Communist Party—these were the ultimate developments of the Mitterrand candidature in 1965.

De Gaulle failed to win outright at the first ballot and this was regarded as something of a shock. His 10·4 million votes were almost 2 million less than the total of those voting Yes at the October 1962 referendum on direct presidential elections. Frank Wilson considers this as the decisive moment when the Prime Minister, Georges Pompidou, seeing the need for organisation to supplement the waning of charismatic authority, turned himself into a party manager to direct the second ballot campaign and subsequent parliamentary elections.[5] One must not exaggerate the de Gaulle 'failure'. He received more votes than the supporters of the Gaullist UNR party at the parliamentary elections of November 1962. He obtained a first ballot overall majority in thirteen *départements,* nearly all in Eastern France or Brittany and Normandy.[6] Moreover he polled very well in working-class industrial districts in northern cities like Lille and Communist suburbs of the Paris 'red belt' like Nanterre and Montreuil. Mitterrand found most of his strength in the southern half of the country where his first ballot score exceeded the General's in twenty *départements*. His total of 7·7 million (32·2%) was still 3·5 million less than the combined parties of the left had obtained in the last parliamentary election of the Fourth Republic. A very large number of traditional Left-wing supporters clearly preferred General de Gaulle as President. The Lecanuet vote was concentrated in the old rural Catholic strongholds of the MRP, particularly in the west of France. This was support that would probably have gone to de Gaulle in the first ballot, but, having prevented his first ballot re-election, two-thirds of it transferred to him at the second.[7] Maître Tixier-Vignancour polled fairly strongly among the white families, mainly on the South coast, who had been resettled in France after independence made them leave Algeria, but he got nowhere near the total of 1·8 million votes cast against Algerian independence in the referendum of April 1962.

Table 12.2
PRESIDENTIAL ELECTION 1965
*(Results—Metropolitan France only)*

|  | First ballot (5 Dec.) | | Second ballot (19 Dec.) | |
|---|---|---|---|---|
| Electorate *(inscrits)* | 28·2 m | | 28·2 m | |
| Abstentions | 15·0 % | | 15·5 % | |
| Spoilt papers *(blancs et nuls)* | 0·2 % | | 0·7 % | |
|  | Million Votes | % of Vote | Million Votes | % of Vote |
| De Gaulle | 10·4 | 43·7 | 12·6 | 54·5 |
| Mitterrand | 7·7 | 32·2 | 10·6 | 45·5 |
| Lecanuet | 3·8 | 15·8 | | |
| Tixier-Vignancour | 1·3 | 5·3 | | |
| Marcilhacy | 0·4 | 1·7 | | |
| Barbu | 0·3 | 1·2 | | |

The electoral turnout, 85%, was very high. The only vote in French electoral history that had attracted similar public interest was the 1958 referendum which consecrated the return to power of General de Gaulle and inaugurated the Fifth Republic.[8] One final comment on the 1965 vote is to note the General's success in the overseas territories (the results of which do not appear in Table 12·2). Of the half million overseas electors who voted, about 450,000 voted for de Gaulle at each ballot. This gives a final score at the second ballot of:

| de Gaulle | 13·1 million votes—55·2% |
|---|---|
| Mitterrand | 10·6 million votes—44·8% |

## 2. The presidential election of 1 and 15 June 1969

Of the three presidential elections that have taken place by universal suffrage in the Fifth Republic, the one in 1969 is the most peculiar. It took place in the strange circumstances of General de Gaulle's abrupt resignation .at midnight on 28 April after his proposed reform of the Senate and the Regions had been defeated by referendum. The opposition forces were completely disunited. Chapter 6 described how the great upheaval known as the Events of May 1968 and then the Soviet invasion of Czechoslovakia in August 1968 had reopened all the old hostility and mistrust between the Communist and non-Communist Left. The election defeat for the Left in 1968 had been very heavy. The FGDS which grouped Radicals and Socialists had collapsed.

There are two points to retain from the 1969 election. The first is the smooth transition from de Gaulle's leadership to that of a less heroic figure. The prophecies of chaos were completely unfounded. The Gaullist electorate did not disintegrate. It remained cohesive and elected Georges Pompidou. The second is that, although presidential candidates like to appear 'above party', party organisation is critically important in a presidential election. The role of the UDR party in this smooth transition from heroic Gaullism was of capital importance.

Georges Pompidou campaigned on the admirably clear slogan '*continuité et ouverture*': continuity of the stability and achievements of the Fifth Republic, and an opening towards a more liberal approach in civil liberties, in European policy and so on. By this means the valuable support of Giscard d'Estaing and the Independent Republicans (which had been denied to the General in the April referendum) was secured, as well as that of some opposition Centrists (though not M. Lecanuet) and the future presidential *Majorité* was widened.[9] His principle opponent turned out to be the President of the Senate Alain Poher. Poher, a Centrist of MRP background, had played a big part in the campaign to defeat the April referendum which had .proposed the virtual abolition of his beloved Senate. The public had rather taken to this amiable figure, fumbling with his notes on television and putting on his glasses to read them better. It was an agreeable and reassuring contrast to the olympian General. After the resignation of de Gaulle, Poher, in conformity with Article 7 of the constitution, became the temporary President of the Republic.[10] Early opinion polls placed him in a favourable position to win: 4% behind Pompidou at the first, and 12% ahead at the second ballot.

The Left in complete disarray had four candidates. The romantic revolutionary Left was represented by Michel Rocard (PSU) and Alain Krivine, who had been active, indeed arrested, in the student revolt of May 1968. The Socialist Party after much dissension agreed to the candidature of Gaston Defferre, mayor of Marseille. No one believed the Communist Party would present a candidate. It was supposed that electors who are quite happy to vote for a hard-working Communist mayor or Member of Parliament would not want a Communist President, and that the extent of their supporters' commitment to the Party would be derisorily revealed for what it was. The PCF did present a candidate, their jovial elder statesman Senator Jacques Duclos, and fought a well-organised and rather successful campaign. Finally there was the *fantaisiste* candidature of M. Ducatel.

According to R. G. Schwartzenburg the results in 1969 proved that three elements are essential to success in a presidential campaign—party support, credibility of policies, and credibility of the candidate.[11] The candidature of Alain Poher, whose star steadily declined as time went on, lacked all these elements. He and Gaston Deferre were extremely vulnerable to the charge that they would have no ministerial team which could command a parliamentary majority, and that they would be unable to continue strong government under presidential leadership, the essential feature of the stability of the Fifth Republic. Poher's emphasis on Gaullist abuses of power—control of television, secret police, and so on—struck a progressively less responsive chord as the campaign developed. The only two candidates to have the support of a large and efficient party organisation were Pompidou and Duclos. Duclos, completely written off at the outset, received more votes than the Communist Party in the 1968 elections and almost defeated Poher for a place in the second ballot. Pompidou polled only half a million fewer than General de Gaulle in the first ballot of 1965. There were local campaign committees for Pompidou, giving an impression of wide support from different sectors, but the organisational effort was contributed by the UDR. In the words of Jacques Duclos: 'Behind the lace curtains of the campaign committees, it was the vast machinery of the UDR party that took on the heavy work.'[12] Poher's campaign committees, by contrast, were no camouflage but all he had.

The election is difficult to analyse in terms of comparison with previous elections mainly because of the collapse of the Socialist candidature. Hardly any of the electors who normally vote Socialist or Radical voted for Defferre. A very large proportion decided to support Poher on the grounds that the main object of the election was to defeat Gaullism. Poher, it was felt, had the best opportunity of gaining wide enough second ballot support to do that. Therefore one voted Poher at the first ballot to ensure he had a place in the second. Some Socialists, on the other hand, felt the need to vote for a genuine candidate of the left in the first ballot and supported Rocard or Duclos. The total vote for the Left at 6·9 million was its worst result since the Second World War—three-quarters of a million fewer than Mitterrand on his own in 1965, 3 million fewer even than in the disastrous parliamentary elections of 1968.

Geographically Poher did best where Lecanuet had done best (Normandy and the Loire country) and in some of the old Socialist and Radical bastions of the south-west. Pompidou did not perform so well in industrial areas as General de Gaulle, but in parts of the rural centre and south he actually did better, reflecting *Majorité* gains in the 1968 parliamentary elections. Poher's second ballot vote was 4 million below the No vote in the April referendum—partly no doubt because the Communist Party advised its supporters to abstain in the second ballot. Pompidou, in the second ballot, received 2 million fewer votes than General de Gaulle in the second ballot of 1965, but about the same number as the Yes-vote in the April referendum and the combined pro-government vote in the 1968 parliamentary elections. The Communist candidate also polled his party's normal electoral score:

Table 12.3
PCF AND GAULLIST VOTES 1967–69

| PCF | | Gaullism | |
|---|---|---|---|
| | *millions* | | *millions* |
| 1967 election | 5·0 | De Gaulle 1965 | 10·4 and 12·6 |
| 1968 election | 4·4 | 1967 election | 8·5 |
| Duclos 1969 | 4·8 | 1968 election | 9·9 |
| | | Pompidou 1969 | 9·8 and 10·7 |

Table 12·4
PRESIDENTIAL ELECTION RESULTS 1969
(*Metropolitan France only*)

| | First ballot (1 June) | Second ballot (15 June) |
|---|---|---|
| Electorate (*inscrits*) | 28·8 m | 28·8 m |
| Abstentions | 21·8 % | 30·9 % |
| Spoilt papers (*blancs et nuls*) | 1·0 % | 4·5 % |

| | Million Votes | % of Vote | Million Votes | % of Vote |
|---|---|---|---|---|
| Pompidou | 9·8 | 44·0 | 10·7 | 57·6 |
| Poher | 5·2 | 23·4 | 7·9 | 42·4 |
| Duclos—PCF | 4·8 | 21·5 | | |
| Defferre—Socialist | 1·1 | 5·1 | | |
| Rocard—PSU | 0·8 | 3·7 | | |
| Ducatel | 0·3 | 1·3 | | |
| Krivine—Trotskyist | 0·2 | 1·1 | | |

The turnout, even at the first ballot, was low for a presidential election. At the second ballot, the big increase of over 2·5 million in the numbers of people not voting or spoiling their ballots was due to the advice of the PCF to its supporters. The PCF takes elections very seriously and always tries to get its supporters to participate in the vote. The 1969 second ballot is the one and only occasion when it has urged Communist electors to stay at home, and even warned that there would be Communist militants at the polling stations watching to see that they did. Pompidou must have been very grateful. Only a massive switch by Communist voters to Poher could have defeated him. It has been maliciously suggested that the Soviet Union, which preferred the continuation of Gaullist foreign policy, played a part in the PCF's decision to deny its votes to the anti-Gaullist candidate. The low second ballot turnout meant that the 10·7 million electors who finally chose Pompidou were only 37·2% of the total electorate.

## 3. *The presidential election of 5 and 19 May 1974*

The election of May 1974, provoked by the sudden death of President Pompidou on 2 April, was much more a war of succession than the 1969 contest. Pompidou, despite his dismissal as Prime Minister in June 1968, had been regarded as the natural successor to General de Gaulle. In 1974 no individual had been anointed or declared to have a 'national destiny'. The first interesting aspect of the 1974 election is therefore the emergence of a champion of the *Majorité*. The second aspect is the great success of the *Union de la Gauche* strategy uniting Socialists, Radicals and Communists behind the single candidature of François Mitterrand, who came within 400,000 votes of victory, in a poll of 26 million. The third point to retain is the immense public interest in the election—huge crowds at meetings and rallies,[13] tremendous audiences for the television coverage especially the face-to-face debates between the leading candidates, and the record voting participation of almost 90% of the electorate.

The rivalry within the ranks of the *Majorité* for the presidential crown is a very interesting story which will not be narrated in detail here.[14] The first candidate to appear, before the late President was cold in his grave, was Jacques Chaban-Delmas. An ardent Gaullist since the wartime Resistance, Mayor of Bordeaux, Prime Minister under President Pompidou from 1969 to 1972, he was endorsed by the UDR Party where orthodox Gaullists rather than Pompidou men had, since the Party conference at Nantes in November 1973, gained the upper hand. He was challenged by Valéry Giscard d'Estaing, President Pompidou's Minister of Finance, and by Edgar Faure, President of the National Assembly and a Prime Minister from the Fourth Republic. The Prime

Minister, Pierre Messmer, expressing the fears of those who thought a division in the ranks of the *Majorité* would lead to a victory of the Left, invited all to withdraw in favour of himself. Jacques Chaban-Delmas was the first to refuse. In consequence, so he said, Giscard d'Estaing retained his candidature. Edgar Faure withdrew. Pierre Messmer withdrew. Two days later another minister, Jean Royer, Mayor of Tours, champion of family life, sexual decency and the small shopkeeper, announced his candidature. His brief and ineffective campaign, never recovered from his first televised meeting when a number of exuberant and nubile students took their clothes off.

The sole significance of the Royer candidature was that it appeared to cut into the support for Chaban-Delmas, thus enabling a large gap to open in the opinion polls between him and Giscard d'Estaing. That gap never closed and Giscard, increasingly judged to have the best second ballot chance against François Mitterrand, grew ever stronger at the expense of the Mayor of Bordeaux.

There were two important pointers to the eventual success of Giscard d'Estaing in rallying an enlarged *Majorité* to his banner. The first was the support of Jean Lecanuet, candidate against de Gaulle in 1965. This was important because his party, the *Centre Démocrate,* which, together with part of the Radical Party, was a component of the Reform Movement, had been an opposition party during the Pompidou Presidency. The second was the declaration of 'the 43' on 13 April. 'The 43' were four ministers, notably Jacques Chirac, Minister of the Interior and protégé of President Pompidou, and thirty-nine members of Parliament, mostly UDR. Their declaration made it clear that a lot of influential people in the UDR, especially the new men who represented 'Pompidolism' rather than orthodox heroic Gaullism, had reservations about the Chaban-Delmas candidature. They would support, they declared, whoever appeared best placed to safeguard the fundamental principles of the Fifth Republic and defeat any 'Socialo-Communist' candidate.[15]

In policy terms Giscard d'Estaing's campaign was very similar to President Pompidou's in 1969: *'continuité et ouverture'*. He would continue the policies of the late President in the spheres of economic and foreign policy, especially European integration. In constitutional matters, in dealings with the opposition and with Parliament, in civil liberties such as freedom from telephone tapping, he would be more liberal. Chaban-Delmas tried desperately to conjure up the genii of heroic Gaullism. He constantly invoked the General's name, national prestige, the Resistance. He even visited the Île de Sein, a bleak, rocky and almost unpopulated islet off West Finistère, which in 1940 had sent all its men to join General de Gaulle and fight for free France. The failure of the Chaban-Delmas campaign marks the end of heroic Gaullism as an electoral force.

In contrast to the divisions within the *Majorité*, and to the divisions within the left at the time of the previous presidential election, the parties of the left were speedily united behind Mitterrand's candidature. Agreement was reached on 5 April, the special conference of the Socialist Party adopted him unanimously on the 8th, the same day the PCF announced that it would not present a separate candidate, and a statement signed by the PS, the PCF, and the MRG (Left-wing Radicals) declared François Mitterrand to be the 'common candidate' of the left. This term was a concession to the PCF since 'sole candidate' would have implied that he was the socialist candidate who happened to be supported by the other parties.

In addition to the rival candidates of the *Majorité* and Mitterrand, there was an unusually large number of *fantaisistes*. There were two Trotskyists from rival chapels, the veteran presidential candidate Alain Krivine, and Arlette Laguiller (Worker's Struggle), an 'ecological' candidate (René Dumont), an extreme Right-wing nationalist (M. le Pen), a royalist (M. Renouvin), an anti-Communist Socialist (Emile Muller), and two European Federalists (MM. Sébag and Héraud) twelve candidates in all.

Table 12·5
PRESIDENTIAL ELECTION RESULTS 1974
*(Metropolitan France only)*

|  | First ballot (5 May) | Second ballot (19 May) |
|---|---|---|
| Electorate (*inscrits*) | 29·8m | 29·8m |
| Abstentions | 15·1% | 12·1% |
| Spoiled papers (*blancs et nuls*) | 0·8% | 1·2% |

|  | Million Votes | % of Vote | Million Votes | % of Vote |
|---|---|---|---|---|
| Mitterrand | 10·9 | 43·4 | 12·7 | 49·3 |
| Giscard d'Estaing | 8·3 | 32·9 | 13·1 | 50·7 |
| Chaban-Delmas | 3·6 | 14·6 |  |  |
| Royer | 0·8 | 3·2 |  |  |
| Laguiller | 0·6 | 2·4 |  |  |
| Dumont | 0·3 | 1·3 |  |  |
| Le Pen | 0·2 | 0·8 |  |  |
| Muller | 0·2 | 0·7 |  |  |
| Krivine | 0·09 | 0·4 |  |  |
| Renouvin | 0·04 | 0·2 |  |  |
| Sébag | 0·04 | 0·2 |  |  |
| Héraud | 0·02 | 0·1 |  |  |

Table 12.6
## PRESIDENTIAL ELECTIONS 1965 AND 1974—COMPARISON
*Départements carried by*

| | De Gaulle 1965 Giscard d'Estaing 1974 | Mitterrand 1965 and 1974 | De Gaulle 1965 Mitterrand 1974 |
|---|---|---|---|
| Brittany | 3 | — | 1 |
| Loire Country | 5 | — | — |
| Lower Normandy | 3 | — | — |
| Upper Normandy | 1 | — | 1* |
| North | — | — | 2* |
| Picardy | — | — | 3* |
| Paris Region | 4 | 2 | 2* |
| Champagne | 3 | — | 1* |
| Lorraine | 3 | — | 1* |
| Alsace | 2 | — | — |
| Centre | 4 | 1 | 1 |
| Burgundy | 2 | 1 | 1 |
| Franche-Comté | 3 | — | 1 |
| (France-North) | (33) | (4) | (14) |
| Poitou-Charentes | 3 | — | 1† |
| Aquitaine | 1 | 2 | 2† |
| Limousin | — | 3 | — |
| Midi-Pyrenees | 1 | 7 | — |
| Languedoc | 1 | 4 | — |
| Auvergne | 3 | 1 | — |
| Rhone-Alpes | 6 | 1 | 1 |
| Provence—Côte d'Azur | 2 | 4 | — |
| Corsica | 1 | — | — |
| (France-South) | (18) | (22) | (4) |
| France | 51 | 26 | 18 |

*Ten of the eighteen *départements* 'gained' by Mitterrand in 1974 contain large industrial cities.

†Three *départements* where Chaban-Delmas (Mayor of Bordeaux) ran ahead of Giscard d'Estaing in the 1974 first ballot and where many of his electors apparently declined to transfer their second ballot votes to Giscard d'Estaing.

The final result was remarkably close—only 400,000 votes between the two candidates in 26 million counted. Mitterrand was the beneficiary of the biggest ever vote for the Left. Some observers see the election as reconstituting the old division of the country into the Right and the classic Left as the Left-wing sympathisers of Gaullism and the Right-wing opponents of Gaullism returned to their traditional camps.[16] This view underestimates Mitterrand's success in urban areas and among working-class voters in parts of the country traditionally associated with the Right. Reims, Beauvais, Le Creusot or Le Mans provide examples. Table 12.6 shows in regional terms where in 1974 Mitterrand improved on his 1965 performance, predominantly in the industrial areas of the north and east.

### 4. Presidential election 1981

In veiled allusions and direct statements, President Giscard d'Estaing has affirmed his intention to serve his full seven-year term whatever the difficulties (like the Left winning a parliamentary majority, for instance). That term expires in 1981. There are numerous aspirants to the throne: François Mitterrand and Jacques Chirac to name but two. The Presidency, even if it has had to adapt to a period of accommodation to a different parliamentary majority, will still represent the pinnacle of political power. A presidential election will give a new start to the institutions and the party system. When a parliamentary majority opposed to a President in mid-term appears, one can debate which mandate is the true expression of universal suffrage. If, however, after a presidential election, a new President has no parliamentary majority to support him, it matters little. The new verdict of universal suffrage would be held to be decisive. Fresh from his triumph, the new President could presumably dissolve the Assembly in the full expectation that the people would confirm their presidential choice in the Parliament they elected. Such, at any rate, is in the logic of the development of institutions in the Fifth Republic and the party system that they have generated.

## NOTES

1. See above, p. 22
2. IFOP (opinion poll) figures quoted in Charlot, *The Gaullist Phenomenon*, p. 56:

Table 12.7

OPINIONS ON DIRECT ELECTION OF PRESIDENT

|  | Nov. 1945 | Nov. 1961 | Dec. 1962 | May. 1964 | Nov. 1965 | May 1969 |
|---|---|---|---|---|---|---|
| Favourable % | 50 | 52 | 46 | 74 | 78 | 81 |
| Unfavourable % | 40 | 17 | 23 | 10 | 6 | 8 |
| Don't know % | 10 | 31 | 31 | 16 | 16 | 11 |

3. General de Gaulle, Press Conference 31 January 1964: 'Who ever believed that General de Gaulle, once called to the helm, would be content with opening flower-shows [*inaugurer les chrysanthèmes*]?'

4. Philip M. Williams, *French Politicians and Elections 1951–1969*, Cambridge University Press 1970, 189. Williams continues: 'his brief announcement of his candidature showed all the old hallmarks: before de Gaulle—nothing; under Gaulle—perfection; if not de Gaulle—catastrophe'.

5. F. L. Wilson, 'Gaullism with de Gaulle', *Western Political Quarterly*, 1973, pp. 485–506.

6. The thirteen were Haut-Rhin and Bas-Rhin, Moselle, Vosges, Meuse, and Haute-Marne (all Eastern France); Ille-et-Vilaine and Morbihan in Britanny with Vendée nearby; Orne and Manche in Normandy; finally Lozère (Rhone Valley) and Corsica.

7. See Deutsch, Lindon, and Weill, *Les Familles Politiques,* Paris: Eds. du Minuit 1966.

8. 84%—see below, Ch. 15.

9. See above Chapter 3.

10. This was not an easy job. It was said that de Gaulle had removed all his records and that Alain Poher could not find out how to activate the French nuclear strike force of which he was nominally in command! He sacked some of de Gaulle's collaborators—notably the mysterious Jacques Foccart who wielded great influence over the leaders of former French colonies, now independent states of Francophone Africa. He kept on the existing government under Maurice Couve de Murville.

11. R. G. Schwartzenburg, *La Guerre de Succession,* Paris; PUF 1969, p. 19.

12. *Ibid.* p. 106.

13. Both François Mitterrand and Valéry Giscard d'Estaing addressed some vast meetings—25,000 at Nantes, 40,000 at Lyon, 100,000 in Paris.

14. For a blow-by-blow account see Roy C. Macridis, *French Politics in Transition: The Years after de Gaulle,* Cambridge, Mass., Winthrop, 1975, pp. 96–128, and, 'L'election presidentielle de Mai 1974', *Le Monde—Dossiers et Documents*.

15. *Le Monde,* 13 April 1974.

16. E.g. Barrillon, in *Le Monde Dossiers et Documents, p. 113.*

# 13

# PARLIAMENTARY ELECTIONS IN THE FIFTH REPUBLIC

## 1. National Assembly elections (élections législatives)

The general characteristics of two-ballot election and electoral procedure outlined in the last chapter apply to parliamentary elections in the Fifth Republic. The obvious and important difference between parliamentary and presidential elections is the division of the country, in the former case, into constituencies (circonscriptions) each returning one member to the National Assembly.[1] The present composition of the Assembly is as follows.

|                                   | Members |
|-----------------------------------|---------|
| Metropolitan France               | 473     |
| Overseas Départements[2]          | 10      |
| Overseas Territories              | 7       |
|                                   | 490     |

The composition is varied as population changes occur. For example a further three constituencies were provided in the rapidly expanding Lyon area before the 1973 elections. The average electorate of a metropolitan constituency is approximately 63,000. Like the States in the United States Senate, each metropolitan département has at least two representatives. This causes some inequality. The Lozére departement for instance has only 52,000 electors but still has two Deputies. The overseas territories of St Pierre-et-Miquelon and Wallis and Futuna send deputies to the National Assembly who each represent less than 3,500 electors. At the other extreme Longjumeau constituency in the Essonne département (Paris region) has over 145,000 electors.

Candidates who wish to contest the election pay a deposit of 1,000 Fr. which is returned to them if they receive 5% of the votes cast. Certain campaign expenses are repaid, up to a defined limit, by the State: posters for official notice boards, distribution of circulars, printing of ballot papers (each candidate produces his own, according to a standard format, for electors to place in the voting envelopes. The elector can either bring his chosen candidate's ballot paper with him on polling day or pick up a selection from the piles placed at the entrance to the polling). Repayment only occurs if the 5% threshold is attained, thus 'the *fantaisiste* candidate is doubly penalised.'[3] If in a constituency no candidate wins an absolute majority at the first ballot, a second ballot is held the following Sunday. No new candidates are allowed at the second ballot (unlike the Third Republic) and no candidate from the first ballot may continue unless he received the votes of at least 12·5% of the registered electorate (not merely votes cast).[4] This hurdle is a severe one. In twenty-one constituencies in 1973 (when the hurdle was 10%) all candidates of the left were eliminated from the second ballot. In one of these St Lô (Manche) the PSU candidate had obtained 11·9% of the votes cast but only 9·6% of the registered electorate. Candidates who are unable or choose not to enter the second ballot may either simply withdraw from the contest or 'desist' in favour of another candidate, urging their supporters to transfer their votes.

National Assembly elections occur every five years unless the President of the Republic, exercising his powers under Article 12 of the constitution, dissolves the Assembly before the five year term is completed. A dissolution cannot be followed by a further dissolution until at least twelve months have elapsed. At the time of writing there have been five National Assembly elections in the Fifth Republic:

November  1958
November  1962 (dissolution)
March       1967 (expiry of five-year term)
June         1968 (dissolution)
March       1973 (expiry of five-year term)

*(a)  The National Assembly election 23 and 30 November 1958.* The 1958 elections were the last of the old and first of the new. That they were the last of the old is reflected in the vast number of Independents and 'moderates' and local notables who were elected, in the numerous party labels and groupings, and in the divisions on the left. They were the first of the new in that one national issue, the return to power of General de Gaulle and the New Republic, dominated the elections. It was the beginning of the 'nationalisation' of French politics, and the beginning of the growth of Gaullism as a disciplined majority which was to have such a profound effect on the Fifth Republic's party system. The election was a disaster for the Communists. They had been the only political party to call for a 'No' vote at the referendum in September 1958 at which the Fifth Republic Constitution was adopted. At 3·9 million their first ballot vote in November was 750,000 less than the total voting 'No' two months before, and their lowest vote since the war. Furthermore the new two-ballot electoral system proved catastrophic for them because they could

not attract extra voters at the second ballot. From 150 seats in the outgoing Parliament, they dropped to 10. By contrast the success of Gaullism at the first ballot established its credentials as a 'serious party' and voters flocked to support its candidates in the second round. 'On the second ballot the full force of attraction to Gaullism and revulsion from the old politicians became plain. Wherever a prominent politician was standing, everyone else (including even some Communists) combined behind the candidate likeliest to throw him out.'[5] Well-known political figures like Gaston Defferre in Marseille were defeated by unknown Gaullist candidates.

Table 13.1
PARLIAMENTARY ELECTIONS 1958

|  | 1st ballot—Metropolitan France | | Seats (Metropolitan and overseas) |
|---|---|---|---|
| Electorate (*inscrits*) | 27·7m | | |
| Abstentions | 22·9% | | |
| Spoilt papers (*blancs et nuls*) | 2·3% | | |
|  | *million votes* | *% of vote* | |
| PCF | 3·9 | 19·2 | 10 |
| SFIO | 3·2 | 15·7 | 44 |
| Radicals | 1·7 | 8·3 | 32 |
| (Total Left) | (8·8) | (43·2) | (86) |
| MRP and Centre | 2·3 | 11·1 | 57 |
| Gaullists (UNR) | 4·0 | 19·5 | 199 |
| Independents (CNI etc.) | 4·7 | 22·9 ⎱ | 133 |
| Other | 0·6 | 3·3 ⎰ | |
| (Algeria and Sahara) | | | (71) |

(b) *National Assembly elections—18 and 25 November 1962.* The 1962 elections resulted from a remarkably timed dissolution by General de Gaulle, the circumstances of which were described in Chapter 2. The ending of the Algerian war, a dramatic summer which included an assassination attempt on the President's life, the proposal to submit to referendum the idea of perpetuating presidential legitimacy by direct election, the motion of censure carried by the traditional parliamentarians against this proposal, the dissolution of Parliament, the victory for 'yes' in the referendum all created the conditions for a remarkable Gaullist electoral victory in October. The UNR won almost 6 million votes at the first ballot, was joined by a further 1·75 million at the second, and, with 233 seats out of 482, almost won a majority on its own without any help from its perfectly dependable allies.

Nineteen-sixty-two marks the emergence of Gaullism as a majority party—the first ever known in Republican France. The Independents and·Moderates who were not prepared to give support to the government were electorally destroyed. In 1958 'people voted for the Independents because they were Gaullists'.[6] Now people voted against them because they had shown that they were not. Opponents of direct presidential elections, most Independents had voted for the motion of censure in September and campaigned unsuccessfully as part of the forlorn and divided *'cartel des non'* in the October referendum. This symbolic attachment to the past was severely punished by the electors in November. Most of the Independents who survived were, by contrast, those who had supported the Government (perhaps, like Valéry Giscard d'Estaing, actually being members of it) and had campaigned for 'Yes' in October. After the election those pro-Government 'Independents' formed the Independent Republican Parliamentary Group which was henceforth to be a loyal and disciplined component of the *Majorité* on whose parliamentary support President and Government depended.

A second group who felt the full force of Gaullism's tidal race was the MRP. In the Catholic bastions of the Fourth Republic's Christian Democracy, electors, having voted 'Yes' to direct presidential elections against the advice of the MRP, transferred their allegience to the UNR. In the northern, more Catholic, half of France the MRP lost half their seats. A third group to feel the effect of a marked popular preference for the new political order were the dissident Gaullists who had not accepted independence for Algeria. Official UNR candidates were run against them and they went down to defeat. Raymond Dronne, for instance, a well-established Gaullist deputy from the Sarthe and a supporter of *Algérie Française* lost 10,000 votes to an official Gaullist opponent. Discipline, appropriate to a new majority party in a new political order, was upheld, and that was the way the voters wanted it to be.

A final noteworthy feature of the 1962 elections was the first attempt, albeit grudging and ill-organised by the parties of the Left, to collaborate at the second ballot as an alternative to slaughter. There were a number of diffident pacts to eliminate competition between Left-wing parties at the second ballot and even the anti-Communist Socialist leader Guy Mollet advised electors to vote Communist at the second ballot if to do otherwise would favour the election of a Gaullist. The Left picked up no extra votes between ballots, and in fact there was a further haemorrhage of 250,000— but by reducing fratricidal strife it managed to salvage some parliamentary representation.

Table 13.2
PARLIAMENTARY ELECTIONS 1962

|  | *1st ballot*<br>*Metropolitan France* | | *Seats—Metropolitan*<br>*and overseas* |
|---|---|---|---|
| Electorate (*inscrits*) | 27·5m. | | |
| Abstentions | 31·3% | | |
| Spoilt papers (*blancs et nuls*) | 2·1% | | |
| | *million votes* | *% of vote* | |
| PCF | 4·0 | 21·7 ( +2·5) | 41 ( +31) |
| Ext. left | 0·4 | 2·4 | — |
| SFIO | 2·3 | 12·6 (−2·9) | 66 ( +22) |
| Radicals | 1·4 | 7·8 (−0·5) | 39 ( +7) |
| (Total Left) | (8·1) | (44·5)( +1·2) | (146) ( +60) |
| MRP and Centre | 1·7 | 9·1 (−2·6) | 55 (−5) |
| UNR/UDT | 5·9 | 31·9 ( +12·4) | 233 ( +34) |
| RI | 1·1 | 5·9 | 35 |
| (*Majorité*) | (7·0) | (37·8) | (268) |
| Others   (CNI, Extreme Right, etc) | 1·6 | 8·6 | 13·(−85)* |

(*not counting the 32 Independents who fought as RI and retained their seats)

*Main regional changes:*

Communists: gains in Paris Region and Industrial North

Non-Communist Left: gains in Central France, Provence and South West.

Centre: losses in Catholic regions e.g. Alsace-Lorraine.

Gaullists: big gains from Independents particularly in large industrial conurbations e.g. Paris or Lyon.

*(c)   The National Assembly elections 5 and 12 March 1967.* From 1962 to 1967 was a period of prosperous calm. The turbulence of the Algerian war and its settlement was over and the rather high-handed exercise of executive power by General de Gaulle that had accompanied that phase was attenuated. It was a period of grandiose and prestigious diplomatic initiatives—reconciliation with Germany, rapprochement with the Soviet Union, sorties against American hegemony in nuclear defence, money and technology, France as the friend of the third world and the Arabs. Throughout the period France had one President, one Prime Minister, and one Foreign Secretary. The 1967 elections were held

at the expiry of a five year term. The electorate in an atmosphere free from crises had an opportunity to judge a stable government and consider the alternatives.

Unlike the previous two elections it is the campaign rather than the result, close and exciting though that was, that ten years later retains our interest. It does so for two reasons: firstly, the campaign had a strongly presidential character, and, secondly, the process of party realignment to a bipolar party system was demonstrated in a very marked way.

The campaign was a long one. It was a continuation of the presidential election campaign of December 1965, and was as personalised as the presidential election had been. Nearly 40% of the candidates of the Socialist-Radical alliance (FGDS)—70% in the Paris region—mentioned François Mitterrand in their election addresses.[7] Posters featured General de Gaulle, Mitterrand, and Lecanuet. Furthermore the successful projection of the presidential candidates during the 1965 campaign gave both Mitterrand and Lecanuet crucial positions in the subsequent party relignment.[8] The Prime Minister, Georges Pompidou, directed the campaign of the *Majorité* and played the leading public part.

The party realignment on the Left has been fully described in Chapter 6. The Mitterrand strategy was to build a strong and united Federation of the non-Communist left, which would then negotiate an alliance with the Communist party, extracting from it certain guarantees on democratic liberties which would make it a less disreputable ally. The Communist Party for its part, had found supporting Mitterrand for President a successful experience, and, under the leadership of its moderate General Secretary Waldeck Rochet, it wanted to pursue the agreeable business of being recognised as a full partner. It wanted to appear modern, responsible, in short a party like the others and not go on being a pariah or an untouchable. "It would give assurances concerning political democracy . . . it would not hestitate to present a deliberately reformist image . . . it desired a common programme of government.'[9] Thus the electoral arrangements of the Left in 1967 prefigured in their composition, their tactics, and their effectiveness the *Union de la Gauche* of the mid 1970s. The Radicals, the Socialists, and Mitterrand's 'Convention of Republican Institutions' ('the clubs') worked well together in the FGDS (Federation of the Democratic and Socialist Left). A single FGDS candidate was designated in 413 constituencies. In the remainder the FGDS was supporting the PSU candidate, a vaguely Radical candidate (like former Prime Minister André Marie in the Seine-Maritime), or no one at all because they had no local strength. Of the 413, 216 were from the Socialist party (SFIO), 79 were Radicals, 21 belonged to no particular party, and 97, after a desperate search by Mitterrand's collaborators for likely candidates, were from the Convention.[10] The principle of designation was that outgoing members of Parliament should be given the FGDS investiture, subject to a written undertaking to join the FGDS parliamentary group after election. In other constituencies a national arbitration committee, on which each group was equally represented, would decide among different contenders for the FGDS investiture. The PCF had a candidate in every constituency except that of Pierre Cot in Paris whom the party supported. The PSU presented 101 candidates in 46 *départements*. The common agreement was for all candidates of the left to withdraw in favour of the one 'best placed' to win. This was normally the one with the highest first ballot score but in thirteen cases the PCF indulgently agreed to withdraw its candidate at the second ballot even though he had been ahead at the first. The main beneficiaries of this interpretation were some of Mitterrand's closest associates like Georges Fillioud or Claude Estier. There was a little indiscipline. Two Communists, four Socialists and a Radical, although behind on the first ballot, refused to withdraw. The second ballot picture on the Left is shown in Table 13.3.

Table 13.3
CANDIDATES OF THE LEFT 1967

|  | 1st ballot | | | 2nd ballot | | | |
|  | candidates | winners | eliminated* | maintained | withdrew in favour of: | | | |
|  | | | | | PCF | FGDS | PSU | Cent |
|---|---|---|---|---|---|---|---|---|
| PCF | 470 | 8 | 117 | 157 | — | 155 | 5 | 0 |
| FGDS | 413 | 1 | 116 | 111 | 98 | — | 0 | 2 |
| PSU | 101 | 0 | 83 | 7 | 11 | 0 | — | 0 |

*Candidates eliminated either because their opponents won outright at the first ballot or because they failed to achieve the qualifying 10%.

The Communists refused to support Centrists even where the Left no longer had a candidate in the contest. In Roland Leroy's phrase 'we refuse to choose between cholera and the plague'.[11] The FGDS was willing to make this dreadful choice where it helped to eliminate a Gaullist such as the unfortunate Couve de Murville, the Foreign Secretary, in Paris.

Where the *Majorité* were concerned there were to be none of these difficult decisions of who should withdraw for whom. It would all be settled before the first ballot. Pompidou declared in June 1966 to the UNR National Council: 'A candidate will be adopted by the *Majorité* in every constituency. There will be only one candidate adopted in each constituency. That there will be dissidents is possible, even probable. But they will be known as dissidents and the electors will be informed.'[12] The *Majorité* was no longer simply under the control of the UNR as it had been in 1962. The Independent Republicans had to be accommodated. The Action Committee for the Fifth Republic, and its special sub-committee on investitures, were formed to designate the single 'Fifth Republic' candidate in each constituency. Not all outgoing members were automatically readopted, There was some conflict here and there. The final outcome was

> UNR/UDT    407 candidates (201 eventually winners)
> RI             79 candidates (42 eventually winners).

The *Centre Démocrate*, created by Jean Lecanuet after his relative success in the presidential election campaign of 1965, presented 390 candidates dedicated to the proposition that the Centre in French politics was a living force and that a substantial body of opinion rejected both Gaullism and Socialism. Of these candidates 133 were former members of the MRP, 97 were former Independents and Moderates, 29 were from the Radical party, thus prefiguring the Reform movement which, as an alliance between the Centre Democrats and part of the Radical Party, was to contest the 1973 elections.

Thus it was a much simplified party system that contested the 1967 elections. Under the single appellation 'Fifth Republic' the Gaullists and their allies fought a well-organised and disciplined campaign, won a close victory and remained in government as a cohesive *Majorité*, so confirming the innovation of majority party rule in Republican France. The parties of the Left, for their part, also found that an effective and disciplined alliance was a profitable experiment. The first ballot vote of all candidates of the Left totalled 43·6% in 1967, against 44·5% in 1962—a slight decline. Yet thanks to effective cooperation at the second ballot, in which the voters willingly played their part, the parliamentary representation of the Left went up from 146 to 196. The *Centre Démocrate* too, though it only won 13% of the first ballot vote, played its part in rationalising the party system by combining moderates from both Catholic and Republican traditions. Its lack of electoral success, is, however, the most eloquent indicator of the bipolarising trend in French political life. The viability of an opposition of the Centre was in question. By 1969 a large part of those who had contested the 1967 elections as Centre Democrats had joined the presidential *Majorité* of Georges Pompidou. In 1974 Lecanuet's followers entered Giscard's presidential fold.

In this most interesting of elections the *Majorité*, while failing to be the great second ballot *rassembleur* of 1958 and 1962, managed to win an overall majority of one seat. The campaign enhanced the legitimacy of Parliament. Not only did government, opposition, and public, by the interest they all showed in the election, contribute to that end, so also did General de Gaulle. Having at the beginning of the Fifth Republic chosen so many of his ministers from outside Parliament he now urged them to make a genuflection to democratic legitimacy by getting themselves elected to the National Assembly.[13] The Prime Minister, Pompidou became a Deputy for the Cantal in the Auvergne; Couve de Murville and Messmer, two future Prime Ministers, failed to win seats. André Malraux, novelist and Minister of Culture, alone disdained electroral contest. This close result, however,

Table 13.4
PARLIAMENTARY ELECTIONS 1967

|  | 1st ballot Metropolitan France | | Seats—Metropolitan and overseas |
|---|---|---|---|
| Electorate (*inscrits*) | 28·2 m. | | |
| Abstentions | 18·9% | | |
| Spoilt papers (*blancs et nuls*) | 1·8% | | |

|  | million votes | % of vote | |
|---|---|---|---|
| PCF | 5·0 | 22·5 ( +0·8) | 73 ( +32) |
| PSU | 0·5 | 2·1 | 4 ( +4) |
| FGDS (Soc. + Rad.) | 4·2 | 19·0 (—1·4) | 116 ( +11) |
| (Total Left) | (9·7) | (43·6) (−0·9) | (193) ( +47) |
| Centre (CD) | 3·0 | 13·4 | 41 |
| *Majorité* (Fifth Republic) | 8·5 | 37·7 (−0·1) | 245 (−24) |
| UNR | 7·3 | 32·2 | 201 (−33) |
| RI | 1·2 | 5·5 | 44 ( +9) |
| Others | 1·1 | 5·4 | 8 |

*Main regional changes:*
Communists: gains in Paris region, industrial North, Languedoc.
Non-Communist Left: steady. Best progress in seats: Marseilles, Lyon, and Bordeaux areas.
Centre: steady. Losses in Lyon area.
Gaullism: main losses in Northern France, especially Paris.

reawakened the executive's suspicion of Parliament. One legislative consequence was the recourse to special powers, under Article 38, to enact unpopular measures by decree and not by the legislative process in Parliament. This executive high-handedness provoked a number of demonstrations in the spring of 1967—the opening chords of May 1968.

*(d) The National Assembly elections of 23 and 30 June 1968.* The extraordinary events of May and June 1968 provoked the election and dictated the result: a landslide victory for the Gaullist forces of law and order. The student revolt, the general strike, the occupations of factories, the demonstrations, the police charges, the breakdown of supplies and services, the near collapse of the regime itself, all produced the inevitable reaction: the fear of chaos, the vote for crisis leadership in the shape of General de Gaulle and his government. The details of the election and the brief campaign need not detain us long.

The parties of the Left maintained their pact but the crisis had strained relations, and the spirit of cooperation, present in 1967 and again in 1973, was absent. The Left lost 1 million votes. If the PSU increased its score from 500,000 to 900,000 it was less because of its fervent identification with the romantic events of May but because it presented three times as many candidates as in 1967. The spirit of unity was less marked in the *Majorité* as well. Giscard d'Estaing, while not of course identifying with the unruly events of recent weeks, wanted his Independent Republicans to challenge the Gaullists in some first ballot primaries in order to build an independent electoral following. As a mild punishment Giscard d'Estaing and some of his friends had their results officially classified among 'other Right' by the Ministry of the Interior, and his lieutenant Michel Poniatowski had an official UDR candidate against him in Pontoise. Lecanuet's Centrists, now called Progress and Modern Democracy experienced a further decline.

The success of the *Majorité* (baptised for the occasion Union for the Defence of the Republic) was remarkable. The Gaullists on their own won 296 seats—the first time in Republican history that a single party had, independently of its allies, however reliable, won an overall majority in the National Assembly. Its allies the Independent Republicans, won 64 seats and formed the second largest parliamentary group. The *Majorité* made gains in every part of the country—the west, the centre, Paris, the industrial area of the north. Above all it broke new ground in the southern bastions of the Left, winning seats in the Pyrenees, the Languedoc, and the Limousin previously undreamed of. It won a record 152 seats at the first ballot (against 63 in 1967), many of them against opposition (especially Communist) incumbents. Indeed anti-Communism was the key note of the *Majorité* campaign. The fears of chaos produced by the disorders of May and June were, turned to fears of Communism despite the indignant protestations of the PCF that it was 'the great and tranquil party of order' and had tried to damp down misplaced revolutionary ardour during the troubles. The anti-Communist card, so triumphantly played in 1968, was to be the basis of the next parliamentary victory in 1973.

Table 13.5
PARLIAMENTARY ELECTIONS 1968

|  | 1st ballot Metropolitan France | Seats—Metropolitan and overseas |
|---|---|---|
| Electorate (*inscrits*) | 28·2m. | |
| Abstensions | 20·0% | |
| Spoilt papers (*blancs et nuls*) | 1·4% | |

|  | million votes | % of vote | |
|---|---|---|---|
| PCF | 4·4 | 20·0 (−2·5) | 34 (−39) |
| PSU and extreme Left | 0·9 | 4·0 | — (−4) |
| FGDS (Soc. + Rad) | 3·7 | 16·5 (−2·4) | 57 (−59) |
| Other Left | 0·2 | 0·7 | — |
| (Total Left) | (9·2) | (41·2) (−2·4) | (91) (−102) |
| | | | |
| Centre (PDM) | 2·3 | 10·3 (−3·1) | 33 (−8) |
| *Majorité* (UDR) | 9·9 | 44·7 (+7·0) | 360 (+116) |
| UDR | 8·2 | 37·0 (+4·8) | 296 (+96) |
| RI | 1·7 | 7·7 (+2·2) | 64 (+20) |
| Others | 0·7 | 3·5 | 3 |

*Main regional changes:*
Communist: main losses where gains had been in 1967—Paris region, the north, south coast.
Non-Communist Left: universal losses. Fewer seats than in 1958 in both northern and southern France.
Centre: steady losses. Worst region—Brittany.
*Majorité:* Strength doubled in southern France; 1967 losses in industrial areas of the north (e.g. Paris) more than recouped.

*(e) The National Assembly election of 5 and 11 March 1973.* The 1973 elections were in many ways similar to those of 1967 and can be compared with them. Firstly both were non-crisis elections held at the expiry of a full parliamentary term after a period of stable government. It is true that a new President, Georges Pompidou,

had been elected in 1969 following the sudden resignation of General de Gaulle. The significant point here is how easily the legitimacy of the Presidency, the loyalty of the large parliamentary majority, and the unity and cohesion of the dominant Gaullist party were maintained after the disappearance of the regime's founding father. Secondly the party realignments which had been so important a feature in 1967, and which, especially on the Left, had subsequently been through a period of eclipse, occupied once again the centre of the political stage. On the left the signature of the *Programme commun* in 1972 prepared the way for the kind of fruitful electoral cooperation known in 1967. In addition François Mitterrand was back playing the prominent leadership role he had played in 1967. With Giscard d'Estaing back in the government, the presidential *Majorité* was cohesive and well organised as in 1967. In the Centre things had changed somewhat. A large part of the Centre had rallied to Pompidou in the 1969 presidential election and had supported the government since then. Those Centrists that remained in opposition, as in 1967, joined those Radicals, now led by Servan-Schreiber, who could not enter an alliance with the PCF. This new grouping contested the election under the title *Mouvement Réformateur*—the Reformers. A third parallel is to be found in the result. It was a close fought election and the different groupings ended up with results very much like those of 1967. This similarity, as Charlot points out,[14] masks more than it reveals, but it does provide a real basis for comparison.

There are also differences between the two elections. In 1973 the Left was believed, on the basis of opinion polls, to have a much better chance of winning. In consequence the threat to liberty from Communism replaced the threat from the 'personal power' of Gaullism as a central theme. So '1967 was the heterogeneous gathering-together of all General de Gaulle's opponents . . . 1973 was the glimpsed possibility of a Left-wing alternative to the *Majorité* which had held power since 1958'.[15] In addition immense stress was placed on the threat to the stability of the regime if a parliamentary majority was elected which was antagonistic to the President's policies. For months on end newspaper commentators endlessly evaluated the presidential options available in such an event. It is of course the great conundrum of the constitution that France will have to resolve one day. The country can have presidential government only if there is a parliamentary majority to sustain a ministry composed of the President's supporters. Nonetheless the two elections stand as normal elections, the only ones in the Fifth Republic not overshadowed by some great de Gaulle initiative, either referendum or crisis leadership. They stand as fixed beacons of normal electoral behaviour in normal times against which electoral stability and change can be measured.

The great public interest in the 1973 elections is indicated by the exceptionally high 81·5% turnout. This characteristic was especially marked in constituencies where the Left was likely to win. The inexorable extinction of small parties continued. The fringes of the extreme Left and extreme Right declined. In the seventy-four constituencies where the PSU presented candidates in all three elections their votes declined on average as follows: 1967:7·1%; 1968:6·9%; 1973:4·1% ( +1·2% for other extreme left candidates).[16] The closeness of the result was reflected in the fact that only fifty-nine seats were decided at the first ballot.

The only party to improve on its 1967 share of the first ballot vote was the UGSD (the new Socialist and Radical alliance that had replaced the defunct FGDS) and it was the Socialist not the Radical component of the UGSD that benefited. The PS, moving strongly towards the role it adopted in the mid-1970s as the biggest party of the Left, narrowed the gap between itself and the Communists, and performed best in those areas where Socialism had traditionally been weak: Normandy, Brittany, Alsace-Lorraine.[17] The Communist Party topped 5 million votes—the sign of a good year—but its share of the vote was slightly down on 1967 and nowhere near the 5·5 million (26%) it had won at the last election of the Fourth Republic in 1956. Its decline between 1967 and 1973 was greatest in those constituencies that the PC normally wins.[18]

The *Majorité* would have been unable to win without the seats won by its ally the CDP, the former opposition Centrists led by Duhamel, who had joined Pompidou's presidential campaign in 1969. The UDR held only 185, the RI 55—in total five short of an overall parliamentary majority.[19] In addition, the only constituencies where the *Majorité* improved its performance compared to 1968 were those where candidates were CDP. This is not very surprising because they were able to add to their local Centrist following many of those electors who in previous elections had voted Gaullist. The *Majorité* won the election but their share of the vote was lower than in 1967, even with the help of the CDP.

At the second ballot the *Majorité* did much better collecting 2 million votes which had gone elsewhere at the first. President Pompidou spoke on television of the threat to freedom and to the ownership of homes and gardens that would immediately follow a victory of the Left. The Prime Minister, Messmer, held urgent discussions with the Reformers to see if some way could be found to stop the advance of the 'Socialo-Communist' coalition. A way was found. Jean Lecanuet agreed to withdraw his candidates wherever their presence, by dividing the anti-Communist vote, would favour the election of a Communist or Socialist. In return the *Majorité* withdrew enough candidates, even where they were ahead, for the Reformers to win the thirty seats necessary to form a parliamentary group. This arrangement, which it is easy to caricature as shabby, indicates the way the Centre in French politics was moving. In 1967, according to calculations made by linear regression analysis, 45% of Centrist electors were prepared to vote Socialist at the second ballot to stop Gaullism, while 47% preferred the *Majorité*. In 1973 the proportions were 22% and 65%.[20] The forces of bipolarisation were at work pushing the leadership and electorate of the Centre towards the *Majorité*. This movement was to be consummated a year later when Lecanuet and Servan-Schreiber joined the presidential *Majorité* of Giscard d'Estaing. Furthermore, and we shall consider this point in the chapter on electoral sociology, many commentators have pointed to a 'restructuration' of the *Majorité* that might 'do away with the originality of Gaullism—a movement cutting across all social classes—in favour of the traditional sociology of conservative electoral forces'.[21] A polarisation by social class was making its appearance: only 49% of manual workers voted for the Left in 1967; now the figure was 64%. It was the middle-class electors and leaders of the Centre, who came to the aid of Pompidou's Gaullism.

The electors of the Left behaved in a reasonably disciplined manner at the second ballot although Lancelot[22] points out numerous cases of failing spirits especially in strong Left-wing areas like Arles or Limoges where there is a venerable tradition of hostility between Socialists and Communists. The PCF (unlike in 1967) insisted on its right to present a candidate at the second ballot in every constituency where it had the leading candidate of the Left at the first. In 184 constituencies, therefore, the Left was represented by a Communist candidate. In 220 cases, however, it was represented by the UGSD. Thus 1973 demonstrated a growing tendency for Socialist candidates to run ahead of the PCF at the first ballot. In 1967 a Communist was the leading candidate of the Left at the first ballot in 261 constituencies, and the FGDS ran ahead of them in only 205. This change round has interesting implications. If the Socialist Party continues to grow in appeal it will tend to outstrip the PCF in more and more constituencies, thus gaining more and more second-ballot candidatures at the expense of the Communists. This tendency was confirmed at the local cantonal (*département* council) elections in 1976. The less the non-communist elector is required to vote Communist at the second ballot to ensure the victory of the Left, the more likely is the victory to occur. Consequently the better the performance of the Socialist Party, the greater the chance of a Left-wing victory, and the more disastrous the consequences for the Communist Party. Socialist

## PARLIAMENTARY ELECTIONS 1973

| | 1st ballot—Metropolitan France | | | | | | Seats—Metropolitan and overseas | | |
|---|---|---|---|---|---|---|---|---|---|
| | million votes | cf. 1967 | cf. 1968 | % of vote | cf. 1967 | cf. 1968 | | cf. 1967 | cf. 1968 |
| Electorate (inscrits) | | | | 29·9m. | | | | | |
| Abstentions | | | | 18·7% | | | | | |
| Spoilt papers (blancs et nuls) | | | | 1·8% | | | | | |
| PCF | 5·1 | (+0·1) | (+0·7) | 21·4 | (−1·1) | (+1·4) | 73 | (±0) | (+34) |
| PSU + extreme left | 0·8 | | | 3·3 | | | 1 | (−3) | (+1) |
| UGSD | | | | | | | | | |
| (PS+MRG) | 4·9 | (+0·7) | (+1·2) | 20·8 | (+1·8) | (+4·3) | 101 | (−15) | (+44) |
| Other Left | 0·1 | | | 0·3 | | | 1 | | |
| (Total Left) | (10·9) | (+1·2) | (+1·7) | (45·8) | (+1·8) | (+4·6) | (176) | (−17) | (+85) |
| Reform Movement | | | | | | | | | |
| (CD+Rad) | 3·1 | | | 13·1 | | | 34 | | |
| Majorité | | | | | | | | | |
| (URP) | 8·5 | (—0) | (−1·4) | 36·0 | (−1·1) | (−8·7) | 268 | (+24) | (−92) |
| UDR | 6·1 | (−1·2) | (−2·1) | 25·7 | (−4·5) | (−11·5) | 183 | (−17) | (−113) |
| RI | 1·6 | (+0·4) | (−0·1) | 6·6 | (+1·1) | (−1·1) | 55 | (−11) | (−9) |
| CDP | 0·9 | | | 3·7 | | | 30 | | |
| Other pro-Majorité | 0·2 | | | 0·7 | | | 5 | | |
| Others | 1·0 | | | 4·4 | | | 7 | | |

*Main regional changes:*

Communists: 1968 losses mainly recovered, declining support most noticeable in Catholic Regions such as Alsace-Lorraine and the Loire country.

Non-Communist Left: Strong Socialist recovery; particular progress in industrial areas and in the traditional Catholic regions of the north-east and north-west: Alsace-Lorraine, Normandy, Brittany; in traditional Socialist bastions in central France (Limousin, Auvergne, Burgundy) 1968 losses were not recovered.

Centre: Composition radically changed between 1968 and 1973 so that comparisons do not have great significance.

Majorité: Big losses in industrial areas of Northern France; the 1968 gains in the rural centre and south west consolidated.

gains are at Communist expense—a 'conflictual alliance' indeed, in Charlot's phase.[23]

*(f) 1978.* Parliament may not, in the Fifth Republic, have the predominant role it had in the Fourth or the Third. Nevertheless the President of the Republic, if he wants to implement the policies upon which he was elected, needs the support of a parliamentary majority, so parliamentary elections are of considerable interest and importance. The five-year term of the 1973 National Assembly is due to end in the spring of 1978. As it watched the Italian general election of 1976, the world will watch France in 1978 with bated breath. Will there be a constitutional crises? Will Communists acquire a place in government? What would they do if they did? All these questions and one or two others are briefly evoked in the concluding chapter of this book. So far as the analyst of elections is concerned, attention should be focused on two aspects: firstly the capacity of the Socialist Party, as indicated for instance by its performance in local elections, to maintain the *élan* of 1974 to 1976 (and in particular their propensity to gain votes at the expense of the PCF), and secondly the arrangements reached by the *Majorité* on single candidatures or primaries. Both aspects affect the outcome. A victory by the Left in which the PCF had a relatively small share would be different in character from one in which it was dominant. As regards the present *Majorité,* its future character will depend on the relative success of hard Gaullism or gentle Centrism.

We must note in conclusion that in parliamentary elections of the Fifth Republic the party system at least permits the elector to make a choice. Some complain the choice is too stark—a 'choice of society', freedom or collectivism, order or chaos. It is however, a vast improvement on the Fourth Republic party system where clandestine negotiations after the election between party groups in Parliament determined the choice of government. It is the job of the elector at the election to choose the government and that is how the French voters now regard their outings to the polling station.

*(g) A note on by-elections (élections partielles).* Occasionally a vacancy in a parliamentary seat has to be filled. In Great Britain by-elections usually occur as a result of the death, ennoblement or resignation of the sitting Member. In France if a Deputy dies or occupies some office which debars him from membership of the Assembly, he is merely replaced by his *suppléant* or substitute who contested the general election as his running-mate. Most by-elections are caused by the curious working of Article 25 of the constitution. This provides that government office is incompatible

with membership of the Assembly. Thus when a Deputy is appointed a minister he has to resign his seat and be replaced automatically by his *suppléant*. However if the minister is dismissed or resigns he naturally wants to regain his parliamentary seat and he is usually able to prevail upon his *suppléant* to resign. It is the resignation of the *suppléant* that provokes a by-election. That is why there is always a flurry of by-elections after a government change—in 1974, for instance, and after the resignation of the Chirac government in 1976. Sometimes ex-ministers cannot prevail upon their *suppléant* to resign. Maurice Couve de Murville's in 1969 would not. Another member sportingly offered the former Prime Minister his seat: A famous by-election occurred and Couve de Murville was beaten by Michel Rocard, the PSU leader. At the subsequent general election Couve de Murville exercised his right to stand for the constituency which originally elected him, so the insubordinate *suppléant* did not last long. On another famous occasion the Prime Minister in office had to contest a by-election. In 1970 Chaban-Delmas' *suppléant* died. Chaban-Delmas contested the by-election in his Bordeaux constituency although he knew that as Prime Minister he would have to give up the seat as he had won it. To stress the ridiculous nature of these rules, the chief opponent of the Prime Minister in that by-election was another candidate who could not have sat as Deputy for Bordeaux either because he was already Deputy for Nancy: Jean-Jacques Servan-Schreiber, leader of the Radical Party.

By-elections, as in Great Britain, are regarded as a live opinion poll on the popularity of government and opposition. Thus they often generate intense public interest all over the country. There is usually the added spice of a well-known political figure, recently resigned or sacked from the government, seeking to regain his influential role in public life and knowing only too well the damaging consequences to his prestige of a defeat or a close shave. The defeats of Couve de Murville (UDR, 1969) and Fontanent (CDP, 1974) damaged their political standing considerably. Pierre Abelin (CD), a minister in the Chirac government, only narrowly retained his seat in the Chatellerault by-election of Oct 1975, caused by the death of his *suppléant,* and his ministerial career very soon came to an end.

In November 1976 there was an important series of seven by-elections caused mainly by the desire of members of the outgoing Chirac government to recover their parliamentary seats. In every case the Socialists did better, in some cases spectacularly better, than they had done in the general election of 1973; in fact they won two seats, both from the RI. The PCF was down in five seats, steady in one, and up only in Versailles in the Paris region.

Centrists, Radicals, and Independent Republicans in the *Majorité* had a difficult time, but not so the two UDR ex-ministers seeking re-election. Jean Tibéri was re-elected at the first ballot in the Latin Quarter of Paris with a big increase on his 1973 score, and Jacques Chirac himself won the spectacular first ballot success to which he has become accustomed since he made rural Corrèze his own in 1967. This success put heart into militant Gaullism and was a suitable prelude to the 5 December rally at which the UDR became the RPR with Chirac as undisputed chieftain.

## 2.  Senate elections

It is often overlooked that the French Parliament has an elected second chamber. The Senate is important for the part it plays in the legislative process, and it is often more disposed than the Assembly to be critical of the government. The two Presidents it has had in the Fifth Republic have made themselves more of a nuisance to the Executive than any Deputy. Gaston Monnerville had the audacity to invoke the Constitutional Council, of which by virtue of his Presidency of the Senate he was a member, to test the constitutionality of the October 1962 referendum on direct presidential elections. Alain Poher we have encountered once or twice in this narrative. He campaigned against the referendum on senate reform in 1969. After General de Gaulle's resignation, and again after the death of Pompidou in 1974, he became, by virtue of his Presidency of the Senate, temporary President of the Republic. In these brief periods of office he sacked various highly placed Gaullist officials, and took steps to end electoral corruption in the overseas territories.

The Senate may be important, but the elections to it attract very little interest, for the very good and simple reason that they are indirect elections, without a direct popular vote. The senators are elected by an electoral college in each *departement* composed of the 490 deputies from the National Assembly, the 3,000 or so *conseillers généraux* (county councillors from the 99 *départements* in France and overseas), and some 100,000 delegates from municipal councils— the size of the delegation depending on the size of the commune. The Senators are elected for nine years. Every three years there is an election for one-third of the seats. Those *départements* which have four senators or fewer elect their senators by the list system. The list with an overall majority at the first ballot, or the most votes at the second wins. Electors can cross names out and vote for individuals on different lists if they wish *(panachage)*. The seven *départements* with the largest population which have five or more senators elect them by proportional representation (highest average system). Here electors can only vote for a list—no *panachage* allowed. Finally the senate itself elects six senators to represent Frenchmen living in foreign countries. The total membership of the Senate is 283.

The Senate is not very representative of public opinion. Firstly its electorate of local worthies is not exactly a cross-section of the populace. Secondly the composition of the electorate is such that the small villages are considerably over-represented as compared with large cities. In 1958 29% of the nation lived in communes with less than 1,500 population and had 53% of senatorial electors; 47% lived in towns over 10,000 in population which had 21% of senatorial electors.[24] In the Fourth Republic the Upper House was known as 'the Chamber of Agriculture'. The same could be said today. Urban industrial, dynamic France is not really present in the Senate. For these reasons, the Senate never went Gaullist. Its stable and traditional-minded electorate has resisted the electoral tide that swept public opinion along throughout the 1960s. That is why it has tended to be more critical of the government than the Assembly. The Senate remains a haven of traditional French parliamentarism where the new party system has not taken root. Most of the Senators are still Independents or Moderates, or Centre-Left. The old radical Party, the essence of the Third Republic, now divided and all but extinct everywhere else, lives on in the Senate. In the country as a whole the Radicals are split between those who have joined the *Union de la Gauche* (and hence remain in the opposition) and those who followed Jacques Servan-Schreiber into the Reform Movement with the Centre Democrats and subsequently into the *Majorité* (and hence support the Government). In the Senate both wings sit happily together in a group called 'Democratic Left'. The group, I am told, practises the principle of the 'freedom of vote'. The Senate has a sense of tradition. The late Jacques Duclos, leader of the Communist group and the party's elder statesman, occupied the seat at the front on the extreme left where Victor Hugo and later Clémenceau sat and are commemorated by brass nameplates.

Stability is not quite as it appears from Table 13.7. In 1974 senatorial elections were due in 88 of the 283 seats. Sixty Senators offered themselves for re-election and fifteen of these were defeated. Thus forty-three of the eighty-eight who emerged from the election were new Senators, though their arrival did not to a vast extent modify the political composition of the chamber.

Table 13.7
## SENATE ELECTIONS IN THE FIFTH REPUBLIC
## COMPOSITION OF SENATE

|  | 1959 | 1962 | 1965 | 1968 | 1971 | 1974 |
|---|---|---|---|---|---|---|
| Communist Group | 14 | .14 | 14 | 18 | 18 | 20 |
| Socialist Group | 51 | 53 | 52 | 52 | 49 | 51 |
| Democratic Left Group | 64 | 50 | 50 | 43 | 38 | 35 |
| MRP/Centre Democrat | 34 | 35 | 38 |  |  |  |
| Centrist Union of Democrats for Progress Group |  |  |  | 47 | 46 | 54 |
| UNR/UDR group | 44 | 31 | 30 | 36 | 38 | 30 |
| Independent Republicans Group* | 74 | 64 | 64 | 54 | 59 | 58 |
| 'Republican Centre for Social Action' Group | 20 | 20 | 17 | 19 |  |  |
| 'Independent Republican for Social Action' Group |  |  |  |  | 16 | 15 |
| Group of *non-inscrits* (politically unattached) | 6 | 6 | 9 | 14 | 19 | 19 |

*The Independent Republican group in the Senate pre-dates the formation of the Independent Republican Party.

## NOTES

1. Except Comores, a remote archipelago in the Indian ocean, which before part of it became independent, was one constituency returning two members. Comores and six other overseas Territories (Afars and Issas, New Caledonia, Polynesia, Wallis and Futuna, and the islands of St Pierre-et-Miquelon in the mouth of Canada's St Lawrence River) have single ballot voting like the British.
2. Martinique, (French) Guiana and Guadeloupe in the Caribbean, and Réunion in the Indian Ocean. St Pierre-et-Miquelon and Mayotte (the non-independent remainder of Comores) have now become *départements*.
3. M. Duverger, *La cinquième République,* Paris: PUF, 4th edition.
4. The hurdle was 5% before 1966, 10% before 1976.
5. Williams, *French Politicians and Elections 1951-1969,* p. 106.
6. M. Chapsal, *La Vie politique en France depuis 1940,* Paris: PUF, 1966, p. 366.
7. Centre d'Etude de la vie politique française, *Les elections législatives de mars 1967,* Paris, Colin: 1970, p. 243.
8. Williams, *French Politicians and elections 1951-1969,* p. 205.

9. Centre d'Etude de la vie politique française: *Les élections législatives de mars 1967*, p. 89.
10. Some of these ninety-seven (including two who won seats in the election) were totally unknown to the Convention and its leaders and had never been seen before, *ibid.*, p. 107.
11. Radio interview – Europe 1, 6 March 1967.
12. Centre d'Etude *Les Élections législatives*, p. 23.
13. This despite the incompatibility rule (Constitution Article 25) under which they would, if they remained in ministerial office, have immediately to resign their parliamentary seats.
14. J. Charlot in Charlot (ed.), *Quand la Gauche peut gagner*, pp. 81-2.
15. *Ibid.*, p. 82.
16. See *Ibid.*, p. 89.
17. See Table 7.2 and also V. Wright and H. Machin, 'The French Socialist Party: success and the problems of success', *Political Quarterly*, Jan-March 1975, p. 44.
18. See Charlot, *Quand la Gauche peut gagner*, pp. 111-12.
19. Actually there would have been enough reliable support from the miscellanous independents to see the *Majorité* through.
20. See tables 11.1 and 11.2 and Charlot, op. cit., pp. 169 and 194.
21. Alain Lancelot, 'La France de M. Bourgeois-République', *Projet*, June 1973, p. 680.
22. *Ibid.*, p. 681.
23. Charlot, *Quand de Gaulle peut gagner*, p. 113.
24. See M. Duverger, *La Cinquième République*, Paris: PUF, 1968, p. 112.

# 14

## LOCAL ELECTIONS

It is commonly believed that since France is so centralised a state, local government, or local administration as the French term it, has no autonomy and hence no importance. There is, it is true, a particularly strong administrative hierarchy in which local officials have a subordinate place. The central government appoints, in each of the ninety-five metropolitan *départements* as well as overseas, a Prefect who, like a colonial governor, represents the state, resides with great official pomp and circumstance in a palace in his provincial capital, presides over all state services in the area, and exercises powers of *tutelle* (somewhere between supervision and control) over the local authorities. Indeed mayors and other elected local officials are, at least for those functions in which they act as the agents of the central government (for instance in the local implementation of central government legislation), directly under the hierarchical authority of the Prefect.

Curiously enough, however, local government always seems a much more vigorous plant in France than in England where its autonomy, for example in matters such as the control of education or the police, is supposed to be much greater. Apart from the fact that British local government has far fewer powers of initiative and is far more subject to control by central government either through legislation, finance, or directive, than is often supposed, there are three reasons for French vigour. Firstly, politics in France has always had a much more local content than in Great Britain. Party, and the propensity of electors to vote for their party whoever the candidate, has always been weaker in France and politicians have always needed a local base of support. The second reason is related: national political leaders in France have not only started life in local politics (that is common to many countries) but remain closely involved throughout their political careers. Whereas British politicians usually drop city council or county council membership after election to Westminster and, *a fortiori*, after being appointed to government, French national leaders traditionally tend to keep their local offices. Giscard d'Estaing remained Mayor of Chamalières, suburb of Clermont-Ferrand and centre of his constituency, while he was Minister of Finance, though as President he has given it up. Chaban-Delmas remained Mayor of Bordeaux as Prime Minister—and being mayor of a large city like Bordeaux is no mere honorific function but an executive job of considerable importance. In 1976 Lecanuet combined the offices of Minister of Justice, Mayor of Rouen, Chairman of the *Conseil Général* (*Département* Council) of Seine-Maritime, and President of the Regional Council of Upper Normandy. The power and importance of a man like Gaston Deferre stems in large part from his role as Mayor of Marseille. Thus it is true to say that nearly all political figures of any substance have a firm base in local government. The third reason for the vigour of French local government is related to the first two. Because local government is regarded as a suitable field for their energies by political leaders of substance, talent and ambition, it is not surprising that the scope for local initiative is greater than the administrative rule-book appears to permit. Indeed a Prefect attaches great importance to good relations with a mayor or chairman of a *département* council who is a Deputy or a Minister or likely to become one. Such people have great influence over the careers of Prefects who are often moved or replaced when a new government takes office. Local government in France is a presidential system—the Mayor is the chief citizen of a community and chief executive of its government. An energetic mayor, particularly one with good ministerial contacts in Paris, has great scope for local initiative, particularly in development projects— industrial or residential—or infrastructure like schools, roads, or water and can leave his mark on a city in a way that, for instance, the leader of the Labour group on Leeds City Council in British local government could never hope to do.

The personal character within a centralised state of local autonomy linked to a prominent and even national personality, explains the nature of French local elections. Three characteristics are particularly noteworthy. One is high voter turnout. In the 1971 municipal elections turnout at 75% was about double the British level and comparable with French national elections. The second is the stability in office of prominent local leaders for considerable periods of time in despite of electoral fluctuations at national level.[1] This is more true of small towns than large ones, where there is an increasing tendency for elections to be fought on national party lines, but there are plenty of examples of cities where non-aligned Centrist mayors like André Morice in Nantes, M. Pradel in Lyon, or André Argant in Epinal survived the tide of Gaullism which carried their cities in national elections. Indeed Gaullism never made the breakthrough in local politics that it did in national. The third charactersistic is the personal character of local electoral alliances. Coalition-building and list-composition constitute an ancient and personal art. The process of balancing one's ticket with a judicious political mixture—a moderate list including a few Socialists if possible—with just the right number of women,

Catholics, grandfathers, shopkeepers, residents of different *quartiers*—has always been a subtle and very personal operation known as electoral *cuisine*. The development on the left of the *Union de la Gauche* strategy into a more comprehensive alliance with a common programme of government has, as we shall see, had important consequences for the electoral *cuisine* in Socialist municipalities. Socialists in 1977 were required by party policy to form coalition lists with Communists and Left-wing Radicals only.

## 1. Local electoral systems

There are two types of local election—cantonal and municipal. The cantonal elections are in fact the elections for the *Conseil Général* in each *Département* (now ninety-six in metropolitan France, six overseas). The *Conseil Général* does not have anything like the range of functions that a municipal council does and its relative lack of importance as a unit of local government explains the rather low turnout at cantonal elections—a mere 50–65% (a fantastic figure if it was ever attained in Great Britain). The cantonal elections are so called because the electoral division represented by a member of the *Conseil Général* is a *canton*. Like a British county councillor's electoral division, it has no particular administrative or community significance.[2] The voting system is like that for parliamentary elections, a two-ballot election for a single councillor in each canton. All the councillors thus elected in a *département* comprise the *Conseil Général* and the party or coalition with a majority of seats is able to take the chairmanship of the council and of the principal committees. The term of office is six years but there are cantonal elections every three, with half of the seats coming up for renewal each time. The size of cantons varies considerably, so inequality of representation as between urban and rural cantons is very great and to the detriment of the urban areas. The elections are *'fortement politisées'* (highly politicised)[3] according to a venerable textbook of administrative law. Certainly they have always been so regarded by the parties of the Left though moderates and the Right, as in other countries, like to claim that politics do not enter into local government and that the elections should be the expression of a natural local consensus. The political or non-political character of cantonal elections was keenly debated in March 1976. It was the first electoral consultation since the presidential election of 1974 and was, despite the protestations of supporters of the President and the government, universally regarded as a test of presidential and government popularity—a vast opinion poll with a sample of several million. There were in fact immense gains for the Left, especially for the Socialist Party which confirmed its strong

Table 14.1

## CANTONAL ELECTIONS IN THE FIFTH REPUBLIC
*(Seats and % of first ballot vote)*

| | 1961 % | 1961 S | 1964 % | 1964 S | 1967 % | 1967 S | 1970 % | 1970 S | 1973 % | 1973 S | 1976 % | 1976 S |
|---|---|---|---|---|---|---|---|---|---|---|---|---|
| Abstentions | 43·5 | | 43·4 | | 42·7 | | 38·2 | | 46·0 | | 34·7 | |
| PCF | 18·6 | 52 | 21·7 | 99 | 26·3 | 131 | 23·8 | 144 | 22·7 | 205 | 22·8 | 249 |
| Ext. Left/PSU | 2·7 | 28 | 2·4 | 40 | 2·0 | 24 | 3·1 | 22 | 1·0 | 9 | 0·8 | 8 |
| SFIO/PS | 16·8 | 271 | 16·6 | 286 } | 21·6 | | 14·8 | 263 | 21·9 | 423 | 26·3 | 520 |
| FGDS | | | | | | 444 | | | | | | |
| Rad/MRG | 7·4 | 211 | 7·0 | 199 } | | 169 } | | 292 | 2·0 | 68 | 2·4 | 84 |
| Other Left | | | | | 6·2 | | 10·5 | | 6·4 | 174 | 4·3 | 100 |
| Centre-Left | 8·4 | 198 | 7·7 | 202 | | | | | | | 5·0 | 116 |
| MRP/CD/Reform | 9·8 | 142 | 9·5 | 148 | 8·1 | 140 | 7·3 | 141 | 6·5 | 123 | 5·0 | 98 |
| UNR/UDR | 12·8 | 166 | 12·2 | 123 | 14·5 | 180 | 15·6 | 206 | 12·7 | 244 | 10·8 | 182 |
| RI | | | 4·0 | 81 | 4·0 | 90 | 5·2 | 110 | 6·2 | 153 | 8·6 | 182 |
| CDP | | | | | | | 1·8 | 42 | 2·1 | 60 | 1·7 | 40 |
| Independents/Moderates | 10·2 | 212 | 7·3 | 165 | 10·0 | 231 } | 17·3 | 383 | 18·5 | 387 | 12·0 | 277 |
| Local Action | 10·4 | 203 | 10·5 | 204 | 6·6 | 135 } | | | | | | |
| Ext. Right | 2·8 | 21 | 1·5 | 15 | 0·5 | 7 | 0·4 | 6 | | | 0·6 | 7 |

showing in opinion polls. Control of many councils passed to the Left. One intriguing electoral trend revealed by the 1976 elections is that the *Union de la Gauche* appears to have reached the stage that further Socialist gains will actually reduce Communist representation since fewer and fewer PCF candidates will reach the second ballot. The first round 'primaries' increasingly show the electors preferring a Socialist, who thus becomes the standard-bearer for the Left as a whole in the final round.

The Left won control—or at any rate a majority sufficient to secure the election of one of their number as Council President—in 41 out of 96 *départements*[4] (a gain of 14 compared with 1973).

Table 14.2
PRESIDENCIES OF CONSEILS GÉNÉRAUX
(DÉPARTEMENT COUNCILS) 1976

| | |
|---|---|
| PCF | 3 (all in Paris Region: Seine St. Denis, Essonne, Val de Marne) |
| PS | 27 |
| MRG | 10 |
| Other Left | 1 |
| Centre Left | 9 |
| CD | 6 |
| UDR | 11 |
| RI | 16 |
| CDP | 3 |
| Ind/Mod | 10 |

## 2. Municipal elections

The vital unit of local government in France is the commune—town or village. The elections for the councils of all the 37,000 communes of France occur on the same day every six years—1965, 1971, 1977 and so on. These elections—the municipal elections—attract much greater public interest than the cantonals. They are politically much more interesting too, because the powers of the municipal council are more important and because the list system of election involves complex coalition-building.

Although the capacity to provide municipal service naturally varies slightly between Marseille (population 1 million) and a tiny hamlet in the Pyrenees with fifty inhabitants, the legal powers and duties of both councils are the same. Only the City Council of Paris traditionally had less municipal powers. Too many governments in the past have been overthrown in the streets of Paris for Parisians to be allowed their own mayor with the municipal powers of every other commune. One of President Giscard d'Estaing's reforms, however, has been to grant Paris a mayor.

The composition and electoral system for councils varies by size of commune. The 4,000 hamlets with a population less than 100 have 9 councillors each, the 20,000 with 100–500 inhabitants 11 councillors, and so on up to the 221 cities with populations over 30,000 who have between 31 and 49 council seats. Exceptions to this rule are the three largest cities, Paris (109 councillors), Marseille (63) and Lyon (61). These, together with Toulouse and Nice, have a separate electoral system from the rest.

For all categories of commune election is by a two-ballot list system. Candidates for the town hall present themselves in lists. In small towns and villages with a population less than 30,000 the elector can of course vote for a whole list, but he can also vote for incomplete lists by crossing names off or by voting for different candidates from several lists (*panachage*). In these smaller communes lists can be modified or merged between ballots, and new candidates are permitted. In the smallest communes of all (under 2,500 population) individual candidates, not on any list, are also allowed at either first or second ballot. Any candidate is elected at the first ballot if he, as an individual or part of a list, has attracted to his name an absolute majority of votes cast, provided of course that the absolute majority is also at least a quarter of the registered electorate. This requirement has an admirably democratic character. Unlike a British parish council or other local election, unopposed candidates still must be positively elected and not merely returned automatically. Most of the elections in these small communes are of non-political character—the victorious lists are usually *action locale,* lists 'for the defence of local interests' and so on. Mayors of small villages express a special local consensus and they go on for years and years— through Vichy, through the fourth Republic, through the Fifth Republic, undisturbed by national convulsions, until infirmity or the grave.

The political interest of municipal elections naturally centres on the 221 larger towns and cities. They all have the two-ballot list system of election but with no crossing-off or *panachage*. Parties or groups contesting the election each present a complete list to fill all the seats on the council. The leader of the victorious list is expected by the citizens to be mayor, and is normally elected to that office by his colleagues at the first council meeting following the election. The elector can only choose a complete list, and lists are 'blocked': they cannot be modified between ballots. Paris and four of the largest provincial cities have the same blocked list system but these cities are divided into sectors each one treated like a city of over 30,000 people. Paris has 18 sectors, Lyon has 9, Marseille 8, Toulouse 3, and Nice 3. The parties or coalitions, therefore, who aspire to govern these cities must present lists in each sector.

The political significance of these electoral provisions is profound. First, since lists are blocked, coalitions must be coherent and, above all, constructed before the campaign begins. They cannot be cooked up between ballots. This is very important for alliances like the *Union de la Gauche* as we shall see. For example in 1971 a Socialist-led list and a Communist list contested the city of Lille as rivals. Just as in a parliamentary election, the Communist list was withdrawn after the first ballot and Communist votes invited to support the Socialists. The Socialist list was elected with Communist support but no Communist had a seat on the council in Lille. Secondly, since the elector can only vote for a whole list, the list with an absolute majority at the first ballot or a relative majority at the second wins all the seats on the council. There is therefore no opposition in the council chamber in large French cities, and this means that in French local government the debate and criticism that is brought to bear in council on the actions and policies of a British city council, for instance, is totally absent. Opposition can only come from dissatisfied segments of the victorious list, who cannot be too opposed to the mayor if they agreed to be on his list for the election and want to be included next time, or from outside the council, or from isolated figures returned at by-elections.

Table 14.3
MUNICIPAL ELECTIONS IN THE FIFTH REPUBLIC
(% *1st Ballot Vote*)

|  | 1965 | 1971 | 1977 |
|---|---|---|---|
| Abstentions % of electorate | 21·8 | 24·9 | |
| Communist lists | | 11·6 | 3·8 |
| Left coalitions | 24·6 | 24·5 | 38·2 |
| Left and Centre, Centrist coalitions | 20·2 | 7·4 | 8·2 |
| *Majorité* coalitions | 28·9 | 40·1 ⎫ | |
| Independent, Local Action, and | | ⎬ | 45·0 |
| other alliances | 26·3 | 16·0 ⎭ | |
| Other | | | 3·7 |

The only exceptions to this rule of no opposition in large cities are the five which are divided into sectors.[6] Thus in 1971 the opposition (Left 31, Centre 13) had 44 of the 90 seats in Paris, and the Communist opposition to Defferre in Marseille won 7 of the 63 seats. In Lyon, however, the artfully constructed list of Pradel containing all the moderate political shades won all nine sectors straight off at the first ballot.

In considering the results of municipal elections in the Fifth Republic it is important to remember that one cannot present them in terms of party shares of the vote. Coalition lists are put together in each town or village before the first ballot and the lists are blocked. Coalitions in 1965 and 1971 were diverse. Sometimes Socialists were allied with Centrists, sometimes with Communists, sometimes with neither. Thus it is impossible to arrive at a figure for the percentage of people voting Socialist. In 1977 it became much easier because the bipolarising trend in French politics had separated *Majorité* and opposition into two separate camps. Even so the lists varied a great deal in their composition.

Table 14.4
MUNICIPAL ELECTIONS IN THE FIFTH REPUBLIC
(*Mayors of cities over 30,000 population*)

|  | 1965 | 1971 | 1977 |
|---|---|---|---|
| PCF | 34 | 45 | 72 |
| Extreme Left | 4 | 1 | – |
| SFIO/PS | 32 | 40 | 81 |
| Radicals | 6 | 4 | 2 (MRG) |
| Other Left | | 8 | 4 |
| Centre Left | 9 | 2 | 7 (inc. ex-PS) |
| MRP/CD/CDS | 13 | 11 | 9 |
| UNR/UDR/RPR | 25 | 30 | 16 |
| RI | 8 | 12 | 13 |
| CDP* | | 12 | |
| Ind., Local Action, etc. | 25 | 27 | 18 |

* Merged with CD to form CDS, 1976.

## 3. The Municipal Elections of March 1977

This brief comment on the interesting municipal elections of 1977 has the nature of a postscript since the rest of the book was completed at the end of 1976.

Municipal elections attract considerable interest in France in their own right—mainly, as suggested at the beginning of this chapter, because of the 'presidential' character of local government. The 1977 elections, however, were regarded nationally and internationally as a dress rehearsal for the 1978 Parliamentary elections. If the *Union de la Gauche* was maintaining the momentum of the 1974 presidential election and the 1976 cantonal elections and by-elections, then surely it was set fair to win in 1978—with all the implications of constitutional difficulties and Communist access to government which so transfix observers. In fact, as a dress rehearsal local elections differ in two important ways from national elections: first, well-entrenched local mayors can often resist the national tide, particularly in the thousands of small towns and villages; secondly, the future character of the regime is not at stake.

Two characteristics of the 1977 municipals were of particular significance. The first was the remarkable success of the *Union de la*

*Gauche,* and the second, related to the first, was the electoral bonus constituted by unity. The *Union de la Gauche* presented joint lists in some 200 of the 221 large cities with over 30,000 inhabitants. In many cases, like Lille, this meant a change of alliance from a Socialist-Centrist coalition to a Socialist-Communist. The number from each party to be included on the new lists was the subject of intense and prolonged local negotiation. Some big cities like Clermont-Ferrand or Limoges, or towns in mining areas of the North, which had been Socialist with virtual exclusivity, now have a number of Communist councillors. Since there were many fewer exclusively Communist councils elected in 1971, the PCF is regarded, in terms of seats gained, as being the principal beneficiary of the *Union de la Gauche* strategy in these elections. The *Majorité* based much of its campaign on supposed fears of a new 'totalitarian presence' in town halls. It was a failure. A tidal wave of votes swept the Left into control of 159 of the 221 cities (a gain of 56). It seemed to matter not a whit to the electors whether the local leader of the Left was a Socialist or a Communist. The stronghold of Michel Durafour, Minister of Finance, in St. Etienne (mayor now PCF), Montpellier (PS), Nantes (PS), Le Mans (PCF) and many other important cities were taken from the *Majorité.* Towns in the Catholic heartlands which had been comfortably carried by Giscard d'Estaing in 1974—like Rennes in Brittany—fell to the Left. Where the Left was disunited, as in Aix-en-Provence, it was, with some important exceptions, less successful in garnering at the second ballot all votes given to the various lists of the Left at the first. In Marseille, a city divided into sectors, Gaston Defferre, in conformity with party policy, severed his local alliance with Centrists. He refused however to include Communists on his lists. He was therefore opposed by PCF lists in all eight sectors and Communist voters were notably reluctant to transfer their second ballot votes to the Socialists.

Public interest of course was centred on the 'battle of Paris'. The government had designated Michel d'Ornano, Minister of Industry, to lead the *Majorité* in Paris and to be the first Mayor of Paris since 1870. However the extraordinary Jacques Chirac, leader of the newly launched Gaullist RPR, flung his hat into the ring. He won. Although the Chirac lists gained only 26% of the Paris first ballot vote against 22% for the d'Ornano lists, the latter were obliged to stand down in favour of their better-placed rivals in eleven of the eighteen sectors. The Chirac lists were thus able to win fifty of the 109 seats, with only sixteen going to their rivals. It was hailed as a great victory for Chirac, for his aggressive style, and for his policy of vigorous attacks upon the Left. Paris certainly enhanced Chirac's reputation as a winner, but the other claims are less able to stand inspection. In the first place, the Left did better in Paris even than it did in the 1974 presidential election (45% at the second ballot compared to 43%—see Appendix 7)—and this in a city which working-class voters are increasingly forced by the high cost of housing to leave. Secondly, the bitter internecine conflict of the *Majorité* in the capital city, contrasted with the serene unity of the opposition, helped the Left to make electoral progress both by the bad impression created and by the reluctance, in areas where first ballot 'primaries' had taken place, of some *Majorité* electors to transfer their votes to the *Majorité* list remaining in the contest. The *Majorité* suffered badly in these elections, but it should not be forgotten that the meagre total of sixty-two out of 221 cities it now controls does nonetheless include Paris, Lyon, Toulouse, Bordeaux, Nice and Strasbourg—six of the ten largest in France.

It is necessary to record briefly the relative success of two new political movements which receive no mention elsewhere in this book. The 'Ecologists' put up lists in Paris and some other cities, and as an environmentalist protest group speaking out on the declining quality of urban life. They did very well: 10% in Paris as a whole, and up to 14% on the Left Bank. The other movement was the '*Jobertistes*'—the *Mouvement des Démocrates,* founded by Michel Jobert, President Pompidou's last Foreign Minister and a vigorous opponent of Giscard d'Estaing. They obtained critical first ballot votes in cities like Nantes and St. Etienne which may have tipped the balance away from the *Majorité*.

Municipal elections in France are a remarkable lesson in political participation. Seventy-eight per cent of the electorate vote in 1977, and even in Paris the turnout was 67%, as against 57% in 1971. In close second-round contests the turnout was even higher. The attraction of local government to leading political figures remains strong: the new Paris City Council includes two Gaullist ex-prime ministers.

## NOTES

1. See Mark Kesselmann: *The Ambiguous Consensus,* Knopf, 1967.
2. Cantons used to have administrative significance. There were cantonal councils until 1926.
3. Charles Debbasch, *Institutions Administratives,* Paris: Librairie Générale de Droit et de Jurisprudence, 1966, p. 68.
4. Corsica was divided into two *départements* in 1975 (Haute-Corse and Corse du Sud) so that Metropolitan France now has 96, not 95.
5. See Chapter 11.
6. At the time of the 1964 law it was maliciously suggested that the special treatment of the largest cities was designed to make life difficult for Gaston Defferre, Mayor of Marseille, who at that time looked likely to be General de Gaulle's opponent in the 1975 presidential election.

# 15

## REFERENDA

The electorate in the Fifth Republic is not only invited to choose its rulers and its representatives at local or national level, it is also periodically called upon to pronounce on laws and policies. Article 11 of the Constitution reads as follows:

On the proposal of the Government during Parliamentary sessions, or on the joint proposal of the two Assemblies, published in the *Journal Officiel*, the President of the Republic may submit to a referendum any Government Bill dealing with the organisation of the public authorities, approving a Community agreement, or authorising the ratification of a treaty which, although not in conflict with the Constitution, would affect the working of institutions.

If the result of the referendum is favourable to the adoption of the Bill, the President of the Republic promulgates it within the time-limit laid down in the preceding article.

Notice that the initiative for a referendum is supposed to come from government or Parliament, not the President—a provision more honoured in the breach than the observance so far. General de Gaulle and his successor Georges Pompidou decided on their own referenda and then asked their Prime Ministers to write a letter suggesting it, beginning 'In conformity with Article 11 of the Constitution I have the honour to propose . . .'. The article also says nothing specific about amending the constitution. Constitutional amendments can be submitted to referendum but only after both houses of Parliament have agreed (Art. 89). As we have seen in Chapter 2, this did not prevent General de Gaulle from submitting two major constitutional revisions directly to the people.

Direct democracy in the form of popular referendum always arouses intense debate. In the United States it is considered appropriate for local issues but not for national policy-making. In Great Britain, despite the intelligent and mature manner in which the British people participated in the referendum on European Community membership in June 1975,[1] the conventional wisdom is to regard the referendum as a threat to the sovereignty of Parliament and to the whole notion of representative government, which declares that the job of an electorate is to choose its representatives and not try to decide complex policy issues. In France, too, this is the traditional 'Republican' view. The referendum is a threat to democracy, according to the Left in

France, principally because it allows authoritarian leaders to obtain plebiscitary votes of confidence for themselves and hence free themselves from the contraints of representative institutions. Memories are long in France. The referendum made an unpromising debut in modern times with the famous question in 1804 'Napoleon Bonaparte, shall he be consul for life?' His nephew Napoleon III also won plebiscitary approval for his dictatorship at a referendum. Some of General de Gaulle's referenda were seen as part of the same tradition of Bonapartist manipulation, notably the controversial one in October 1962 on direct presidential elections. At the height of the turbulent Events of May 1968 de Gaulle proposed a referendum on participation and the comment of Pierre Mendès-France, one of the Left's most distinguished leaders, was: 'Plebiscites? You don't discuss them, you fight them.'[2] In other words the referendum was merely a device for de Gaulle, threatening chaos if he were to depart, to renew his mystical communion with the people and obtain a personal vote of confidence at the expense of intermediaries who were trying to represent the discontents of the nation.

So these are the main democractic objections to referenda: ignorance and prejudice would inevitably carry the day against wisdom and reason, and they would lead to the abuse of power by demagogic leaders who would influence the hysterical mob to vote for dictatorship and repressive laws. It is a view, one is compelled to remark, that expresses remarkably little confidence in the perspicacity of the common people. In fact in reasonably mature democracies people have proved much less malleable than critics of referenda imagined. The British would vote 'No' to Europe because the price of butter had risen and they hate foreigners. They voted 'Yes'. The Italians would vote 'Yes' to the petition outlawing divorce because they would docilely do what the Church told them to do. They voted 'No'. The Swiss (after a few valiant years of irrational prejudice) voted responsibly on feminine suffrage and on the rights of foreign workers. The French too have supported measures they really wanted to support and which have turned out very well—colonial independence, directly elected Presidency, or the constitution of the Fifth Republic. They have withheld their support from more dubious measures—the constitution of the Fourth Republic which was very narrowly adopted with a third of the nation in favour, a third against, and third abstaining, and the two most recent referenda of the Fifth Republic, April 1969 and April 1972, both of which smacked of abusive attempts to get presidential votes of confidence or bad laws. In both cases the French administered a raspberry to executive power: in the first by voting 'No' and provoking the resignation of General de Gaulle, in the second by abstaining in millions

There have been nine referenda in France since the liberation. The three in the Fourth Republic were all related to the adoption of a new constitution. Did the people want one? (Yes.)[3] Did they like the constitution eventually proposed? (No.) Did they, having elected a new constituent Assembly in June 1946, like the constitution it eventually proposed? (Only just: 9 million in favour, 8 million against, 8 million abstentions and spoilt papers.) In the Fifth Republic there have been six (if we include the referendum of September 1958 setting up the Republic and exclude the referendum of July 1962 in which Algerian voters only were asked whether they wanted independence for their nation), five under General de Gaulle, one in the Presidency of Georges Pompidou, and, by the end of 1976 at any rate, none in the reign of President Giscard d'Estaing. There is a profound difference between the Fourth and Fifth Republics as far as referenda are concerned. The Fourth Republic constitution, once legitimised by adoption at a referendum, was very much the constitution of 'parliamentary sovereignty'—no question of further recourse to direct democracy. The Fifth Republic on the other hand, as we have seen, retains the referendum as a normal constitutional device and, indeed, as a powerful weapon in the armoury of the President of the Republic.

## 1. *The referendum of 28 September 1958*
The constitution of the Fifth Republic, sweeping away the impotent and ever-changing governments of the Fourth Republic at the mercy of their over-mighty Parliaments, conferring real powers on the Executive—in particular those of the President of the Republic—and cutting Parliament down to size, was massively adopted in September 1958 by a majority of four to one. The constitution had been drawn up very much along the lines of General de Gaulle's famous speech at Bayeux in 1946. The powers of the Presidency were somewhat ambiguous in relation to those of the Prime Minister and of the government, but in his hands were special powers in an emergency (Art. 16), recourse to referendum (Art. 11), dissolution of Parliament (Art. 12), and the power to appoint the Prime Minister (Art. 8). In addition, all kinds of restrictions were to be put on Parliament's capacity to impede or overthrow the executive (Arts. 24–51).

The new constitution was presented to the people at a massive rally (tickets by invitation only) in the Place de la République by General de Gaulle in early September. These were troubled times. It was only four months since the *coup d'état* in Algiers had caused the collapse of the Fourth Republic. Its last President, M. Coty, turned to 'the most illustrious of Frenchmen' to form a government and prepare a new constitution. If ever there was a vote of confidence referendum this was it: the heroic war-time leader called back from the wilderness to save his people again. The whole enterprise, crisis leadership and the type of constitution now presented, was condemned as Bonapartist by the Communist Party, the CGT, about half of the Socialist SFIO (though not its leaders like Guy Mollet) and other important figures on the Left, François Mitterrand and Pierre Mendés-France. Despite their campaign, however, only 5 million people (less than the Communist vote alone in 1956) voted against the Constitution. It has been estimated that at least 1·5 million Communist voters voted 'Yes', as majorities were recorded in even the most solid Communist municipalities of the Paris suburbs.

In overseas territories the electors were asked a second question: did they want independence or membership of a new organisation called the French Community. Only Guinea in West Africa chose independence.

## 2. *The referendum of 8 January 1961*
The referendum on the policy of self-determination for Algeria fits into the dramatic story, already briefly recounted,[4] of how General de Gaulle, brought back to power by those who wanted to keep Algeria French, was able to lead the nation, and his own supporters in particular, to acceptance of the need for Algerian independence. The January 1961 referendum lies between two Algiers revolts— the 'week of the barricades' in January 1960, and the *'putsch des généraux'* of 22 April 1961 when four army leaders seized the city. The result of the referendum was a victory for self-determination by a majority of three to one. The Communist suburbs of Paris voted 'No' and so did some economically backward areas of the Centre and South. These areas were traditionally Left but had become rather Poujadist in expression in the 1950s. The Moderate and Conservative regions gave massive support to the General and his policy.

## 3. *The referendum of 8 April 1962*
The 90% Yes-vote in April 1962 represents the apogee of support for General de Gaulle who had held the country together through the difficult times in the previous year when important parts of the army had been in revolt against Algerian independence and the emergency powers under Article 16 had been invoked. In the April referendum the people were asked to approve the Evian Agreement—the independence negotiations completed with the Algerian Independence movement (FLN). The referendum was surrounded by some worries about the abuse of power by General de Gaulle. The period of emergency powers (April to September 1961) had been very long and had included some arbitrary acts of

government. The Evian negotiations had been very secret—even the government had not been privy to them. The referendum text would confer additional powers on the President to take the regulatory measures required to implement Evian. The PSU campaigned for a blank vote as a way of saying 'Yes' to peace and 'No' to Gaullist abuse of power. It was however the desire for peace, an end to the long Algerian conflict, and an end to the terrorism of the extremist supporters of *Algérie Française*, the OAS, that carried the day by a crushing majority.

## 4. The referendum of 28 October 1962

This is the most far-reaching and controversial of the referenda since the inauguration of the Fifth Republic. We have encountered it in Chapter 2 and again, as an issue overshadowing the November 1962 elections, in Chapter 13 by proposing the direct election of the President of the Republic by universal suffrage, it advanced a constitutional amendment that would fundamentally alter the regime because a directly elected President, would, in addition to General de Gaulle's lofty conception of that office, officially incarnate a higher legitimacy than any other institution. We looked earlier at the General's masterly sense of when the right moment had come to put to the people the question of how to maintain the authority of the Presidency when charismatic legitimacy was exhausted. After the settlement of the Algerian crisis with a 90% majority in April, after the drama of the Petit Clamart assassination attempt in August, the time had come to use charismatic authority to shift the regime on to a new basis. A referendum was declared in a quite unconstitutional manner (changes to the constitution must be approved by Parliament first: Art. 89). An outraged Assembly passed a motion of censure on 4 October. The government resigned. Parliament was dissolved. All the traditional parties campaigned to defeat the referendum. The Conservative Independents, the MRP, the Radicals, and the Socialists formed a *Cartel des Non*. A cartel of the Noes is not the same as cartel for No—it suggests a variety of different reasons for voting No. The only thing that united them was a preference for the traditional conception of parliamentary democracy as enshrined in the discredited Fourth Republic. It was thus a straight confrontation: 'de Gaulle specifically put the issue in terms of himself or the parties of the bad old times'.[5] The threat that he would resign if the vote was unsatisfactory unleashed claims that this was another plebiscitary Bonapartist operation. It was, of course, but this view overlooks the important fact that the people had demonstrated, on the evidence of opinion polls since 1945, their preference for stable executive leadership based on a directly elected Presidency.[6]

The result was not the triumph of April 1962—under two-thirds (62%) of those voting, themselves under half (47%) of those entitled to vote, voted 'Yes'. There was a No-majority in fifteen *départements,* all in the economically backward Centre and South. However, the Left-wing strongholds in prosperous industrial areas like the Paris region and the North voted 'Yes'. The leaders of the Right and Centre who had campaigned for No did disastrously badly against Gaullists and their reliable Yes-voting allies in the elections a month later.[7] The October referendum was the last stand of the 'third force' of the Fourth Republic—the bloc of Moderates of the Centre-Right, Centre-Left and Socialists who, excluding only the Fourth Republic's anti-parliamentary forces of Communism on their Left and Gaullism and Poujadism on their Right, had governed France from 1947 to 1958. Attempts to resuscitate the 'third force'—the abortive Defferre candidature for the Presidency in 1964-5[8] and the limbless Poher candidature for the Presidency in 1969[9]—have been doomed to failure. The people in the autumn of 1962 chose majority government under a strong Presidency which gave a better chance of effectiveness and stability. In future only an opposition which looked like a coherent alternative majority would have any chance of winning.

## 5. *The referendum of 27 April 1969*

After the Algerian crisis and the reform of the constitution had been disposed of in 1962, there followed six years of 'normal' times in which the Fifth Republic settled down to its cruising speed. When this was shattered by the romantic folklore events of May 1968, General de Gaulle decided to call a referendum. People were discontented, he thought, because the state attended to their every need without giving them a chance to have a say. There was to be participation. The proposal did nothing to calm perturbed spirits and General de Gaulle, announcing in his famous radio broadcast of 30 May, that there would be elections instead, said of his referendum: 'I defer its date.' True to his word, almost a year later he called a referendum for 27 April 1969. It was not really on participation, more a kind of corporatism. It proposed, firstly, a reform of the Senate in which economic and social interests, such as unions, education, industry and agriculture, would be directly represented alongside the present type of geographical representation. The second proposal was to create twenty-one regional councils (based on the programme regions set up in 1964) also containing designated representatives of social and economic interest groups as well as of local councils.

This referendum and its campaign had three attributes making it more objectionable than its predecessors. In the first place it was unconstitutional because it involved constitutional changes which, according to Article 89, should be voted by Parliament first. In this respect it was, of course, following the precedent of October 1962. But it was possible to argue, and subsequent events have borne this out, that the 1962 referendum had a saving grace in that it proposed a measure, direct election of the Presidency, desired by the nation whose will would have been frustrated by Parliament, rooted in the effete and rejected traditions of the Fourth Republic. In 1969 there was no evidence that any group wanted the Senate to be converted into a corporatist chamber. The regional reforms were a little more popular but only 33% of those interviewed in an opinion poll during the campaign thought them really important for the future.[10]

The second objectionable attribute was that it was much more like a plebiscite and less like a referendum. The actual text on which the people were required to vote, sixty-nine articles of detailed proposals and technical amendments to the constitution, were virtually incomprehensible to all but constitutional lawyers. In addition there were two separate proposals—reform of the Senate, and reform of the regions—lumped into one question. 'To separate the two propositions would of course have been possible, but it might have resulted in a mixture of victory and defeat which was incompatible with General de Gaulle's intentions. An artificial agglomeration of issues has at all times been the characteristic of a plebiscite.'[11] The General wanted the people 'to give to the state, and, in the first place to its leader, a mandate for renewal'. The plebiscitary character of the referendum became increasingly marked. In repeated broadcasts the General made it clear he would resign if the referendum was not carried and in a final, almost pathetic appeal, that his present term of office would be his last.

The third noteworthy and objectionable characteristic of the campaign was the abuse of executive power that it revealed. The public authorities and public funds were pressed into the service of the campaign for Yes. Every voter received a letter from General de Gaulle explaining why he or she should vote for the reform proposals. The entire resources of television and radio appeared to have been consecrated to the task of securing an affirmative result. An extraordinary atmosphere of secrecy and nervousness pervaded the whole ORTF building. The audience research departments were instructed to conduct telephone polls to measure the penetration of General de Gaulle's last broadcast. Interviews, news bulletins, regional information centres set up by the ORTF for audiences to telephone, were yes-oriented.[12] The opposition parties divided the lean crust of a single hour's official television time, which as it turned out, proved unexpectedly nutritious. It was here that Alain Poher, President of the Senate and soon to be a Presidential candidate, who, amiable, fumbling with his notes, and thus presenting a striking contrast with the olympian General, made so favourable an impact on the public. The opposition also gave some of their time to well-remembered TV personalities like Maurice Sévéno, sacked after the 1968 events of May, who appeared denouncing not the text of the referendum but the distortion of news and stifling of information. In the subsequent Presidential campaign the liberalisation of television and radio from executive interference became a leading issue.

Unconstitutional, plebiscitary, abusive of executive power and unsuccessful—that was the character of the 1969 referendum. The people voted No by 53% to 47% and General de Gaulle immediately resigned. Many leading political figures who had supported General de Gaulle in the past withheld their support on this occasion. The most notable was Giscard d'Estaing, who had a wide audience among Moderate electors, and who proclaimed at a press conference that he would not be voting Yes. Gaullists still blame Giscard d'Estaing for the General's resignation. Another candidate for their bitterness was the man who, as Prime Minister, had saved the day during the events of May. If only he had declared that he would not be a presidential candidate if de Gaulle resigned, Georges Pompidou could have contributed to fears of chaos and hence to a plebiscitary vote of confidence in the General. This time there was a Yes majority only in the Catholic and Gaullists bastions of Brittany, Alsace-Lorraine, and the Massif Central. Industrial France voted No.

Many people have asked themselves why General de Gaulle staked all on success in this unnecessary and unconvincing referendum.[13] It seems as though he needed, after the regime's great difficulties in 1968, a restatement of public confidence in his personal leadership or a pretext to leave office. De Gaulle and popular confidence are like the poet Walter Savage Landor and the 'fire of life': 'It sinks, and I am ready to depart.'

## 6. *The referendum of 23 April 1972*

Not a spectacular failure, merely a damp squib, the referendum of April 1972 need not detain us. The French people were asked if they would be good enough to allow Great Britain, Denmark, the Irish Republic, and Norway to join the European Community. From President Pompidou's point of view a referendum seemed an excellent idea. It was perfectly constitutional—indeed, as the President pointed out, the phrase in Article 11 about 'the ratification of a treaty which . . . would affect the working of institutions' might have been written with the enlargement of the EEC in mind. It was an opportunity to take an important presidential constitutional weapon out of the armoury, dust it down, and make sure it was still in working order. France would be able to show

how democratic it was by involving the people in decisions on the European Community. Since very few people were opposed to the British and the others joining the EEC, the result was bound to be satisfactory. This could be displayed as a vote of confidence in the President personally and as approval for his handling of a European policy markedly different from that of his illustrious predecessor. Finally it would have the advantage of sowing discord amongst the opposition who were trying actively to pursue a strategy of alliance and unity—*Union de la Gauche*. The Socialists had always wanted the British in the EEC, the Communists had always wanted them to stay out. The referendum therefore seemed a wonderful idea. It would give the President greatly reinforced authority at the Paris summit in October.[14]

The Socialist party very sensibly suggested to the PCF that both parties should recommend abstention. If the Socialists declined to vote Yes, despite their feelings on British membership, and the Communists declined to vote No despite theirs, both could concentrate on attacking the referendum as a cheap presidential popularity device. Furthermore if the Communists abstained there would be no opposition at all and there could therefore be no presidential victory. The PCF refused. It would campaign for No. It looked as if the Pompidou stratagem might work. The satirical weekly *Le Canard Enchaîné* published an imaginary letter from President Pompidou to the General Secretary of the PCF: 'Dear Georges, Thank you for coming to my help as you have done so often in the past . . .'

Despite the obliging decision of the PCF to let the match go on by fielding an opposition, the referendum attracted very little interest: 40% of the electorate abstained and a further 7% spoilt their ballots. Although this 47% no doubt included many who were indifferent to the whole issue, it looked like a great success for the Socialist Party who stuck to their line of recommending abstention as a way of saying 'Yes' to Great Britain and 'No' to President Pompidou. The abstentions were the highest in any national vote since universal manhood suffrage was introduced in 1848. Only 36% of the electorate (68% of those voting) voted Yes. The Communists saw a reasonably satisfactory 5 million vote No.

April 1972 was President Pompidou's only referendum and at the end of 1976 Giscard d'Estaing had not yet used that particular presidential instrument. However, Jean-Luc Parodi's interesting assessment of referenda[15] would indicate that we might expect them at regular intervals. He points to the repeated phenomenon in the Fifth Republic of 'referenda of confirmation'. The seven-year term of presidential office is a very long one and there is a need to recharge the batteries of presidential authority in mid-term. This would be particularly important if an anti-presidential

majority won a parliamentary election. It would be claimed that
the parliamentary vote is the up-to-date expression of the popular
will and not the President's yellowing mandate. Parodi points to
the referendum of 1961 (on the principle of Algerian self-
determination), the attempted referendum on participation
proposed during the events of May 1968 and held after a fashion in
April 1969, and the referendum on EEC enlargement of 1972 as
examples of 'referenda of confirmation'. None of them was
necessary in the sense of being a vital issue that had to be decided—
as for instance the adoption of the constitution was, or the granting
of independence to Algeria. All of them fell three years after a
presidential election—mid-term. In late 1976 President Giscard
d'Estaing was clearly experiencing that certain mid-term attrition
of authority experienced by his predecessors, and there was talk of
a referendum on direct elections to the European Parliament. The
weakest and least convincing referenda of the Fifth Republic, 1969
and 1972, have both been referenda of confirmation. One of the
differences between the two most controversial and unconstitutional referenda of the Fifth Republic—October 1962 on
direct presidential elections and April 1969 on Senate and regional
reform—is that the earlier was not a referendum of confirmation.
Presidential power was at its zenith and did not need a vote of
confidence. The objectionable plebiscitary character of the later
referendum was much more evident.

One final word: the most significant feature of the last two
referenda, 1969 and 1972, both 'referenda of confirmation' seeking
plebiscitary votes of confidence, is that they both failed. In a
democracy people are not so easily taken in as is commonly
supposed.

### Table 15.1 REFERENDUM RESULTS
*Metropolitan France, 1945-72*

| | *Yes* | *No* | *Abstentions and Spoilt Votes (% of electorate)* |
|---|---|---|---|
| **Fourth Republic** | | | |
| **21 Oct. 1945** | | | |
| (a) Desire for a new constitution | 96.4% (18 m.) | 3.6% (0.7 m.) | 24.2% (6 m.) |
| (b) Limited powers for constituent Assembly | 66.3% (12.3 m.) | 33.7% (6.3 m.) | 24.4% (6 m.) |
| **5 May 1946** Adoption of constitution | 47.0% (9.1 m.) | 53.0% (10.3 m.) | 21.3% (5.3 m.) |
| **13 Oct. 1946** Adoption of constitution | 53.5% (9 m.) | 46.5% (7.8 m.) | 32.5% (8.1 m.) |
| **Fifth Republic** | | | |
| **28 Sept. 1958** Adoption of constitution | 79.2% (17.1 m.) | 20.7% (4.6 m.) | 16.2% (4.3 m.) |
| **8 Jan. 1961** Self-determination for Algeria | 75.2% (15.2 m.) | 24.7% (5 m.) | 25.6% (7 m.) |
| **8 April 1962** Algerian independence | 90.7% (17.5 m.) | 9.3% (1.8 m.) | 28.4% (7.7 m.) |
| **28 Oct. 1962** Direct election of President | 61.7% (12.8 m.) | 38.2% (7.9 m.) | 24.7% (6.9 m.) |
| **28 April 1969** Reform of Senate and Regions | 46.7% (10.5 m.) | 53.2% (11.9 m.) | 21.6% (6.2 m.) |
| **23 April 1972** Enlargement of Common Market | 67.7% (10.5 m.) | 32.3% (5 m.) | 46.6% (13.6 m.) |

NOTES

1 For a view on this see J. R. Frears, 'A re-appraisal of referenda', *Socialist Commentary*, Oct. 1975. Note also that Great Britain has long used referenda in local government to decide local issues such as Sunday opening for pubs in Wales, whether or not to have a municipal lottery in Manchester, etc—not to mention the major constitutional issue of devolution for Scotland and Wales.

2 'Le plébiscite, ça ne se discute pas, ça se bat', Radio interview.

3 This referendum, in October 1945, asked the people two questions: Did they want the Assembly elected that day to draw up a new constitution? And did they want the powers of that Assembly to be limited along the lines of a plan proposed by General de Gaulle, head of the Provisional Government?

4 See Chapter 2.

5 Michael Steed in S. Henig and J. Pinder, eds, *European Political Parties*, PEP, 1969, p. 132.

6 See p. 192n, and Charlot, *The Gaullist Phenomenon*, p. 56.

7 See p. 210.

8 See p. 90.

9 See p.199.

10 *Sondages*, 1969, p. 10. In Oct. 1962 53% considered direct election of the President an issue of great importance.

11 H. W. Ehrmann, *Politics in France*, Little, Brown & Co., 2nd edn., 1971 p. 112.

12 See J. R. Frears, *The Listener*, 29 May 1969, p. 746.

13 E.g. J. E. S. Hayward 'Presidential suicide by plebiscite', *Parliamentary Affairs 1969*, pp. 289-319, and Frédéric Bon: 'Le Référendum du 27 avril 1969: Suicide politique ou nécessité stratégique', *Revue Française de Sciences Politiques*, 1970, pp. 205-23

14 See Michael Leigh, 'Linkage politics: the French referendum and the Paris summit of 1972', *Journal of Common Market Studies*, Dec. 1975, pp. 157-70

15 In his 'La Cinquième République et le Système majoritaire', Thèse pour le Doctorat de Recherches, Paris 1973, unpublished.

# 16

## ASPECTS OF ELECTORAL BEHAVIOUR

### 1. *Abstention*

We have already encountered various aspects of electoral behaviour: the transfer of first ballot votes for one party to second ballot votes for another, the social characteristics of the *Majorité* or Communist electorate, the regional variations in party support. Another aspect of electoral behaviour has so far not been examined at all: abstention, the behaviour that consists in not voting at all.

There are clearly many possible reasons for not voting in an election. It may be a positive act in that an elector does not wish to support any of the election candidates or referendum measures proposed for his consideration. This was the case, for instance, with Communist supporters in the second ballot of the 1969 presidential election. Their party urged them to boycott a choice between what it saw as two Right-wing candidates. It was the case, no doubt, for a large number of those who abstained in the 1972 referendum on enlargement of the European Community. The Socialist Party campaigned strongly on the theme that the referendum was merely a popularity device for President Pompidou. The French, however, are very fortunate in that the elector can abstain in a more positive way than staying at home: he can cast a blank or spoilt paper knowing that these are given as a separate total. A blank is a more positive abstention than spoilt papers which appear more often to be the work of deranged electors who scrawl offensive observations on their voting slip. Perhaps they should be counted separately.

Abstention, however, is often not a positive political act but a negative one. Some people cannot vote—they may not have been included on the register, they may be ill, they may have moved away from where they are registered, they may be away and unable to return. Some people do not bother to vote because they would rather go fishing, or because they do not feel like going out in the rain, or because they are just not interested. The categories of positive and negative abstainers are very indistinct. How does one assess the precise difference between one individual who is uninterested in an election and another who feels that no candidate is worth supporting?

Alain Lancelot has done a major study on the phenomenon of abstention which looks carefully at all the possible variables.[1] Firstly, abstention has a 'geography'. Broadly speaking the north

250

votes more than the south, with Corsica invariably having the worst record. These regional variations seem to be remarkably persistent as do 'micro-variations' from town to town, village to village. 'Political' explanations of abstention revolve round the number of candidates (up to a point the more there are the more electors will find someone to identify with), the frequency of elections (if they come too often, as in Autumn 1962, people grow tired of voting), and, above all, the extent to which an election is crucial and keenly contested. Very few people abstain in a presidential election. Very few people in small villages abstain in their local council elections which are seen as important. Many abstain in Cantonal elections for the *département* council and in pre-Chirac Paris City Council elections because they were seen as unimportant. When an election is keenly fought, regarded as likely to produce a close result, and presented as an election on the outcome of which profound social and political change depends, abstention is low. For instance the 1973 parliamentary and the 1974 presidential election campaigns centred on the profound effects that would result from a victory of the left at the polls. The election was a 'choice of society'. In both elections more electors were mobilised to vote at the second ballot than had turned out at the first. Usually the reverse happens: the limited choice at the second ballot keeps people at home. 1973 and 1974, however, were exciting elections. The record turnout of all, the second ballot of 1974 (12·1% abstention, 1·2% spoilt papers) was the prelude to the closest imaginable finish—less than 400,000 in 26 million separating the two candidates.

Abstention has certain sociological characteristics. Women abstain more than men, very young and very old electors abstain more than those who are neither, the educated vote more than the less-educated, the well-to-do vote more than those on low incomes, workers abstain more than those in middle-class occupations, those who go to church on a Sunday seem more willing to move on to the polling station than the irreligious who do not. The final sociological conclusion reached by Lancelot[2] is that citizens who are well integrated into the community, who do not occupy isolated or subordinate social roles, who participate in community activities like church, local clubs, or unions, are less likely to be drawn into abstention. These findings are close to those of most political sociologists in Europe and America from Siegfried to Lazarsfeld.

The final point which Lancelot seeks to establish is whether there is a regular standing army of abstainers augmented from time to time by people who sometimes abstain and sometimes vote. In France, as we saw in Chapter 11, the electoral lists recording who has been to vote are available for inspection. Lancelot has done a detailed study based on these lists covering a number of elections, municipal, parliamentary, and referenda, in two localities. He found that 45·5% of electors always voted and that only 5·2% never voted. The remaining 49·3% abstained on one or more occasions.[3] He also found that in a two-ballot election, although the crude figures usually show such little variation in the total number of abstentions from one ballot to another that one would be tempted to conclude that the same body of electors abstained at both, in fact there is wide movement in both directions between voting and non-voting. He found slightly over 70% of first ballot abstainers continuing to abstain in the second ballot. Consequently nearly 30% of first ballot abstainers turned out in the decisive ballot, while among those who did not vote in the second ballot almost 30% had voted at the first.[4] Thus it is of capital importance in a close election to mobilise potential supporters who do not turn out at the first ballot and to maintain the support of those who do because they cannot be taken for granted.

## 2. *Religion*

The remainder of this chapter will summarise very briefly (because these characteristics have been evoked in the chapters on the parties) three other important aspects of electoral behaviour in France: religion, social class, and region. Religion used to be a powerful explanatory factor in French voting behaviour— Catholics voted against the godless Republic and the atheist Republicans, Radicals, Socialists, Communists and other heathens. A vote for the Left was a vote against the forces of reaction led by the Catholic Church. Religion no longer explains voting behaviour—France is a modern secular state where religious belief has long since ceased to be an issue—but there is still a remarkable correlation between religious practice and voting. Where the Church is strong (Brittany, Lower Normandy, Alsace-Lorraine) the *Majorité* is most successful. Where the Church is weakest are the traditional bastions of Left-wing strength (Limousin or Languedoc). Vincent McHale showed how closely in 1965 and 1967 what he calls 'religiosity' (intensity of religious practice) correlated with voting: [5]

Table 16·1
RELIGION AND VOTING 1967

| (% of population) | Catholics who go to church: | | | Without religion |
| | Regularly (25%) | Occasionally (22%) | Never (16%) | (37%) |
|---|---|---|---|---|
| | % | % | % | % |
| Majorité | 53 | 47 | 29 | 13 |
| Centre | 35 | 21 | 10 | 4 |
| | (88) | (68) | (39) | (17) |
| Non-Communist Left | 8 | 23 | 29 | 23 |
| PCF | 4 | 10 | 32 | 59 |
| | (12) | (33) | (61) | (82) |

By 1973 the position had changed a little but not very much:[6]

Table 16·2
RELIGION AND VOTING 1973

| | Regular churchgoers | Occasional churchgoers | Non-churchgoers |
|---|---|---|---|
| | % | % | % |
| Majorité | 70 | 47 | 20 |
| Centre | 16 | 13 | 11 |
| | (86) | (60) | (31) |
| Non-Communist Left | 12 | 24 | 34 |
| PCF | 1 | 14 | 32 |
| | (13) | (38) | (66) |

In 1968 the *Majorité* had considerable electoral success in some of the old rural anticlerical strongholds of the Left in' the centre and south-west of the country—and these gains were retained to a considerable extent in 1973. By contrast, we have seen in Chapter 7 the progress made by the Socialist Party in Catholic areas, and the very high proportion of Catholics among new party members.

## 3. Social class

The growing tendency for industrial workers to vote for the Left means that class is displacing religion as the most significant factor in voting behaviour. As Table 4·2 on page 54 showed, the Gaullist electorate in the days of the General was an almost perfect cross-section of the population and Gaullism received the support of more workers than did the Communist Party. This is not true of today's industrial and clerical workers, particularly the male, the young, and the urban, as is shown by Table 16·3 which takes the total percentage vote for the Left in 1973 as an index of 100 and

Table 16·3

LEFT-VOTING 1973[7]

| Total vote for Left 100 | | | | Urban / Rural |
|---|---|---|---|---|
| Manual and clerical workers 118 | Men 131 | Under 45 | 135 | Urban 136 / Rural 134 |
| | | Over 45 | 122 | Urban 127 / Rural 112 |
| | Women 106 | Under 45 | 106 | Urban 106 / Rural 106 |
| | | Over 45 | 105 | Urban 114 / Rural 99 |
| Other occupations 81 | Men 89 | Under 45 | 93 | Urban 98 / Rural 86 |
| | | Over 45 | 88 | Urban 99 / Rural 77 |
| | Women 72 | Under 45 | 79 | Urban 92 / Rural 63 |
| | | Over 45 | 68 | Urban 67 / Rural 66 |

expresses the percentages of Left-voting in the different categories of voters as variations from that figure. Thus class (as expressed by occupation) is a factor in voting behaviour of growing importance and, within the overall factor of class, sex, age and habitat are important variables.

## 4. *Regional variations*

Regional variations in voting behaviour have a long history but they represent to a large extent a synthesis of the last two factors: religion and class. Regions where the Catholic Church has always been strong vary in their traditional voting behaviour from regions which the Church has been forced to regard as 'mission territory'—for instance the remote rural backwaters of the south-west. Industrial regions, where there are numerous manual workers, vote differently from rural regions where there are not. These two variables are overlaid in for example, industrial areas with a strong tradition of churchgoing like north-eastern France. The electoral map of France, however, despite the recent changes just mentioned still looks, as it has done since manhood suffrage began in 1849, more like a map of religious practice than a map of urban settlement. Figures showing regional patterns of voting behaviour conceal the variations within regions. For example in 1974 within the Languedoc Region the Aude *département* preferred Mitterrand to Giscard d'Estaing by sixty-two to thirty-eight, whereas in the Lozère *département* (equally rural but traditionally Catholic) the proportions were almost exactly the reverse.

Religion, social class, and region are obviously not the whole story as far as variables in the explanation of voting behaviour are concerned. Why people vote the way they do, and indeed the whole attitude of the individual to the political process and to his role in it have been the subject of endless speculation and research in many countries. A Sofres opinion poll in 1970 found that 72% of French voters agreed with the statement 'Affairs of state are too complicated, you need to be a specialist to understand', and the same proportion answered the question 'Do you think you personally can exercise any influence on state decisions?' in the negative. Not surprisingly, therefore, in France as in other countries, voters pass general judgement on national leadership as they perceive it. Opinion polls in 1967[8] found 26% of voters indicating that their vote in the parliamentary elections of that year was a pronouncement directly for or against General de Gaulle (who, naturally, was not a candidate).

In France, as in America but not Great Britain, the candidate himself counts for a good deal in electoral choice. The local 'favourite son' seems always to do well. In presidential elections, candidates do best in their own locality. In 1974 Chaban-Delmas

Table 16·4
ELECTORAL PERFORMANCE OF MAJORITÉ BY REGION
*% of vote—suffrages exprimés*

| | 1967 1st ballot | 1968 1st ballot | 1969 (P) Pompidou 1st ballot★ | 1973 1st ballot | 1974 (P) Giscard 2nd ballot |
|---|---|---|---|---|---|
| *Regions of Strength†* | | | | | |
| N. Lower Normandy | 48·6 | 56·2 | 51·1 | 47·3 | 60·4 |
| Brittany ( +) | 40·3 | 49·8 | 51·3 | 45·3 | 58·1 |
| Loire Country | 45·3 | 55·6 | 51·2 | 48·8 | 60·1 |
| Alsace | 52·7 | 64·9 | 58·7 | 51·3 | 66·6 |
| Lorraine ( −) | 46·4 | 56·4 | 48·2 | 41·1 | 52·6 |
| Champagne | 39·7 | 43·5 | 44·3 | 39·5 | 50·2 |
| Franche-Comté | 44·2 | 48·9 | 46·3 | 41·2 | 50·9 |
| Burgundy | 38·5 | 48·8 | 42·8 | 42·5 | 48·6 |
| Centre | 40·8 | 47·5 | 41·2 | 39·0 | 52·0 |
| S. Poitou–Charentes | 38·0 | 45·4 | 44·2 | 40·1 | 51·3 |
| Auvergne ( +) | 34·0 | 46·4 | 47·6 | 38·8 | 52·8 |
| Corsica ( −) | 46·5 | 55·2 | 53·6 | 42·5 | 53·6 |
| *Average or below* | | | | | |
| *Average Regions†* | | | | | |
| N. Upper Normandy | | | | | |
| ( −) | 38·5 | 45·7 | 41·8 | 33·4 | 47·8 |
| Paris Region ( −) | 37·7 | 43·5 | 41·3 | 31·9 | 49·3‡ |
| North ( −) | 36·9 | 44·1 | 41·5 | 31·1 | 44·5 |
| Picardy ( −) | 38·9 | 43·4 | 40·9 | 29·8 | 45·8 |
| S. Aquitaine ( +) | 33·2 | 42·1 | 42·8 | 37·5 | 47·6 |
| Midi-Pyrenees ( +) | 30·9 | 37·2 | 41·7 | 35·1 | 46·1 |
| Rhone-Alps | 35·1 | 42·9 | 43·3 | 35·2 | 51·9 |
| Languedoc ( +) | 25·4 | 42·1 | 39·8 | 31·8 | 44·3 |
| Limousin ( +) | 25·7 | 38·7 | 40·8 | 31·1 | 42·2 |
| Provence-Côte | | | | | |
| d'Azur | 29·9 | 40·1 | 37·2 | 29·5 | 47·7‡ |
| France-Metropolitan | 37·7 | 44·7 | 44·0 | 36·0 | 50·7 |

(P) Presidential election.

★The high level of abstentions and the lack of a candidate of the Left make the second ballot in 1969 highly atypical.

†Based on 1973 parliamentary elections.

‡Regions where Giscard d'Estaing was exceptionally successful compared to the *Majorité* in 1973.

+/− Areas of above average gain(loss) 1967–73. Note how exceptional losses have been confined almost exclusively to industrial areas in the north and east, and how gains have been mainly in the traditional rural left-wing areas of the south-west.

Table 16·5
# UNION DE LA GAUCHE BY REGIONS—1967–74
*(% of votes—suffrages exprimés—1st ballot)*

|  | 1967 FGDS+ PCF | 1968 FGDS+ PCF | 1973 UGSD+ PCF | 1974 (P) Mitterrand |
|---|---|---|---|---|
| *Regions of strength*★ |  |  |  |  |
| N. North | 54·6 | 49·4 | 53·5 | 51·3 |
| Picardy | 46·8 | 39·2 | 46·5 | 47·1 |
| S. Limousin (−) | 62·8 | 55·9 | 55·2 | 51·5 |
| Languedoc | 53·6 | 49·6 | 55·2 | 50·3 |
| Provence-Côte d'Azur | 49·8 | 43·4 | 50·5 | 47·9 |
| Midi-Pyrenees | 46·6 | 43·9 | 47·6 | 47·4 |
|  |  |  |  |  |
| *Average regions*★ |  |  |  |  |
| N. Paris Region | 42·3 | 34·9 | 41·9 | 44·4 |
| Upper Normandy | 42·6 | 36·7 | 42·5 | 42·8 |
| Champagne | 42·0 | 37·4 | 43·1 | 44·1 |
| Centre | 43·4 | 37·4 | 40·0 | 39·8 |
| Burgundy (−) | 51·3 | 43·8 | 45·2 | 46·1 |
| Franche-Comté | 41·8 | 35·2 | 41·4 | 43·5 |
| S. Poitou-Charente | 38·1 | 35·5 | 39·2 | 40·5 |
| Aquitaine | 44·8 | 42·0 | 44·7 | 43·0 |
| Auvergne (−) | 49·0 | 43·7 | 44·6 | 42·3 |
| Rhone-Alps | 37·6 | 32·3 | 40·5 | 42·4 |
| Corsica | 41·3 | 43·3 | 42·0 | 44·6 |
|  |  |  |  |  |
| *Regions of weakness*★ |  |  |  |  |
| N. Alsace | 17·8 | 16·2 | 20·3 | 30·2† |
| Lorraine | 29·2 | 27·5 | 35·5 | 43·2† |
| Lower Normandy | 24·2 | 19·7 | 29·4 | 34·0† |
| Brittany | 26·4 | 22·9 | 33·1 | 37·2† |
| Loire Country | 27·6 | 25·3 | 30·7 | 36·1† |
|  |  |  |  |  |
| France-Metropolitan | 41·5 | 36·5 | 42·1 | 43·4 |

(P) Presidential election.

★Based on 1973 election.

†Note how the Left has been improving in these regions of traditional weakness, and the exceptional gains made by Mitterrand in 1974.

(−) Note how the Left has declined since 1967 in the old strongholds of rural central France.

ran well ahead of Giscard d'Estaing in Aquitaine and was top of the poll in his own city of Bordeaux. Mitterrand carried his province of Burgundy and got 1,200 out of 1,500 votes in the little town of Château-Chinon of which he is mayor. Even the luckless Royer carried his own city of Tours in the first ballot. In marked contrast to Great Britain, local connections are considered essential for parliamentary candidates. Much of a candidate's time is spent trying to win over local opinion leaders like mayors of villages in their constituency because they are presumed to exercise a decisive influence over their own electors. Despite the Fifth Republic's great upheaval in the party system and the electoral slaughter of non-Gaullists that occurred on numerous occasions, especially 1962 and 1968, eighty-eight deputies re-elected in 1968 had been in Parliament since before 1951, fourteen since the Third Republic.

If positive identification with a local candidate or national leader is an element of electoral behaviour, so too is the negative phenomenon of rejection.[9] Large numbers of voters for the Left in 1968 gave negative reasons for their choice. Nothing had been done for workers or the small man. Prices were too high. Nothing had been done for the farmer. When asked in 1970 why people might vote Communist only 5% of respondents thought French Communist voters wanted a Communist regime in France; 53% thought people would vote Communist in order to express general discontent.[10] By the same token the *Majorité* benefits electorally from feelings of dislike or fear of Communism and the Left. It has already been observed that the recent elections in which the Left were thought to have a good chance of winning, 1973 and 1974, were elections where, in contrast to usual practice, turnout increased slightly at the second ballot.

In addition one must consider the different 'political resources' of candidates and parties—though their effect on electoral choice is hard to assess. The public relations agency *Services et Méthodes* is considered to have played an important part in the successful way Jean Lecanuet was projected as a presidential candidate in 1965. It played a big part in campaign planning and presentation for the Gaullists in 1967 and for Pompidou in the presidential election of 1969. In the 1970s one has seen a growing awareness in the parties of the Left of the importance of their 'image' as a determinant of electoral choice.

To the great honour of France, election campaigns remain political. The image of the candidate as a family man is not sickeningly overdone. Candidates are not pre-packaged by market research and publicity men who, having discovered what the public wants said on any issues, produce their marionette to utter the correct sounds. The negative vote against probably outweighs the positive vote for in the balance of the Frenchman's electoral choice, and the negative campaign against probably outweighs the positive campaign for. However the campaigns are at least vigorous and neither local nor national nor indeed international issues are ignored.

## NOTES

1. *L'Abstentionnisme électorale en France*, Fondation Nationale des Sciences Politiques, Paris: Armand Colin, 1968.
2. *Ibid.*, pp. 216–26.
3. *Ibid.*, p. 237.
4. *Ibid.*, pp. 228–30.
5. 'Religion and electoral politics in France', *Canadian Journal of Political Science, Sept. 1969* pp. 292–311 (figures from IFOP, 1967).
6. IFOP February 1973—voting intentions in Charlot (ed.), *Quand la Gauche peut gagner*, p. 66.
7. IFOP March 1973 in ibid., p. 20.
8. *Sondages*, p. 27.
9. see Philippe Braud *Le Comportement électoral en France*, Paris: PUF, 1973.
10. *Sondages*, 1970, 1–2, p. 36.

# 17

# CONCLUSION: THE ALTERNATION OF POWER

Concluding a book on French political parties is an even more hazardous enterprise than beginning it. A child playing with toy soldiers finds that when he has nearly finished standing them all up the first ones in the line have started to fall down again. During the composition of this book two important new political parties have been formed—the CDS *(Centre des Démocrates Sociaux)* and RPR *(Rassemblement pour la République).* Before publication undreamed-of upheavals could occur.

Many observers predict a difficult time ahead for France. The dependence on imported supplies of energy and a worry that the forces of inflation may, despite the efforts of the President and his Prime Minister Raymond Barre, prove too strong, lead some to suppose that France will enter economically troubled times. Against that pessimistic view, it is important not to forget that the French state machine, expertly staffed, has been a good deal more effective in the Fifth Republic than most democracies at making policy decisions and seeing that they are implemented. Of considerable help has been the fact that France, unlike Great Britain or the United States, has not yet had the problem of interest groups acquiring a virtual power of veto over large areas of public policy. In this respect French democracy differs from the Anglo-Saxon version of a pluralist society. President Giscard d'Estaing in his book pleads for a genuinely pluralist and liberal society based on restraint and tolerance. Groups that push their demands to an excessive extent are committing 'an act of social violence'.[1] Up to now, however, except in sporadic outbursts like May 1968, 'acts of social violence' have had remarkably little impact on the capacity of the government to govern.

Nonetheless the French could be entering a period of economic difficulty, which, in contrast to the last twenty years, would mean an interruption in the steady and continuous improvement in living standards which they have experienced. This could impose political strains and indicate the limits of the increased social cohesion and political consensus that have characterised France in the Fifth Republic. The first big test for the character of French democracy will be the next parliamentary election, which, unless it is precipitated by a dissolution, will occur in 1978. The great question that the French themselves and foreign observers are asking themselves about that election is, of course: 'What happens if it is won by the Left?'

This subdivides into further questions. Firstly would there be a constitutional crisis? Up to now in the Fifth Republic there has always been a parliamentary majority in support of the President of the Republic. The constitutional practice that developed under Presidents de Gaulle and Pompidou was to regard them as leaders of the executive and leaders of the *Majorité*. This has changed slightly under President Giscard d'Estaing who has found himself in a less dominant position with regard to his *Majorité*. This process would go infinitely further if the parliamentary majority was composed of Socialists and Communists who remained committed to a *Union de la Gauche* alliance, under which they had just successfully fought election. The President could try to continue with a government that supported the policies supported by universal suffrage in his own election in 1974. A parliamentary vote of censure, however, would bring about its early defeat and, under Article 50 of the constitution, the government would have to tender its resignation (though no mention is made of the President having to accept it). The President himself could resign. That course of action would however, seem pointless as it would probably give the victorious Left an easy triumph and, in any case, Giscard d'Estaing during his bicentenary visit to the United States in 1976 specifically declared that he would serve his full seven-year term until 1981.

He could try to detach the Socialists from the Communists and put together a coalition that excluded the latter. Such a solution would depend on parliamentary arithmetic, the state of harmony or discord between the parties of the Left, a reversal of the bipolarising logic of the Fifth Republic party system, and upon an excessively high degree of political dishonesty by leading figures in the opposition.

Finally he could appoint François Mitterrand Prime Minister. It would not be the end of presidential power.[2] The President would have to approve laws voted by parliament, which he might not care for in some cases. However, using his constitutional powers, he could withhold his signature from non-legislative decrees and regulations, and block nominations to senior posts in the public service such as ambassadors, prefects, or senior administrative officials. The constitution also gives him the right to address Parliament, and of course he could give interviews and press conferences. All this would allow him to express in a spectacular way any reservations he felt about his government and he would retain the power to dissolve parliament if he felt the public was ready to throw the government out. In consequence there is no necessity for a constitutional crisis if the Left wins the next election, nor is there a necessity for a total eclipse of presidential authority.

There are however other questions which flow from the hypothesis of a victory of the Left at the next parliamentary election. One that preoccupies people most is the question of Communist participation in ministerial office. Would they be given only 'safe' ministries like Health or Labour, or would they get 'sensitive' ones like the Ministry of the Interior? Should they get them? If they obtained important posts in government would they set about undermining democratic liberties and creating a totalitarian regime? Would they pass Western defence secrets to the Soviet Union? There was a lot of hysterical speculation on these issues at the time of the Italian general election of June 1976. It is not possible to give rational answers to such questions. One point perhaps should be borne in mind. Even if one supposes that the leaders of the French Communist Party would like to have a Soviet-type dictatorship in France, it is placing remarkably little confidence in the democratic traditions of other parties and of the French people as a whole to imagine that they would be able to do so. In a democracy the wish is by no means father to the deed.

Another question is the whole issue of the peaceful alternation of power. Having won an election, would the Left be allowed to take over the government? Would everyone take their money out of the country, thus precipitating a severe economic collapse? Would there be a sort of *coup d'état* whereby the President and his supporters would abrogate the constitution rather than hand over power to the Left? Would the army and the civil service accept the political leadership of the Left? The combative style of the new Gaullist RPR indicates the presence of a large and militant body of opinion determined to resist the introduction of 'collectivism' in France. There has been, however, no suggestion of violent action to overturn an electoral verdict. There is no doubt that attempts to introduce radically socialist economic measures would meet extremely determined and well-organised opposition but there is nothing *a priori* undemocratic about that. President Giscard d'Estaing himself has declared that he will respect the constitution whatever the verdict of the electors. An interesting feature of his book is the longing it expresses for a peaceful democratic system where the alternation of power would not be 'a series of chaotic upheavals, foreseen as great dramas, experienced as revolutions'.[3]

The President is a great admirer of the British concept of a 'loyal opposition' where political conflict occurs against a background of consensus about the fundamentals of the democratic political order, where each side acknowledges that its opponents will maintain the country's political institutions. He argues that the basis for this consensus now exists in France. The social progress of the last twenty years in terms of living standards and education have removed much potential conflict; the traditional divisions of French political life—clericals and anticlericals, monarchists and republicans—have long since disappeared; there is widespread agreement about the nature of political institutions such as the directly elected presidency; all the major parties, including the Communists, claim to reject the violent overthrow of the social and political order and to be committed to a pluralist democracy. Yet the normal functioning of political life is still prevented, he complains, by the 'needlessly dramatic nature of political debate in our country': 'The political élite is in a constant state of fever', he declared on radio in December 1976, 'but France itself is not in a fever'. 'Alternation of power is fundamental to advanced democratic societies', but unfortunately in France 'it is as though' political debate was not a competition between two points of view but the confrontation of two rival and mutually exclusive truths.' 'Its style is that of a war of religion.'[4]

The President is right. The basic lack of trust between political adversaries, undeniably exacerbated by the importance in the opposition of a Communist party with a particularly Stalinist past, is the great problem of democracy in France. The Left of course, is by no means assured of winning Parliament in 1978 or the Presidency in 1981. Neither the present alliance of the Left nor the present bipolar configuration of the party system as a whole are irrevocably bound to continue for ever. Despite conflicts of personality, of style, and of policy, of fluctuating severity within each camp, this bipolar structure reflects the inherent logic of a directly elected Presidency and the emergence in the Fifth Republic for the first time in French history of majority government. The party system, as befits democratic government, has been greatly strengthened and simplified, and thus enabled to carry out more effectively than before its function of providing a mechanism through which the people can choose their government. Some day, however, French democracy has got to submit to the test of the peaceful alternation of power. The constitution of the Fifth Republic has endowed France with institutions that have permitted effective and democratic government for two decades. It is true that this process has been greatly helped by a party system which has always produced a parliamentary majority in support of the President of the Republic. To assert, however, that the institutions can only function if President and parliamentary majority are in permanent mutual agreement, that power must never change hands, that no way can be found to make alternative democratic choice work, that no adaptation of political institutions and political attitudes is conceivable, is to pronounce that democracy in France is a house of cards indeed. The author of this book, aware of the dangers, is not prepared to be so pessimistic.

## NOTES

1   *Démocratie française*, p. 141
2   See Jean-Luc Parodi, *La Vème République et le système majoritaire*; M. Duverger *La Monarchie Républicaine*, Paris: Editions Robert Laffont, 1974 and 'Le pouvoir modérateur', *Le Monde*, 28 May 1976.
3   *Démocratie française*, p. 154.
4   *Ibid.*, p. 155.

# ABBREVIATIONS
## POLITICAL PARTIES (IV = Fourth Republic only)

*Majorité*
Ve Rép.   *Vème République (Fifth Republic) (1967)*
UDR     *Union pour la Defense de la République (1968)*
URP     *Union des Républicains pour le Progrès (1973)*

*Gaullism*
RPF     *Rassemblement du Peuple Français (IV)*
UNR     *Union pour la Nouvelle République*
UDVe   *Union des Démocrates pour la Vème République*
UDR     *Union des Démocrates pour la République*
RPR     *Rassemblement pour la République*

*Centrists, Independents, etc.*
RI       *Républicains Indépendents*
CNIP    *Centre Nationale des Indépendents et Paysans*
MRP    *Mouvement Républicain Populaire*
CD      *Centre Démocrate*
PDM    *Progrès et Démocratie Moderne*
CDP     *Centre pour la Démocratie et le Progrès*
UC      *Union Centriste*
CDS     *Centre des Démocrates Sociaux*
REF     *Mouvement Réformateur*
RAD     Radical Party (*Parti Républicain Radical et Radical-Socialiste*)
MSDF   *Mouvement Démocrate Socialiste de France*
UDSR   *Union Démocrate et Socialiste de la Résistance (IV)*
RGR     *Rassemblement des Gauches Républicaines (IV)*

*Socialists and allies*
SFIO    *Section Française de l'Internationale Ouvrière (Socialist Party 1905-69)*
PS      *Parti Socialiste*
MRG    *Mouvement des Radicaux de Gauche*
FGDS   *Fédération de la Gauche Démocrate et Socialiste*
UGSD   *Union de la Gauche Socialiste et Démocrate*
PSU     *Parti Socialiste Unifié*
CIR     *Convention des Institutions Républicaines*
CERES  *Centre d'Etude de Recherche et d'Education Socialistes (Left wing of PS)*

*Communists*
PCF        *Parti Communiste Français*

## UNIONS AND OTHER ORGANISATIONS
CGT        *Confédération Générale du Travail*
CFDT       *Confédération Française Démocratique du Travail*
CFTC       *Confédération Française des Travailleurs Chrétiens*
FO         *Force Ouvrière*
FEN        *Fédération de l'Education Nationale*
JAC        *Jeunesse Agricole Chrétienne*
JOC        *Jeunesse Ouvrière Chrétienne*
JEC        *Jeunesse Etudiante Chrétienne*
CNPF       *Conseil National du Patronat Français*
MODEF      *Mouvement de Défense de l'Exploitation Familiale*
CGC        *Confédération Générale des Cadres* (Managers)
CID-       *Comité d'Information et de Défense—Union Nationale des*
   UNATI   *Artisans et Travailleurs Indépendents*

## APPENDIX II
# 1. DÉPARTEMENTS OF METROPOLITAN FRANCE

PARIS AND
SUBURBS

*In 1976 Corsica was divided into the *départements* of Haute–Corse and Corse du Sud.

# 2. REGIONS

## Regional capitals

**NORTH**

*Champagne:* Châlons-sur–Marne
   (Marne)
*North:* Lille (Nord)
*Picardy:* Amiens (Somme)
*Upper Normandy:* Rouen
   (Seine-Maritime)
*Lower Normandy:* Caen (Calvados)
*Brittany:* Rennes (Ille-et-Vilaine)
*Loire Country:* Nantes
   (Loire-Atlantique)
*Paris Region (Ile de France):* Paris
*Centre:* Tours (Indre et Loire)
*Burgundy:* Dijon (Côte d'Or)
*Alsace:* Strasbourg (Bas-Rhin)
*Lorraine:* Metz (Moselle)
*Franche-Comté:* Besançon (Doubs)

**SOUTH**

*Poitou-Charentes:* Poitiers (Vienne)
*Limousin:* Limoges (Haute-Vienne)
*Aquitaine:* Bordeaux (Gironde)
*Midi-Pyrenees:* Toulouse
   (Haute-Garonne)
*Languedoc:* Montpellier (Hérault)
*Auvergne:* Clermont-Ferrand
   (Puy de Dôme)
*Rhone-Alps:* Lyon (Rhône)
*Provence-Côte d'Azur:* Marseille
   (Bouches du Rhône)
*Corsica:* Ajaccio (Corse du Sud)

## APPENDIX III

### PARLIAMENTARY ELECTION 1973—REGIONAL SUMMARY

(% of 1st ballot vote and Seats won)

*(Regions and parliamentary constituencies, Metropolitan France)*

| | PCF | | UGSD | | CD/Rad. | | Majorité | | Other | Second ballot contests* | | | |
| | | | | | | | | | | Majorité represented by | | Left represented by | |
| | % | S | % | S | % | S | % | S | S | UDR | RI CDP | PC | UGSD |
|---|---|---|---|---|---|---|---|---|---|---|---|---|---|
| *France—North* | | | | | | | | | | | | | |
| Champagne (12) | 22·4 | — | 20·7 | 2 | 10·5 | — | 39·5 | 10 | — | 11 | — | 6 | 5 |
| Picardy (15) | 28·0 | 3 | 18·6 | 2 | 15·1 | 2 | 29·8 | 8 | — | 12 | 1 | 12 | 3 |
| North (37) | 26·9 | 12 | 26·6 | 15 | 9·4 | 1 | 31·1 | 9 | — | 32 | 3 | 16 | 21 |
| Upper Normandy (14) | 25·7 | 2 | 16·8 | 2 | 17·4 | 3 | 33·4 | 7 | — | 8 | 2 | 9 | 4 |
| Lower Normandy (13) | 11·7 | — | 17·7 | 2 | 17·3 | 2 | 47·3 | 8 | 1 | 9 | 2 | 1 | 9 |
| Brittany (25) | 16·0 | — | 17·1 | 3 | 12·9 | 2 | 45·3 | 19 | 1 | 13 | 3 | 6 | 9 |
| Loire Country (26) | 11·7 | — | 19·0 | 2 | 13·0 | 1 | 48·8 | 22 | 1 | 14 | 3 | 1 | 15 |
| Paris Region (83) | 27·1 | 31 | 14·9 | 3 | 14·6 | 3 | 31·9 | 46 | — | 61 | 13 | 58 | 14 |
| Alsace (13) | 7·9 | — | 12·4 | — | 23·0 | 4 | 51·3 | 9 | — | 11 | — | — | 5 |
| Lorraine (21) | 16·9 | 2 | 18·5 | 1 | 16·3 | 4 | 41·1 | 14 | — | 8 | 8 | 7 | 9 |
| Franche-Comté (9) | 14·0 | — | 27·4 | 3 | 10·2 | — | 41·2 | 6 | — | 3 | 5 | — | 8 |
| Burgundy (15) | 19·3 | — | 26·0 | 5 | 8·9 | — | 42·5 | 10 | — | 10 | 1 | 3 | 8 |
| Centre (20) | 21·3 | 1 | 18·7 | 2 | 12·4 | — | 39·0 | 17 | — | 13 | 4 | 9 | 8 |
| (303 seats) | (21·3) | (51) | (18·8) | (42) | (13·8) | (22) | (37·5) | (185) | (3) | (205) | (45) | (128) | (118) |

| | PCF | | UGSD | | CD/Rad. | | Majorité | | Other | Second ballot contests* | | | |
| | | | | | | | | | | Left represented by | | Majorité represented by | |
| | % | S | % | S | % | S | % | S | S | UDR | RI CDP | PC | UGSD |
|---|---|---|---|---|---|---|---|---|---|---|---|---|---|
| *France—South* | | | | | | | | | | | | | |
| Poitou–Charentes (14) | 18·0 | — | 21·1 | 2 | 14·7 | 2 | 40·1 | 10 | — | 8 | 3 | 6 | 6 |
| Limousin (8) | 29·9 | 3 | 25·3 | 3 | 6·1 | — | 31·1 | 2 | — | 5 | 1 | 4 | 3 |
| Aquitaine (24) | 17·5 | 2 | 27·1 | 9 | 12·6 | 1 | 37·5 | 12 | — | 18 | 5 | 3 | 20 |
| Midi-Pyrenees (22) | 16·3 | — | 31·3 | 15 | 9·3 | 1 | 35·1 | 6 | — | 12 | 10 | — | 22 |
| Auvergne (13) | 20·2 | 1 | 24·4 | 4 | 9·6 | 1 | 38·8 | 6 | 1 | 7 | 2 | 5 | 5 |
| Rhône-Alps (42) | 19·6 | 2 | 20·8 | 7 | 14·4 | 3 | 35·2 | 28 | 2 | 21 | 16 | 17 | 23 |
| Languedoc (16) | 28·2 | 6 | 27·0 | 8 | 8·8 | — | 31·8 | 2 | — | 14 | 1 | 6 | 9 |
| Provence-Côte d'Azur (28) | 28·2 | 8 | 22·3 | 9 | 13·1 | 1 | 29·5 | 9 | 1 | 17 | 9 | 15 | 12 |
| Corsica (3) | 14·5 | — | 27·5 | 2 | 11·3 | — | 42·5 | 1 | — | 2 | — | — | 2 |
| (170 seats) | (21·6) | (22) | (24·6) | (59) | (11·9) | (9) | (34·7) | (76) | (4) | (104) | (47) | (56) | (102) |
| Metropolitan France (473 seats) | 21·4% | 73 | 20·8% | 101 | 13·1% | 31 | 36·0% | 261 | 7 | 309 | 92 | 184 | 220 |

*Note that in some constituencies there was no second ballot, in some the *Majorité* withdrew in favour of the Reform Movement (CD or Rad.), and in some the Left was entirely eliminated at the first ballot with no candidate receiving the support of 10% of the registered electorate.

## APPENDIX IV
### PARLIAMENTARY ELECTIONS IN THE FOURTH REPUBLIC
(% of vote, Metropolitan France; seats won, Metropolitan and overseas)

|  | Oct. 1945 | | June 1945 | | Oct. 1946 | | June 1951 | | Jan. 1956 | |
|---|---|---|---|---|---|---|---|---|---|---|
|  | % | S. | % | S. | % | S. | % | S. | % | S. |
| Abstentions (% of electorate) | 20·1 | | 18·1 | | 21·9 | | 19·8 | | 17·2 | |
| PCF | 26·2 | 161 | 25·9 | 153 | 28·2 | 183 | 26·9 | 101 | 25·9 | 150 |
| SFIO | 23·4 | 150 | 21·1 | 129 | 17·8 | 105 | 14·6 | 107 | 15·2 | 99 |
| Rad., UDSR, RGR | 10·5 | 57 | 11·6 | 53 | 11·1 | 70 | 10·0 | 95 | 15·2b | 94 |
| MRP | 23·9 | 150 | 28·2 | 169 | 25·9 | 167 | 12·6 | 96 | 11·1 | 84 |
| Ind./Con. | 15·6 | 64 | 12·8 | 67 | 12·9 | 71 | 14·1 | 108 | 15·3 | 97 |
| Gaullists | | | | | 3·0 | | 21·6a | 120 | 3·9 | 22 |
| Others | 0·1 | 4 | 0·1 | 15 | 0·8 | 22 | | | 13·2c | 50 |

(a) RPF; (b) Radicals split into two factions; (c) mainly Poujadists.

# APPENDIX V
## PARLIAMENTARY ELECTIONS IN THE FIFTH REPUBLIC

(% 1st ballot vote—metropolitan France only; National Assembly seats—metropolitan and overseas)

| | Oct. 1958 | | Nov. 1962 | | Mar. 1967 | | June 1968 | | Mar. 1973 | |
|---|---|---|---|---|---|---|---|---|---|---|
| | % | Seats | % | Seats | % | Seats | % | Seats | % | Seats |
| PCF | 19·2 | 10 | 21·7 | 41 | 22·5 | 73 | 20·0 | 34 | 21·4 | 73 |
| PSU | — | — | 2·4 | — | 2·1 | 4 | 4·0 | — | 3·3 | 1 |
| Socialists | 15·7 | 44 | | | | | | | | |
| FGDS/UGSD (PS +MRG) | | | 12·6 | 66 | 19·0 | 116 | 16·5 | 57 | 20·8 | 101 |
| Radicals | 8·3 | 32 | 7·8 | 39 | | | | | | |
| (Total Left) | (43·2) | (86) | (44·5) | (146) | (43·6) | (193) | (41·2)★ | (91) | (45·8)★ | (176)★ |
| *Réformateurs* (Rad. +CD) | | | | | | | | | 13·1 | 34 |
| MRP | 11·1 | 57 | 9·1 | | | | | | | |
| Opposition-Centre—CD/PDM | | | | | 13·4 | 41 | 10·3 | 33 | CIDP *(Maj.)* | 30 |
| Independents | 22·9 | 133 | 7·7 | 55 | | | | | | |
| RI | | | 5·9 | 35 | | 44 | | 64 | | 55 |
| 5th Repub/URP UNR/UDR | 19·5 | 199 | 31·9 | 233 | 37·7 | 201 | 44·7 | 296 | 36·0 | 183 |
| (Total *Majorité*) | | | (37·8) | (268) | (37·7) | (245) | (44·7) | (360) | (36·0) | (268) |
| Other | 3·3 | | 8·6 | 13 | 5·4 | 8 | 3·5 | 3 | 5·1 | 12 |

★includes 'other Left': 0·7% in 1968, 0·3% (1 seat) in 1973.

## APPENDIX VI
## PARLIAMENTARY ELECTORAL SYSTEMS IN FRANCE
### SINCE 1848*

| Date of law | Type of constituency | No. of ballots | Method of allocating seats |
|---|---|---|---|
| 1848 | Multi-member | One | Simple majority of the electors voting |
| 1849 | Multi-member | One | As in 1848 |
| 1852 | Single-member | Two | First ballot: absolute majority of electors voting<br>Second ballot: relative majority of votes cast |
| 1871 | Multi-member | One | As in 1848 |
| 1873 | Multi-member | Two | As in 1852 |
| 1875 | Single-member | Two | As in 1852 |
| 1885 | Multi-member | Two | As in 1852 |
| 1889 | Single-member | Two | As in 1852 |
| 1919 | Multi-member | One | List system; candidates with the votes of an absolute majority of the electors voting were declared elected; any remaining seats were allocated to the lists by means of a quotient; any seats still remaining went to the list with the highest average of votes per candidate |
| 1927 | Single-member | Two | As in 1852 |
| 1945 | Multi-member | One | List system of proportional representation by quotient and highest average of votes per seat won |
| 1946 | Multi-member | One | List system of proportional representation by highest average of votes per seat won |

| 1951 | Multi-member | One | Paris region: list system of proportional representation by the greatest remainder; Provinces: list system; in any constituency an isolated list or an alliance of lists winning an absolute majority of the votes cast won all the seats; if an alliance won all the seats they were distributed among the allies by the system of proportional representation by the highest average; if no isolated list or alliance won an absolute majority the seats were distributed by the system of proportional representation by the highest average |
|------|--------------|-----|---|
| 1958 | Single-member | Two | Substantially as in 1852 |

*P. Campbell, *Electoral Systems in France since 1789*, op. cit., pp 134-5.

# APPENDIX VI
## HOW PARIS VOTES

M = municipal election, Pres. = presidential, P = parliamentary
(% of votes, first ballot—except 1971 and 1977)

| | M. 1965 | Pres. 1965 | P. 1967 | 2. 1968 | Pres. 1969 | M. 1971 | P. 1973 | Pres. 1974 1st ballot | P. 1977 2nd ballot* |
|---|---|---|---|---|---|---|---|---|---|
| Left | 35·2 | 30· | 38·6 | 34·2 | 30·4 | 34·8 | 37·5 | 4?· | 44·0 |
| Centre | 16·6 | 19·6 | 15·9 | 6·5 | 23·5 | 18·2 | 17·2 | — | — |
| Majorité | 38·2 | 4·0 | 43·0 | 5?·8 | 45·2 | 43·1 | 33·9 | 55·2 | 55·6 |

*There was no second ballot in the 5th sector of Paris (as the first ballot) and the Majorité alone was present in the second ballot in the 6th and 10th sectors. If first ballot votes are substituted in these three sectors the score for the Left comes out at 44·0%.

APPENDIX VII

# GLOSSARY

ELECTIONS

| | |
|---|---|
| *Ballotage* | Requirement for a second ballot |
| *Blancs et nuls* | Blank and spoilt votes |
| *Bulletin de vote* | Voting paper |
| *Bureau de vote* | Polling station |
| *Circonscription* | Constitutency |
| *Dépouillement du scrutin* | Counting of votes |
| *Désistement* | Withdrawal by a first ballot candidate in favour of another |
| *Elections: Cantonales* | Cantonal (*Département* Council) elections |
| *Législatives* | Parliamentary (National Assembly) elections |
| *Municipales* | Local (town or village) elections |
| *Partielles* | By-elections |
| *Présidentielles* | Presidential elections |
| *au Sénat* | Senate elections |
| *Forfait* | Deposit |
| *Inscrits* | Registered electors |
| *Investiture* | Adoption of a candidate |
| *Isoloir* | Polling booth |
| *Panachage* | Voting for candidates on different lists |
| *Suffrages exprimés* | Valid votes |
| *Tour (premier ou second)* | (First or second) ballot |
| *Transfert (report) de voix* | Transfer of votes (between ballots) |
| *Urne* | Ballot box |
| *Voix* or *vote* | Vote |
| *Votants* | Turnout |

ASSEMBLIES, OFFICIALS, ETC.

| | |
|---|---|
| *Apparenté* | Attached to a political group |
| *Assemblée Nationale* | National Assembly |
| *Commission* or *Comité* | Committee |
| *Commune* | Town or Village |
| *Conseil(ler) Général* | *Département* Council(lor) |
| *Conseil(ler) Municipal* | Local council(lor) (town or village) |
| *Conseil(ler) Régional* | Regional council(lor) |

| | |
|---|---|
| *Deputé* | Deputy, Member of the National Assembly |
| *Deputé-Maire* | Deputy and mayor |
| *Maire* | Mayor |
| *Maire-Adjoint* | Assistant mayor and committee chairman |
| *Préfet (Sous-Préfet)* | Prefect (Sub-prefect) |
| *Sénat Sénateur* | Senate, Senator |
| *Suppléant* | Substitute |

# SELECT BIBLIOGRAPHY

(For general works of political and sociological theory cited, and for publications by political parties, see notes, above.)

FNSP = Fondation Nationale des Sciences Politiques
PUF = Presses Universitaires de France
RFSP = *Revue Française de Science Politique*
PEP = Political and Economic Planning

## 1. *French Politics and Government (general)*

Ardagh, John, *The New France,* London: Penguin (2nd ed.), 1973.

Aron, Raymond, *An Explanation of de Gaulle,* New York: Harper and Row, 1966.

Cayrol, Roland, Parodi, Jean-Luc and Ysmal, Colette, *Le Député Français,* Paris: FNSP, Travaux et Recherches, 23, 1973.

Cerny, P., 'Cleavage, aggregation, and change in French politics' *British Journal of Political Science,* October 1972, pp. 443–56.

Chapsal, M. *La Vie politique en France depuis 1940,* Paris: PUF, 1966.

Cohen, Stephen S., *Modern Capitalist Planning: the French model,* London: Weidenfeld and Nicolson, 1969.

Crawley, Aidan, *De Gaulle,* London: Collins, 1969.

Debbasch, Charles, *Institutions Administratives,* Paris: Lib. Gén. de Droit et de Jurisprudence, 1966.

Duclos, Jacques, *Mémoires (6 vols.),* Paris: Fayard, 1968–73.

Duverger, Maurice, *La V$^e$ République,* Paris: PUF (5th ed.), 1974.

Duverger, Maurice, *La Monarchie Républicaine,* Paris: Robert Laffont, 1974.

Ehrmann, H. W., *Politics in France,* Chicago: Little, Brown, (2nd ed.), 1972.

Ferniot, Jean, *Mort d'une révolution,* Paris: Denoël, 1968.

Finer, S. E., *Comparative Government,* London: Allen Lane, 1970.

Fougeyrollas, Pierre, *La Conscience politique dans la France contemporaine,* Paris: Denoël, 1963.

Frears, J. R., 'Conflict in France: the decline and fall of a stereotype', *Political Studies,* March 1972, pp. 31–41.

——'The French Parliament and the European Community', *Journal of Common Market Studies,* December 1975, pp. 140–56.

Garaudy, Roger, *Toute la vérité,* Paris: Grasset, 1970.

De Gaulle, Charles, *Le Fil de l'épée* Paris: Berger-Levrault, 1944.

——*Mémoires de Guerre:* Vol. 1: *L'Appel 1940–1942,* Vol. 2: *L'Unité 1942–1944;* Vol. 3: *Le Salut 1944–1946,* Paris: Plon, 1954, 1956, 1959.

——*Mémoires d'Espoir:* Vol. 1: *Le Renouveau 1958–1966;* Vol. 2: *L'Effort 1962—,* Paris: Plon, 1970, 1971.

Giscard d'Estaing, V., *Démocratie Française,* Paris: Fayard, 1976.

Goguel, François and Grosser, Alfred, *La Politique en France,* Paris: A. Colin, 1964.

Greenstein, F. and Tarrow, Sidney, 'The study of French political socialisation', *World Politics,* 1969, pp. 95–137.

Hayward, Jack, *The One and Indivisible French Republic,* London: Weidenfeld and Nicolson, 1973.

Hoffman, S., 'Heroic leadership: the case of modern France' in L. J. Edinger, ed., *Political Leadership in Advanced Industrial Societies,* New York: Wiley, 1967.

Kesselmann, Mark *The Ambiguous Consensus: a study of local government in France* New York: Knopf, 1967.

Kolinsky, Martin and Paterson, William E., eds., *Social and Political Movements in Western Europe* London: Croom Helm, 1976.

Luthy, H., *The State of France,* London: Secker and Warburg, 1955.

Macridis, Roy C., *French Politics in Transition,* Cambridge, Mass.: Winthrop, 1975.

Marchais, Georges, *Le Défi démocratique,* Paris: Grasset, 1973.

Mitterrand, François, *Le Coup d'état permanent,* Paris: Plon, 1965.

——, *Ma Part de vérité,* Paris: Fayard, 1969.

Morin, Edgar, *La Brèche,* Paris: Fayard, 1968.

Noonan, Lowell G., *France: the politics of continuity in change,* New York: Holt, Rinehart and Winston, 1970.

Pickles, Dorothy, *The Fifth French Republic,* London: Methuen, 3rd ed., 1965.

——, *The Government and Politics of France,* Vol. 1: *Institutions and Parties;* Vol. 2: *Politics,* London: Methuen, 1973.

Pierce, Roy, *French Politics and Political Institutions,* New York, Harper and Row (2nd ed.), 1973.

Poniatowski, Michel, *Cartes sur table,* Paris: Fayard, 1972.

Rochet, Waldeck, *Qu'est-ce qu'un révolutionnaire dans la France de notre temps?,* Paris: Eds. Sociales, 1968.

Roig, C., and Billon–Grand, F., *La Socialisation politique des enfants,* Cahiers de la FNSP, 1968.

Séguy, Georges, *Lutter,* Paris: Stock, 1975.

Suleiman, Ezra, 'The French Bureaucracy and its students', *World Politics,* 1970–1, pp. 121–70.

——, 'L'Administrateur et le Député en France', *RFSP,* 1973, pp. 729–57.

——, *Politics, Power, and Bureaucracy in France,* Princeton University Press, 1974.

Thompson, David, *Democracy in France,* Oxford University Press, 1958.

Waterman, Harvey, *Political Change in Contemporary France,* Columbus, Ohio: Merrill, 1969.

Williams, Philip M., *Crisis and Compromise: politics in the Fourth Republic,* London: Longmans, (3rd ed.), 1964.

——, *The French Parliament 1958–67,* London: Allen and Unwin 1968.

——, and Harrison, Martin, *De Gaulle's Republic,* London: Longman, 1961.

——, *Politics and Society in de Gaulle's Republic*, London: Longman, 1971.

Wright, Gordon, *Rural Revolution in France*, Stanford, Calif.: Stanford University Press, 1964.

Wright, Vincent, 'Politics and administration under the Fifth French Republic', *Political Studies* 1974, pp. 44–65.


## 2. Political Parties (general)

Allardt, E. and Rokkan, S., *Mass Politics: studies in political sociology*, New York: Free Press, 1970.

Almond, Gabriel A., *The Appeals of Communism*, Princeton University Press, 1954.

Borella, F., *Les Partis politiques dans la France d'aujourd'hui*, Paris: Eds. du Seuil, 1973.

Burkett, Tony, *Parties and Elections in West Germany: the search for stability*, London: Hurst, 1975.

Caute, David, *The Left in Europe*, London: Weidenfeld and Nicolson, 1966.

Charlot, J., *Les Partis politiques*, Paris: A. Colin, 1971.

Duverger, Maurice, *Les Partis politiques*, Paris: A. Colin, 7th edition, 1969.

——, *Party Politics and Pressure Groups*, London: Nelson, 1972.

Goguel, F., *La Politique des partis sous la III$^e$ République*, Paris: Eds. du Seuil, 1948.

Henig, Stanley and Pinder, John, (eds.), *European Political Parties* London: PEP—Allen and Unwin, 1969 (chapter on France by Michael Steed).

Kesselmann, Mark, 'Changes in the French party system', *Comparative Politics*, January, 1972, pp. 281–301.

Kraehe, R., *Le Financement des partis politiques*, Paris: PUF, 1972.

Lagroye, Jacques, Lord, Guy, Mounier-Chazel, Lise and Palard, Jacques, *Les Militants politiques dans trois partis français*, Paris: Pédone 1976.

Lapalombara, J. and Weiner, M., *Political Parties and Political Development*, Princeton University Press, 1966.

McHale, V. and Paranzino, D., 'Developmental change and electoral cleavage in France: government and opposition in the Fifth Republic', *Canadian Journal of Political Science 1975*, pp. 431–53.

MacRae, Duncan, Jr. *Parliament, Parties, and Society in France, 1946–58*, New York: St Martin's; London: Macmillan, 1967.

Parodi, J.-L., 'La Ve République et le système majoritaire', Paris: unpublished doctoral thesis, 1973.

Rose, Richard, 'The variability of party Government: a theoretical and empirical critique', *Political Studies*, Dec. 1964, pp. 413–45.

——, *The Problem of Party Government*, London: Macmillan, 1974.

Tarrow, Sidney, *Peasant Communism in Southern Italy*, New Haven: Yale University Press, 1967.

Wright, Vincent, 'Presidentialism and the parties in the French Fifth Republic', *Government and Opposition*, 1975, pp. 24–45.


### 3. *Political Parties (specific)*

Anderson, Malcolm, *Conservative Politics in France*, London: Allen and Unwin, 1973.

Andreu, Anne, and Mignalon, Jean-Louis, *L'Adhésion*, Paris: Calmann-Lévy, 1975.

Barjonet, André, *Le Parti Communiste Français*, Paris: Didier, 1969.

Bizot, Jean-François, *Au Parti des Socialistes: plongée libre dans les courants d'un grand parti*, Paris: Grasset, 1975.

Blackmer, Donald L. M., and Tarrow, Sidney, (eds.), *Communism in Italy and France*, Princeton University Press, 1975.

Bon, F. *et al. Le Communisme en France*, Paris: FNSP, 1969.

Cameron, D. R. and Hofferbert, R. I., 'Continuity and change in Gaullism', *American Journal of Political Science*, Feb. 1973, pp. 77–98.

Campbell, Ian, 'The French Communists and the union of the Left', *Parliamentary Affairs*, Summer 1976, pp. 246–63.

Caute, David, *Communism and the French Intellectuals*, London: Deutsch, 1964.

Charlot, J. *L'UDR: Étude du pouvoir au sein d'un parti politique*, Paris: Cahiers de la FNSP, no. 153, 1967.

——, *Le Gaullisme*, Paris: A. Colin, 1970.

——, *The Gaullist Phenomenon*, London: Allen and Unwin, 1971.

Colliard, Jean-Claude, *Les Républicains Indépendents: Valéry Giscard-d'Estaing*, Paris: PUF, 1971.

Fauvet, Jacques, *Histoire du Parti Communiste Français*, Vol. 1: *1917–1939*, Vol. 2: *1939–1965*, Paris: Fayard, 1965.

Fejto, François, *The French Communist Party and the Crisis of International Communism*, Cambridge, Mass.: MIT Press, 1967.

Greene, T. H., 'The Communist Parties of Italy and France', *World Politics*, 1968–9, pp. 1–38.

Harris, André and De Sédouy, Alain, *Voyage à l'intérieur du Parti Communiste*, Paris: Eds. du Seuil, 1974.

Hartley, Anthony, *Gaullism—the rise and fall of a political movement*, London: Routledge and Kegan Paul, 1972.

Hoffman, S., *Le Mouvement Poujade*, Paris: A. Colin, 1956.

Hurtig, Christiane, *De la SFIO au nouveau parti socialiste*, Paris: A. Colin, 1970.

Irving, R. E. M., *Christian Democracy in France*, London: Allen and Unwin, 1973.

——, 'The Centre Parties in the Fifth French Republic', *Parliamentary Affairs*, Summer 1976, pp. 264–80.

Jaffré, Jérome, La concurrence au sein de la Gauche en 1967 et en 1968', *RFSP*, 1973 pp. 110–18.

Kriegel, Annie, 'The present theory of power in the Fren[c]
Party', in *Government and Opposition, 1967*, pp. 253–6[

———, *The French Communists*, University of Chicago Pr[

Laurens, A. and Pfister, T., *Les Nouveaux Communistes*, Pari[s

Le Calloch, Bernard, *La Révolution silencieuse: du Gaullis[m
Paris: Didier, 1971.

Lichtheim, George, *Marxism in Modern France*, New York: Columbia University Press, 1966.

Lyra, Rubens Pinto, *Le Parti Communiste français et l'intégration Européenne (1957–1973)* Nancy: Centre Européen Universitaire, 1974.

Macridis, R. C., 'Oppositions in France: an interpretation', in *Government and Opposition*, 1972, pp. 166–85.

Nicolet, Claude, *Le Radicalisme*, Paris: PUF, 1961.

Poperen, Jean, *L'Unité de la Gauche 1965–1973*, Paris: Fayard, 1975.

*Programme Commun de Gouvernement du Parti Socialiste, Parti Communiste, et Mouvement des Radicaux de Gauche*, Paris: Flammarion, 1973.

Quilliot, Roger, *La SFIO et l'exercise du pouvoir 1944–1958*, Paris: Fayard, 1972.

Rémond, René, *The Right Wing in France from 1815 to de Gaulle*, Philadelphia: University of Pennsylvania Press, (2nd ed.), 1966.

Rocard, Michel, *Les Militants du PSU*, Paris: Epi, 1971.

Rochet, Waldeck, *L'Avenir du Parti Communiste français*, Paris: Eds. Sociales, 1969.

Routier-Preuvost, André, *Lettre inquiète à François Mitterrand*, Nantes: Eds. Europlan, 1976.

Simmons, Harvey G., *French Socialists in search of a Role 1956–1967*, Ithaca: Cornell University Press, 1970.

Tarr, Francis de, *The French Radical Party from Herriot to Mendès-France*, Oxford University Press, 1961.

Tiersky, R., *French Communism 1920–1972*, New York: Columbia University Press, 1974.

———, 'French Communism in 1976', *Problems of Communism*, February, 1976, pp. 20–47.

Willard, Claude, *Socialisme et Communisme français*, Paris: A. Colin, 1967.

Wilson, Frank L., *The French Democratic Left 1963–1969: towards a modern party system*, Stanford, Calif.: Stanford University Press, 1971.

———, 'The club phenomenon in France', *Comparative Politics*, July, 1971, pp. 517–28.

———, 'Gaullism without de Gaulle', *Western Political Quarterly*, 1973, pp. 485–506.

Wright, V. and Machin, H., 'The French Socialist Party in 1973: performance and prospects', in *Government and Opposition*, Spring, 1974, pp. 123–45.

———, 'The French Socialist Party: success and the problems of success', *Political Quarterly*, Jan.–March 1975, pp. 36–52.

Ysmal, Colette, 'Adhérent et dirigeants du Centre Démocrate', RFSP, 1972, pp. 77–88.

## 4. Elections and Electoral Behaviour

Association Française des Sciences Politiques (AFSP) Les Élections du 2 janvier 1956, Cahiers de la FNSP, 82, 1957.

——, l'Etablissement de la Vème République: le Référendum de septembre et les élections de novembre 1958, Cahiers de la FNSP, 109, 1960.

Centre d'Étude de la Vie Politique Française (CEVPF) Le Référendum du 8 janvier 1961, Cahiers de la FNSP, 19, 1962.

——, Le Référendum du 8 avril 1962, Cahiers de la FNSP, 124, 1963.

——, Le Référendum d'octobre et les élections de novembre 1962, Cahiers de la FNSP, 142, 1965.

——, L'Élection présidentielle des 5 et 12 décembre 1965, Cahiers de la FNSP, 169, 1970.

——, Les Élections législatives de mars 1967, Cahiers de la FNSP, 170, 1971.

Bon, Frédéric, 'Le référendum du 27 avril 1969: suicide politique ou nécessité stratégique', RFSP, April 1970, pp. 205–23.

Bortoli, Gilbert, Sociologie du référendum dans la France moderne, Paris: Lib. Gén. de Droit et de Jurisprudence, 1965.

Braud, Philippe, Le Comportement électoral en France, Paris: PUF, 1973.

Cameron, D. R., 'Stability and change in patterns of French partisanship', Public Opinion Quarterly, 1972, pp. 19–30.

Campbell, Bruce A., 'On the prospects of polarisation in the French electorate', Comparative Politics, Jan. 1976, pp. 227–90.

——, 'The future of the Gaullist Majority in France', American Journal of Political Science, Feb. 1974, pp. 67–94.

Campbell, Peter, French Electoral Systems and Elections since 1789, London: Faber and Faber, 1958.

Charlot, J., ed., 'Quand la Gauche peut Gagner . . .', Paris: Eds. A. Moreau, 1973.

Converse P. and Dupeux, G., 'Politicisation of the electorate in France and the United States', Public Opinion Quarterly, Spring 1962, pp. 1–23.

Criddle, Byron, 'Distorted representation in France', Parliamentary Affairs, 1975, pp. 154–79.

Dennis, N., 'Du 5 mai 1946 au 19 mai 1974', RFSP 1974, pp. 893–910.

Deutsch, E., Lindon, D., and Weill, P. Les Familles Politiques, Paris: Eds. du Minuit, 1966.

Goguel, F., 'Combien y-a-t-il eu d'électeurs de gauche parmi ceux qui ont voté le 5 décembre 1965 pour le Général de Gaulle', RFSP, Feb. 1967, pp. 65–9.

——, Modernisation économique et comportement politique, Paris: FNSP, Travaux et recherches de sciences politiques, 1969.

Goldey, D. B., and Johnson, R. I. W., 'The French general election of 1973', Political Studies, 1973, pp. 321–42.

Hayward, J. E. S., 'Presidential suicide by plebiscite', *Parliamentary Affairs*, 1969, pp. 289–317.

——, and Wright, V., 'The 37,708 microcosms of an Indivisible Republic: the local elections of March 1971', *Parliamentary Affairs*, 1971, pp. 284–311.

——, 'les deux France and the presidential elections of May 1974', *Parliamentary Affairs*, 1974, pp. 208–36.

——, 'Presidential supremacy and the French general elections of March 1973', *Parliamentary Affairs*, 1973, pp. 274–306 and 372–401.

Jackson, R. J., 'The succession of Georges Pompidou', *Political Quarterly*, 1970, pp. 156–68.

Lancelot, Alain, *l'Abstentionnisme électoral en France*, Paris: Cahiers de la FNSP, 162, 1970.

——, 'Les élections des 5 et 12 mars 1967', *Projet*, May 1967, pp. 549–62.

——, 'Les élections des 23 et 30 juin 1968', *Projet*, Sept.–Oct., 1968, pp. 935–52.

——, 'Comment ont voté les Français', *Projet*, Sept.–Oct., 1969, pp. 926–47.

——, 'La France de M. Bourgeois-République', *Projet*, June 1973, pp. 670–84.

——, 'Elections: la relève et le suris', *Projet*, Sept.–Oct., 1974, pp. 941–58.

——, and Lancelot, Marie-Thérèse, *Atlas des circonscriptions électorales en France depuis 1875*, Paris: FNSP 1970.

Le Gall, G., and Riglet, M., 'Les circonscriptions marginales aux élections législatives de 1967 et 1968', *RFSP*, 1973, pp. 86–109.

Leigh, Michael, 'Linkage politics: the French referendum and the Paris Summit of 1972', *Journal of Common Market Studies*, Dec. 1975, pp. 157–70.

Lord, H. G., Petrie, A. J., and Whitehead, L. A., 'Political change in rural France: the 1967 election in a Communist stronghold', *Political Studies*, 1968, pp. 153–76.

McHale, Vincent, 'Religion and electoral politics in France', *Canadian Journal of Political Science*, Sept. 1969, pp. 292–311.

——, 'Electoral traditions and opposition-building in France', *Comparative Politics*, July 1971, pp. 499–516.

*Monde, Le, Dossiers et Documents*, 'L'élection présidentielle de mai 1974'.

Penniman, Howard R., ed. *France at the Polls: the presidential election of 1974* [articles by R. Pierce, J. Blondel, J. Charlot, A. and M.-T. Lancelot, and others], Washington, DC: American Enterprise Institute of Policy Research, 1975.

Schwartzenburg, R. G. *La Guerre de Succession*, Paris: PUF, 1969.

Williams, Philip M., *French Politicians and Elections 1951–1969*, Cambridge University Press, 1970.

Wilson, F. L. 'The French Left and the elections of 1968', *World Politics*, 1968–9, pp. 539–74.

Wolf, M., 'Lille 1973: choix de société ou élection de quartier?, *RFSP*, April 1975, pp. 259–90.
Ysmal, Colette, 'L'élection de M. Gaston Defferre à Marseille', *RFSP*, April 1972, pp. 319–47.
——, et al., 'L'élection présidentielle de mai 1974: la redistribution des électeurs de droite', *RFSP*, April 1975, pp. 222–58.

*For further electoral analysis see:*
*RFSP*, April 1972, Municipal elections of 1971 (articles by F. Bon, J. Ranger and others).
*RFSP*, Dec. 1974, Presidential election of 1974 (articles by J. Jaffré, J. Ranger and others).

## 5. *Sources for Election Statistics*

FNSP—Centre d'Étude de la Vie Politique Française Contemporaine.
Ministère de l'Intérieur, *Les Elections Législatives* 1958, 1962, 1967, 1968.
*L'Année Politique.*
*Le Monde.*
*Cahiers du Communisme,* Elections Législatives 1967, 1968, 1973.
Charlot J., (ed.), *Quand la Gauche peut gagner . . . ,* Paris: Moreau, 1973.
Goguel, François, and Grosser, Alfred, *la Politique en France,* Paris: A. Colin, 1964.
Sénat—Service du Séance.

No two sources agree, so the election statistics published in this book represent the author's conclusions.

# INDEX